D1243484

POPULAR
MUSIC

Other Books by Nat Shapiro

Popular Music
An Annotated Index of American Popular Songs
Volume 1, 1950-1959
Volume 2, 1940-1949

Hear Me Talkin' to Ya (Co-Editor)

The Jazz Makers (Co-Editor)

VOLUME 3
1960-1964

POPULAR MUSIC

An Annotated Index of American Popular Songs

Edited by

NAT SHAPIRO

ADRIAN PRESS

Library of Congress Catalog Card Number 64-23761

Jacket designed by Robert Cato

Printed in the United States of America
by the Lerman Printing Co., New York, N.Y.

 426

Acknowledgments

The Editor is particularly indebted to Betty Martone, Miles Kreuger, Hal B. Cook, Russell Sanjek, Saul Weinbaum, Elias Feilich, Mark Sikelianos, Sylvia Rosenberg, Rebecca L. Socolow, Barbara Davies, Amy L. Shapiro, the Index Department of the American Society of Composers, Authors and Publishers (ASCAP), the Index Department of Broadcast Music, Inc. (BMI), and the numerous publishers, authors, and composers who took the time to remember, correspond, confirm, and correct. Felice Faust Ascher's research assistance was invaluable because of her specialized experience in the popular music field. As with the earlier volumes of *Popular Music*, Dr. Vera Miller (Mrs. Nat Shapiro) was responsible for the organization and production of the book. Her research training, knowledge, editorial meticulousness, enthusiasm for the project, and stamina made it all possible.

Table of Contents

About the Book and How To Use It

This volume is the third of a series, the aim of which is to set down in permanent and practical form a selective, annotated list of the significant popular songs of our times. Previous indexes of popular music have either dealt with special areas, such as jazz or theater and film music, or been concerned chiefly with songs which achieved a degree of popularity, as measured by the variably reliable music business trade indicators. And, unfortunately, the basic records kept by the active participants in the music business are often casual, inaccurate, and transitory.

There is no single source of comprehensive information about popular songs, and those sources which do exist do not publish complete material about even the musical works with which they are directly concerned. Two of the primary proprietors of basic information about our popular music are the major performing rights societies—the American Society of Composers, Authors and Publishers (ASCAP) and Broadcast Music, Inc. (BMI). Although each of these organizations has considerable information about the songs of its own writer and publisher members and has also issued indexes of its own songs, their files and published indexes are designed primarily for clearance identification by the commercial users of music. Their publications of annual or periodic lists of their "hits" necessarily include only a small fraction of their songs, and the facts given about these are also limited. Both ASCAP and BMI are, however, invaluable and indispensable sources of data about popular music. It is just that their data and special knowledge are not readily accessible to the researcher.

About the Book

Another basic source of information about musical compositions and their creators and publishers is the *Catalog of Copyright Entries* issued by the Copyright Office of The Library of Congress. Each year, two massive volumes are published by the Copyright Office, listing each published, unpublished, republished, and renewed copyright of songs registered with the Office. While these volumes are helpful in determining the precise date of the declaration of the original ownership of musical works, they contain no other information, are unwieldy, and, lacking a unified index, difficult to use. To complicate matters further, some authors, composers, and publishers have been known to employ rather makeshift methods of protecting their works legally, and there are several songs listed in *Popular Music* which are not to be found in The Library of Congress files.

In preparing this series, the Editor was faced with a number of separate problems. The first and most important of these was the basic one of selection. In this regard, the solution was determined by adherence to the stated aim of the project itself—to offer the user of the Index as comprehensive and accurate a listing of significant popular songs as possible. Significance was decided objectively and without any editorial prejudice for or against any type of popular music. It was not the Editor's intention to evaluate the importance or quality of rock and roll, show tunes, Blue Grass music, movie themes, or nonsense songs. Rather, it was the purpose of *Popular Music* to document those musical works which (1) achieved a substantial degree of popular acceptance, (2) were exposed to the public in especially notable circumstances, or (3) were accepted and given important performances by influential musical and dramatic artists.

Another problem was whether or not to classify the songs as to type. The first half of the 1960's was characterized by a continuation of the integration of several divergent streams of creative musical activity—country and western songs, rhythm and blues, authentic folk music, and jazz and the inception of new permutations and combinations of styles of which folk-rock is the most notable. (These significant developments are discussed in the introduction, "Popular Music, 1960-1964.") Under these circumstances, it seemed arbitrary and misleading to label a given song as "rhythm and blues," "country and western," "folk," or "jazz." Most works of music are subject to any number of interpretations and, although it is possible to describe a particular performance, it is more difficult to give a musical composition a label applicable not only to its origin but to its subsequent musical history. In fact, the most significant versions of some songs are often quite at variance with their origins. It is believed, however, that the information in *Popular Music* for such songs indicates the important facts about not only their origins but also their subsequent lives.

The principal sources of information for the titles, authors, composers, publishers, and dates of copyright of the songs in this volume were the Copyright Office of The Library of Congress, ASCAP, BMI, and individual writers and publishers. Data about best-selling recordings were obtained principally from two of the leading music business trade journals—*Billboard* and *Cash Box*. For the historical notes; anecdotes; information about foreign, folk, public domain, and classical origins; and identification of theatrical, film, and television introducers of songs, the Editor relied upon his own and the New York Public Library's collection of record album notes, theater programs, sheet music, newspaper and magazine articles, and other material.

The information for each song in Volume 3, published in 1960-1964, is listed under the year of its original published copyright. The reader is, therefore, advised to consult the List of Titles to determine the year of the song's original published copyright. Songs are occasionally registered with the Copyright Office of The Library of Congress before publication, but, in almost all cases, the copyright year given in Volume 3 is that of the original *published* copyright and not the year of the original registration by the writer.

The primary listing for a song published in 1960-1964 includes, first of all, the full title and alternate title or titles, exactly as they appear on The Library of Congress copyright card or, in some cases, the sheet music. Since even a casual perusal of the List of Titles indicates considerable variation in spelling and punctuation, it should be noted that these are neither editorial nor typographical errors but the colloquialisms of the music trade. The title of a given song as it appears in this volume is the one under which it is legally registered.

About the Book

In all cases, the primary listing reports the author or authors and the composer or composers. Here, too, the reader will find variations in the spelling of a song writer's name. Again, the form of the name of a writer used in connection with any particular song is the form under which that copyright was registered. In addition to this kind of variation in the spelling of writers' names, the reader will also notice that, in some cases, where the writer is also the performer, his name as a writer may differ from the form of the name he used as a performer.

The publisher listed is the current publisher. Since *Popular Music* is designed as a practical reference work rather than an academic study, and since copyrights more than occasionally change hands, the current publisher is given instead of the original holder of the copyright. If a publisher has, for some reason, copyrighted a song more than once, the years of the significant copyrights, subsequent to the year of the original published copyright, are listed after the publisher's name.

If the song is of foreign origin, the primary listing indicates the country of origin after the title. Additional information about the original title, copyright date in country of origin (if other than copyright date in the United States), writers, publisher, and other facts about the adaptation are noted.

The primary listing also includes first or best-selling records, indicating the performer and the record company; the production in which the song was introduced and, where important, by whom it was introduced in the case of theater, film, and television songs; any other performers identified with the song; and other relevant data. The name of a performer may be listed differently in connection with different songs, especially over a period of years. The name listed is the form of the name given in connection with a particular record or performance. It should be noted that the designation, "best-selling record," does not mean that the record was a "hit." It means, simply, that the record or records noted as "best-selling" were the best-selling record or records of that particular song, in comparison with the sales of other records of the same song.

In all cases, if any fact about a song relates to a year other than the year of the original copyright, the year of such fact is noted in the primary listing. Cross-references to such songs appear under the other years in which there are significant facts for them. The one exception is that there are no cross-references to best-selling records appearing in the year immediately following the copyright year. Since many songs become popular in the year following the copyright year, such cross-references would have cluttered the book to the point of distracting the reader. The year of any annotation, including those of best-selling records, subsequent to the copyright year is, of course, noted in the primary listing. Cross-references for all important alternate titles of songs are also listed.

Volume 3 also includes a Supplement of information about songs copyrighted before 1960 that became significant in 1960-1964. For songs copyrighted in the 1940's and 1950's, for which there was no significant development up to the time of the preparation of Volumes 1 and 2 of *Popular Music,* complete information is listed in the Supplement. For songs copyrighted in the 1940's and 1950's, for which the basic data appear in Volume 1 or 2, the subsequent information is listed in this Supplement, with a reference to the year in Volume 1 or 2 under which the basic information appears. For songs copyrighted before 1940, the facts relating to 1960-1964 are given, with a reference to the copyright year under which the basic information will be listed in subsequent volumes of *Popular Music* covering the years before 1940. While there may be some temporary inconvenience until this material is published, it seemed cumbersome and inconsistent to duplicate full listings for such songs. Songs copyrighted in the 1940's and 1950's, for which complete data, including that for 1960-1964, appear in Volume 1 or 2, are not listed in this Supplement but under the year in 1960-1964 in which the development occurred, with a reference to the year in Volume 1 or 2 in which all the information appears. They may be located by consulting the List of Titles.

The List of Publishers, which is alphabetically arranged, includes the performing rights affiliation (ASCAP, BMI, or SESAC) and current address of each publisher of a song appearing in Volume 3.

Popular Music, 1960-1964

By 1965, the annual gross income derived from the sale and dissemination of popular music in the United States was well over one billion dollars. Record sales alone amounted to $693,000,000 in 1964, with additional sources of directly related income from jukeboxes, sheet music sales, and performance royalties paid to music publishers, composers, and lyric writers by the radio, television, and motion picture industries. This estimate does not take into account box office receipts for theatrical and concert presentations of individual performers and vocal and instrumental groups or sales of musical instruments, phonographs, tape recorders, transistor and other radios, and other products and services related to the creation, promotion, distribution, sale, and performance of music.

Since the rates of economic growth of the "industry" and the consumption of popular music have been exceeding those of almost all other industrial and commercial products and because the social, cultural, and economic dynamics of American life indicate similar development in the future, we can safely assume that popular music will continue to serve as a lively and sometimes disturbing accompaniment to, and reflection of, the life of this and other countries.

The influence of American urban and rural Negro folk music continued, in the early 1960's, to dominate popular music, a trend that had become evident in the early 1950's when rock and roll first began to take hold. If anything, the degree and potency of the ingredients of Negro rhythm and blues that have filtered into the mainstream of popular music intensified in the most recent period. The wide acceptance of "soul" music; the enormous popularity of the "Detroit" sound,

1

exemplified by The Supremes and other similar groups; and the adoption by white vocal and instrumental recording artists, such as The Rolling Stones, The Animals, and The Righteous Brothers, of the mannerisms, inflections, and devices of pure rhythm and blues are of considerable interest and are testimony to the vitality and appeal of this music, especially for young people.

The most notable and unexpected development in the world of popular music in the first five years of the 1960's was the emergence of England as a major source of performers, composers, and lyric writers. Led by the extraordinary Beatles, a colorfully garbed, cleverly named, and sometimes talented parade of young writers, singers, and instrumentalists began to capture the imagination and enthusiastic support of pre-teens and teen-agers not only in England but in the United States and the rest of the world as well. By the end of 1964, British performing artists, singing and playing British songs, were represented on the best-selling record lists in dozens of countries. Groups like The Beatles, The Rolling Stones, Herman's Hermits, The Animals, Gerry and The Pacemakers, The Dave Clark Five, The Kinks, Manfred Mann, Peter and Gordon, Chad and Jeremy, The Searchers, and dozens of others were challenging and often exceeding American rock and roll groups in popularity.

Despite promotional attempts to localize or nationalize the sounds and styles of The Beatles and their followers with slogans referring to "The Liverpool Sound" and "The Mersey Beat," the music that came from and, at this writing, is still coming from England was and is nothing more than popular music derived from the identical sources that American "teen-beat" music is derived from—American Negro rhythm and blues and, to a lesser extent, American country and western music.

Another, and not too surprising, development that came to the fore in the early 1960's was the appearance and acceptance of such poet-troubadours as Bob Dylan, Phil Ochs, Tom Paxton, Paul Simon, and Richard Fariña, along with a group of singers, among them Joan Baez; Peter, Paul, and Mary; Judy Collins; and Chad Mitchell, who began to insist upon broader, more profound, more poetic, and more socially-oriented material. In a sense, this was a logical evolution. Youngsters who had progressed from the compelling sounds and rhythms of "hard" rock and roll were demanding—in keeping with their "new freedom" and with what was apparently an almost universal reaction against conformity—music and lyrics to meet their emotional and intellectual requirements. It was evident to them that the Tin Pan Alley, Broadway, and Hollywood "establishment" did not, and probably could not, understand them or their musical needs.

As the first five years of the 1960's came to a close, folk-rock, a loose amalgam of the rock and roll beat and the poetic, unconfined content of the contemporary folk song movement, began to make itself felt, and groups like The Beatles in England and The Byrds in the United States began experimenting with new musical forms, advanced harmonies, unusual instrumentation, and, most important, lyrics that reached beyond the traditional patterns of the popular music of the past. Almost all of Bob Dylan's lyrics; Pete Seeger's "Turn! Turn! Turn!", "Guantanamera," and "Where Have All the Flowers Gone?"; Malvina Reynolds' "Little Boxes"; and scores of other songs previously limited to very small audiences began to find their way to the best-selling record lists.

The Broadway theater continued to be the principal source of the most interesting, literate, and entertaining songs written and composed in standard patterns during the first five years of the 1960's. The work of new and younger composers and lyricists, however, took precedence in popular acceptance over scores by such stalwarts as Irving Berlin, Frank Loesser, Alan Jay Lerner and Frederick Loewe, Harold Rome, Harold Arlen, Arthur Schwartz and Howard Dietz, and Noël Coward. From the standpoint of consistent quality, the most successful scores produced from 1960 to 1965 were those for *Bye Bye Birdie,* by Lee Adams and Charles Strouse; *Fiddler on the Roof,* by Sheldon Harnick and Jerry Bock; *Little Me,* by Carolyn Leigh and Cy Coleman; and *No Strings,* by Richard Rodgers. Other scores of particular but mixed merit by writers new to the theater were those for *The Fantasticks* and *110 in the Shade* (Tom Jones and Harvey Schmidt), *Hello, Dolly!* (Jerry Herman), and *What Makes Sammy Run?* (Ervin Drake).

Perhaps the most spectacular new arrivals—from Eng-

3

land, interestingly enough—were Anthony Newley and Leslie Bricusse, whose lyrics, music, and books for *Stop the World— I Want To Get Off* and *The Roar of the Greasepaint* brought new excitement not only to the theater but to the popular music marts as well. "What Kind of Fool Am I?", "Who Can I Turn To," "Once in a Lifetime," "Gonna Build a Mountain," "The Joker," and other songs from their two shows either became hits or were recorded widely enough to become accepted into the standard popular repertoire.

The film industry's dominant contribution to popular music was a continuation of the steady flow of film title songs and lyric versions or adaptations of principal themes from motion picture scores. Apart from the promotional values derived from widespread exposure of the names of films in song titles or on the covers of record albums, all the major and most of the independent producers also looked to extra profits from their own companies' music publishing and record divisions or subsidiary firms.

The biggest hits from films during the years 1960-1964 were "Exodus," composed by Ernest Gold; "Never on Sunday," by the Greek composer, Manos Hadjidakis; "More," which was adapted from a theme from the Italian documentary film, *Mondo Cane*, and composed by Riz Ortolani and N. Oliviero; "Moon River," with lyrics by Johnny Mercer and music by Henry Mancini, featured in *Breakfast at Tiffany's*; and "Goldfinger," with words by Anthony Newley and Leslie Bricusse to music by John Barry.

Apart from the highly successful film versions of such major Broadway musicals as *The Sound of Music, My Fair Lady*, and *West Side Story*, the motion picture industry's involvement in original musical films was negligible. Only three pictures of merit, two of them produced outside the United States, seem worthy of mention. From England came the inventive, *avant-garde*-influenced *A Hard Day's Night*, featuring The Beatles and a score of rock and roll songs by Paul McCartney and John Lennon. It is probable that what was significant about this film was not so much the music but rather the interesting and original ways in which the music was used. From France came the experimental *The Umbrellas of Cherbourg*, a quite successful attempt at a popular opera on film. Michel

Legrand's melodic score, with a libretto by writer-director Jacques Demy, was both distinguished and charming, and two of the songs, as adapted into English by Norman Gimbel, "I Will Wait for You" and "Watch What Happens," are becoming standards. The third musical film of note was the American-made *Mary Poppins*, with a score by the talented brothers, Richard and Robert Sherman. Unpretentious, tuneful, and literate, the score and the film were a tremendous success and apparently stimulated Hollywood producers to renew their efforts in the direction of original musical film production. Several major pictures were promised for the second half of the decade.

Despite sporadic and, we suspect, sentimental attempts to revive them, dance bands continued to fall off in popularity, a trend completely consistent with a now long-evident preference for television and phonograph records to "live" presentations of musical entertainment. Symptomatic of this condition was the virtual disappearance of the ballroom as a social center for young people. Further, the sponsors of the periodic dance band revivals evidently could not come to terms with the overwhelming orientation of the new music audience to the small-band vocal and electronic sounds of rock and roll. In addition, and of major importance, social dancing itself underwent a profound change in the early 1960's, one that could perhaps be best evaluated by sociologists and psychologists. The shift from the traditional fox-trot and variations thereof to the non-tactile sensuality of such dances as the twist, frug, Madison, monkey, fish, Watusi, etc. produced, inevitably, a long stream of rhythmic songs dedicated as much to the promotion of as to the accompaniment for the new dances. The titles of the more popular songs of this genre are listed in this volume.

As the first five years of the 1960's came to a close, it was clear that not only had the market for popular music changed but the marketplace as well. The writers, producers, and performers of nearly all the hit songs and records were under the age of thirty, and very many of them even younger. A large portion of the billion dollars a year spent for popular music came from America's junior citizens, and the aging, conservative commercial establishment was having some difficulty in understanding and communicating with a generation of consumers that was adopting a whole new set of cultural clichés in exchange for those that comforted their parents. The language, the beat, and the sound of the discothèque, the protest march, the coffee house, the "happening," LSD, and sexual freedom belonged to the young.

The tempo of change in popular music has been a quickening one. As the second half of the 1960's began, several positive trends were discernible, the most important of which was the acceptance by the public of more intelligent lyrics and more subtle musical settings. All indications were and, at the time of writing, are that a new and higher level of popular music will be achieved before the decade is over.

Nat Shapiro

February 1967

1960

Aching, Breaking Heart
Words and music by Roe E. Hall.
Big Bopper Music Co./Tune Publishers, Inc.
Best-selling record in 1962 by George Jones (Mercury).

Alabam
Words and music by Lloyd Copas.
Starday Music.
Best-selling record by Cowboy Copas (Starday).

All I Could Do Was Cry
Words and music by Berry Gordy, Jr., Gwendolyn B. Gordy, and
    Roquel Davis.
Fidelity Music Co.
Best-selling record by Etta James (Argo).

(You Were Made For) All My Love
Words and music by Jackie Wilson and Billy Myles.
Pearl Music Co., Inc.
Best-selling record by Jackie Wilson (Brunswick).

All You Need Is a Quarter
Words by Betty Comden and Adolph Green, music by Jule Styne.
Stratford Music Corp.
Introduced by chorus in *Do Re Mi* (musical).

Alley Oop
Words and music by Dallas Frazier.
Maverick Music, Inc./Kavelin Music/T.M. Music, Inc.
Best-selling record by The Hollywood Argyles (Lute).

Alone at Last
Words and adaptation of music by Johnny Lehmann.
Pearl Music Co., Inc.
Melody based on theme from First Movement of Tchaikovsky's
    "Piano Concerto No. 1 in B-flat Minor." Best-selling record by
    Jackie Wilson (Brunswick).

Alvin's Orchestra
Words and music by Ross Bagdasarian.
Monarch Music Corp.
Best-selling record by The Chipmunks and David Seville (Liberty).

Amigo's Guitar, see 1959.

Angel Baby
Words and music by Rose Hamlin.
Figure Music, Inc.
Best-selling record by Rosie and The Originals (Highland).

Any Way the Wind Blows, see 1959.

Anybody but Me
Words and music by Ronnie Self and Dub Allbritten.
Champion Music Corp.
Best-selling record by Brenda Lee (Decca).

Anymore
Words and music by Roy Drusky, Vic McAlpin, and Marie Wilson.
Moss Rose Publications, Inc.
Best-selling record by Roy Drusky (Decca).

Apache (English)
Music by Jerry Lordan.
Francis, Day & Hunter, Ltd., London, England/Regent Music Corp.
Best-selling record in England by The Shadows (English Columbia);
   best-selling record in United States in 1961 by Jorgen Ingmann
   (Atco).

Apple Green
Words and music by Charlie Singleton.
Hollis Music, Inc.
Best-selling record by June Valli (Mercury).

Are You Sure
Words and music by Meredith Willson.
Frank Music Corp./Rinimer Corp.
Introduced by Tammy Grimes, Jack Harrold, and chorus in *The Un-
   sinkable Molly Brown* (musical).

Artificial Flowers
Words by Sheldon Harnick, music by Jerry Bock.
Sunbeam Music Corp.
Introduced by Ron Husmann and The Parishioners in *Tenderloin*
   (musical). Best-selling record by Bobby Darin (Atco).

As Long As He Needs Me (English)
Words and music by Lionel Bart.
Lakeview Music Co., Ltd., London, England/Hollis Music, Inc.
Introduced by Georgia Brown in London production and New York
   production (1963) of *Oliver!* (musical). Best-selling record in
   England by Shirley Bassey (Columbia).

Ask Anyone in Love
Words and music by Mr. and Mrs. Ted Shapiro.
Valiant Music Co., Inc.
Introduced by Tony Bennett (Columbia).

Asking for You
Words by Betty Comden and Adolph Green, music by Jule Styne.
Stratford Music Corp.
Introduced by John Reardon in *Do Re Mi* (musical).

Baby Sittin' Boogie
Words and music by Johnny Parker.
Herb Reis Music Corp.
Best-selling record in 1961 by Buzz Clifford (Columbia).

Baby, Talk to Me
Words by Lee Adams, music by Charles Strouse.
Edwin H. Morris & Co., Inc.
Introduced by Dick Van Dyke and quartet in *Bye Bye Birdie* (musical).

Baby (You've Got What It Takes), see 1959.

Bad and the Beautiful, The
Words by Dory Langdon, music by David Raksin.
Robbins Music Corp., 1953, 1960.
Melody, originally subtitled "Love Is for the Very Young," introduced as theme for *The Bad and the Beautiful* (film, 1953).

Badman's Blunder
Words and music by Lee Hays and Cisco Houston.
Sanga Music, Inc.
Best-selling record by The Kingston Trio (Capitol).

Ballad of Lady Jane, The, see My Love Doesn't Love Me at All.

Ballad of the Alamo
Words by Paul Francis Webster, music by Dimitri Tiomkin.
Leo Feist, Inc.
Introduced in *The Alamo* (film). Best-selling record by Marty Robbins (Columbia).

Ballad of Wild River, The
Words and music by Marshall T. Pack.
Mountain City Publishing Co.
Best-selling record by Gene Woods (Hap).

Banjo-Boy (German)
English words by Buddy Kaye, German words and music by Charly Niessen.
Edition Montana, Germany, 1959/Edition Tonleiter Gemeinschafts-Produktion, Germany, 1959/Budd Music Corp., 1960, 1961.
From *Kein Mann zum Heiraten* (German film). Best-selling record by Jan and Kjeld (Kapp). English words added in 1961.

Beatnik Fly
Words and music by Ira Mack and Tom King.
Duchess Music Corp.
Best-selling record by Johnny and The Hurricanes (Warwick).

Because They're Young
Words by Aaron Schroeder and Wally Gold, music by Don Costa.
Columbia Pictures Music Corp.
Introduced by Duane Eddy in *Because They're Young* (film). Best-
selling record by Duane Eddy (Jamie).

Before I Gaze at You Again
Words by Alan Jay Lerner, music by Frederick Loewe.
Chappell & Co., Inc.
Introduced by Julie Andrews in *Camelot* (musical).

Before This Day Ends
Words and music by Roy Drusky, Vic McAlpin, and Marie Wilson.
Moss Rose Publications, Inc.
Best-selling record by George Hamilton IV (ABC-Paramount).

Beggar to a King, also known as **From a Beggar to a King**
Words and music by J. P. Richardson.
Starrite Publishing Co.
Best-selling record in 1961 by Hank Snow (RCA Victor).

Belly Up to the Bar, Boys
Words and music by Meredith Willson.
Frank Music Corp./Rinimer Corp.
Introduced by Tammy Grimes, Joseph Sirola, and chorus in *The Un-
sinkable Molly Brown* (musical). Sung by Debbie Reynolds in film
version (1964).

Big Hurt, The, see 1959.

Blanket Roll Blues, see **Not a Soul.**

Blue Angel
Words and music by Roy Orbison and Joe Melson.
Acuff-Rose Publications, Inc.
Best-selling record by Roy Orbison (Monument).

Blue Rondo a la Turk
Music by Dave Brubeck.
Derry Music Co.
Introduced by The Dave Brubeck Quartet (Columbia).

Blue Train, The
Words by Paul Manning and Jim Harbert, music by Paul Manning.
Daywin Music, Inc.
Introduced by Doris Day (Columbia).

Boll Weevil Song
Words and music by Clyde Otis and Brook Benton.
Play Music, Inc.
Adapted from traditional American folk song. Introduced and best-selling record in 1961 by Brook Benton (Mercury).

Bonanza
Words and music by Jay Livingston and Ray Evans.
Livingston & Evans, Inc.
Theme of *Bonanza* (television series).

Boys
Words and music by Luther Dixon and Wes Farrell.
Ludix Publishing Co., Inc.
Introduced by The Shirelles (Scepter). Best-selling record in 1964 by The Beatles (Vee Jay and Capitol).

Broken Heart and a Pillow Filled with Tears, A
Words and music by Paul Anka.
Spanka Music Corp.
Best-selling record by Patti Page (Mercury).

Burning Bridges
Words and music by Melvin Miller.
Becks Music Co.
Best-selling record by Jack Scott (Top Rank).

But I Do
Words and music by Robert Guidry and Paul Gayten.
Arc Music Corp., 1960, 1961.
Best-selling record in 1961 by Clarence "Frogman" Henry (Argo).

Bye Bye Johnny
Words and music by Chuck Berry.
Arc Music Corp.
Introduced by Chuck Berry (Chess).

Calcutta (German)
English words by Lee Pockriss and Paul J. Vance, music by Heino Gaze.
Edition Takt und Ton GmbH., Berlin, Germany, 1958, 1960/Symphony House Music Publishers Corp./George Pincus & Sons Music Corp.
Introduced in Germany, in 1958, as "Tivoli Melody"; shortly thereafter as "Take Me Dreaming"; then as "Nicolette"; finally, in 1960, as "Kalkutta Liegt am Ganges." Best-selling instrumental recording in 1961 by Lawrence Welk and his Orchestra (Dot). Vocal version introduced by The Four Preps (Capitol).

Camelot
Words by Alan Jay Lerner, music by Frederick Loewe.
Chappell & Co., Inc.
Introduced by Richard Burton in *Camelot* (musical).

Captain Buffalo
Words by Mack David, music by Jerry Livingston.
M. Witmark & Sons.
From *Sergeant Rutledge* (film).

Cast Your Fate to the Wind
Words by Carel Werber, music by Vincent Guaraldi.
Atzal Music, Inc.
Best-selling record in 1962 by Vince Guaraldi (Fantasy). Winner of
    National Academy of Recording Arts and Sciences Award for
    "Best Original Jazz Composition," 1962. Revived and best-selling
    record in 1965 by Sounds Orchestral (Parkway). Vocal version
    introduced in 1965 by Steve Alaimo (ABC-Paramount).

Cathy's Clown
Words and music by Don Everly and Phil Everly.
Acuff-Rose Publications, Inc.
Best-selling record by The Everly Brothers (Warner Bros.).

Chain Gang, see 1956.

China Doll
Words and music by Cindy Walker.
Paxwin Music Corp.
Best-selling record by The Ames Brothers (RCA Victor).

Ching Ching, see **Ding Ding.**

Clementine
New words and adaptation of music by Woody Harris.
Towne Music Corp./Darwood Music Corp.
Based on American folk song, "Clementine." Best-selling record by
    Bobby Darin (Atco).

Cloud Song, The, see **Suzie Wong.**

Colorado, My Home
Words and music by Meredith Willson.
Frank Music Corp./Rinimer Corp.
Introduced by Tammy Grimes, Harve Presnell, and chorus in *The
    Unsinkable Molly Brown* (musical). Sung by Harve Presnell in
    film version (1964).

Consider Yourself (English)
Words and music by Lionel Bart.
Lakeview Music Co., Ltd., London, England/Hollis Music, Inc.
    Introduced by Keith Hamshere, Martin Horsey, and crowd in Lon-
    don production and sung by Paul O'Keefe, David Jones, and crowd
    in New York production (1963) of *Oliver!* (musical).

Country Girl, see 1959.

Cradle of Love
Words and music by Jack Fautheree and Wayne Gray.
Big Bopper Music Co./Tree Publishing Co., Inc.
Best-selling record by Johnny Preston (Mercury).

Cry Like the Wind
Words by Betty Comden and Adolph Green, music by Jule Styne.
Stratford Music Corp.
Introduced by Nancy Dussault in *Do Re Mi* (musical).

Dance On, Little Girl
Words and music by Paul Anka.
Spanka Music Corp., 1960, 1961.
Best-selling record in 1961 by Paul Anka (ABC-Paramount).

Delaware
Words and music by Irving Gordon.
Gunston Music, Inc.
Best-selling record by Perry Como (RCA Victor).

Ding Ding, also known as Ching Ching
Words and music by Bob Sherman and Dick Sherman.
Music World Corp./Annette Music, Inc.
Best-selling record by Hayley Mills (Vista).

Ding-a-Ling
Words and music by Kal Mann, Bernie Lowe, and Dave Appell.
Lowe Music Corp.
Best-selling record by Bobby Rydell (Cameo).

Dis-Donc, Dis-Donc, see 1958.

Do You Ever Dream of Vienna?
Words and music by Rick Besoyan.
Sunbeam Music Corp.
Introduced by Elizabeth Parrish and Mario Siletti in *Little Mary Sunshine* (off-Broadway musical).

Do You Mind? (English)
Words and music by Lionel Bart.
The Peter Maurice Music Co., Ltd.
From *Let's Get Married* (film). Introduced by Anthony Newley. Best-selling record by Andy Williams (Cadence).

Doggin' Around
Words and music by Lena Agree.
Lena Music, Inc.
Best-selling record by Jackie Wilson (Brunswick).

Dolce Far Niente
Words and music by Meredith Willson.
Frank Music Corp./Rinimer Corp.
Introduced by Mitchell Gregg in *The Unsinkable Molly Brown* (musical).

Dollar Down, A
Words and music by Cisco Houston.
Sanga Music, Inc., 1960, 1961.
Introduced by The Limeliters (RCA Victor).

Dondi
Words by Earl Shuman, music by Mort Garson.
Lear Music, Inc.
Based on comic-strip character, "Dondi." Introduced by Patti Page
   in *Dondi* (film, 1961).

Don't Come Knockin'
Words and music by Antoine Domino.
Travis Music Co.
Best-selling record by Fats Domino (Imperial).

Don't Cry No More
Words and music by Deadric Malone.
Don Music Co.
Best-selling record in 1961 by Bobby "Blue" Bland (Duke).

Don't Worry
Words and music by Marty Robbins.
Marty's Music Corp.
Introduced and best-selling record in 1961 by Marty Robbins (Co-
   lumbia).

Down by the Station, see Early in the Morning.

Dreamin'
Words and music by Ted Ellis and Barry De Vorzon.
Sherman-De Vorzon Music Corp.
Best-selling record by Johnny Burnette (Liberty).

Dreamy
Words by Sydney Shaw, music by Erroll Garner.
Octave Music Publishing Corp., 1956, 1960.
Introduced instrumentally in 1956 by Erroll Garner. Lyrics added in
   1960. First recording by Adam Wade (Epic).

Each Moment Spent with You
Words and music by Billy Worth (pseudonym for Ernest Ashworth)
   and Billy Hogan.
Acuff-Rose Publications, Inc.
Best-selling record by Ernest Ashworth (Decca).

Early in the Morning, also known as Down by the Station
Words and music adapted by Bruce Belland and Glen Larson.
Lar-Bell Music Corp.
Based on traditional song. Original title, "Down by the Station,"
   changed to "Early in the Morning." Best-selling record by The
   Four Preps (Capitol).

Eddie, My Darling
Words and music by Kathy Young.
Blue Indigo Music Co.
Best-selling record by Kathy Young (Indigo).

El Paso, see 1959.

Emotions
Words and music by Mel Tillis and Ramsey Kearney.
Cedarwood Publishing Co., Inc.
Best-selling record in 1961 by Brenda Lee (Decca).

Enchanted Melody, The
Music by Vic Mizzy.
Miller Music Corp., 1960, 1962.
Theme of *The Shirley Temple Show* (television series).

English Teacher, An
Words by Lee Adams, music by Charles Strouse.
Edwin H. Morris & Co., Inc.
Introduced by Chita Rivera and Dick Van Dyke in *Bye Bye Birdie*
    (musical).

Especially for the Young
Words by Manny Curtis, music by Ben Weisman.
Roncom Music Co.
Introduced by Perry Como (RCA Victor).

Ev'rybody's Somebody's Fool
Words by Howard Greenfield, music by Jack Keller.
Screen Gems-Columbia Music, Inc./Efsee Music, Inc.
Best-selling record by Connie Francis (MGM).

Excuse Me (I Think I've Got a Heartache)
Words and music by Harlan Howard and Alvis E. Owens.
Briarcliff Music, Inc.
Best-selling record by Buck Owens (Capitol).

Exodus
Music by Ernest Gold.
Chappell & Co., Inc.
Main theme from *Exodus* (film). Best-selling instrumental records
    in 1960-61 by Ferrante and Teicher (United Artists) and Eddie
    Harris (Vee Jay). Lyrics added in 1961 by Pat Boone under title,
    "The Exodus Song (This Land Is Mine)"; introduced by Pat
    Boone (Dot). Winner of National Academy of Recording Arts and
    Sciences Award for "Song of the Year," 1960.

Exodus Song, The (This Land Is Mine), see **Exodus.**

Face to the Wall, see 1959.

Facts of Life, The
Words and music by Johnny Mercer.
Commander Publications.
Introduced by Steve Lawrence and Eydie Gormé on soundtrack of
The Facts of Life (film). Nominated for Academy Award, 1960.

Fallen Angel
Words and music by Wayne Walker, Marijohn Wilkin, and Webb
Pierce.
Cedarwood Publishing Co., Inc.
Best-selling record by Webb Pierce (Decca).

Fame and Fortune
Words by Fred Wise, music by Ben Weisman.
Gladys Music, Inc.
Best-selling record by Elvis Presley (RCA Victor).

Family Bible
Words and music by Walt Breeland, Claude Gray, and Paul Buskirk.
Glad Music Co.
Best-selling record by Claude Gray (Decca).

Fannie Mae
Words and music by Waymon Glasco.
Frost Music Corp./Olivia Publishing Co.
Best-selling record by Buster Brown (Fire).

Faraway Boy, see 1959.

Faraway Part of Town, The
Words by Dory Langdon, music by André Previn.
Columbia Pictures Music Corp.
Introduced by voice of Judy Garland on soundtrack of Pepe (film).
Nominated for Academy Award, 1960.

Faucets Are Dripping, The
Words and music by Malvina Reynolds.
Schroder Music Co.
Introduced by Malvina Reynolds.

Feel So Fine (Feel So Good)
Words and music by Leonard Lee.
Travis Music Co./Big Bopper Music Co.
Best-selling record by Jo Hallyday (Philips).

Fie on Goodness!
Words by Alan Jay Lerner, music by Frederick Loewe.
Chappell & Co., Inc.
Introduced by The Knights (John Cullum, James Gannon, and Bruce
Yarnell) in Camelot (musical).

Finger Poppin' Time
Words and music by Hank Ballard.
Lois Publishing Co.
Introduced and best-selling record by Hank Ballard and The Mid-nighters (King).

Fings Ain't Wot They Used T'Be (English)
Words and music by Lionel Bart.
The Peter Maurice Music Co., Ltd., London, England/The Peter Maurice Music Co., Ltd.
From *Fings Ain't Wot They Used T'Be* (British musical). Best-sell-ing record in England by Max Bygraves (Decca).

Fireworks
Words by Betty Comden and Adolph Green, music by Jule Styne.
Stratford Music Corp.
Introduced by John Reardon and Nancy Dussault in *Do Re Mi* (musi-cal).

Follow Me
Words by Alan Jay Lerner, music by Frederick Loewe.
Chappell & Co., Inc.
Introduced by Marjorie Smith in *Camelot* (musical). Best-selling record by Tony Bennett (Columbia).

Food, Glorious Food (English)
Words and music by Lionel Bart.
Lakeview Music Co., Ltd., London, England/Hollis Music, Inc.
Introduced by Keith Hamshere and boys in London production and sung by Paul O'Keefe and boys in New York production (1963) of *Oliver!* (musical).

Fool in Love (Tell Me What's Wrong), A
Words and music by Ike Turner.
Saturn Music, Inc.
Best-selling record by Ike and Tina Turner (Sue).

Fool Too Long, A, see Poor Fool.

Footsteps
Words and music by Barry Mann and Hank Hunter.
Screen Gems-Columbia Music, Inc.
Best-selling record by Steve Lawrence (ABC-Paramount).

Forty Winks Away
Words by Larry Kolber, music by Barry Mann.
Screen Gems-Columbia Music, Inc.
Best-selling record by Neil Sedaka (RCA Victor).

From a Beggar to a King, see Beggar to a King.

From the Terrace (Love Theme)
Music by Elmer Bernstein.
Miller Music Corp.
From *From the Terrace* (film).

Gee Whiz! (Look at His Eyes)
Words and music by Carla Thomas.
East Publications/Bais Music.
Best-selling record in 1961 by Carla Thomas (Atlantic).

Gimme That Wine
Words and music by Jon Hendricks.
Hendricks Music, Inc.
Introduced by Lambert, Hendricks, and Ross (Columbia).

Gina
Words and music by Paul Vance and Leon Carr.
Elm Drive Music Corp.
Introduced by Johnny Janis (Columbia). Best-selling record in 1962
   by Johnny Mathis (Columbia).

Give a Little Whistle
Words by Carolyn Leigh, music by Cy Coleman.
Edwin H. Morris & Co., Inc.
Introduced by Lucille Ball, Keith Andes, The Crew, and Townspeople
   in *Wildcat* (musical).

Gloria
Words by Mack David, music by Bronislau Kaper.
Robbins Music Corp.
Adapted from a theme from *Butterfield 8* (film).

Go, Jimmy, Go, see 1959.

Gone Is My Love
Words and music by Paul Vance and Leon Carr.
Roncom Music Co.
Introduced by Perry Como (RCA Victor).

Good Clean Fun
Words by Sheldon Harnick, music by Jerry Bock.
Sunbeam Music Corp.
Introduced by Maurice Evans and The Parishioners in *Tenderloin*
   (musical).

Good Timin'
Words and music by Clint Ballard, Jr. and Fred Tobias.
Post Music, Inc.
Best-selling record by Jimmy Jones (Cub).

Got My Mojo Working
Words and music by McKinley Morganfield.
Arc Music Corp.
Introduced by Muddy Waters.

Green Fields, see 1956.

Green Leaves of Summer, The
Words by Paul Francis Webster, music by Dimitri Tiomkin.
Leo Feist, Inc.
From *The Alamo* (film). Nominated for Academy Award, 1960. Best-selling record by The Brothers Four (Columbia).

Greener Pastures
Words and music by Marijohn Wilkin.
Cedarwood Publishing Co., Inc.
Best-selling record in 1961 by Stonewall Jackson (Columbia).

Guenevere
Words by Alan Jay Lerner, music by Frederick Loewe.
Chappell & Co., Inc.
Introduced by ensemble in *Camelot* (musical).

G'Won Train
Music by Patti Bown.
Duchess Music Corp., 1960, 1963.
Introduced by Patti Bown (Columbia).

Handbag Is Not a Proper Mother, A
Words by Anne Croswell, music by Lee Pockriss.
Edwin H. Morris & Co., Inc.
Introduced by Sara Seegar and John Irving in *Ernest in Love* (off-Broadway musical).

Handy Man, see 1959.

Happiness
Words and music by Fred Darian and Joseph Van Winkle.
Criterion Music Corp.
Best-selling record by Teddy Tanaka (Cordak).

Happy Birthday to Me
Words and music by Bill Anderson.
Tree Publishing Co., Inc./Champion Music Corp.
Best-selling record in 1961-62 by Hank Locklin (RCA Victor).

Happy Go Lucky Me
Words by Al Byron, music by Paul Evans.
Pambill Music, Inc./Lyle Music, Inc.
Introduced and best-selling record by Paul Evans (Guaranteed).

He Will Break Your Heart
Words and music by Jerry Butler, Calvin Carter, and Curtis Mayfield.
Conrad Publishing Co., Inc.
Best-selling record by Jerry Butler (Vee Jay).

Heart to Heart Talk
Words and music by Lee Ross.
Loring Music Co.
Best-selling record by Bob Wills and Tommy Duncan (Liberty).

Heartaches by the Number, see 1959.

Heartbreak (It's Hurting Me)
Words and music by John Thomas and C. Hoyles.
Pamco Music, Inc.
Best-selling record by Jon Thomas (ABC-Paramount).

Heartbreak, U.S.A.
Words and music by Harlan Howard.
Pamper Music, Inc., 1960, 1961.
Best-selling record in 1961 by Kitty Wells (Decca).

He'll Have To Go, see 1959.

He'll Have To Stay
Words by Charles Grean, music by Charles Grean, Audrey Allison, and Joe Allison.
Central Songs, Inc.
Introduced by Corina Minette (ABC-Paramount). Best-selling record by Jeanne Black (Capitol).

Hennesey
Music by Sonny Burke.
Crystal Music Publishers, Inc.
From *Hennesey* (television series).

Hey, Look Me Over
Words by Carolyn Leigh, music by Cy Coleman.
Edwin H. Morris & Co., Inc.
Introduced by Lucille Ball and Paula Stewart in *Wildcat* (musical).

Honestly Sincere
Words by Lee Adams, music by Charles Strouse.
Edwin H. Morris & Co., Inc.
Introduced by Dick Gautier and chorus in *Bye Bye Birdie* (musical). Sung by Jesse Pearson in film version (1963).

Hop, Skip, Jump
Music by Robert Ascher.
Devon Music, Inc.
From *Miracle on 34th Street* (television special).

How Lovely To Be a Woman
Words by Lee Adams, music by Charles Strouse.
Edwin H. Morris & Co., Inc.
Introduced by Susan Watson in *Bye Bye Birdie* (musical). Sung by Ann-Margret in film version (1963).

How To Handle a Woman
Words by Alan Jay Lerner, music by Frederick Loewe.
Chappell & Co., Inc.
Introduced by Richard Burton in *Camelot* (musical).

Hymn for a Sunday Evening
Words by Lee Adams, music by Charles Strouse.
Edwin H. Morris & Co., Inc.
Introduced by Paul Lynde, Marijane Maricle, Susan Watson, and
 Johnny Borden in *Bye Bye Birdie* (musical). Sung by Ann-
 Margret, Paul Lynde, Mary La Roche, and Bryan Russell in film
 version (1963).

I Ain't Down Yet
Words and music by Meredith Willson.
Frank Music Corp./Rinimer Corp.
Introduced by Tammy Grimes and Harve Presnell in *The Unsinkable
 Molly Brown* (musical). Sung by Debbie Reynolds and Harve
 Presnell in film version (1964).

I Belong to Your Heart (French)
English words by Carl Sigman, French words and music by Jacques
 Brel.
Éditions Tropicales, Paris, France, 1956/Sigma Music, Inc.
Original French title, "Quand On n'a Que l'Amour." Best-selling
 record by Sam Cooke (RCA Victor).

I Can See It
Words by Tom Jones, music by Harvey Schmidt.
Chappell & Co., Inc.
Introduced by Kenneth Nelson and Rita Gardner in *The Fantasticks*
 (off-Broadway musical).

I Can't Help You, I'm Falling Too, see Please Help Me, I'm Falling (In Love with You).

I Cry Alone
Words by Hal David, music by Burt Bacharach.
Mansion Music Corp., 1960, 1963.
Best-selling record by Dionne Warwick (Scepter).

I Don't Believe I'll Fall in Love Today
Words and music by Harlan Howard.
Central Songs, Inc.
Best-selling record by Warren Smith (Liberty).

I Fall to Pieces
Words by Hank Cochran, music by Harlan Howard.
Pamper Music, Inc.
Best-selling record in 1961 by Patsy Cline (Decca).

I Know about Love
Words by Betty Comden and Adolph Green, music by Jule Styne.
Stratford Music Corp.
Introduced by John Reardon in *Do Re Mi* (musical).

I Know One
Words and music by Jack Clement.
Jack Music, Inc.
Best-selling record by Jim Reeves (RCA Victor).

I Love the Way You Love
Words and music by Berry Gordy, Jr. and Mikaljohn.
Jobete Music Co., Inc.
Best-selling record by Marv Johnson (United Artists).

I Loved You Once in Silence
Words by Alan Jay Lerner, music by Frederick Loewe.
Chappell & Co., Inc.
Introduced by Julie Andrews in *Camelot* (musical).

I May Never Get to Heaven
Words and music by Buddy Killen and Bill Anderson.
Tree Publishing Co., Inc.
Introduced by Don Gibson (RCA Victor).

I Missed Me
Words and music by Bill Anderson.
Tree Publishing Co., Inc./Champion Music Corp.
Introduced by Jim Reeves (RCA Victor).

I Must Be Dreaming
Words and music by Neil Sedaka and Howard Greenfield.
Screen Gems-Columbia Music, Inc.
Best-selling record by Neil Sedaka (RCA Victor).

I Pity the Fool
Words and music by Deadric Malone.
Lion Publishing Co., Inc.
Best-selling record in 1961 by Bobby Bland (Duke).

I Think I Know
Words and music by Claude Putnam.
Travis Music Co.
Best-selling record by Marion Worth (Columbia).

I Want To Be Wanted (Italian)
English words by Kim Gannon, Italian words by A. Testa, music by
  Pino Spotti.
Casa Editrice Santa Cecilia, Milan, Italy, 1959, 1960/Leeds Music
  Corp.
Original Italian title, "Per Tutta la Vita." Best-selling records by
  Brenda Lee (Decca) and Andy Williams (Columbia).

I Want To Know
Words and music by Pylia Parham, Robert Geddins, and Ronald
    Badger.
B-Flat Publishing Co.
Best-selling record by Sugarpie Desanto (Check).

I Wish I Could Fall in Love Today
Words and music by Harlan Howard.
Central Songs, Inc.
Best-selling record by Ray Price (Columbia).

I Wish I'd Never Been Born
Words and music by Jack Keller and Howard Greenfield.
Screen Gems-Columbia Music, Inc.
Introduced by Patti Page (Mercury).

I Wonder What It's Like?
Words by Sheldon Harnick, music by Jerry Bock.
Sunbeam Music Corp., 1959, 1960.
Written for, but deleted from, *Tenderloin* (musical).

I Wonder What the King Is Doing Tonight?
Words by Alan Jay Lerner, music by Frederick Loewe.
Chappell & Co., Inc.
Introduced by Richard Burton in *Camelot* (musical).

I'd Do Anything (English)
Words and music by Lionel Bart.
Lakeview Music Co., Ltd., London, England/Hollis Music, Inc.
Introduced by Martin Horsey, Georgia Brown, Keith Hamshere, and
    cast in London production and sung by David Jones, Georgia
    Brown, Paul O'Keefe, and cast in New York production (1963) of
    Oliver! (musical).

I'd Rather Loan You Out
Words and music by Roy Drusky, Vic McAlpin, and Lester Vanadore.
Moss Rose Publications, Inc.
Best-selling record in 1961 by Roy Drusky (Decca).

If Ever I Would Leave You
Words by Alan Jay Lerner, music by Frederick Loewe.
Chappell & Co., Inc.
Introduced by Robert Goulet in *Camelot* (musical).

If I Can't Have You
Words and music by Harvey Fuqua and Etta James.
Arc Music Corp.
Best-selling record by Etta and Harvey (Chess).

If I Had a Girl, see 1959.

If I Knew
Words and music by Meredith Willson.
Frank Music Corp./Rinimer Corp.
Introduced by Harve Presnell in *The Unsinkable Molly Brown* (musical).

If I Lost Your Love
Words and music by Wayne P. Walker.
Cedarwood Publishing Co., Inc.
Best-selling record by Mel Tillis (Columbia).

If She Should Come to You (La Montaña) (Spanish)
English words by Alec Wilder, Spanish words by G. Moreu, music by Augusto Alguero.
Canciones Del Mundo, Barcelona, Spain, 1959/Hollis Music, Inc.
English-language version introduced by Anthony Newley (London).

I'll Be There
Words and music by Bobby Darin.
T. M. Music, Inc., 1960, 1964.
Introduced by Bobby Darin (Atco). Best-selling record in 1964 by Gerry and The Pacemakers (Laurie).

I'll Have Another Cup of Coffee, Then I'll Go, also known as I'll Just Have a Cup of Coffee
Words and music by Bill Brock.
Mixer Music/Tree Publishing Co., Inc.
Best-selling record in 1961 by Claude Gray (Mercury).

I'll Just Have A Cup of Coffee, see I'll Have Another Cup of Coffee, Then I'll Go.

I'll Never Say No
Words and music by Meredith Willson.
Frank Music Corp./Rinimer Corp.
Introduced by Harve Presnell in *The Unsinkable Molly Brown* (musical). Sung by Harve Presnell and Debbie Reynolds in film version (1964).

I'm a Fool for Loving You
Words and music by Bob Edwards and Fred Henley.
Vogue Music Co.
Introduced by Bobby Edwards (Crest).

I'm Gettin' Better
Words and music by Jim Reeves.
Tuckahoe Music, Inc.
Best-selling record by Jim Reeves (RCA Victor).

I'm So Miserable without You, see 1964.

I'm Sorry
Words and music by Ronnie Self and Dub Allbritten.
Champion Music Corp.
Best-selling record by Brenda Lee (Decca).

Image of a Girl
Words by Marvin Rosenberg, music by Richard Clasky.
Eldorado Music Co.
Best-selling record by The Safaris (Eldo).

Irma la Douce, see 1958.

It's Now or Never
Words and music by Aaron Schroeder and Wally Gold.
Gladys Music, Inc.
Adapted from Italian song, "O Solo Mio," with lyrics by G. Capurro
and music by Eduardo Di Capua. Best-selling record by Elvis
Presley (RCA Victor).

It's Time To Cry, see 1959.

Itsy Bitsy Teenie Weenie Yellow Polkadot Bikini
Words and music by Paul J. Vance and Lee Pockriss.
George Pincus & Sons Music Corp.
Best-selling record by Brian Hyland (Kapp).

Jimmy's Girl
Words and music by Paul J. Vance and Lee Pockriss.
Skidmore Music Co. Inc.
Best-selling record by Johnny Tillotson (Cadence).

Jousts, The
Words by Alan Jay Lerner, music by Frederick Loewe.
Chappell & Co., Inc.
Introduced by Richard Burton and Julie Andrews in *Camelot* (musical).

Just for Old Times' Sake
Words and music by Hank Hunter and Jack Keller.
Screen Gems-Columbia Music, Inc., 1960, 1961.
Best-selling record by The McGuire Sisters (Coral).

Just One Time
Words and music by Don Gibson.
Acuff-Rose Publications, Inc.
Best-selling record by Don Gibson (RCA Victor).

Kids
Words by Lee Adams, music by Charles Strouse.
Edwin H. Morris & Co., Inc.
Introduced by Paul Lynde in *Bye Bye Birdie* (musical). Sung by
Dick Van Dyke, Paul Lynde, Maureen Stapleton, and Bryan Russell
in film version (1963).

King of Holiday Island, The
Words by Bob Hilliard, music by Milton De Lugg.
Shapiro, Bernstein & Co., Inc.
Best-selling record by Don Rondo (Carlton).

Kissin' on the Phone
Words by Earl Wilson, music by Leonard Whitcup.
Brighton Music Co., Inc./Flanka Music Corp.
Best-selling record in 1961 by Paul Anka (ABC-Paramount).

Kookie Little Paradise, A
Words by Bob Hilliard, music by Lee Pockriss.
Skidmore Music Co., Inc.
Best-selling record by Jo Ann Campbell (ABC-Paramount).

La Dolce Vita (The Sweet Life) (Italian)
English words by Les Vandyke, Italian words by Dino Verde, music
by Nino Rota.
Edizioni Mus. G. Campi e Nord-Sud, Rome, Italy/Robbins Music Corp.
Adapted from a theme from *La Dolce Vita* (film).

La Montaña, see If She Should Come to You.

Lady Luck
Words and music by Lloyd Price and Harold Logan.
Prigan Music Corp.
Best-selling record by Lloyd Price (ABC-Paramount).

Last Date
Words and music by Floyd Cramer.
Acuff-Rose Publications, Inc.
Best-selling instrumental record by Floyd Cramer (RCA Victor);
best-selling vocal record by Pat Boone (Dot).

(I'd Be) A Legend in My Time
Words and music by Don Gibson.
Acuff-Rose Publications, Inc.
Introduced by Don Gibson.

Lemon Tree
Words and music by Will Holt.
Boulder Music Corp./Dolfi Music, Inc.
Best-selling records in 1961 by Peter, Paul, and Mary (Warner Bros.)
and in 1964-65 by Trini Lopez (Reprise).

Let's Get Together
Words and music by Richard Sherman and Robert Sherman.
Wonderland Music Co., Inc., 1960, 1961.
Introduced in *The Parent Trap* (film, 1961). Best-selling record in
1961 by Hayley Mills (Vista).

Let's Go, Let's Go, Let's Go
Words and music by Hank Ballard.
Lois Publishing Co.
Best-selling record by Hank Ballard and The Midnighters (King).

Let's Slip Away (English)
Words by David Dearlove, music by Johnny Dankworth.
B. Feldman & Co., Ltd., London, England/Harvard Music, Inc.
From *Saturday Night and Sunday Morning* (British film).

Let's Think about Living
Words and music by Boudleaux Bryant.
Acuff-Rose Publication, Inc.
Best-selling record by Bob Luman (Warner Bros.).

Like Love
Words by Dory Langdon, music by André Previn.
Andor Music Co.
First recording by Jack Jones (Kapp).

Little Bitty Girl
Words and music by Clint Ballard, Jr. and Fred Tobias.
Post Music, Inc.
Best-selling record by Bobby Rydell (Cameo).

Little Bitty Tear, A
Words and music by Hank Cochran.
Pamper Music, Inc.
Best-selling record in 1962 by Burl Ives (Decca).

Little Boy Lost (Australian)
Words and music by Tony Withers and Johnny Ashcroft.
Leeds Music Pty., Ltd., Sydney, Australia/Leeds Music Corp.

Little Boy Sad
Words and music by Wayne P. Walker.
Cedarwood Publishing Co., Inc.
Best-selling records by Johnny Burnette (Liberty) and in 1966 by
  Herman's Hermits (MGM).

Little Old New York
Words by Sheldon Harnick, music by Jerry Bock.
Sunbeam Music Corp.
Introduced by Eileen Rodgers, Lee Becker, and The Tenderloin
  Crowd in *Tenderloin* (musical).

Little Space Girl, see 1959.

Little Susie, see 1958.

Loco Weed
Words and music by Mel Tillis and Jim Denny.
Cedarwood Publishing Co., Inc.
Best-selling record by Mel Tillis (Columbia).

Lollipops and Roses
Words and music by Tony Velona.
Cavalcade Music Corp.
Best-selling record by Jack Jones (Kapp). Winner of National Academy of Recording Arts and Sciences Award for "Best Solo Vocal Performance—Male," 1961.

Lonely Blue Boy, see 1958.

Lonely Teenager
Words and music by Salvatore Pippa, Alfred Di Paolo, and Silvio Faraci.
Lola Publishing Corp.
Best-selling record in 1961 by Dion (Laurie).

Lonely Weekends
Words and music by Charlie Rich.
Hi Lo Music, Inc.
Best-selling record by Charlie Rich (Phillips International).

Lonely Woman
Words by Margo Guryan, music by Ornette Coleman.
M.J.Q. Music, Inc.
Introduced by Ornette Coleman (Atlantic). First vocal version by June Christy (Capitol).

Long Gone
Words and music by Alfonso "Sonny" Thompson and Lewis Simkins.
Arc Music Corp.
Best-selling record in 1948 by Sonny Thompson (Miracle). Not copyrighted until 1960.

Look for a Sky of Blue
Words and music by Rick Besoyan.
Sunbeam Music Corp.
Introduced by Eileen Brennan and chorus in *Little Mary Sunshine* (off-Broadway musical).

Look for a Star (English)
Words and music by Mark Anthony (pseudonym for Tony Hatch).
Filmusic Publishing Co., Ltd., London, England/Harborn Music, Inc./Dijon Music.
Introduced by Garry Mills on soundtrack of *Circus of Horrors* (British film).

Lot of Livin' To Do, A
Words by Lee Adams, music by Charles Strouse.
Edwin H. Morris & Co., Inc.
Introduced by Dick Gautier and The Teenagers in *Bye Bye Birdie* (musical). Sung by Jesse Pearson, Ann-Margret, and Bobby Rydell in film version (1963).

Love Has Laid Her Hands on Me
Words and music by Margie Singleton.
Tree Publishing Co., Inc.
Introduced by Damita Jo (Mercury).

Love Has Made You Beautiful
Words and music by Merle Kilgore.
Bayou State Publishing Co.
Best-selling record by Merle Kilgore (Starday).

Love Me Some More (French)
English words by Mitchell Parish, French words by Henri Contet,
    music by Paul Durand.
La Societé Éditions Paris-Étoile, Paris, France/Mills Music, Inc.
Original French title "Les Mains du Vent." From *The Cow and the
    Prisoner* (French film).

(I Wanna) Love My Life Away
Words and music by Gene Pitney.
Sea-Lark Enterprises, Inc.
Introduced and best-selling record by Gene Pitney (Musicor).

Love Theme from *One-Eyed Jacks*
Music by Hugo W. Friedhofer.
Famous Music Corp., 1960, 1961.
From *One-Eyed Jacks* (film).

Love Theme from *The Rat Race*
Music by Elmer Bernstein.
Famous Music Corp.
From *The Rat Race* (film).

Love Theme from *The World of Suzie Wong*
Music by George Duning.
Famous Music Corp.
From *The World of Suzie Wong* (film).

Lovely Laurie
Words by Sheldon Harnick, music by Jerry Bock.
Sunbeam Music Corp.
Written for, but deleted from, *Tenderloin* (musical).

Lovely Work of Art, A
Words and music by James Joiner.
Newkeys Music, Inc./Tune Publishers, Inc.
Best-selling record by Jimmy Newman (MGM).

Loving You (Was Worth This Broken Heart)
Words and music by Helen Carter.
Acuff-Rose Publications, Inc.
Best-selling records by Bob Gallion (Hickory) and Porter Wagoner
    (RCA Victor).

Lusty Month of May, The
Words by Alan Jay Lerner, music by Frederick Loewe.
Chappell & Co., Inc.
Introduced by Julie Andrews and ensemble in *Camelot* (musical).

(Girls, Girls, Girls Were) Made To Love
Words and music by Phil Everly.
Acuff-Rose Publications, Inc.
Best-selling record in 1962 by Eddie Hodges (Cadence).

Madison Time
Words by Eddie Morrison, music by Ray Bryant.
Ludlow Music, Inc.
Best-selling record by Ray Bryant (Columbia).

Magnificent Seven, The
Music by Elmer Bernstein.
United Artists Music Co., Inc.
From *The Magnificent Seven* (film).

Main Title Theme from *The Rat Race*
Music by Elmer Bernstein.
Famous Music Corp.
From *The Rat Race* (film).

Make Someone Happy
Words by Betty Comden and Adolph Green, music by Jule Styne.
Stratford Music Corp.
Introduced by John Reardon in *Do Re Mi* (musical).

Manhã de Carnaval, see 1959.

Many Tears Ago
Words and music by Winfield Scott.
Roosevelt Music Co., Inc./Efsee Music, Inc.
Best-selling record by Connie Francis (MGM).

Maria Ninguem (Brazilian)
Portuguese words and music by Carlos Lyra.
Editora de Musica Brasilera e Internacional S.A., Brazil/Peer
    International Corp.
Introduced in United States by The Paul Winter Quintet (Columbia).

Marriage-Go-Round, The
Words and music by Alan Bergman, Marily Keith, and Lew Spence.
Robbins Music Corp.
Introduced by voice of Tony Bennett on soundtrack of *The Marriage-Go-Round* (film, 1961).

Mental Cruelty
Words and music by Larry Davis and Dixie Davis.
Les Kangas Music Publishing Co./Blue Book Music Co.
Best-selling record in 1961 by Buck Owens and Rose Maddox (Capitol).

Mess o' Blues, A
Words and music by Doc Pomus and Mort Shuman.
Elvis Presley Music, Inc.
Best-selling record by Elvis Presley (RCA Victor).

Midnight Lace
Words and music by Jerome Howard and Joe Lubin.
Daywin Music, Inc.
Theme from *Midnight Lace* (film). Best-selling record by Ray Coniff
  and his Orchestra and Chorus (Columbia).

Million to One, A
Words and music by Phil Medley.
Starflower Music Co.
Best-selling record by Jimmy Charles (Promo).

Miracles
Words and music by Bart Howard.
Elm Drive Music Corp.
Introduced by Johnny Mathis (Columbia).

Mission Bell
Words and music by William Michael.
Bamboo Music, Inc.
Best-selling record by Donnie Brooks (Era).

Mister Custer
Words and music by Fred Darian, Al De Lory, and Joseph Van
  Winkle.
Pattern Music, Inc.
Best-selling record by Larry Verne (Era).

Mr. Lucky
Words by Jay Livingston and Ray Evans, music by Henry Mancini.
Southdale Music Corp.
Theme from *Mr. Lucky* (television series). Best-selling record by
  Henry Mancini and his Orchestra (RCA Victor). Winner of Na-
  tional Academy of Recording Arts and Sciences Awards for "Best
  Performance by an Orchestra" and "Best Arrangement," 1960.

Moment of Fear
Music by Vic Mizzy.
Miller Music Corp., 1960, 1962.
From *Moment of Fear* (television drama).

Much More
Words by Tom Jones, music by Harvey Schmidt.
Chappell & Co., Inc.
Introduced by Rita Gardner in *The Fantasticks* (off-Broadway musi-
  cal). Popularized in 1963 by Barbra Streisand (Columbia).

Much Too Well
Words and music by Roger Miller.
Tree Publishing Co., Inc.
Introduced by Hawkshaw Hawkins (Columbia).

Music of Home, The, see 1959.

Muss I Denn, see **Wooden Heart.**

Must Be Santa
Words and music by Hal Moore and Bill Fredricks.
Hollis Music, Inc.
Introduced by Mitch Miller and his Orchestra and Chorus (Columbia).

Mustafa, see **The Sheik of Chicago.**

My Dearest Darling
Words and music by Paul Gayten and E. Bocage.
Arc Music Corp.
Best-selling record by Etta James (Argo).

My Empty Arms
Words and adaptation of music by Al Kasha and Hank Hunter.
Merrimac Music Corp.
Adapted from an aria from Leoncavallo's opera, *Pagliacci*. Best-selling record in 1961 by Jackie Wilson (Brunswick).

My Gentle Young Johnny
Words by Sheldon Harnick, music by Jerry Bock.
Sunbeam Music Corp.
Introduced by Eileen Rodgers and The Girls in *Tenderloin* (musical).

My Heart Has a Mind of Its Own
Words by Howard Greenfield, music by Jack Keller.
Screen Gems-Columbia Music, Inc.
Best-selling record by Connie Francis (MGM).

My Heart Was an Island, see **Swiss Family Theme.**

My Home Town
Words and music by Paul Anka.
Spanka Music Corp.
Best-selling record by Paul Anka (ABC-Paramount).

My Last Date (With You)
Words by Boudleaux Bryant and Skeeter Davis, music by Floyd Cramer.
Acuff-Rose Publications, Inc.
Best-selling record in 1961 by Skeeter Davis (RCA Victor).

My Little Corner of the World
Words by Bob Hilliard, music by Lee Pockriss.
Shapiro, Bernstein & Co., Inc./Lewis Music Publishing Co., Inc.
Best-selling record by Anita Bryant (Carlton).

My Love Doesn't Love Me at All (The Ballad of Lady Jane)
Words and music by Irving Gordon.
Shapiro, Bernstein & Co., Inc.
Identified with Jane Morgan (Kapp).

My Miss Mary
Words by Sheldon Harnick, music by Jerry Bock.
Sunbeam Music Corp.
Introduced by Ron Husmann, Wynne Miller, and ensemble in *Tenderloin* (musical).

My Old Man's a Dustman (English)
Words and music adapted by Lonnie Donegan, Peter Buchanan, and
Beverley Thorn.
Tyler Music, Ltd., London, England/Hollis Music, Inc.
Based on traditional song. Best-selling record by Lonnie Donegan
(Atlantic).

Need for Love, The, see **The Unforgiven.**

Never on Sunday (Greek)
English words by Billy Towne, Greek words and music by Manos
Hadjidakis.
Éditions Associées, Paris, France/Éditions Musicales Eddie Barclay,
Paris, France/Unart Music Corp./Llee Corp.
Introduced in Greek under original title, "Ta Pedia Tou Pirea"
("The Children of Piraeus") by Melina Mercouri in *Never on
Sunday* (Greek film). Academy Award-winning song, 1960. Originally copyrighted in France under title, "Les Enfants du Pirée,"
with French lyrics by Jacques Larue. Best-selling records by Don
Costa and his Orchestra (United Artists) and The Chordettes
(Cadence).

(Down in) New Orleans
Words and music by Frank J. Guida and Joseph F. Royster.
Rock Masters, Inc.
Best-selling record by U. S. Bonds (LeGrand).

Next Time I Love, The
Words and music by Jerry Herman.
Vogue Music Co.
Introduced in *Jerry Herman's Parade* (revue).

Nice 'n' Easy
Words by Marilyn Keith and Alan Bergman, music by Lew Spence.
Eddie Shaw Music Co.
Introduced by Frank Sinatra (Capitol).

No Love Have I
Words and music by Mel Tillis.
Cedarwood Publishing Co., Inc.
Introduced by Mel Tillis (Columbia).

Non, Je Ne Regrette Rien, see **No Regrets,** 1961.

Normal American Boy
Words by Lee Adams, music by Charles Strouse.
Edwin H. Morris & Co., Inc.
Introduced by Chita Rivera, Dick Van Dyke, and chorus in *Bye Bye Birdie* (musical).

North to Alaska
Words and music by Mike Phillips.
Robbins Music Corp.
Introduced by Johnny Horton in *North to Alaska* (film). Best-selling record by Johnny Horton (Columbia).

Not a Soul (Blanket Roll Blues)
Words by Tennessee Williams, music by Kenyon Hopkins.
United Artists Music Co., Inc.
Introduced by Marlon Brando in *The Fugitive Kind* (film).

Not Me
Words and music by Gary Anderson and Frank Guida.
Rock Masters, Inc.
Best-selling record by U.S. Bonds (LeGrand).

O Dio Mio
Words and music by Al Hoffman and Dick Manning.
Topper Music Publishing Corp.
Best-selling record by Annette (Vista).

Oh, Oh, Rosie (Belgian)
English words by Bob Merrill, Italian words and music by Rocco Granata.
Class Music-V, Antwerp, Belgium, 1959/Ivan Mogull Music Corp.
Origin of song is Belgium, although lyrics are Italian. Introduced in Europe by Rocco Granata. English-language version introduced by Lou Monte (RCA Victor).

On the Rebound
Words and music by Floyd Cramer.
Cigma Music Co., Inc.
Best-selling record in 1961 by Floyd Cramer (RCA Victor).

Once in a Blue Moon
Words and music by Rick Besoyan.
Sunbeam Music Corp.
Introduced by Jack McMartin and Elmarie Wendel in *Little Mary Sunhine* (off-Broadway musical).

One Boy
Words by Lee Adams, music by Charles Strouse.
Edwin H. Morris & Co., Inc.
Introduced by Susan Watson, Jessica Albright, Sharon Lerit, and Chita Rivera in *Bye Bye Birdie* (musical). Sung by Ann-Margret, Janet Leigh, and Bobby Rydell in film version (1963).

One Last Kiss
Words by Lee Adams, music by Charles Strouse.
Edwin H. Morris & Co., Inc.
Introduced by Dick Gautier and company in *Bye Bye Birdie* (musical). Sung by Jesse Pearson in film version (1963).

One More Time
Words and music by Mel Tillis.
Cedarwood Publishing Co., Inc.
Best-selling record by Ray Price (Columbia).

One of Us (Will Weep Tonight)
Words and music by Clint Ballard, Jr. and Fred Tobias.
Post Music, Inc.
Introduced by Patti Page (Mercury).

Only the Lonely (Know the Way I Feel)
Words and music by Roy Orbison and Joe Melson.
Acuff-Rose Publications, Inc.
Best-selling record by Roy Orbison (Monument).

Our Concerto (Italian)
English words by Hal David, Italian words by Giorgio Calabrese, music by Umberto Bindi.
Ariston Edizioni Musicali, Milan, Italy/Shapiro, Bernstein & Co., Inc.
Original title "Il Nostro Concerto." Introduced by Umberto Bindi (Jamie). First recording in English by Al Martino (20th Century-Fox).

Our Language of Love, see 1958.

Paper Roses
Words by Janice Torre, music by Fred Spielman.
Lewis Music Publishing Co., Inc.
Best-selling record by Anita Bryant (Carlton).

Partin' Time
Words and music by B.B. King.
Modern Music Publishing Co.
Best-selling record by B.B. King (Kent).

Passing Through
Words by Sydney Shaw, music by Erroll Garner.
Octave Music Publishing Corp.
Version, with lyrics, of instrumental introduced in 1956.

Pastures of Plenty
Words and music by Woody Guthrie.
Ludlow Music, Inc.
Introduced by Woody Guthrie.

Patches
Words and music by Barry Mann and Larry Kolber.
Screen Gems-Columbia Music, Inc., 1960, 1962.
Introduced and best-selling record in 1962 by Dickey Lee (Smash).

Pepe (German)
English words by Dory Langdon, music by Hans Wittstatt.
Ed. Kassner & Co. Musikverlag, Berlin, Germany, 1957, 1960/
　　Shapiro, Bernstein & Co., Inc.
Original title, "Andalusian Girl." Introduced by Shirley Jones in
　　Pepe (film).

Petite Fleur, see 1952.

Picture, The
Words and music by Jim Howell.
Yonah Music, Inc.
Best-selling record by Roy Godfrey (J & J and Savoy).

Pinball Machine
Words and music by Lonnie Irving.
Starday Music.
Best-selling record by Lonnie Irving (Starday).

Pineapple Princess
Words and music by Dick Sherman and Bob Sherman.
Music World Corp.
Introduced by Annette (Vista).

Playboy's Theme
Words by Carolyn Leigh, music by Cy Coleman.
Edwin H. Morris & Co., Inc.
From *Playboy Penthouse Party* (television series).

Please Don't Eat the Daisies
Words and music by Joe Lubin.
Daywin Music, Inc., 1959, 1960.
Introduced by Doris Day in *Please Don't Eat the Daisies* (film).

Please Help Me, I'm Falling (In Love with You), also known as I Can't Help You, I'm Falling Too
Words and music by Don Robertson and Hal Blair.
Ross Jungnickel, Inc.
Best-selling records by Skeeter Davis (RCA Victor) and Hank Lock-
　　lin (RCA Victor).

Poetry in Motion
Words and music by Paul Kaufman and Mike Anthony.
Vogue Music Co.
Best-selling record by Johnny Tillotson (Cadence).

Pony Time
Words and music by Don Covay and J. Berry.
Harvard Music, Inc.
Best-selling record in 1961 by Chubby Checker (Parkway).

Poor Fool, also known as **A Fool Too Long**
Words and music by Ike Turner.
Saturn Music, Inc./Placid Music.
Best-selling record in 1962 by Ike and Tina Turner (Sue).

Pretty Blue Eyes, see 1959.

Puppy Love, see 1959.

Put On a Happy Face
Words by Lee Adams, music by Charles Strouse.
Edwin H. Morris & Co., Inc.
Introduced by Dick Van Dyke in *Bye Bye Birdie* (musical). Sung
by Dick Van Dyke and Janet Leigh in film version (1963).

Question
Words and music by Lloyd Price and Harold Logan.
Lloyd and Logan, Inc.
Best-selling record by Lloyd Price (ABC-Paramount).

Quien Sabe? (Who Knows? Who Knows?)
Words and music by Fred Tobias and Leon Carr.
Larry Taylor Music Corp.
Introduced by The Secrets (Columbia).

Rat Race, The, see **Main Title Theme from *The Rat Race.***

Right or Wrong, I'll Be with You
Words and music by Wanda Jackson.
Combine Music Corp.
Best-selling record in 1961 by Wanda Jackson (Capitol).

River Boat, see 1959.

Roaring Twenties, The
Words and music by Mack David and Jerry Livingston.
M. Witmark & Sons.
From *The Roaring Twenties* (television series).

Roll Muddy River
Words and music by Betty Sue Perry.
Sure-Fire Music Co., Inc.
Best-selling record in 1963 by The Wilburn Brothers (Decca).

Rosie
Words by Lee Adams, music by Charles Strouse.
Edwin H. Morris & Co., Inc.
Introduced by Dick Van Dyke and Chita Rivera in *Bye Bye Birdie*
(musical). Sung by Ann-Margret, Janet Leigh, Dick Van Dyke,
and Bobby Rydell in film version (1963).

Rubber Ball
Words and music by Aaron Schroeder and Anne Orlowski.
Arch Music Co., Inc.
Best-selling record by Bobby Vee (Liberty).

Ruby-Duby-Du
Words by Sunny Skylar, music by Charles Wolcott.
Robbins Music Corp.
From *Key Witness* (film). First vocal recording by Joanie Sommers
(Warner Bros.).

Run Samson Run
Words by Howard Greenfield, music by Neil Sedaka.
Screen Gems-Columbia Music, Inc.
Introduced by Neil Sedaka (RCA Victor).

Running Bear, see 1959.

Sailor (Your Home Is the Sea) (Austrian)
English words by Alan Holt, German words by Fini Busch, music by
Werner Scharfenberger.
Gemeinschaftsproduktion Hermann Schneider Bühnen u.
Musikalienverlage KG, Vienna, Austria/Cavalcade Music Corp.
Original German title, "Seemann." Best-selling record by Lolita
(Polydor, Germany) and (Kapp, United States).

Samba de Orfeu, see 1959.

Same Old Me, see 1959.

Sandy, see 1959.

Save the Last Dance for Me
Words and music by Doc Pomus and Mort Shuman.
Rumbalero Music, Inc./Progressive Music Publishing Co., Inc./
Trio Music Co., Inc.
Best-selling record by The Drifters (Atlantic).

Say You
Words and music by Johnnie B. Hicks.
T. M. Music, Inc., 1960, 1964.
Best-selling record in 1964 by Ronnie Dove (Diamond).

Sea of Heartbreak
Words and music by Hal David and Paul Hampton.
Shapiro, Bernstein & Co., Inc., 1960, 1961.
Best-selling record in 1961 by Don Gibson (RCA Victor).

Sealed with a Kiss
Words by Peter Udell, music by Gary Geld.
Post Music, Inc.
Best-selling record in 1962 by Brian Hyland (ABC-Paramount).

Sea-Shell
Words by Sheldon Harnick, music by Jerry Bock.
Sunbeam Music Corp.
Written for, but deleted from, *Tenderloin* (musical).

Second Time Around, The
Words by Sammy Cahn, music by James Van Heusen.
Miller Music Corp.
Introduced by Bing Crosby in *High Time* (film). Nominated for
Academy Award, 1960. Best-selling record by Frank Sinatra (Reprise).

Seven Deadly Virtues, The
Words by Alan Jay Lerner, music by Frederick Loewe.
Chappell & Co., Inc.
Introduced by Roddy McDowall in *Camelot* (musical).

She Can't Find Her Keys
Words by Roy Alfred, music by Wally Gold.
Arch Music Co., Inc.
Best-selling record by Paul Petersen (Colpix).

Sheik of Chicago (Mustafa), The
Words and adaptation of music by Bob Merrill.
Ivan Mogull Music Corp.
Adapted from traditional near-Eastern melody. Best-selling French
version introduced by Bob Azzam (Barclay, France). English-
language version introduced by The Four Lads (Columbia).

She's Just a Whole Lot Like You
Words and music by Hank Thompson.
Texoma Music Corp.
Best-selling record by Hank Thompson (Capitol).

Shimmy, Shimmy Ko-Ko Bop, see 1959.

Show Time
Words and music by Joe Lubin.
Daywin Music, Inc.
Introduced by Doris Day (Columbia).

Simple Joys of Maidenhood, The
Words by Alan Jay Lerner, music by Frederick Loewe.
Chappell & Co., Inc.
Introduced by Julie Andrews in *Camelot* (musical).

Since I Made You Cry, see 1959.

Sink the Bismarck
Words and music by Tillman Franks and Johnny Horton.
Cajun Publishing Co., Inc.
"Inspired" by *Sink the Bismarck* (film). Best-selling record by
Johnny Horton (Columbia).

Six-Pack To Go, A
Words and music by Hank Thompson, Johnny Lowe, and Dick Hart.
Brazos Valley Music, Inc.
Best-selling record by Hank Thompson (Capitol).

Smokie, Part II, see 1959.

So Sad (To Watch Good Love Go Bad)
Words and music by Don Everly.
Acuff-Rose Publications, Inc.
Best-selling record by The Everly Brothers (Warner Bros.).

Softly and Tenderly (I'll Hold You in My Arms)
Words by Red Bailey, music by Jim Howell.
Yonah Music, Inc.
Best-selling record by Lewis Pruitt (Decca).

Softly, As I Leave You (Italian)
English words by Hal Shaper, Italian words by G. Calabrese, music
    by A. DeVita.
Edizioni Curci, Milan, Italy, 1960, 1962/Miller Music Corp.
Original Italian title, "Piano."

Solitaire, see 1955.

Somebody
Words by Jack Brooks, music by Harry Warren.
Famous Music Corp.
Introduced by Jerry Lewis in *Cinderfella* (film). First recording by
    Tony Bennett (Columbia).

Something Special
Words and music by Mac Rebennack.
Ace Publishing Co., Inc.
Best-selling record by Roland Stone (Ace).

Song without End
Words by Ned Washington, music by Morris Stoloff and George
    W. Duning.
Columbia Pictures Music Corp.
From *Song without End* (film). Based on "Un Sospiro" by Franz
    Liszt.

Soon It's Gonna Rain
Words by Tom Jones, music by Harvey Schmidt.
Chappell & Co., Inc.
Introduced by Kenneth Nelson and Rita Gardner in *The Fantasticks*
    (off-Broadway musical). Popularized by Barbra Streisand.

Spanish Harlem
Words and music by Jerry Leiber and Phil Spector.
Progressive Music Publishing Co., Inc./Trio Music Co., Inc., 1960,
    1961.
Best-selling record in 1961 by Ben E. King (Atco).

Spanish Rose
Words by Lee Adams, music by Charles Strouse.
Edwin H. Morris & Co., Inc.
Introduced by Chita Rivera in *Bye Bye Birdie* (musical).

Spartacus—Love Theme
Music by Alex North.
Northern Music Corp.
From *Spartacus* (film).

Stairway to Heaven
Words by Howard Greenfield, music by Neil Sedaka.
Screen Gems-Columbia Music, Inc.
Best-selling record by Neil Sedaka (RCA Victor).

Starbright, see 1959.

Starry Eyed
Words by Earl Shuman, music by Mort Garson.
Mansion Music Corp.
First recording by Gary Stites (Carlton).

Stay
Words and music by Maurice Williams.
Windsong Music.
Best-selling record by Maurice (Williams) and The Zodiacs (Herald).

Stay Here with Me (Italian)
English words by Milt Gabler, Italian words by Verde and Domenico
    Modugno, music by Domenico Modugno.
Edizioni Curci, Milan, Italy, 1957, 1958, 1960/Leeds Music Corp.
Original title "Resta Cu' Mme." From *Bay of Naples* (film).

Step by Step
Words and music by Ollie Jones and Billy Dawn Smith.
Paxwin Music Corp.
Best-selling record by The Crests (Co-ed).

Sticks and Stones
Words and music by Titus Turner.
Tangerine Music Corp.
Not copyrighted until 1965. Best-selling record in 1960 by Ray
    Charles (ABC-Paramount).

Strange Feeling
Words by Mort Goode, music by Joseph Liebman.
Chappell & Co., Inc.
Adapted from a theme from *Force of Impulse* (film).

Strangers When We Meet
Words by Richard Quine, music by George Duning.
Columbia Pictures Music Corp./Soon Music Co.
Adapted from the theme from *Strangers When We Meet* (film).

Stuck on You
Words and music by Aaron Schroeder and J. Leslie McFarland.
Gladys Music, Inc.
Best-selling record by Elvis Presley (RCA Victor).

Summer's Gone
Words and music by Paul Anka.
Spanka Music Corp.
Best-selling record by Paul Anka (ABC-Paramount).

Summertime Love, see 1959.

Surfside 6
Words and music by Mack David and Jerry Livingston.
M. Witmark & Sons.
From *Surfside 6* (television series).

Surrender (Italian)
English words and adaptation by Doc Pomus and Mort Shuman,
    Italian words by G. B. De Curtis, music by E. De Curtis.
Edizioni Bideri, S.p.a., Naples, Italy/Elvis Presley Music, Inc.
An adaptation of "Torna a Sorrento." Best-selling record in 1961
    by Elvis Presley (RCA Victor).

Suzie Wong (The Cloud Song)
Words by Sammy Cahn, music by James Van Heusen.
Famous Music Corp.
From *The World of Suzie Wong* (film, 1961).

Sweet Life, The, see La Dolce Vita.

Sweet Nothin's, see 1959.

Swingin' on a Rainbow, see 1959.

Swingin' School
Words by Kal Mann, music by Bernie Lowe and Dave Appell.
Columbia Pictures Music Corp.
Introduced in *Because They're Young* (film). Best-selling record by
    Bobby Rydell (Cameo).

Swiss Family Theme (My Heart Was an Island)
Words and music by Terry Gilkyson.
Wonderland Music Co., Inc.
Theme from *Swiss Family Robinson* (film).

T.L.C., see 1959.

Ta Ta
Words and music by Jimmy Oliver and Clyde McPhatter.
Olimac Music, Inc.
Introduced by Clyde McPhatter (Mercury).

Take Five
Music by Paul Desmond.
Derry Music Co.
Introduced and best-selling record by The Dave Brubeck Quartet
(Columbia). Lyrics added in 1962 by Iola Brubeck; introduced by
Carmen McRae with The Dave Brubeck Quartet (Columbia).

Talk That Talk, see 1959.

Tall Hope
Words by Carolyn Leigh, music by Cy Coleman.
Edwin H. Morris & Co., Inc.
Introduced by Bill Walker, Swen Swenson, Ray Mason, Charles Bras-
well, and The Crew in *Wildcat* (musical).

Tarnished Angel
Words and music by Roger Miller.
Tree Publishing Co., Inc.
Introduced by George Jones (Mercury).

Taste of Honey, A
Words by Ric Marlow, music by Bobby Scott.
Songfest Music Corp., 1960, 1962.
Introduced instrumentally as interlude music by Bobby Scott (piano)
and combo in New York production of *A Taste of Honey* (play).
First recording by Victor Feldman (Infinity). Best-selling record
in 1962 by Martin Denny (Liberty). Winner of National Academy
of Recording Arts and Sciences Award for "Best Instrumental
Theme," 1962. Revived and best-selling record in 1965-66 by Herb
Alpert and The Tijuana Brass (A&M). Winner of National Aca-
demy of Recording Arts and Sciences Awards for "Record of the
Year," "Best Instrumental Performance—Non-Jazz," and "Best
Instrumental Arrangement," 1965.

Teddy, see 1959.

Teen Angel, see 1959.

Teen Beat, see 1959.

Telephone Hour, The
Words by Lee Adams, music by Charles Strouse.
Edwin H. Morris & Co., Inc.
Introduced by The Sweet Apple Kids in *Bye Bye Birdie* (musical).
Sung by Bobby Rydell and The Sweet Apple Teenagers in film
version (1963).

Tell Her for Me
Words and music by Selma Craft and Morty Craft.
Paxwin Music Corp.
Best-selling record by Adam Wade (Co-ed).

Tell Laura I Love Her
Words and music by Jeff Barry and Ben Raleigh.
Edward B. Marks Music Corp.
Best-selling record by Ray Peterson (RCA Victor).

Tell the World, see Wheels.

Tempo of the Times, The
Words by Carolyn Leigh, music by Cy Coleman.
Edwin H. Morris & Co., Inc.
Introduced in *Medium Rare* (cabaret revue).

Tender Love and Care, see T.L.C., 1959.

That's How It Went, All Right
Words by Dory Langdon, music by André Previn.
Columbia Pictures Music Corp.
Introduced by Bobby Darin in *Pepe* (film).

That's My Kind of Love
Words and music by Marion Worth.
Travis Music Co.
Best-selling record by Marion Worth (Guyden).

Theme for a Dream
Words by Earl Shuman, music by Mort Garson.
Mansion Music Corp.
Introduced and best-selling record in England and United States
    by Cliff Richard (Epic).

Theme from an Un-filmed Movie
Music by Robert Maxwell.
Shapiro, Bernstein & Co., Inc.

Theme from *Route 66*
Music by Nelson Riddle.
Screen Gems-Columbia Music, Inc., 1960, 1963.
Theme from *Route 66* (television series). Best-selling record by
    Nelson Riddle and his Orchestra (Capitol). Lyrics by Stanley
    Styne added in 1963 to new title, "Open Highway"; introduced
    by Teri Thornton (Columbia).

Theme from *Sons and Lovers*
Music by Mario Nascimbene.
Leo Feist, Inc.
From *Sons and Lovers* (film).

Theme from *Stowaway in the Sky* (French)
Words by Eddy Marnay, music by Jean Prodromides.
Éditions Philippe Pares, Paris, France, 1960, 1962/Piedmont Music
    Co., Inc.
Theme from *Stowaway in the Sky* (*Voyage en Ballon*) (French
    film).

Theme from *The Apartment,* see **Jealous Lover,** 1949.

Theme from *The Dark at the Top of the Stairs*
Music by Max Steiner.
M. Witmark & Sons.
Theme from *The Dark at the Top of the Stairs* (film).

Theme from *The Misfits*
Music by Alex North.
United Artists Music Co., Inc.
From *The Misfits* (film, 1961).

Theme from *The Sundowners*
Music by Dimitri Tiomkin.
M. Witmark & Sons.
Theme from *The Sundowners* (film).

Then You May Take Me to the Fair
Words by Alan Jay Lerner, music by Frederick Loewe.
Chappell & Co., Inc.
Introduced by Julie Andrews, John Cullum, James Gannon, and
   Bruce Yarnell in *Camelot* (musical).

There Goes My Baby, see 1959.

There's a Big Wheel, see 1959.

There's a Moon Out Tonight
Words and music by Al Striano, Joe Luccisano, and Al Gentile.
Rob-Ann Music, Inc./Maureen Music, Inc.
Best-selling record in 1961 by The Capris (Old Town).

They Were You
Words by Tom Jones, music by Harvey Schmidt.
Chappell & Co., Inc.
Introduced by Kenneth Nelson and Rita Gardner in *The Fantasticks*
   (off-Broadway musical).

Think Twice
Words and music by Joe Shapiro, Jimmy Williams, and Clyde Otis.
Play Music, Inc.
Best-selling record in 1961 by Brook Benton (Mercury).

This Bitter Earth
Words and music by Clyde Otis.
Play Music, Inc.
Best-selling record by Dinah Washington (Mercury).

This Land Is Mine, see **Exodus.**

This Magic Moment
Words and music by Doc Pomus and Mort Shuman.
Rumbalero Music, Inc./Tiger Music, Inc./Tredlew Music, Inc.
Best-selling record by The Drifters (Atlantic).

Thousand Stars, A
Words and music by Eugene Pearson.
Bryden Music, Inc.
Best-selling record by Kathy (Young) and The Innocents (Indigo).

Three Hearts in a Tangle
Words and music by Ray Pennington and Sonny Thompson.
Lois Publishing Co.
Best-selling record in 1961 by Roy Drusky (Decca).

Three Nights a Week
Words and music by Antoine Domino.
Travis Music Co.
Best-selling record by Fats Domino (Imperial).

Time and the River, see 1959.

Time and Time Again (French)
English words by Carl Sigman, French words by Pierre Dorsey,
    music by Hubert Giraud.
Éditions Do Re Mi, Paris, France/Les Nouvelles Éditions Meridian,
    Paris, France/Shapiro, Bernstein & Co., Inc.
Original French title, "Comme Au Premier Jour."

Tip of My Fingers, The
Words and music by Bill Anderson.
Tree Publishing Co., Inc./Champion Music Corp.
Best-selling records by Bill Anderson (Decca) and in 1963 by Roy
    Clark (Capitol).

Tobacco Road
Words and music by John D. Loudermilk.
Cedarwood Publishing Co., Inc.
Best-selling record, produced in England, in 1964 by The Nashville
    Teens (London).

Togetherness
Words and music by Russell Faith.
Debmar Publishing Co.
Best-selling record by Frankie Avalon (Chancellor).

Tommy, Tommy
Words by Sheldon Harnick, music by Jerry Bock.
Sunbeam Music Corp.
Introduced by Wynne Miller in *Tenderloin* (musical).

Tomorrow, see **Will You Love Me Tomorrow.**

Too Much To Lose
Words and music by Tommy Blake and Lester Vanadore.
Moss Rose Publications, Inc.
Best-selling record by Carl Belew (Decca).

Tracy's Theme, see 1959.

Travelin' Man
Words and music by Jerry Fuller.
Golden West Melodies, Inc., 1960, 1961.
Best-selling record in 1961 by Ricky Nelson (Imperial).

Trouble in Paradise
Words and music by Allison R. Khent and Billy Dawn Smith.
Paxwin Music Corp.
Best-selling record by The Crests (Co-ed).

Try To Remember
Words by Tom Jones, music by Harvey Schmidt.
Chappell & Co., Inc.
Introduced by Jerry Orbach in *The Fantasticks* (off-Broadway musi-
cal). Best-selling records in 1965-66 by The Brothers Four (Co-
lumbia) and Ed Ames (RCA Victor).

Turn on the Sunshine
Words by Howard Greenfield, music by Neil Sedaka.
Screen Gems-Columbia Music, Inc.
Introduced by Connie Francis in *Where the Boys Are* (film).

Twelfth Rose, The
Words and music by Marvin Moore and Buddy Killen.
Tree Publishing Co., Inc.
Introduced by The Browns (RCA Victor).

Twist and Shout
Words and music by Bert Russell and Phil Medley.
Robert Mellin, Inc./Progressive Music Publishing Co., Inc.
Best-selling records in 1962 by The Isley Brothers (Wand) and in
1964 by The Beatles (Tollie and Capitol).

Twistin' U.S.A.
Words and music by Kal Mann.
Kalmann Music, Inc.
Best-selling record by Danny and The Juniors (Swan).

Two of a Kind
Words by Johnny Mercer, music by Bobby Darin.
Commander Publications, 1960, 1963.
Introduced by Johnny Mercer and Bobby Darin (Atco).

Unchain My Heart
Words and music by Agnes Jones (pseudonym for Bobby Sharp)
and Freddy James (pseudonym for Teddy Powell).
Tee Pee Music Co., Inc.
Best-selling record in 1962 by Ray Charles (ABC-Paramount).

Unforgiven, The (The Need for Love)
Words by Ned Washington, music by Dimitri Tiomkin.
Colby Music, Inc.
Adapted from theme from *The Unforgiven* (film). Best-selling record,
  instrumental, by Don Costa and his Orchestra (United Artists).
  First vocal recording by The McGuire Sisters (Coral).

Utopia
Words and music by Aaron Schroeder, Wally Gold, and Martin
  Kalmanoff.
Arch Music Co., Inc.
Introduced by Frank Gari (Crusade).

Village of St. Bernadette, The, see 1959.

Volare, see 1958.

Wake Me When It's Over
Words by Sammy Cahn, music by James Van Heusen.
Robbins Music Corp.
From *Wake Me When It's Over* (film).

Walk, Don't Run
Words and music by John H. Smith, Jr.
Forshay Music.
Best-selling record by The Ventures (Dolton). Best-selling record
  in 1964 of updated version entitled "Walk—Don't Run '64," by
  The Ventures (Dolton).

Walk On, Boy
Words and music by Mel Tillis and Wayne P. Walker.
Cedarwood Publishing Co., Inc.
Best-selling records by Mel Tillis (Columbia) and Jimmy Dean
  (Columbia).

Walk Out Backwards
Words and music by Bill Anderson.
Champion Music Corp./Tree Publishing Co., Inc.
Best-selling record in 1961 by Bill Anderson (Decca).

Walk Right Back
Words and music by Sonny Curtis.
Cricket Music, Inc.
Best-selling record in 1961 by The Everly Brothers (Warner Bros.).

Walkin' Down to Washington
Words and music by Dick Sanford and Sammy Mysels.
Valiant Music Co., Inc.
Introduced and best-selling record by Mitch Miller and his Orchestra
  and Chorus (Columbia).

Walking Away Whistling, see 1959.

Walking to New Orleans
Words and music by Antoine Domino, Dave Bartholomew, and
Robert Guidry.
Travis Music Co.
Best-selling record by Fats Domino (Imperial).

Waltz de Funk
Music by Patti Bown.
Duchess Music Corp., 1960, 1963.
Introduced by Patti Bown (Columbia).

Wanderer, The
Words and music by Ernest Maresca.
Marimba Music Corp./Schwartz Music Co., Inc.
Best-selling record in 1962 by Dion (Laurie).

Way Down East
Music by Larry Adler.
Saunders Publications, Inc., 1960, 1962, 1963.
Theme from *The Great Chase* (film, 1962), introduced on soundtrack
by Larry Adler.

Way of a Clown, The
Words and music by Barry Mann and Howard Greenfield.
Screen Gems-Columbia Music, Inc.
Introduced by Teddy Randazzo and Barry Mann (Am-Par).

We Got Us
Words by Chuck Sweeney, music by Moose Charlap.
Maxana Music Corp.
Introduced by Eydie Gormé and Steve Lawrence (United Artists).

We Shall Overcome
New words and music arrangement by Zilphia Horton, Frank Hamil-
ton, Guy Carawan, and Pete Seeger.
Ludlow Music, Inc., 1960, 1963.
Believed to have originated as religious folk song later turned into
a formal Baptist hymn, entitled "I'll Overcome Some Day," by C.
Albert Tindley, copyrighted in 1901.

What a Wonderful World, see Wonderful World.

What Did I Ever See in Him?
Words by Lee Adams, music by Charles Strouse.
Edwin H. Morris & Co., Inc.
Introduced by Chita Rivera and Susan Watson in *Bye Bye Birdie*
(musical).

What Do the Simple Folks Do?
Words by Alan Jay Lerner, music by Frederick Loewe.
Chappell & Co., Inc.
Introduced by Julie Andrews and Richard Burton in *Camelot* (musi-
cal).

What in the World's Come Over You, see 1959.

What's New at the Zoo?
Words by Betty Comden and Adolph Green, music by Jule Styne.
Stratford Music Corp.
Introduced by Nancy Dussault and chorus in *Do Re Mi* (musical).

Wheels, also known as **Tell the World**
Words and music by Jimmy Torres and Richard Stephens.
Dundee Music/Selma Music Corp.
Best-selling records in 1961 by The String-A-Longs (Warwick) and
    in 1962 by Billy Vaughn and his Orchestra (Dot).

When Will I Be Loved
Words and music by Phil Everly.
Acuff-Rose Publications, Inc.
Best-selling record by The Everly Brothers (Cadence).

Where Is Love? (English)
Words and music by Lionel Bart.
Lakeview Music Co., Ltd., London, England/Hollis Music, Inc.
Introduced by Keith Hamshere, and reprised by Madeleine Newbury,
    in London production, and sung by Paul O'Keefe, and reprised by
    Dortha Duckworth, in New York production (1963) of *Oliver!*
    (musical).

Where the Boys Are
Words by Howard Greenfield, music by Neil Sedaka.
Screen Gems-Columbia Music, Inc.
Introduced by Connie Francis in *Where the Boys Are* (film). Best-
    selling record in 1961 by Connie Francis (MGM).

Where the Hot Wind Blows
Words by Buddy Kaye, music by Jimmy McHugh.
Levine-McHugh Music International, Inc.
Introduced by The Ames Brothers on soundtrack over credits of
    Where the Hot Wind Blows (French-Italian film).

White Silver Sands, see 1957.

Who Will Buy? (English)
Words and music by Lionel Bart.
Lakeview Music Co., Ltd., London, England/Hollis Music, Inc.
Introduced by Keith Hamshere and chorus in London production and
    sung by Paul O'Keefe and chorus in New York production (1963)
    of *Oliver!* (musical).

(It All Depends) Who Will Buy the Wine, see **Who'll Buy
    the Wine.**

Who'll Buy the Wine, also known as **(It All Depends) Who Will Buy the Wine**
Words and music by Billy Mize.
Penny Music Co./Kentucky Music, Inc.
Best-selling record in 1960 by Charlie Walker (Columbia). Apparently not copyrighted, but cleared by BMI in 1965.

Why
Words by Bob Marcucci, music by Peter De Angelis.
Debmar Publishing Co., Inc.
Best-selling record by Frankie Avalon (Chancellor).

Why I'm Walkin'
Words and music by Stonewall Jackson and Melvin Endsley.
Ernest Tubb Music, Inc./Acuff-Rose Publications, Inc.
Best-selling record by Stonewall Jackson (Columbia).

Wild One
Words and music by Bernie Lowe, Kal Mann, and Dave Appell.
Lowe Music Corp.
Best-selling record by Bobby Rydell (Cameo).

Wild Weekend, also known as **Wild Weekend Cha Cha**
Words and music by Tom Shannon and Phil Todaro.
Tupper Publishing Co./Embassy Music Corp.
Best-selling record in 1963 by The Rebels (Swan).

Wild Weekend Cha Cha, see **Wild Weekend.**

Will You Love Me Tomorrow?
Words and music by Gerry Goffin and Carole King.
Screen Gems-Columbia Music, Inc., 1960, 1961.
Best-selling record in 1961 by The Shirelles (Scepter).

Wonderful World, also known as **What a Wonderful World**
Words and music by Barbara Campbell, Lou Adler, and Herb Alpert.
Kags Music.
Best-selling record by Sam Cooke (Keen).

Wonderland by Night (German)
Words by Lincoln Chase, music by Klauss-Gunter Neuman.
Musikverlag Lutz Templin, Germany, 1959/Roosevelt Music Co., Inc.
Original German title, "Wunderland bei Nacht." Best-selling instrumental recording by Bert Kaempfert (Decca); best-selling vocal recording by Anita Bryant (Carlton).

Wooden Heart (German)
Words and adaptation of music by Fred Wise, Ben Weisman, Kay Twomey, and Berthold Kaempfert.
Gladys Music, Inc.
Based on German folk song, "Muss I Denn zum Stadtele Haus." Introduced by Elvis Presley in *G.I. Blues* (film). Best-selling records by Elvis Presley (RCA Victor) and in 1961 by Joe Dowell (Smash).

Work Song
Words by Oscar Brown, Jr., music by Nat Adderley.
Upam Music Co.
Adapted from jazz instrumental. Vocal version introduced by Oscar Brown, Jr. (Columbia). Best-selling record in 1966 by Herb Alpert and The Tijuana Brass (A&M).

World I Can't Live In, A
Words and music by Roger Miller.
Tree Publishing Co., Inc.
Introduced by Jaye P. Morgan (MGM).

World So Full of Love, A
Words and music by Roger Miller and Faron Young.
Tree Publishing Co., Inc.
Introduced by Faron Young (Capitol).

Yellow Bandana, The
Words and music by Al Gorgoni, Steve Karliski, and Larry Kolber.
Screen Gems-Columbia Music, Inc., 1960, 1963.
Best-selling record in 1963 by Faron Young (Mercury).

Yogi
Words and music by Lou Stallman, Sid Jacobson, and Charles Koppelman.
Saxon Music Corp.
Best-selling records by Bill Black (Hi) and Ivy Three (Shell).

You Can Have Her
Words and music by Bill Cook.
Big Billy Music Co.
Best-selling record in 1961 by Roy Hamilton (Epic).

You Can't Sit Down
Words and music by Dee Clark, Cornell Muldrow, and Kal Mann.
Conrad Publishing Co., Inc.
Best-selling record in 1963 by The Dovells (Parkway).

(In the Summer Time) You Don't Want My Love
Words and music by Roger Miller.
Tree Publishing Co., Inc.
Best-selling records by Andy Williams (Cadence) and Roger Miller (RCA Victor).

You Mean Everything to Me
Words and music by Neil Sedaka and Howard Greenfield.
Screen Gems-Columbia Music, Inc.
Introduced by Neil Sedaka (RCA Victor).

You Talk Too Much
Words and music by Joe Jones and Reginald Hall.
Nom Music, Inc./Ben-Ghazi Enterprises, Inc.
Best-selling record by Joe Jones (Roulette).

You Were Made for All My Love, see **All My Love.**

Young Emotions, see 1962.

Your Old Used To Be
Words by Hilda M. Young, music by Faron Young.
Moss Rose Publications, Inc.
Best-selling record by Faron Young (Capitol).

You're Sixteen, You're Beautiful and You're Mine
Words and music by Dick Sherman and Bob Sherman.
Blue Grass Music Co.
Best-selling record by Johnny Burnette (Liberty).

You're the Reason
Words and music by Bobby Edwards, Mildred Imes, Fred Henley,
   and Terry Fell.
American Music, Inc.
Best-selling record in 1961 by Bobby Edwards (Crest).

You've Come Home
Words by Carolyn Leigh, music by Cy Coleman.
Edwin H. Morris & Co., Inc., 1960, 1961.
Introduced by Keith Andes in *Wildcat* (musical).

1961

Above the Stars
Music by Bob Merrill.
Robbins Music Corp.
"Wilhelm's Theme" from *The Wonderful World of the Brothers Grimm* (film).

Ada
Words by Mack David, music by Bronislau Kaper.
Miller Music Corp., 1961, 1962.
Adapted from a theme from *Ada* (film).

Adios, My Love (The Song of Athens) (Greek)
English words by Norman Newell, Greek words by Nikos Gatsos, German words by Hans Bradtke, music by Manos Hadjidakis.
Ed. Kassner & Co., Berlin, Germany/Peter Schaeffers Music Corp.
Introduced on soundtrack of *Dreamland of Desire* (German film) by Nana Mouskouri (President). English-language version introduced by Jo Stafford (Colpix).

African Waltz, The
Words by Mel Mitchell and Norman Sachs, music by Galt MacDermot.
Key Music, Ltd., London, England/Musical Comedy Productions, Inc.
Best-selling instrumental version by Julian "Cannonball" Adderley (Riverside). Winner of National Academy of Recording Arts and Sciences Awards for "Best Instrumental Theme" and "Best Original Jazz Composition," 1961.

Afrikaan Beat
Music by Bert Kaempfert.
Roosevelt Music Co., Inc., 1961, 1962.
Best-selling record in 1963 by Bert Kaempfert (Decca).

Ain't That Just Like Me
Words and music by Earl Carroll and Billy Guy.
Trio Music Co., Inc./Progressive Music Publishing Co., Inc.
Best-selling record in 1964 by The Searchers (Kapp).

Ain't That Loving You
Words and music by Deadric Malone.
Lion Publishing Co., Inc.
Best-selling record in 1962 by Bobby Bland (Duke).

Air Mail to Heaven
Words and music by Kent Westberry.
Cedarwood Publishing Co., Inc.
Best-selling record by Carl Smith (Columbia).

Al Di Là (Italian)
English words by Ervin Drake, Italian words by Mogo, music by
    C. Donida.
Fono Film Ricordi, Italy/M. Witmark & Sons.
Winner of San Remo (Italy) Song Festival, 1961. Sung by Emilio
    Pericoli in *Rome Adventure* (film, 1962). Best-selling record in
    1962 by Emilio Pericoli (Warner Bros.).

All Night Long
Words and music by Curtis R. Lewis.
Sea-Lark Enterprises, Inc.
Best-selling record by Gloria Lynn (Everest).

Allison's Theme from *Parrish*
Music by Max Steiner.
M. Witmark & Sons.
From *Parrish* (film).

Angel or Devil
Words and music by Winfield Scott.
Gower Music, Inc.
Best-selling record by Bobby Keene (Coral).

Annie Get Your Yo-Yo
Words and music by Deadric Malone and Joseph Scott.
Don Music Co.
Best-selling record in 1962 by Little Junior Parker (Duke).

Another Time, Another Place
Words and music by Richard Adler.
Sahara Music, Inc.
Introduced by Sally Ann Howes in *Kwamina* (musical).

Anytime At All
Words and music by Baker Knight.
Duchess Music Corp.
Best-selling record by Frank Sinatra (Reprise).

Are You Sure? (English)
Words and music by John Allison and Bob Allison.
Marlyn Music Co., Ltd., London, England/Burlington Music Corp.
Song, winner of second place, Eurovision Song Contest, 1961. Best-
    selling record in England by The Allisons (Fontana).

As If I Didn't Know
Words and music by Scott David (pseudonym for Jerry Samuels) and Larry Kusik.
Paxwin Music Corp.
Best-selling record by Adam Wade (Co-ed).

As Simple As That
Words and music by Jerry Herman.
Jerryco Music Co.
Introduced by Mimi Benzell and Robert Weede in *Milk and Honey* (musical).

Asia Minor, see 1951.

Ask Me Nice
Words and music by Mose Allison.
Audre Mae Music.
Introduced by Mose Allison (Columbia).

Athina (White Rose of Athens) (Greek)
English words by Norman Newell, Greek words by Nikos Gatsos, German words by Hans Bradtke, music by Manos Hadjidakis.
Ed. Kassner & Co., Berlin, Germany/Peter Schaeffers Music Corp.
Original title, "Weisse Rosen aus Athen." From *Dreamland of Desire* (German film). Introduced by Nana Mouskouri (Riverside). Best-selling records by David Carroll (Mercury) and The Chordettes (Cadence).

Baby Elephant Walk
Words by Hal David, music by Henry Mancini.
Famous Music Corp., 1961, 1962.
From *Hatari!* (film, 1962). Record by Henry Mancini and his Orchestra (RCA Victor) winner of National Academy of Recording Arts and Sciences Award for "Best Instrumental Arrangement," 1962. Vocal version introduced by Pat Boone (Dot). Best-selling record in 1962-63 by Lawrence Welk and his Orchestra (Dot).

Baby, It's You
Words and music by Mack David, Burt F. Bacharach, and Barney Williams.
Dolfi Music, Inc./Mary Jane Music.
Best-selling record in 1962 by The Shirelles (Scepter).

Baby, You're Right
Words and music by James Brown and Joe Tex.
Lois Publishing Co.
Best-selling record by James Brown (King).

Bachelor in Paradise
Words by Mack David, music by Henry Mancini.
Robbins Music Corp.
From *Bachelor in Paradise* (film). Nominated for Academy Award, 1961.

Back on the Corner
Words and music by Mose Allison.
Audre Mae Music.
Introduced by Mose Allison (Columbia).

Back Street
Words by Ken Darby, music by Frank Skinner.
Northern Music Corp.
Adapted from a theme from *Back Street* (film).

Back-Track
Words and music by Faron Young and Alex Zanetis.
Vanadore Publications, Inc.
Best-selling record by Faron Young (Capitol).

Barbara Ann
Words and music by Fred Fassert.
Cousins, Inc./Shoe-String Music, Inc.
Best-selling record in 1965-66 by The Beach Boys (Capitol).

Be a Santa
Words by Betty Comden and Adolph Green, music by Jule Styne.
Stratford Music Corp.
Introduced by Sydney Chaplin and chorus in *Subways Are for Sleeping* (musical).

Be Quiet, Mind
Words and music by Liz Anderson.
Yonah Music, Inc.
Best-selling record by Del Reeves (Decca).

Beautiful Candy
Words and music by Bob Merrill.
Robbins Music Corp.
Introduced by Anna Maria Alberghetti, Puppets, and Carnival People in *Carnival!* (musical).

Being in Love
Words and music by Meredith Willson.
Frank Music Corp.
Introduced by Shirley Jones in *The Music Man* (film version, 1962).

Berlin Melody, The (German)
Music by Heino Gaze.
Symphony House Music Publishers Corp.
Best-selling record by Billy Vaughn and his Orchestra (Dot).

Big Bad John
Words and music by Jimmy Dean.
Cigma Music Co., Inc.
Best-selling record by Jimmy Dean (Columbia). Winner of National
Academy of Recording Arts and Sciences Award for "Best Coun-
try and Western Recording," 1961.

Big, Cold Wind
Words and music by Robert Mosely and Bob Elgin.
Gil Music Corp.
Best-selling record by Pat Boone (Dot).

Big Daddy
Words and music by John D. Loudermilk.
Acuff-Rose Publications, Inc.
Introduced by John D. Loudermilk (RCA Victor).

Big John (Ain't You Gonna Marry Me?)
Words and music by John Patton and Amiel Summers.
Ludix Publishing Co., Inc./Betalbin Music Publishing Corp.
Best-selling record by The Shirelles (Scepter).

Big River, Big Man
Words and music by Mike Phillips and George Watson.
Robbins Music Corp.
Best-selling record by Claude King (Columbia).

Bilbao Song, The (German)
English words by Johnny Mercer, German words by Bertolt Brecht,
music by Kurt Weill.
Universal Editions, London, England, 1929/Harms, Inc., 1961.
Introduced in *Happy End* ("a play with music") in Berlin, Germany
in 1929. First recording in United States by Lotte Lenya. English
lyrics written in 1961. Introduced by Andy Williams (Cadence).

Bit of Soul, A
Music by Ray Charles.
Progressive Music Publishing Co., Inc.
Introduced by Ray Charles (Atlantic).

Bless You
Words and music by Barry Mann and Cynthia Weil.
Screen Gems-Columbia Music, Inc.
Best-selling record by Tony Orlando (Epic).

Blizzard, The
Words and music by Harlan Howard.
Red River Songs, Inc./Tuckahoe Music, Inc.
Introduced by Jim Reeves (RCA Victor).

Blues I Got Comin' Tomorrow, The
Words by Mort Goode, music by Joseph Liebman.
Chappell & Co., Inc.
Introduced by Lionel Hampton in *Force of Impulse* (film).

Bom Di Di Bom
Words and music by Stu Phillips, Howard Berk, and Paul Wexler.
Screen Gems-Columbia Music, Inc.
Best-selling record by Billy Sills (Colpix).

Born To Wander
Words and music by Al Peterson.
Genius Music Corp./Gavadima Music, Inc.
Best-selling record in 1964 by The Four Seasons (Philips).

Break It to Me Gently
Words and music by Diane Lampert and Joe Seneca.
Northern Music Corp.
Best-selling record in 1962 by Brenda Lee (Decca).

Breaking In a Brand New Broken Heart
Words and music by Howard Greenfield and Jack Keller.
Screen Gems-Columbia Music, Inc.
Best-selling record by Connie Francis (MGM).

Bright Lights, Big City
Words and music by Jimmy Reed.
Conrad Publishing Co., Inc.
Best-selling record by Jimmy Reed (Vee Jay).

Bristol Stomp, The
Words by Kal Mann, music by Dave Appell.
Kalmann Music, Inc.
Best-selling record by The Dovells (Parkway).

Brotherhood of Man
Words and music by Frank Loesser.
Frank Music Corp.
Introduced by Robert Morse, Sammy Smith, Ruth Kobart, and company in *How To Succeed in Business without Really Trying* (musical).

Burning of Atlanta, The
Words and music by Chuck Taylor.
Conrad Publishing Co., Inc.
Best-selling record in 1962 by Claude King (Columbia).

By Love Possessed
Words by Sammy Cahn, music by Elmer Bernstein.
United Artists Music Co., Inc.
Title song from *By Love Possessed* (film).

Calendar Girl
Words and music by Howard Greenfield and Neil Sedaka.
Screen Gems-Columbia Music, Inc.
Best-selling record by Neil Sedaka (RCA Victor).

California Sun
Words and music by Morris Levy and Henry Glover.
Lloyd and Logan, Inc./Nom Music, Inc.
Best-selling record in 1964 by The Rivieras (Riviera).

Candy Man
Words and music by Fred Neil and Beverly Ross.
January Music Corp.
Best-selling record by Roy Orbison (Monument).

Can't Help Falling in Love
Words and music by George Weiss, Hugo Peretti, and Luigi
  Creatore.
Gladys Music, Inc.
Introduced by Elvis Presley in *Blue Hawaii* (film). Best-selling
  record in 1961-62 by Elvis Presley (RCA Victor).

Chapel by the Sea, The
Words by Mary Margaret Hadler Gilbert, music by Vivian Clark
  Gilbert.
Sun-Vine Music Co.
Best-selling record by Billy Vaughn (Dot).

Charlesville
Music by Ray Charles.
Progressive Music Publishing Co., Inc.
Introduced by Ray Charles (Atlantic).

Charlie's Shoes
Words and music by Roy Baham.
Pamper Music, Inc.
Best-selling record in 1962 by Billy Walker (Columbia).

Cherie
Words by Kal Mann, music by Bernie Lowe and Dave Appell.
Kalmann Music, Inc.
Best-selling record by Bobby Rydell (Cameo).

Chime In!
Words and music by Robert Wright and George Forrest.
Empress Music, Inc.
Introduced by Alfred De Sio, Christopher Hewett, Robert Penn,
  Arthur Rubin, and ensemble in *Kean* (musical).

Chip Chip
Words and music by Jeff Barry, Cliff Crawford, and Arthur Resnick.
T.M. Music, Inc./Glo-Mac Music.
Introduced and best-selling record in 1962 by Gene McDaniels
  (Liberty).

Comancheros, The
Words and music by Tillman Franks.
Robbins Music Corp.
"Inspired" by *The Comancheros* (film). Best-selling record by
  Claude King (Columbia).

Comes Once in a Lifetime!
Words by Betty Comden and Adolph Green, music by Jule Styne.
Stratford Music Corp.
Introduced by Sydney Chaplin and Carol Lawrence in *Subways Are
  for Sleeping* (musical).

Company Way, The
Words and music by Frank Loesser.
Frank Music Corp.
Introduced by Robert Morse, Sammy Smith, Charles Nelson Reilly,
  and company in *How To Succeed in Business without Really Try-
  ing* (musical).

Conscience
Words and music by Barry Mann and Cynthia Weil.
Screen Gems-Columbia Music, Inc.
Best-selling record by James Darren (Colpix).

Crazy
Words and music by Willie Nelson.
Pamper Music, Inc.
Best-selling record by Patsy Cline (Decca).

Cry to Me
Words and music by Bert Russell.
Robert Mellin, Inc./Progressive Music Publishing Co., Inc.
Best-selling record in 1962 by Solomon Burke (Atlantic).

Crying
Words and music by Roy Orbison and Joe Melson.
Acuff-Rose Publications, Inc.
Best-selling record by Roy Orbison (Monument).

Crying in the Rain
Words and music by Howard Greenfield and Carole King.
Screen Gems-Columbia Music, Inc.
Best-selling record in 1962 by The Everly Brothers (Warner Bros.).

Cuando Caliente El Sol, also known as Love Me with All Your Heart (Mexican)
English words by Michael Vaughn, Spanish words by Mario Rigual,
  music by Carlos Rigual.
Editorial Mexicana De Musica Internacional, S.A., Mexico/Peer
  International Corp.
Best-selling record in 1964 by The Ray Charles Singers (Command).

Cupid
Words and music by Sam Cooke.
Kags Music.
Best-selling record by Sam Cooke (RCA Victor).

Daddy's Home
Words and music by James Sheppard and William Miller.
Nom Music, Inc.
Best-selling record by Shep and The Limelites (Hull).

Darling (Gonna Work Out Fine), see It's Gonna Work Out Fine.

Dawn Ray
Music by Ray Charles.
Progressive Music Publishing Co., Inc.
Introduced by Ray Charles (Atlantic).

Day into Night
Words and music by Don Gibson.
Acuff-Rose Publications, Inc.
Best-selling record in 1962 by Kitty Wells (Decca).

Daydreams
Words and music by Al Hazan.
Johnstone-Montei, Inc./Maravilla Music, Inc.
Best-selling record by Johnny Crawford (Del-Fi).

Dear Ivan
Words and music by Jimmy Dean.
Plainview Music, Inc.
Best-selling record in 1962 by Jimmy Dean (Columbia).

Dear Lady
Words and music by Frank J. Guida.
Rock Masters, Inc.
Best-selling record in 1962 by Gary "U.S." Bonds (LeGrand).

Dear One
Words and music by John Lawrence Finneran and Vincent Finneran.
Maureen Music, Inc.
Best-selling record in 1962 by Larry Finnegan (Old Town).

Deportee, see Plane Wreck at Los Gatos.

Diamond Head
Words by Mack David, music by Hugo Winterhalter.
Columbia Pictures Music Corp., 1961, 1962.
Adapted from a theme from *Diamond Head* (film, 1963).

Don't Bet Money, Honey
Words and music by Linda Scott.
Figure Music, Inc.
Introduced and best-selling record by Linda Scott (Canadian American).

Don't Call Me from a Honky Tonk
Words and music by Harlan Howard.
Pamper Music, Inc.
Best-selling record in 1963 by Johnny and Jonie Mosby (Columbia).

Don't Read the Letter
Words by Howard Greenfield, music by Jack Keller.
Screen Gems-Columbia Music, Inc.
Introduced by Patti Page (Mercury).

(He's My) Dreamboat
Words and music by John D. Loudermilk.
Acuff-Rose Publications, Inc.
Best-selling record by Connie Francis (MGM).

Dreamstreet
Music by Erroll Garner.
Octave Music Publishing Corp.
Introduced by Erroll Garner (ABC-Paramount).

Driving Wheel
Words and music by Roosevelt Sykes.
Lion Publishing Co., Inc.
Best-selling record by Little Junior Parker (Duke).

Duke of Earl
Words and music by Earl Edwards, Bernie Williams, and Eugene
    Dixon.
Conrad Publishing Co., Inc./Aba, Inc.
Best-selling record in 1962 by Gene Chandler (Vee Jay).

Dum Dum
Words and music by Jackie De Shannon and Sharon Sheeley.
Metric Music Co.
Best-selling record by Brenda Lee (Decca).

Ebony Eyes
Words and music by John Loudermilk.
Acuff-Rose Publications, Inc.
Best-selling record by The Everly Brothers (Warner Bros.).

Elena
Words and music by Robert Wright and George Forrest.
Empress Music, Inc.
Introduced by Alfred Drake, Arthur Rubin, and ensemble in *Kean*
    (musical).

Eventually
Words and music by Ronnie Self and Dub Allbritten.
Champion Music Corp.
Best-selling record by Brenda Lee (Decca).

Every Breath I Take
Words and music by Gerry Goffin and Carole King.
Screen Gems-Columbia Music, Inc.
Best-selling record by Gene Pitney (Musicor).

Every Which-a-Way
Words and music by Roger Miller.
Tree Publishing Co., Inc.
Introduced by Roger Miller (RCA Victor).

Ev'rything Beautiful
Words and music by Jay Livingston and Ray Evans.
Livingston & Evans, Inc.
Introduced by George Gobel and Birthday Girls in *Let It Ride!*
  (musical).

Fair Swiss Maiden
Words and music by Roger Miller.
Tree Publishing Co., Inc.
Introduced by Roger Miller (RCA Victor).

Falcon and the Dove, The, see **Love Theme from** *El Cid.*

Familiar
Words and music by George Weiss.
Abilene Music, Inc.

Fanny, see 1954.

Find Another Girl
Words and music by Jerry Butler and Curtis Mayfield.
Conrad Publishing Co., Inc.
Best-selling record by Jerry Butler (Vee Jay).

First Lady Waltz, The
Words by Ned Washington, music by Jimmy McHugh.
Jimmy McHugh Music, Inc.
Dedicated to Mrs. John F. Kennedy.

Fish, The
Words by Kal Mann, music by Bernie Lowe and Dave Appell.
Lowe Music Corp.
Best-selling record by Bobby Rydell (Cameo).

Fishin' Hole, The
Words by Everett Sloane, music by Earle Hagen and Herb Spencer.
Larrabee Music, Inc.
Theme from *The Andy Griffith Show* (television series).

Flat Top
Words and music by Cowboy Copas and Tommy Hill.
Starday Music.
Best-selling record by Cowboy Copas (Starday).

Fly, The
Words and music by John Madara and Dave White.
Woodcrest Music, Inc./Mured Publishing Co.
Best-selling record by Chubby Checker (Parkway).

Fly by Night
Words and music by Ritchie Adams and Neval Nader.
Sea-Lark Enterprises, Inc.
Introduced by Andy Williams (Cadence).

Fog and the Grog, The
Words and music by Robert Wright and George Forrest.
Empress Music, Inc.
Introduced by Christopher Hewett, Robert Penn, Arthur Rubin,
    Alfred Drake, and ensemble in *Kean* (musical).

Fool Number One, also known as Fool No. 1
Words and music by Kathryn R. Fulton.
Sure-Fire Music Co., Inc.
Introduced by Loretta Lynn. Best-selling record by Brenda Lee
    (Decca).

Foolin' 'Round
Words and music by Harlan Howard and Buck Owens.
Central Songs, Inc.
Best-selling record by Buck Owens (Capitol).

For the First Time
Words and music by Howard Dietz and Arthur Schwartz.
Harms, Inc.
Introduced by Walter Chiari in *The Gay Life* (musical).

Forever My Love
Words by Hal David, music by Burt F. Bacharach.
Famous Music Corp.
Introduced in *Forever My Love* (film, 1962).

Fortune Teller (Canadian)
Words and music by Basil Hurdon and Dyer Hurdon.
Hurdon Music Publishers, Canada/Kemo Music Co.
Best-selling record in 1962 by Bobby Curtola (Del-Fi).

Funny, also known as Funny How Time Slips Away
Words and music by Willie Nelson.
Pamper Music, Inc.
Best-selling record in 1964 by Joe Hinton (Back Beat).

Funny How Time Slips Away, see Funny.

Genius after Hours, The
Music by Ray Charles.
Progressive Music Publishing Co., Inc.
Introduced by Ray Charles (Atlantic).

Get a Little Dirt on Your Hands
Words and music by Bill Anderson.
Champion Music Corp./Tree Publishing Co., Inc., 1961, 1962.
Best-selling record in 1962 by Bill Anderson (Decca).

Ginny Come Lately, also known as **Johnny Come Lately**
Words by Peter Udell, music by Gary Geld.
George Pincus & Sons Music Corp.
Best-selling record by Brian Hyland (ABC-Paramount).

Girls Like Me
Words by Betty Comden and Adolph Green, music by Jule Styne.
Stratford Music Corp.
Introduced by Carol Lawrence in *Subways Are for Sleeping* (musical).

Go Home
Words and music by Onie Wheeler.
Four Star Music Co., Inc.
Best-selling record by Lester Flatt and Earl Scruggs (Columbia).

Go Slow, Johnny (English)
Words and music by Noël Coward.
Operating Company Salina, Ltd., Jamaica, British West Indies/
    Chappell & Co., Inc.
Introduced by James Hurst in *Sail Away* (musical).

Gonna Build a Mountain (English)
Words and music by Leslie Bricusse and Anthony Newley.
Essex Music, Ltd., London, England/Ludlow Music, Inc.
Introduced by Anthony Newley in London and New York (1962)
    productions of *Stop the World — I Want To Get Off* (musical).

Good Time Baby
Words by Kal Mann, music by Bernie Lowe and Dave Appell.
Lowe Music Corp./Fajob Music Publishing Co.
Best-selling record by Bobby Rydell (Cameo).

Goodbye Cruel World
Words and music by Gloria Shayne.
Screen Gems-Columbia Music, Inc.
Best-selling record by James Darren (Colpix).

Goodbye Is a Lonesome Sound
Words by Alan Bergman and Marilyn Keith, music by Paul Weston.
Empress Music, Inc., 1961, 1963.
Introduced by The Three Young Men (from Montana) (Columbia).

Goodbye, Juan, see **Plane Wreck at Los Gatos.**

Grand Old Ivy
Words and music by Frank Loesser.
Frank Music Corp.
Introduced by Robert Morse and Rudy Vallee in *How To Succeed in Business without Really Trying* (musical).

Guilty of Loving You
Words and music by Jerry Fuller.
Four Star Music Co., Inc.
Best-selling record by Jerry Fuller (Challenge).

Guns of Navarone, The
Words by Paul Francis Webster, music by Dimitri Tiomkin.
Columbia Pictures Music Corp.
Adapted from a theme from *The Guns of Navarone* (film).

Gypsy Woman
Words and music by Curtis Mayfield.
Curtom Publishing Co., Inc.
Best-selling record by The Impressions (ABC-Paramount).

Halfway to Paradise
Words and music by Gerry Goffin and Carole King.
Screen Gems-Columbia Music, Inc.
Best-selling record by Tony Orlando (Epic).

Happy Birthday, Sweet Sixteen
Words and music by Neil Sedaka and Howard Greenfield.
Screen Gems-Columbia Music, Inc.
Best-selling record by Neil Sedaka (RCA Victor).

Happy Journey (German)
English words by Fred Jay, German words by Nicola Wilke (pseudonym for Lale Andersen), music by Charles Nowa.
Carlton Musikverlag Hans Gerig, KG, Cologne, Germany/Regent Music Corp.
Original German title, "Wenn Du Heimkommst." Best-selling record in 1962 by Hank Locklin (RCA Victor).

Happy Times (Are Here To Stay)
Words and music by Gerry Goffin, Cynthia Weil, and Carole King.
Screen Gems-Columbia Music, Inc.
Best-selling record by Tony Orlando (Epic).

Happy To Be Unhappy
Words and music by Bobby Bare.
Central Songs, Inc.
Best-selling record in 1963 by Gary Buck (Petal).

Happy To Keep His Dinner Warm
Words and music by Frank Loesser.
Frank Music Corp.
Introduced by Bonnie Scott in *How To Succeed in Business without Really Trying* (musical).

Hard Times (No One Knows Better Than I)
Words and music by Ray Charles.
Progressive Music Publishing Co., Inc.
Introduced by Ray Charles (Atlantic).

Hatari!
Music by Henry Mancini.
Famous Music Corp., 1961, 1962.
Title theme from *Hatari!* (film, 1962). Best-selling record by Henry
  Mancini and his Orchestra (RCA Victor).

Hats Off to Larry
Words and music by Del Shannon.
Vicki Music, Inc./McLaughlin Publishing Co.
Best-selling record by Del Shannon (Big Top).

Hawaii Tattoo (Belgian)
Words and music by Michael Thomas.
World Music Co., Brussels, Belgium/Zodiac Music Corp.
Best-selling record in 1965 by The Waikikis (Kapp Winner's Circle).

He Cried
Words and music by Ted Daryll and Greg Richards.
Trio Music Co., Inc.
Best-selling record in 1966 by The Shangri-Las (Red Bird).

Heart over Mind
Words and music by Mel Tillis.
Cedarwood Publishing Co., Inc.
Best-selling record by Ray Price (Columbia).

Hello Fool
Words and music by Willie Nelson and Jim Coleman.
Pamper Music, Inc.
Best-selling record by Ralph Emery (Liberty).

Hello, Mary Lou
Words and music by Gene Pitney.
January Music Corp.
Introduced by Ricky Nelson (Imperial).

Hello Walls
Words and music by Willie Nelson.
Pamper Music, Inc.
Best-selling record by Faron Young (Capitol).

Her Face
Words and music by Bob Merrill.
Robbins Music Corp.
Introduced by Jerry Orbach in *Carnival!* (musical).

Her Royal Majesty
Words and music by Gerry Goffin and Carole King.
Screen Gems-Columbia Music, Inc.
Best-selling record in 1962 by James Darren (Colpix).

Hide Away — 1962
Words and music by Freddy King and Sonny Thompson.
Sonlo Publishing Co.
Title changed from "Hide Away" to "Hide Away — 1962" in 1962.
  Best-selling record by Freddy King (Federal).

His Latest Flame, also known as (Marie's the Name) His Latest Flame
Words and music by Doc Pomus and Mort Shuman.
Elvis Presley Music, Inc.
Best-selling record by Elvis Presley (RCA Victor).

Hit the Road, Jack
Words and music by Percy Mayfield.
Tangerine Music Corp.
Best-selling record by Ray Charles (ABC-Paramount). Winner of
  National Academy of Recording Arts and Sciences Award for
  "Best Rhythm and Blues Recording," 1961.

Hollywood
Words and music by John D. Loudermilk.
Acuff-Rose Publications, Inc.
Best-selling record by Connie Francis (MGM).

How Can I Tell Her It's Over
Words and music by Barry Mann and Cynthia Weil.
Screen Gems-Columbia Music, Inc.

How Can I Write on Paper What I Feel in My Heart, see What I Feel in My Heart.

How Can You Describe a Face?
Words by Betty Comden and Adolph Green, music by Jule Styne.
Stratford Music Corp.
Introduced by Sydney Chaplin in *Subways Are for Sleeping* (musical).

How Do You Talk to a Baby?
Words and music by Wayne P. Walker and Webb Pierce.
Cedarwood Publishing Co., Inc.
Best-selling record by Webb Pierce (Decca).

How Many Tears
Words and music by Gerry Goffin and Carole King.
Screen Gems-Columbia Music, Inc.
Best-selling record by Bobby Vee (Liberty).

How To Succeed in Business without Really Trying
Words and music by Frank Loesser.
Frank Music Corp.
Introduced by Robert Morse in *How To Succeed in Business without
Really Trying* (musical).

How Wonderful To Know (Italian)
English words by Kermit Goell, Italian words by Tito Manlio, music
by Salve d'Esposito.
Edizioni Musical Film, Milan, Italy, 1950/Leeds Music Corp., 1954,
1961.
Original Italian title, "Ànema e Core." Introduced by Ferruccio
Tagliavini in *Ànema e Core* (Italian film). Under titles, "Until"
and "With All My Heart and Soul," earlier English-language versions recorded by Dinah Shore and Eddie Fisher. Best-selling
record of this version by Andy Williams (Cadence). See "Ànema
e Core," 1954.

Humpty Dumpty
Music by Alex North.
North & Son Music, Inc.
From *The Misfits* (film).

Hundred Pounds of Clay, A
Words and music by Bob Elgin, Luther Dixon, and Kay Rogers.
Gil Music Corp.
Best-selling record by Gene McDaniels (Liberty).

I Believe in You
Words and music by Frank Loesser.
Frank Music Corp.
Introduced by Robert Morse and company in *How To Succeed in
Business without Really Trying* (musical).

I Don't Mind
Words and music by James Brown.
Lois Publishing Co.
Best-selling record by James Brown (King).

I Don't Want To Cry No More
Words and music by Luther Dixon and Charles Jackson.
Ludix Publishing Co., Inc./Betalbin Music Publishing Corp.
Best-selling record by Chuck Jackson (Wand).

I Fought the Law
Words and music by Sonny Curtis.
Acuff-Rose Publications, Inc.
Best-selling record in 1966 by Bobby Fuller (Mustang).

I Guess I'll Never Learn
Words and music by John Hathcock and Weldon Allard.
Neillrae Music.
Best-selling record in 1962 by Charlie Phillips (Columbia).

I Just Don't Understand
Words and music by Marijohn Wilkin and Kent Westbury.
Cedarwood Publishing Co., Inc.
Best-selling record by Ann-Margret (RCA Victor).

I Know (You Don't Want Me No More)
Words and music by Barbara George.
Saturn Music, Inc./At Last Publishing Co.
Best-selling record in 1962 by Barbara George (AFO).

I Let It Slip Away
Words and music by Jan Crutchfield.
Tree Publishing Co., Inc.
Introduced by Faron Young (Capitol).

I Like It Like That
Words and music by Chris Kenner and Alan Toussaint.
Tune-Kel Publishing Co., Inc.
Best-selling records by Chris Kenner (Instant) and in 1964 by The
    Dave Clark Five (Epic).

I Love How You Love Me
Words and music by Barry Mann and Larry Kolber.
Screen Gems-Columbia Music, Inc.
Best-selling record by The Paris Sisters (Gregmark).

I Understand Just How You Feel, see 1953.

I Went Out of My Way
Words by Vic McAlpin, music by Roy Drusky and Jean Elrod.
Moss Rose Publications, Inc.
Best-selling record by Roy Drusky (Decca).

I Will Follow You
Words and music by Jerry Herman.
Jerryco Music Co.
Introduced by Tommy Rall in *Milk and Honey* (musical).

I Wonder Who
Words and music by Ray Charles.
Progressive Music Publishing Co., Inc.
Introduced by Ray Charles (Atlantic).

If Only Tomorrow (Could Be Like Today)
Words and music by Warner McPherson and Mike Terry.
Valley Publishers, Inc.
Introduced by Buddy Thomas (Todd).

I'm a Woman
Words and music by Mike Stoller and Jerry Leiber.
Trio Music Co., Inc.
Best-selling record in 1963 by Peggy Lee (Capitol).

I'm Blue (The Gong Gong Song)
Words and music by Ike Turner.
Progressive Music Publishing Co., Inc./Placid Music/Valley Spring
    Music Corp.
Best-selling record in 1962 by The Ikettes (Atco).

I'm Gonna Knock on Your Door
Words and music by Aaron Schroeder and Sid Wayne.
Sigma Music, Inc.
Best-selling record by Eddie Hodges (Cadence).

I'm Just Taking My Time
Words by Betty Comden and Adolph Green, music by Jule Styne.
Stratford Music Corp.
Introduced by Sydney Chaplin and chorus in *Subways Are for Sleeping* (musical).

I'm Yours
Words and music by Don Robertson and Hal Blair.
Gladys Music, Inc.
Best-selling record in 1965 by Elvis Presley (RCA Victor).

Imitation
Words and music by Wayne P. Walker and Irene Stanton.
Cedarwood Publishing Co., Inc.
Introduced by Marion Worth (Columbia).

In All My Wildest Dreams
Words and music by Jack Wolf.
Integrity Music Corp.

In the Middle of a Heartache
Words and music by Laurie Christenson, Pat Franzese, and Wanda
    Jackson.
Central Songs, Inc.
Best-selling record by Wanda Jackson (Capitol).

It Keeps Right On A-Hurtin' Since I Left
Words and music by Johnny Tillotson and Lorene Mann.
Ridge Music Corp.
Introduced and best-selling record in 1962 by Johnny Tillotson
    (Cadence).

It Takes All Kinds To Make a World
Words and music by Roger Miller.
Tree Publishing Co., Inc.
Introduced by Roger Miller.

It Was a Very Good Year
Words and music by Ervin Drake.
Dolfi Music, Inc.
Introduced by The Kingston Trio (Capitol). Best-selling record in
1965-66 by Frank Sinatra (Reprise). Winner of National Academy
of Recording Arts and Sciences Award for "Best Vocal Perform-
ance—Male," 1965. Best-selling record in 1966 by Della Reese
(RCA Victor).

It Was Always You
Words and music by Bob Merrill.
Robbins Music Corp.
Introduced by James Mitchell and Kaye Ballard in *Carnival!* (musi-
cal).

It's a Raggy Waltz
Music by Dave Brubeck.
Derry Music Co.
Best-selling record by Dave Brubeck (Columbia). Featured in *All
Night Long* (British film).

It's Gonna Work Out Fine, also known as Darling (Gonna Work Out Fine)
Words and music by Rose Marie McCoy and Sylvia McKinney.
Ben-Ghazi Enterprises, Inc./Saturn Music, Inc.
Best-selling record by Ike and Tina Turner (Sue).

It's Your World
Words and music by Marty Robbins.
Marizona Music.
Best-selling record by Marty Robbins (Columbia).

I've Got Bonnie
Words and music by Gerry Goffin and Carole King.
Screen Gems-Columbia Music, Inc.
Best-selling record by Bobby Rydell (Cameo).

Jamie
Words and music by Barrett Strong and William Stevenson.
Jobete Music Co., Inc.
Best-selling record in 1962 by Eddie Holland (Motown).

Jeremiah Peabody's Poly-Unsaturated, Quick Dissolving, Fast Acting, Pleasant Tasting, Green and Purple Pills
Words and music by Ray Stevens.
Lowery Music Co., Inc.
Best-selling record by Ray Stevens (Mercury).

Joey Baby
Words and music by Jane Connell.
Tree Publishing Co., Inc.
Introduced by Anita and The So and So's (RCA Victor).

John Birch Society, The
Words and music by Michael Brown.
Sunbeam Music Corp.
Introduced in *Seven Come Eleven* (nightclub revue). Best-selling
  record by The Chad Mitchell Trio (Kapp).

John Riley
Words and music by Bob Gibson and Ricky Neff.
Sanga Music, Inc./Harvard Music, Inc.
Introduced by Bob Gibson (Riverside).

Johnny Come Lately, see **Ginny Come Lately.**

Joy Ride
Music by Ray Charles.
Progressive Music Publishing Co., Inc.
Introduced by Ray Charles (Atco).

Just an Honest Mistake
Words and music by Jay Livingston and Ray Evans.
Livingston & Evans, Inc.
Introduced by Ted Thurston, Stanley Simmonds, and company in *Let
  It Ride!* (musical).

King of Kings Theme, also known as **Theme from
  King of Kings**
Music by Miklos Rozsa.
Robbins Music Corp.
Theme from *King of Kings* (film).

Kiss Me Quick
Words and music by Doc Pomus and Mort Shuman.
Gladys Music, Inc.
Best-selling record by Elvis Presley (RCA Victor).

La Novia, see **The Wedding.**

Last Kiss
Words and music by Wayne Cochran.
Macon Music Co., 1961, 1964.
Introduced by Wayne Cochran (Gala). Best-selling record in 1964 by
  J. Frank Wilson with The Cavaliers (Josie).

Last Night
Words and music by T. Johnson and The Mar-Keys.
East Publications/Bais Music.
Best-selling record by The Mar-Keys (Satellite).

Later Than Spring (English)
Words and music by Noël Coward.
Operating Company Salina, Ltd., Jamaica, British West Indies/
  Chappell & Co., Inc.
Introduced by James Hurst in *Sail Away* (musical).

Let Me Belong to You
Words by Peter Udell, music by Gary Geld.
East-West Music, Inc.
Best-selling record by Brian Hyland (ABC-Paramount).

Let Me In
Words and music by Yvonne Baker.
Arc Music Corp./Kae Williams Music, Inc., 1961, 1962.
Best-selling record in 1962 by The Sensations (Argo).

Let the Four Winds Blow
Words and music by Dave Bartholomew and Antoine Domino.
Travis Music Co.
Introduced and best-selling record by Fats Domino (Imperial).

Let There Be Drums
Music by Sandy Nelson and Richard Podolor.
Travis Music Co.
Introduced by Sandy Nelson (Imperial).

Let's Not Waste a Moment (A Short Forever)
Words and music by Jerry Herman.
Jerryco Music Co.
Introduced by Robert Weede in *Milk and Honey* (musical).

Let's Twist Again
Words by Kal Mann, music by Kal Mann and Dave Appell.
Kalmann Music, Inc.
Best-selling record by Chubby Checker (Parkway). Winner of Na-
tional Academy of Recording Arts and Sciences Award for "Best
Rock and Roll Recording," 1961.

Like a Young Man
Words and music by Jerry Herman.
Jerryco Music Co.
Introduced by Robert Weede in *Milk and Honey* (musical).

Lion Sleeps Tonight, The, see **Wimoweh,** 1951.

Little Bird, The
Words and music by John D. Loudermilk.
Acuff-Rose Publications, Inc.
Best-selling record in 1965 by Marianne Faithfull (London).

Little Bit of Soap, A
Words and music by Bert Russell.
Robert Mellin, Inc.
Best-selling record by The Jarmels (Laurie).

Little Devil
Words and music by Howard Greenfield and Neil Sedaka.
Screen Gems-Columbia Music, Inc.
Introduced by Neil Sedaka (RCA Victor).

Little Drops of Rain
Words by E. Y. Harburg, music by Harold Arlen.
Harwin Music Corp.
Introduced by voice of Judy Garland, and reprised by voice of Robert
  Goulet, in *Gay Purr-ee* (cartoon feature film).

Little Red Rooster
Words and music by Willie Dixon.
Arc Music Corp.
Introduced by Sam Cooke (RCA Victor).

Little Sister
Words and music by Doc Pomus and Mort Shuman.
Elvis Presley Music, Inc.
Best-selling record by Elvis Presley (RCA Victor).

Lonesome Number One
Words and music by Don Gibson.
Acuff-Rose Publications, Inc.
Best-selling record in 1962 by Don Gibson (RCA Victor).

Lonesome Whistle Blues
Words and music by Rudy Toombs and Elson Teat.
Lois Publishing Co.
Best-selling record by Freddy King (Federal).

Look in My Eyes
Words and music by Richard Barrett.
Atlantic Music Corp.
Best-selling record by The Chantels (Carlton).

Losing Your Love
Words and music by Bill Anderson and Buddy Killen.
Champion Music Corp./Tree Publishing Co., Inc.
Best-selling record in 1962 by Jim Reeves (RCA Victor).

Loss of Innocence
Music by Richard S. Addinsell.
Columbia Pictures Music Corp.
Theme from *Loss of Innocence* (film).

Louisiana Man
Words and music by Doug Kershaw.
Acuff-Rose Publications, Inc.
Best-selling record by Rusty and Doug (Hickory).

Love from a Heart of Gold.
Words and music by Frank Loesser.
Frank Music Corp.
Introduced by Rudy Vallee and Virginia Martin in *How To Succeed
  in Business without Really Trying* (musical).

Love Makes the World Go 'Round, see Theme from *Carnival!*.

Love Me Warm and Tender
Words and music by Paul Anka.
Spanka Music Corp., 1961, 1962.
Best-selling record in 1962 by Paul Anka (RCA Victor).

Love Me with All Your Heart, see **Cuando Caliente El Sol.**

Love Theme from *El Cid* (The Falcon and the Dove)
Words by Paul Francis Webster, music by Miklos Rozsa.
Robbins Music Corp.
Adapted from a theme from *El Cid* (film). Nominated for Academy
    Award, 1961.

Lover Come Back
Words by Alan Spilton, music by Alan Spilton and Frank De Vol.
Daywin Music, Inc.
Introduced by Doris Day in *Lover Come Back* (film, 1962).

Lover, Please
Words and music by Bill Swan.
Lynlou Music, Inc.
Best-selling record in 1962 by Clyde McPhatter (Mercury).

Lucy's Theme from *Parrish*
Music by Max Steiner.
M. Witmark & Sons.
From *Parrish* (film).

Lumbered (English)
Words and music by Leslie Bricusse and Anthony Newley.
Essex Music, Ltd., London, England/Ludlow Music, Inc.
Introduced by Anthony Newley in London and New York (1962)
    productions of *Stop the World — I Want To Get Off* (musical).

Magic Moment
Words and music by Howard Dietz and Arthur Schwartz.
Harms, Inc.
Introduced by Barbara Cook in *The Gay Life* (musical).

Mama Said, see **Momma Said.**

Mama Sang a Song
Words and music by Bill Anderson.
Champion Music Corp./Tree Publishing Co., Inc.
Best-selling record in 1962 by Bill Anderson (Decca).

Marvelous Toy, The
Words and music by Tom Paxton.
Teena Music Corp.
Best-selling record by The Chad Mitchell Trio (Mercury).

Mewsette
Words by E. Y. Harburg, music by Harold Arlen.
Harwin Music Corp.
Introduced by voice of Robert Goulet in *Gay Purr-ee* (cartoon feature film).

(My Heart's in) Mexico
Words by Felice Bryant and Boudleaux Bryant, music by Boudleaux Bryant.
Acuff-Rose Publications, Inc.
Best-selling instrumental record by Bob Moore (Monument).

Michael (Row the Boat Ashore)
New words and music arrangement by Dave Fisher.
United Artists Music Co., Inc., 1960, 1961.
Adapted from traditional work-spiritual, which first appeared in print in *Slave Songs of the United States* by Charles Pickard Ware (1867). Best-selling record by The Highwaymen (United Artists).

Midnight in Moscow, also known as Moscovian Nights, also known as Moscow Nights (Russian)
New music and arrangement by Kenny Ball and Jan Burgers.
Tyler Music, Ltd., London, England/Les Editions Int. Basart N.V., Holland/Melody Trails, Inc.
Based on song by Vassili Soloviev-Sedoy and M. Matusovsky, entitled "Padmaskoveeye Vietchera." Best-selling instrumental recording in 1961-62 by Kenny Ball (Kapp).

Milk and Honey
Words and music by Jerry Herman.
Jerryco Music Co.
Introduced by Tommy Rall, Juki Arkin, and company in *Milk and Honey* (musical).

Mira (Can You Imagine That?)
Words and music by Bob Merrill.
Robbins Music Corp.
Introduced by Anna Maria Alberghetti in *Carnival!* (musical).

Misery Loves Company
Words and music by Jerry Reed.
Lowery Music Co., Inc.
Best-selling record in 1962 by Porter Wagoner (RCA Victor).

Missing Angel
Words and music by Dale Noe.
Tuckahoe Music, Inc.
Best-selling record by Jim Reeves (RCA Victor).

Mr. Charles' Blues
Words and music by Ray Charles.
Progressive Music Publishing Co., Inc.
Introduced by Ray Charles (Atlantic).

Misterioso
Music by Thelonious Monk.
Thelonious Music.
First recording in 1948 by Thelonious Monk (Blue Note).

Moliendo Cafe (Venezuelan)
Music by José Munzo.
Morro Music Corp.
Introduced and best-selling record in South America by Hugo Blanco
    and his Orchestra. First United States recording by Ray Anthony
    and his Orchestra (Capitol).

Momma Said, also known as **Mama Said**
Words and music by Luther Dixon and Willie Dennson.
Ludix Publishing Co., Inc./Betalbin Music Publishing Corp.
Best-selling record by The Shirelles (Scepter).

Mon Amour Perdu (My Lost Love)
Words and music by Richard M. Sherman and Robert B. Sherman.
Wonderland Music Co., Inc., 1961, 1962.
From *Big Red* (film, 1962).

Moody River
Words and music by Gary D. Bruce.
Keva Music Co.
Best-selling record by Pat Boone (Dot).

Moon Is High and So Am I, The
Words and music by Roger Miller.
Tree Publishing Co., Inc.
Introduced by Roger Miller (RCA Victor).

Moon River
Words by Johnny Mercer, music by Henry Mancini.
Famous Music Corp.
Introduced by Audrey Hepburn in *Breakfast at Tiffany's* (film).
    Academy Award-winning song, 1961. Best-selling records by
    Henry Mancini and his Orchestra (RCA Victor), Andy Williams
    (Columbia), and Jerry Butler (Vee Jay). Winner of National
    Academy of Recording Arts and Sciences Awards for "Song of
    the Year," "Record of the Year" (Mancini version), and "Best
    Arrangement" (Mancini version), 1961.

Moscovian Nights, see **Midnight in Moscow.**

Moscow Nights, see **Midnight in Moscow.**

Most People Get Married
Words by Earl Shuman, music by Leon Carr.
Famous Music Corp., 1961, 1962.
Introduced by Patti Page (Mercury).

Mother-in-Law
Words and music by Alan Toussaint.
Minit Music Co.
Best-selling record by Ernie K-Doe (Minit).

Mountain's High, The
Words and music by Dick Gosting.
Odin Music Co.
Best-selling record by Dick and Deedee (Liberty).

Multiplication
Words and music by Bobby Darin.
Adaris Music, Inc.
Introduced by Bobby Darin in *Come September* (film).

Murder, She Said (English)
Music by Ron Godwin.
Robbins Music Corp., Ltd., London, England/Robbins Music Corp.
Theme from *Murder, She Said* (British film, 1962).

My Boomerang Won't Come Back (English)
Words and music by Max Diamond and Charlie Drake.
Kaye Music Co., Ltd., London, England/Piccadilly Music Corp.
Best-selling record by Charlie Drake (United Artists).

My Ears Should Burn (When Fools Are Talked About)
Words and music by Roger Miller.
Tree Publishing Co., Inc.
Best-selling record by Claude Gray (Mercury).

My Kind of Girl (English)
Words and music by Leslie Bricusse.
Essex Music, Ltd., London, England/Hollis Music, Inc.
Best-selling record by Matt Monro (Warwick).

My Lost Love, see Mon Amour Perdu.

My Name Is Mud
Words and music by Bill Anderson.
Tree Publishing Co., Inc./Champion Music Corp.
Best-selling record in 1962 by James O'Gwynn (Mercury).

My State, My Kansas, My Home
Words and music by Meredith Willson.
Frank Music Corp./Rinimer Corp.
Written for Centennial of State of Kansas. Sung by Janis Paige,
    Paul Reed, Fred Gwynne, Arthur Rubin, and Cliff Hall in *Here's
    Love* (musical, 1963).

My True Story
Words and music by Eugene Pitt and Oscar Waltzer.
Lescay Music, Inc.
Best-selling record by The Jive Five and Joe Rene (Beltone).

Naked City Theme, also known as Somewhere in the Night
Words by Milton Raskin, music by Billy May.
Gower Music, Inc., 1961, 1962, 1963.
Theme of *Naked City* (television series). Words added in 1962 and
  introduced as "Somewhere in the Night" by Teri Thornton
  (Dauntless).

Nick Teen and Al K. Hall (Australian)
Words and music by Rolf Harris.
Castle Music Pty., Ltd., Sydney, Australia, 1960/Beechwood Music
  Corp.
Introduced by Rolf Harris (Epic).

No One
Words and music by Doc Pomus and Mort Shuman.
Efsee Music, Inc.
Best-selling record in 1962 by Ray Charles (ABC-Paramount).

No Regrets (French)
English words by Hal David, French words by Michel Vaucaire,
  music by Charles Dumont.
Éditions Musicales Eddie Barclay, Paris, France, 1960, 1961, 1963/
  The Barclay Music Corp.
English lyrics added in 1961. Original French title, "Non, Je Ne
  Regrette Rien." Introduced by Edith Piaf.

Nobody Cares
Words and music by Ray Charles.
Progressive Music Publishing Co., Inc.
Introduced by Ray Charles (Atco).

Norman
Words and music by John D. Loudermilk.
Acuff-Rose Publications, Inc.
Best-selling record in 1962 by Sue Thompson (Hickory).

Nothing More To Look Forward To
Words and music by Richard Adler.
Sahara Music, Inc.
Introduced by Robert Guillaume and Ethel Ayler in *Kwamina*
  (musical).

Now and Forever (German)
Words by Milton Gabler, music by Bert Kaempfert.
Roosevelt Music Co., Inc.
Introduced by Bert Kaempfert and his Orchestra (Decca).

Oceans of Love
Words and music by Carl Sigman.
Edwin H. Morris & Co., Inc.

Odds and Ends, Bits and Pieces
Words and music by Harlan Howard.
Central Songs, Inc.
Best-selling record by Warren Smith (Liberty).

Oh Love, Hast Thou Forsaken Me
Words and music by William Bowers.
Denslow Music, Inc.
Introduced by Peggy Lee (Capitol).

Old Man Time
Words and music by Cliff Friend and Jack Reynolds.
Miller Music Corp., 1961, 1962.
Introduced by Jimmy Durante (Warner Bros.).

Once in a Lifetime (English)
Words and music by Leslie Bricusse and Anthony Newley.
Essex Music, Ltd., London, England/Ludlow Music, Inc.
Introduced by Anthony Newley in London and New York (1962)
    productions of *Stop the World — I Want To Get Off* (musical).

One Mint Julep, see 1952.

One Note Samba (Samba De Uma Nota So) (Brazilian)
English words by Jon Hendricks, Portuguese words and music by
    N. Mendonca and Antonio Carlos Jobim.
Antonio Carlos Jobim and Mrs. N. Mendonca, Brazil, 1961, 1962/
    Duchess Music Corp.
Introduced by João Gilberto (Capitol). First recording of Hendricks
    version introduced by Pat Thomas (Verve). Another English-
    language version, with lyrics by Jobim, introduced by Jobim with
    Herbie Mann (Atlantic).

One Track Mind
Words and music by Bobby Lewis and Malou Rene.
Viva Music, Inc./Harvard Music, Inc.
Best-selling record by Bobby Lewis (Beltone).

One, Two, Three Waltz, The
Words by Dory Langdon Previn, music by André Previn.
United Artists Music Co., Inc.
Adapted from a theme from *One, Two, Three* (film).

Optimistic, also known as **Optomistic**
Words and music by Aubrey Freeman.
Big "D" Music, Inc./Neillrae Music.
Best-selling record by Skeeter Davis (RCA Victor).

Optomistic, see **Optimistic.**

Ordinary People
Words and music by Richard Adler.
Sahara Music, Inc.
Introduced by Sally Ann Howes and Terry Carter in *Kwamina*
  (musical).

P. T. 109
Words and music by Marijohn Wilkin and Fred Burch.
Cedarwood Publishing Co., Inc.
Best-selling record in 1962 by Jimmy Dean (Columbia).

Paris Blues
Words by Billy Strayhorn and Harold Flender, music by Duke
  Ellington.
United Artists Music Co., Inc./Tempo Music.
Introduced by Duke Ellington with orchestra in *Paris Blues* (film).

Paris Is a Lonely Town
Words by E. Y. Harburg, music by Harold Arlen.
Harwin Music Corp.
Introduced by voice of Judy Garland in *Gay Purr-ee* (cartoon fea-
  ture film).

Paris Original
Words and music by Frank Loesser.
Frank Music Corp.
Introduced by Bonnie Scott, Claudette Sutherland, Mara Landi, and
  company in *How To Succeed in Business without Really Trying*
  (musical).

Peace of Mind
Words and music by Riley King and Joe Josea.
Modern Music Publishing Co.
Best-selling record by B. B. King (Kent).

Peanut Butter
Words and music by H. B. Barnum, Martin J. Cooper, Clifford
  Goldsmith, and Fred Smith.
Arvee Music.
Best-selling record by The Marathons (Arvee).

Peppermint Twist
Words and music by Joey Dee and Henry Glover.
Frost Music Corp.
Best-selling record in 1961-62 by Joey Dee and The Starlighters
  (Roulette).

Percolator
Music by Lou Bideu and Ernie Freeman.
Meadowlark Music, 1961, 1962.
Best-selling record by Billy Joe and The Checkmates (Dore).

Pianissimo (French)
English words by Jimmy Kennedy, French words by André Tabet
  and Alex Alstone, music by Alex Alstone.
Éditions Salabert S.A., Paris, France/Regent Music Corp.
Best-selling record by Jackie Wilson (Brunswick).

Plane Wreck at Los Gatos, also known as **Deportee,** also
  known as **Goodbye, Juan**
Words by Woody Guthrie, music by Martin Hoffman.
Ludlow Music, Inc.
Best-selling record by Judy Collins (Elektra).

Playboy
Words and music by Brian Holland, Robert Bateman, and William
  Stevenson.
Jobete Music Co., Inc.
Best-selling record in 1962 by The Marvelettes (Tamla).

Please Don't Ask about Barbara
Words and music by Bill Buchanan and Jack Keller.
Screen Gems-Columbia Music, Inc.
Best-selling record by Bobby Vee (Liberty).

(Don't Go) Please Stay
Words by Bob Hilliard, music by Burt F. Bacharach.
Eleventh Floor Music, Inc./Quartet Music, Inc./Walden Music Corp.
Best-selling record by The Drifters (Atlantic).

Pleasure of His Company, The
Words by Sammy Cahn, music by Alfred Newman.
Famous Music Corp.
From *The Pleasure of His Company* (film).

Po' Folks
Words and music by Bill Anderson.
Tree Publishing Co., Inc./Champion Music Corp.
Best-selling record by Bill Anderson (Decca).

Pocketful of Miracles
Words by Sammy Cahn, music by James Van Heusen.
Maraville Music Corp.
Introduced by voice of Frank Sinatra on soundtrack of *Pocketful of
  Miracles* (film). Nominated for Academy Award, 1961.

Point of No Return
Words and music by Gerry Goffin and Carole King.
Screen Gems-Columbia Music, Inc.
Best-selling record by Gene McDaniels (Liberty).

Poor Little Puppet
Words and music by Howard Greenfield and Jack Keller.
Screen Gems-Columbia Music, Inc.
Best-selling record by Cathy Carroll (Warner Bros.).

Portrait of My Love (English)
Words by David West, music by Cyril Ornadel.
Edward Kassner Music Co., Ltd., London, England, 1960/Piccadilly
    Music Corp.
Best-selling record by Steve Lawrence (United Artists).

Pretty Boy Floyd
Words and music by Woody Guthrie.
Fall River Music, Inc.
Introduced by Woody Guthrie (Folkways).

Pretty Little Angel Eyes (Australian)
Words and music by Tommy Boyce and Curtis Lee.
Belinda Music, Sydney, Australia/S-P-R Music Corp.
Best-selling record by Curtis Lee (Dunes).

Pretty Little Girl in the Yellow Dress
Words by Ned Washington, music by Dimitri Tiomkin.
Leeds Music Corp.
From *The Last Sunset* (film).

Quarter to Three
Words and music by Frank Guida, Joe Royster, Gene Barge, and
    Gary Anderson.
Rock Masters, Inc.
Best-selling record by Gary "U.S." Bonds (LeGrand).

Raindrops
Words and music by Dee Clark.
Conrad Publishing Co., Inc.
Best-selling record by Dee Clark (Vee Jay).

(Love Is Like a) Ramblin' Rose
Words and music by Marijohn Wilkin, Fred Burch, and Obrey Wilson.
Cedarwood Publishing Co., Inc.
Best-selling record by Ted Taylor (Okeh).

Ray's Blues
Words and music by Ray Charles.
Progressive Music Publishing Co., Inc.
Introduced by Ray Charles.

Reach for the Stars
Words by David West, music by Udo Jergens.
Piccadilly Music Corp.
Introduced by Shirley Bassey (United Artists).

Revenge
Words and music by Brook Benton, Marnie Ewald, and Oliver Hall.
Raleigh Music, Inc./Benday Music Corp.
Best-selling record by Brook Benton (Mercury).

Ride through the Night
Words by Betty Comden and Adolph Green, music by Jule Styne.
Stratford Music Corp.
Introduced by Sydney Chaplin, Carol Lawrence, and chorus in *Subways Are for Sleeping* (musical).

Rock-A-Hula Baby
Words and music by Fred Wise, Ben Weisman, and Dolores Fuller.
Gladys Music, Inc.
Best-selling record by Elvis Presley (RCA Victor). Featured in *Blue Hawaii* (film.)

Roses Are Red (My Love)
Words and music by Al Byron and Paul Evans.
Lyle Music, Inc.
Best-selling record in 1962 by Bobby Vinton (Epic).

Rules of the Road, The
Words by Carolyn Leigh, music by Cy Coleman.
Melrose Music Corp., 1961, 1963.
Introduced by Tony Bennett (Columbia).

Run to Him
Words and music by Gerry Goffin and Jack Keller.
Screen Gems-Columbia Music, Inc.
Best-selling record by Bobby Vee (Liberty).

Runaround Sue
Words and music by Dion Di Mucci and Ernest Maresca.
Disal Music Corp./Schwartz Music Co., Inc.
Best-selling record by Dion (Laurie).

Runaway
Words by Del Shannon, music by Max Crook and Del Shannon.
Vicki Music, Inc.
Best-selling record in 1961-62 by Del Shannon (Big Top).

Sacred
Words by William Landau, music by Adam Ross.
Daywin Music, Inc./Bamboo Music, Inc.
Introduced by The Castells (Era).

Sad Movies (Make Me Cry)
Words and music by John D. Loudermilk.
Acuff-Rose Publications, Inc.
Best-selling record by Sue Thompson (Hickory).

Sail Away, see 1950.

San-Ho-Zay
Music by Freddy King and Sonny Thompson.
Lois Publishing Co.
Best-selling record by Freddy King (Federal).

Satan Never Sleeps
Words by Harold Adamson and Leo McCarey, music by Harry
Warren.
Leo Feist, Inc., 1961, 1962.
From *Satan Never Sleeps* (film, 1962). Best-selling record by Timi
Yuro (Liberty).

School Is Out
Words and music by Gary Anderson and Gene Barge.
Rock Masters, Inc.
Best-selling record by U.S. Bonds (LeGrand).

Senza Fine, see The Phoenix Love Theme, 1964.

Shake the Hand of a Fool
Words and music by Margie Singleton.
Ponderosa Music Co., Inc./Jamie Music Publishing Co.
Best-selling record by Johnny Hallyday (Philips).

Shalom
Words and music by Jerry Herman.
Jerryco Music Co.
Introduced by Robert Weede and Mimi Benzell in *Milk and Honey*
(musical).

She's Got You
Words and music by Hank Cochran.
Pamper Music, Inc.
Best-selling record in 1962 by Patsy Cline (Decca).

She's My Love
Words and music by Bob Merrill.
Robbins Music Corp.
Introduced by Jerry Orbach in *Carnival!* (musical).

Shop Around
Words and music by Berry Gordy, Jr. and Bill "Smokie" Robinson.
Jobete Music Co., Inc.
Best-selling record by The Miracles (Tamla).

Should I Surrender
Words by Bill Landau, music by Adam Ross.
Daywin Music, Inc.
From *Lover Come Back* (film, 1962).

Soft Rain
Words and music by Ray Price.
Pamper Music, Inc.
Best-selling record by Ray Price (Columbia).

Soldier Boy
Words and music by Florence Green and Luther Dixon.
Ludix Publishing Co., Inc.
Best-selling record in 1962 by The Shirelles (Scepter).

Some Day Baby
Words and music by Ray Charles.
Progressive Music Publishing Co., Inc.
Introduced by Ray Charles.

Some Kind-a Wonderful
Words and music by Gerry Goffin and Carole King.
Screen Gems-Columbia Music, Inc.
Best-selling record by The Drifters (Atlantic).

Someone Nice Like You (English)
Words and music by Leslie Bricusse and Anthony Newley.
Essex Music, Ltd., London, England/Ludlow Music, Inc.
Introduced by Anthony Newley in London and New York (1962)
    productions of *Stop the World — I Want To Get Off* (musical).

Something Big
Words and music by Richard Adler.
Sahara Music, Inc.
Introduced by company in *Kwamina* (musical).

Something Very Strange (English)
Words and music by Noël Coward.
Operating Company Salina, Ltd., Jamaica, British West Indies/
    Chappell & Co., Inc.
Introduced by Elaine Stritch in *Sail Away* (musical).

Something You Never Had Before
Words and music by Howard Dietz and Arthur Schwartz.
Harms, Inc.
Introduced by Barbara Cook in *The Gay Life* (musical).

Somewhere in the Used To Be
Words by Mack David, music by Elmer Bernstein.
Columbia Pictures Music Corp., 1961, 1962.
From *Walk on the Wild Side* (film, 1962).

Song of Athens, The, see **Adios, My Love.**

Sorry Willie
Words and music by Roger Miller.
Tree Publishing Co., Inc.
Introduced by Roger Miller (RCA Victor).

Speedy Gonzales
Words and music by Buddy Kaye, David Hill, and Ethel Lee.
Budd Music Corp., 1961, 1962.
First recording made in France by Dalida (Barclay). Best-selling
    record in 1962 by Pat Boone (Dot).

Stand by Me
Words and music by Ben E. King, Jerry Leiber, and Mike Stoller.
Progressive Music Publishing Co., Inc./Trio Music Co., Inc.
Best-selling record by Ben E. King (Atco).

Stick Shift
Music by Henry Bellinger.
Saturn Music, Inc./Hidle Music.
Best-selling record by The Duals (Sue).

Stranger on the Shore (English)
Words by Robert Mellin, music by Acker Bilk.
Robert Mellin, Inc., 1961, 1962.
Introduced in England by Acker Bilk. Originally entitled and re-
leased on records as "Jenny." Retitled for signature theme for
British TV series, *Stranger on the Shore*. Best-selling instru-
mental record by Acker Bilk (Atco). Lyrics added in 1962. Best-
selling vocal record by Andy Williams (Columbia).

Stripper, The
Music by David Rose.
David Rose Publishing Co., 1961, 1962.
Best-selling record in 1962 by David Rose and his Orchestra (MGM).

Success
Words and music by Johnny Mullins.
Sure-Fire Music Co., Inc.
Best-selling record in 1962 by Loretta Lynn (Decca).

Summer Sunday
Words by Earl Shuman, music by Leon Carr.
Mansion Music Corp.
Introduced by Zabethe Wilde (Capitol).

Summertime Lies
Words by Bob Hilliard, music by Milton De Lugg.
International Korwin Corp./Phalanx Music, Inc.
Introduced by Kitty Kallen (Columbia).

Sweet Danger
Words and music by Robert Wright and George Forrest.
Empress Music, Inc.
Introduced by Joan Weldon and Alfred Drake in *Kean* (musical).

Sweet Lips
Words and music by Webb Pierce, Doug Tubb, and Wayne P. Walker.
Cedarwood Publishing Co., Inc.
Best-selling record by Webb Pierce (Decca).

Sweet Little You
Words and music by Barry Mann and Larry Kolber.
Screen Gems-Columbia Music, Inc.
Best-selling record by Neil Sedaka (RCA Victor).

Sweets for My Sweet
Words and music by Doc Pomus and Mort Shuman.
Brenner Music, Inc./Progressive Music Publishing Co., Inc./Trio
    Music Co., Inc.
Best-selling record by The Drifters (Atlantic).

Switcharoo
Words and music by Al Kasha, Gordon Evans, and Alonzo Tucker.
Merrimac Music Corp.
Best-selling record by Hank Ballard and The Midnighters (King).

Take Good Care of Her
Words and music by Ed Warren and Arthur Kent.
George Paxton Corp./Recherche Music Corp.
Best-selling record by Adam Wade (Co-ed).

Take Good Care of My Baby
Words and music by Gerry Goffin and Carole King.
Screen Gems-Columbia Music, Inc.
Best-selling record by Bobby Vee (Liberty).

Take My Hand, Paree
Words by E. Y. Harburg, music by Harold Arlen.
Harwin Music Corp.
Introduced by voice of Judy Garland in *Gay Purr-ee* (cartoon feature film).

Take My Love, I Want To Give It All to You
Words and music by Mertis John, Jr.
Lois Publishing Co.
Best-selling record by Little Willie John (King).

Take Time
Words and music by Mel Tillis and Marijohn Wilkin.
Cedarwood Publishing Co., Inc.
Best-selling record in 1962 by Webb Pierce (Decca).

Tears and Laughter
Words and music by Miriam Lewis.
Gll Music Corp.
Introduced by Dinah Washington (Mercury).

Tears Break Out on Me
Words and music by Hank Cochran.
Pamper Music, Inc.
Best-selling record in 1962 by Eddy Arnold (RCA Victor).

Tell Her I Said Hello, see Tell Him I Said Hello.

Tell Him I Said Hello, also known as Tell Her I Said Hello
Words by Johnny Lehman, music by Don Costa.
Westside Music, Inc.
Introduced by Steve Lawrence (Columbia).

Tender Is the Night
Words by Paul Francis Webster, music by Sammy Fain.
Miller Music Corp.
Introduced by Earl Grant in *Tender Is the Night* (film, 1962). Nominated for Academy Award, 1962. Best-selling record by Tony Bennett (Columbia).

Tender Years
Words and music by Darrell Edwards.
South Coast Music.
Best-selling record by George Jones (Mercury).

Tennessee Flat-Top Box
Words and music by Johnny Cash.
Johnny Cash Music, Inc.
Best-selling record by Johnny Cash (Columbia).

That Was Yesterday
Words and music by Jerry Herman.
Jerryco Music Co.
Introduced by Mimi Benzell and company in *Milk and Honey* (musical).

That's My Pa
Words and music by Sheb Wooley.
Channel Music Co.
Best-selling record in 1962 by Sheb Wooley (MGM).

That's What Girls Are Made For
Words and music by Harvey Fuqua and Gwen Gordy.
Jobete Music Co., Inc.
Best-selling record by The Spinners (Tri-Phi).

Theme from *A Summer Place,* see 1959.

Theme from *Ben Casey*
Music by David Raksin.
Morley Music Co., Inc.
Theme from *Ben Casey* (television series).

Theme from *By Love Possessed*
Words by Sammy Cahn, music by Elmer Bernstein.
United Artists Music Co., Inc.
Adapted from a theme from *By Love Possessed* (film).

Theme from *Carnival!,* also known as Love Makes the World Go 'Round
Words and music by Bob Merrill.
Robbins Music Corp.
Introduced by Anna Maria Alberghetti in *Carnival!* (musical).

Theme from *Come September*
Music by Bobby Darin.
Adaris Music, Inc.
From *Come September* (film). Introduced by Bobby Darin and his Orchestra (Atco).

Theme from *Dr. Kildare* (Three Stars Will Shine Tonight)
Words by Hal Winn, music by Jerrald Goldsmith and Pete Rugolo.
Hastings Music Corp., 1961, 1962.
Theme from *Dr. Kildare* (television series). Best-selling record in 1962 by Richard Chamberlain (MGM).

Theme from *Goodbye Again*
Words by Dory Langdon, music by Georges Auric.
United Artists Music Co., Inc.
From *Goodbye Again* (film).

Theme from *King of Kings,* see *King of Kings* Theme.

Theme from *My Geisha*
Music by Franz Waxman.
Famous Music Corp., 1961, 1962.
From *My Geisha* (film, 1962).

Theme from *Romanoff and Juliet*
Music by Mario Nascimbene.
Northern Music Corp.
Theme from *Romanoff and Juliet* (film).

Theme from *Summer and Smoke*
Music by Elmer Bernstein.
Famous Music Corp.
Theme from *Summer and Smoke* (film, 1962).

Theme from *The Andy Griffith Show,* see The Fishin' Hole.

There's No Other
Words and music by Phil Spector and Leroy Bates.
Mother Bertha Music, Inc.
Best-selling record by The Crystals (Philles).

There's No Reason in the World
Words and music by Jerry Herman.
Jerryco Music Co.
Introduced by Robert Weede in *Milk and Honey* (musical).

Things
Words and music by Bobby Darin.
Adaris Music, Inc./Cherio Music Publishers, Inc., 1961, 1962.
Best-selling record in 1962 by Bobby Darin (Atco).

This White Circle on My Finger
Words and music by Margie Bainbridge and Dorothy Lewis.
Sure-Fire Music Co., Inc.
Best-selling record in 1964 by Kitty Wells (Decca).

Those Oldies but Goodies Remind Me of You
Words and music by Paul Politti and Nick Curinga.
Maravilla Music, Inc.
Best-selling record by Little Caesar and The Romans (Del-Fi).

Three Days
Words and music by Willie Nelson and Faron Young.
Pamper Music, Inc., 1961, 1962.
Best-selling record in 1962 by Faron Young (Capitol).

Three Stars Will Shine Tonight, see **Theme from *Dr. Kildare.***

Three Steps to the Phone
Words and music by Harlan Howard.
Acuff-Rose Publications, Inc.
Best-selling record by George Hamilton IV (RCA Victor).

Tie Me Kangaroo Down, Sport (Australian)
Words and music by Rolf Harris.
Castle Music Pty., Ltd., Sydney, Australia, 1960/Beechwood Music
    Corp.
Introduced in Australia by Rolf Harris. Best-selling record in
    United States in 1963 by Rolf Harris (Epic).

To Look upon My Love
Words and music by Robert Wright and George Forrest.
Empress Music, Inc.
Introduced by Alfred Drake and Truman Smith in *Kean* (musical).

Tonight, see 1957.

Too Big for Her Bikini
Words by Oromay Diamond, music by Ben Weisman.
Roncom Music Co.
Introduced by Gerry Granahan (Caprice).

Too Many Times
Words and music by Don Winters.
Tannen Music Enterprises.
Best-selling record by Don Winters (Decca).

Tossin' and Turnin'
Words and music by Malou Rene and Ritchie Adams.
Harvard Music, Inc./Viva Music, Inc.
Best-selling record by Bobby Lewis (Beltone).

Touch Me
Words and music by Willie Nelson.
Pamper Music, Inc.
Best-selling record in 1962 by Willie Nelson (Liberty).

Tower of Strength
Words by Bob Hilliard, music by Burt F. Bacharach.
Famous Music Corp.
Best-selling record by Gene McDaniels (Liberty).

Town without Pity
Words by Ned Washington, music by Dimitri Tiomkin.
United Artists Music Co., Inc.
Introduced by Gene Pitney in *Town without Pity* (film). Nominated
   for Academy Award, 1961. Best-selling record by Gene Pitney
   (Musicor).

Transistor Sister
Words and music by Frank C. Slay, Jr. and Chuck Dougherty.
Claridge Music, Inc.
Best-selling record by Freddie Cannon (Swan).

Trouble's Back in Town
Words and music by Dick Flood.
Sure-Fire Music Co., Inc.
Best-selling record in 1962 by The Wilburn Brothers (Decca).

Tuff
Music by Ace Cannon.
Jec Publishing Corp.
Best-selling record in 1962 by Ace Cannon (Hi).

Turn On Your Love Light
Words and music by Deadric Malone and Joseph Scott.
Don Music Co.
Best-selling record in 1962 by Bobby Bland (Duke).

Typically English (English)
Words and music by Leslie Bricusse and Anthony Newley.
Essex Music, Ltd., London, England/Ludlow Music, Inc.
Introduced by Anna Quayle in London and New York (1962) pro-
   ductions of *Stop the World — I Want To Get Off* (musical).

Under the Influence of Love
Words by Buck Owens, music by Harlan Howard.
Central Songs, Inc.
Best-selling record by Buck Owens (Capitol).

Unsquare Dance
Music by Dave Brubeck.
Derry Music Co.
Best-selling record by The Dave Brubeck Quartet (Columbia).

Venus in Blue Jeans
Words and music by Howard Greenfield and Jack Keller.
Screen Gems-Columbia Music, Inc.
Best-selling record in 1962 by Jimmy Clanton (Ace).

Walk On By
Words and music by Kendall Hayes.
Lowery Music Co., Inc.
Best-selling record by Leroy Van Dyke (Mercury).

Walk on the Wild Side
Words by Mack David, music by Elmer Bernstein.
Columbia Pictures Music Corp., 1961, 1962.
From *Walk on the Wild Side* (film, 1962). Nominated for Academy Award, 1962. Best-selling record by Jimmy Smith (Verve).

Walkin' Back to Happiness (English)
Words by John Schroeder, music by Mike Hawker.
Filmusic Publishing Co., Ltd., London, England/Bourne-Rank Music, Inc.
From *Look at Life* (British film). Best-selling record in England by Helen Shapiro (English Columbia).

Wedding, The (La Novia) (Argentine)
English words by Fred Jay, Spanish words and music by Joaquin Prieto.
Ediciones Internacionales Fermata, Buenos Aires, Argentina/Regent Music Corp.
Original Spanish-language version introduced in Argentina by Joaquin Prieto. Introduced on records in United States by Anita Bryant (Columbia). Best-selling record in England and United States in 1964 by Julie Rogers (Mercury).

Welcome to My World
Words and music by Ray Winkler and John Hathcock.
Neillrae Music/Tuckahoe Music, Inc.
Best-selling record in 1964 by Jim Reeves (RCA Victor).

What a Sweet Thing That Was
Words and music by Gerry Goffin and Carole King.
Screen Gems-Columbia Music, Inc.
Best-selling record by The Shirelles (Scepter).

What Happened to Me Tonight?
Words and music by Richard Adler.
Sahara Music, Inc.
Introduced by Sally Ann Howes in *Kwamina* (musical).

(How Can I Write on Paper) What I Feel in My Heart
Words and music by Danny Harrison, Don Carter, George Kent, and Jim Reeves.
Tuckahoe Music, Inc.
Best-selling record in 1962 by Jim Reeves (RCA Victor).

What Is This Feeling in the Air?
Words by Betty Comden and Adolph Green, music by Jule Styne.
Stratford Music Corp.
Introduced by Carol Lawrence and company in *Subways Are for Sleeping* (musical).

What Kind of Fool Am I? (English)
Words and music by Leslie Bricusse and Anthony Newley.
Essex Music, Ltd., London, England/Ludlow Music, Inc.
Introduced by Anthony Newley in London and New York (1962) productions of *Stop the World — I Want To Get Off* (musical). Best-selling record in 1962 by Sammy Davis, Jr. (Reprise). Winner of National Academy of Recording Arts and Sciences Award for "Song of the Year," 1962.

What Will My Mary Say?
Words and music by Paul Vance and Eddie Snyder.
Elm Drive Music Corp.
Best-selling record in 1963 by Johnny Mathis (Columbia).

What's Wrong with Me?
Words and music by Richard Adler.
Sahara Music, Inc.
Introduced by Sally Ann Howes in *Kwamina* (musical).

What's Your Name?
Words and music by Claude Johnson.
Hill and Range Songs, Inc., 1961, 1962.
Best-selling record in 1962 by Don and Juan (Big Top).

When My Little Girl Is Smiling
Words and music by Gerry Goffin and Carole King.
Screen Gems-Columbia Music, Inc.
Best-selling record by The Drifters (Atlantic) and Jimmy Justice (Kapp).

When the Boy in Your Arms Is the Boy in Your Heart, also known as When the Girl in Your Arms Is the Girl in Your Heart
Words and music by Sid Tepper and Roy C. Bennett.
Pickwick Music, Ltd., London, England/MCA, Inc.
From *The Young Ones* (British film, 1962). Best-selling record in 1962 by Connie Francis (MGM).

When the Girl in Your Arms Is the Girl in Your Heart, see When the Boy in Your Arms Is the Boy in Your Heart.

When Two Worlds Collide
Words and music by Roger Miller and Bill Anderson.
Tree Publishing Co., Inc.
Best-selling record by Roger Miller (RCA Victor).

When We Get Married
Words and music by Donald Hogan.
Elsher Music Co.
Best-selling record by The Dreamlovers (Heritage).

When Will I Find Love (German)
English words by Marcel Stellman, German words by Johannes
Brandt, music by Nikolaus Brodszky.
Beboton-Verlag, Hans Sikorski GmbH, Hamburg, Germany, 1932,
1956/Fred Fisher Music Co., Inc., 1961, 1964.
Original German title, "Was Kann So Schoen Sein Wie Deine Liebe."

When You Want Me (English)
Words and music by Noël Coward.
Operating Company Salina, Ltd., Jamaica, British West Indies/
Chappell & Co., Inc.
Introduced by Grover Dale and Patricia Harty in *Sail Away* (musi-
cal).

When You're in Love (The Whole World Is Jewish)
Words and music by Mark Bucci.
'62 Revue Publishers, Inc.
Introduced in *New Faces of '62* (revue, 1962).

Where Have All the Flowers Gone?
Words and music by Peter Seeger.
Fall River Music, Inc.
Inspired by passage from Mikhail Sholokhov's novel, *And Quiet
Flows the Don*. Additional verses by Jod Hickerson. Best-selling
records by The Kingston Trio (Capitol) and in 1965 by Johnny
Rivers (Imperial).

Where Shall I Find Him? (English)
Words and music by Noël Coward.
Operating Company Salina, Ltd., Jamaica, British West Indies/
Chappell & Co., Inc.
Introduced by Patricia Harty in *Sail Away* (musical).

White Rose of Athens, see Athina.

Who Knows What Might Have Been?
Words by Betty Comden and Adolph Green, music by Jule Styne.
Stratford Music Corp.
Introduced by Sydney Chaplin and Carol Lawrence in *Subways Are
for Sleeping* (musical).

Who Put the Bomp (In the Bomp Ba Bomp Ba Bomp)
Words and music by Barry Mann and Gerry Goffin.
Screen Gems-Columbia Music, Inc.
Best-selling record by Barry Mann (ABC-Paramount).

Why Do the Wrong People Travel? (English)
Words and music by Noël Coward.
Operating Company Salina, Ltd., Jamaica, British West Indies/
Chappell & Co., Inc.
Introduced by Elaine Stritch in *Sail Away* (musical).

Wild in the Country
Words and music by George Weiss, Hugo Peretti, and Luigi
Creatore.
Gladys Music, Inc.
Best-selling record by Elvis Presley (RCA Victor).

Will Your Lawyer Talk to God
Words and music by Harlan Howard and Richard Johnson.
Pamper Music, Inc.
Best-selling record in 1962 by Kitty Wells (Decca).

Willingly
Words and music by Hank Cochran.
Pamper Music, Inc.
Best-selling record in 1962 by Shirley Collie and Willie Nelson
(Liberty).

Willow, Willow, Willow
Words and music by Robert Wright and George Forrest.
Empress Music, Inc.
Introduced by Lee Venora in *Kean* (musical).

Window Up Above, The
Words and music by George Jones.
Glad Music Co./Starday Music.
Best-selling record by George Jones (Mercury).

Without You
Words and music by Johnny Tillotson.
Ridge Music Corp.
Best-selling record by Johnny Tillotson (Cadence).

Writing on the Wall
Words and music by Sandy Baron, Mark Barkan, and George Eddy
(pseudonym for George Paxton).
Paxwin Music Corp.
Best-selling record by Adam Wade (Co-ed).

Ya Ya
Words and music by Lee Dorsey, Clarence Lewis, and Morgan
Robinson.
Frost Music Corp.
Best-selling record by Lee Dorsey (Fury).

Yassu
Words by Ned Washington, music by Dimitri Tiomkin.
Columbia Pictures Music Corp.
Based on traditional Greek song. Wedding song from *The Guns of
Navarone* (film).

Yellow Bird, see 1957.

Yes, My Heart
Words and music by Bob Merrill.
Robbins Music Corp.
Introduced by Anna Maria Alberghetti and Roustabouts in *Carnival!*
  (musical).

You Can't Take a Dream from a Dreamer
Words and music by Redd Evans, Jack Perry, and Harry Sims.
Valiant Music Co., Inc.
Introduced by Tony Bennett (Columbia).

You Don't Know (English)
Words and music by John Schroeder and Michael Hawker.
Lorna Music Co., Ltd., London, England/Edward B. Marks Music
  Corp.
Best-selling record in England by Helen Shapiro (English Columbia).

You Don't Know What You've Got
Words and music by Paul Hampton and George Burton.
Post Music, Inc.
Best-selling record by Ral Donner (Gone).

You'll Answer to Me
Words by Hal David, music by Sherman Edwards.
Shapiro, Bernstein & Co., Inc.
Best-selling record by Patti Page (Mercury).

Young Ones, The
Words and music by Sid Tepper and Roy C. Bennett.
Harms-Witmark, Ltd., London, England/M. Witmark & Sons.
Introduced by Cliff Richard with The Shadows in *The Young Ones*
  (British film, 1962).

1962

Aching, Breaking Heart, see 1960.

Addio, Addio (Italian)
English words by Carl Sigman, Italian words by Migliacci and
   Domenico Modugno, music by Domenico Modugno.
Edizioni Curci, Milan, Italy/Miller Music Corp.
Introduced by Domenico Modugno and Claudio Villa. Winner of San
   Remo (Italy) Song Festival, 1962.

Adios Amigo
Words and music by Ralph Freed and Jerry Livingston.
Randy-Smith Music Corp.
Best-selling record by Jim Reeves (RCA Victor).

After Loving You
Words and music by Eddie Miller and Johnny Lantz.
Red River Songs, Inc.
Best-selling record by Eddy Arnold (RCA Victor).

Ah! Camminare
Words by Ronny Graham, music by Milton Schafer.
Giovanni Music, Inc./Mayfair Music Corp.
Introduced by Gene Varrone, Cesare Siepi, and company in *Bravo
   Giovanni* (musical).

Ahab the Arab
Words and music by Ray Stevens.
Lowery Music Co., Inc.
Introduced and best-selling record by Ray Stevens (Mercury).

Ain't Nothing but a Man
Words and music by Merle Kilgore.
Painted Desert Music Corp.
Best-selling record by Merle Kilgore (Mercury).

Aladdin (Canadian)
Words by Basil Hurdon, music by Dyer Hurdon.
Kemo Music Co.
Best-selling record by Bobby Curtola (Del-Fi).

100

All Alone Am I (Greek)

English words by Arthur Altman, Greek words by Jean Ioannidis,
  music by Manos Hadjidakis.
SOPE, Athens, Greece, 1959, 1962/Duchess Music Corp.
Best-selling record by Brenda Lee (Decca).

All Over the World

Words by Charles Tobias, music by Al Frisch.
Comet Music Corp.
Best-selling record by Nat "King" Cole (Capitol).

Alla My Love

Words and music by Jimmy Gately and Harold Donny.
Champion Music Corp.
Best-selling record by Webb Pierce (Decca).

Alley Cat (Danish)

English words by Jack Harlen (pseudonym for Britt Simonson),
  music by Frank Bjorn.
Eureka Anstalt, Switzerland, 1961, 1962/ Metorion Music Corp.
Original Danish title, "Omkring et Flygel" ("Around the Piano").
  Introduced in 1961 on Danish television by Bent Fabric (Bent
  Fabricius-Bjerre). Best-selling record by Bent Fabric (Metro-
  nome, Denmark) (Atco, United States). Winner of National Acad-
  emy of Recording Arts and Sciences Award for "Best Rock and
  Roll Recording," 1962. Vocal version introduced by David Thorne
  (Riverside) as "The Alley Cat Song."

Alley Cat Song, The, see Alley Cat.

Anna (Go to Him)

Words and music by Arthur Alexander.
Painted Desert Music Corp./Keva Music Co.
Introduced by Arthur Alexander (Dot). Best-selling record in 1964
  by The Beatles (Vee Jay).

Any Day Now

Words and music by Bob Hilliard and Burt F. Bacharach.
Plan Two Music, Inc.
Best-selling record by Chuck Jackson (Wand).

Anything That's Part of You

Words and music by Don Robertson.
Gladys Music, Inc.
Best-selling record by Elvis Presley (RCA Victor).

Bachelor Boy (English)

Words and music by Bruce Welch and Cliff Richard.
Elstree Music, Ltd., London, England/Ross Jungnickel, Inc./Harms,
  Inc.
Best-selling record in England and United States by Cliff Richard
  and The Shadows (Epic).

Bag's Groove
Music by Milt Jackson.
Wemar Music Corp.
Jazz instrumental first recorded in 1954 by Miles Davis, Milt Jackson, Thelonious Monk, Percy Heath, and Kenny Clarke (Prestige).

Bald Headed Lena
Words by Edward Sneed, music by Willie Perryman.
Hill and Range Songs, Inc.
Best-selling record in 1966 by The Lovin' Spoonful (Kama Sutra).

Ballad of Ira Hayes
Words and music by Peter La Farge.
Edward B. Marks Music Corp.
Dedicated to Ira Hayes, American Pima Indian hero credited with raising the American flag at Iwo Jima in World War II. Introduced by Peter La Farge (Columbia). Best-selling record in 1964 by Johnny Cash (Columbia).

Ballad of Jed Clampett
Words and music by Paul Henning.
Carolintone Music Co., Inc.
Theme of *The Beverly Hillbillies* (television series). Best-selling record by Flatt and Scruggs (Columbia).

Barabbas (Italian)
English words by Earl Shuman, Italian words by G. C. Testoni, music by M. Nascimbene.
Dino De Laurentiis, Rome, Italy, 1961, 1962/Columbia Pictures Music Corp.
Adapted from a theme from *Barabbas* (film).

Bayou Talk
Words and music by Jimmy Newman.
Newkeys Music, Inc.
Best-selling record by Jimmy "C" Newman (Decca).

Be a Performer
Words by Carolyn Leigh, music by Cy Coleman.
Edwin H. Morris & Co., Inc.
Introduced by Joey Faye, Mort Marshall, and Virginia Martin in *Little Me* (musical).

Be My Host
Words and music by Richard Rodgers.
Williamson Music, Inc.
Introduced by Richard Kiley, Bernice Massi, Don Chastain, Alvin Epstein, and Ann Hodges in *No Strings* (musical).

Beautiful
Words and music by James Goldman, John Kander, and William Goldman.
Sunbeam Music Corp.
Introduced by Shelley Berman in *A Family Affair* (musical).

Beechwood 4-5789
Words and music by William Stevenson, George Gordy, and Marvin Gaye.
Jobete Music Co., Inc.
Best-selling record by The Marvelettes (Tamla).

Before I'm Over You
Words and music by Betty Sue Perry.
Sure-Fire Music Co., Inc.
Best-selling record in 1963 by Loretta Lynn (Decca).

Beggar to a King, see 1960.

Best Dressed Beggar in Town, The
Words and music by Houston Turner.
Ashna Music Corp./Troy Martin Music, Inc.
Best-selling record by Carl Smith (Columbia).

Big Girls Don't Cry
Words and music by Bob Crewe and Bob Gaudio.
Claridge Music, Inc.
Best-selling record by The Four Seasons (Vee Jay).

Big Wide World
Words and music by Teddy Randazzo, Bobby Weinstein, and Billy Barberis.
South Mountain Music Corp.
Best-selling record by Teddy Randazzo (Colpix).

Bird Man, The
Words by Mack David, music by Elmer Bernstein.
United Artists Music Co., Inc.
From *Birdman of Alcatraz* (film). Introduced by The Highwaymen (United Artists).

Blame It on the Bossa Nova
Words and music by Cynthia Weil and Barry Mann.
Screen Gems-Columbia Music, Inc.
Best-selling record in 1963 by Eydie Gormé (Columbia).

Blowin' in the Wind
Words and music by Bob Dylan.
M. Witmark & Sons, 1962, 1963.
Introduced by Bob Dylan. Best-selling record in 1963 by Peter, Paul, and Mary (Warner Bros.). Winner of National Academy of Recording Arts and Sciences Awards for "Best Folk Recording" and "Best Performance by a Vocal Group," 1963.

Blue Genius
Music by Ray Charles.
Progressive Music Publishing Co., Inc.
Introduced by Ray Charles and Milt Jackson (Atlantic).

Boa Constrictor
Words and music by Shel Silverstein.
Hollis Music, Inc.
Introduced by Shel Silverstein.

Bobby's Girl
Words and music by Henry Hoffman and Gary Klein.
American Metropolitan Enterprises of New York, Inc.
Best-selling record by Marcie Blane (Seville).

Bossa Nova U.S.A.
Music by Dave Brubeck.
Derry Music Co.
Introduced by The Dave Brubeck Quartet (Columbia).

Boys' Night Out, The
Words by Sammy Cahn, music by James Van Heusen.
Miller Music Corp.
From *The Boys' Night Out* (film). First recording by Patti Page
(Mercury).

Breaking Up Is Hard To Do
Words and music by Neil Sedaka and Howard Greenfield.
Screen Gems-Columbia Music, Inc.
Best-selling record by Neil Sedaka (RCA Victor).

Bring It On Home to Me
Words and music by Sam Cooke.
Kags Music.
Introduced and best-selling record by Sam Cooke (RCA Victor).
Revived in 1965 with best-selling record in England and United
States by The Animals (MGM).

Brown Baby
Words and music by Oscar Brown, Jr.
Edward B. Marks Music Corp.
Introduced by Oscar Brown, Jr. (Columbia).

Busted
Words and music by Harlan Howard.
Pamper Music, Inc., 1962, 1963.
Introduced by Johnny Cash (Columbia). Best-selling record in 1963
by Ray Charles (ABC-Paramount). Winner of National Academy
of Recording Arts and Sciences Award for "Best Rhythm and
Blues Recording," 1963.

Bye Bye Birdie
Words by Lee Adams, music by Charles Strouse.
Edwin H. Morris & Co., Inc., 1962, 1963.
Introduced by Ann-Margret in *Bye Bye Birdie* (film, 1963).

Cajun Queen, The
Words and music by Wayne Walker.
Cedarwood Publishing Co., Inc.
Best-selling record by Jimmy Dean (Columbia).

Call Me Irresponsible
Words by Sammy Cahn, music by James Van Heusen.
Paramount Music Corp., 1962, 1963.
Introduced by Jackie Gleason in *Papa's Delicate Condition* (film, 1963). Academy Award-winning song, 1963. Best-selling records by Frank Sinatra (Reprise) and Jack Jones (Kapp).

Call Me Mr. In-Between
Words and music by Harlan Howard.
Pamper Music, Inc.
Best-selling record by Burl Ives (Decca).

Call on Me
Words and music by Deadric Malone.
Lion Publishing Co., Inc.
Best-selling record in 1963 by Bobby Bland (Duke).

Can't Get Used To Losing You
Words and music by Doc Pomus and Mort Shuman.
Brenner Music, Inc.
Best-selling record in 1963 by Andy Williams (Columbia).

Can't Take No More
Words and music by Ted Taylor.
Ronnat Music Co.
Best-selling record by Ted Taylor (Okeh).

Carina Marie
Words by Sunny Skylar, music by Ettore Stratta.
Southern Music Publishing Co., Inc.
Introduced instrumentally by Horace Diaz (Amy-Mala).

Carousels (French-Belgian)
English words by Eric Blau, French words and music by Jacques Brel.
Les Éditions Musicales Tutti, Paris, France, 1959, 1962, 1964/ Leeds Music Corp.
Original French title, "La Valse à Mille Temps." Introduced in France by Jacques Brel (Philips). Introduced in United States by Elly Stone in *O, Oysters!* (off-Broadway revue). Another version, with English lyrics by Will Holt, introduced in 1964 by Felicia Sanders. See "The Days of the Waltz," 1964.

Cast Your Fate to the Wind, see 1960.

Caterina
Words and music by Earl Shuman and "Bugs" Bower.
Roncom Music Co.
Best-selling record by Perry Como (RCA Victor).

Cha Cha Cha, The
Words and music by Kal Mann and Dave Appell.
Fajob Music Publishing Co./Kalmann Music, Inc.
Best-selling record by Bobby Rydell (Cameo). Not copyrighted until
    1965.

Chains
Words and music by Gerry Goffin and Carole King.
Screen Gems-Columbia Music, Inc.
Best-selling records by The Cookies (Dimension) and in 1964 by
    The Beatles (Vee Jay and Capitol).

Cindy's Birthday
Words and music by Jeff Hooven and Hal Winn.
Maravilla Music, Inc.
Best-selling record by Johnny Crawford (Del-Fi).

Cinnamon Cinder (It's a Very Nice Dance)
Words and music by Russ Regan.
Algrace Music Co.
Best-selling record by The Cinders (Warner Bros.).

Cleo's Mood
Music by William Woods and Junior Walker.
Jobete Music Co., Inc.
Best-selling record by Junior Walker and The All Stars (Harvey).

Clinging Vine
Words and music by Earl Shuman, Leon Carr, and Grace Lane.
The Peter Maurice Music Co., Ltd., 1962, 1964.
Best-selling record in 1964 by Bobby Vinton (Epic).

Close to Cathy
Words by Earl Shuman, music by Bob Goodman.
Arch Music Co., Inc.
Best-selling record by Mike Clifford (United Artists).

Cold Dark Waters Below
Words and music by Don Owens.
Don Owens Music, Inc.
Best-selling record by Porter Wagoner (RCA Victor).

Come and Get These Memories
Words and music by Brian Holland, Lamont Dozier, and Eddie
    Holland.
Jobete Music Co., Inc.
Best-selling record in 1963 by Martha and The Vandellas (Gordy).

Come Away Melinda
Words and music by Fred Hellerman and Fran Minkoff.
Appleseed Music, Inc.
Introduced by Harry Belafonte (RCA Victor).

Comeback, The
Words and music by Danny Dill.
Cedarwood Publishing Co., Inc.
Best-selling record by Faron Young (Capitol).

Comedy Tonight
Words and music by Stephen Sondheim.
Burthen Music Co., Inc.
Introduced by Zero Mostel and company in *A Funny Thing Happened on the Way to the Forum* (musical).

Comin' Home Baby
Words by Bob Dorough, music by Ben Tucker.
Cotillion Music, Inc.
Best-selling record by Mel Tormé (Atlantic).

Control Yourself
Words by Dory Langdon, music by André Previn.
Artists Music, Inc.
Introduced by Doris Day (Columbia).

Corcovado, see Quiet Nights of Quiet Stars.

Cotton Fields
Words and music by Huddie Ledbetter.
Folkways Music Publishers, Inc.
Written in the 1940's and introduced by Huddie "Leadbelly" Ledbetter. Best-selling record in 1962 by The Highwaymen (United Artists). Not copyrighted until 1962.

Crazy Wild Desire
Words and music by Mel Tillis and Webb Pierce.
Cedarwood Publishing Co., Inc.
Best-selling record by Webb Pierce (Decca).

Criss-Cross
Music by Thelonious Monk.
Thelonious Music.
Introduced by Thelonious Monk (Columbia).

Crowd, The
Words and music by Roy Orbison and Joe Melson.
Acuff-Rose Publications, Inc.
Best-selling record by Roy Orbison (Monument).

Cuttin' In
Words and music by John Watson.
Lois Publishing Co.
Best-selling record by Johnny "Guitar" Watson (King).

Dancin' Party
Words by Kal Mann, music by Dave Appell.
Kalmann Music, Inc.
Best-selling record by Chubby Checker (Parkway).

Darkest Street in Town, The
Words and music by Howard Greenfield and Kenny Karen.
Screen Gems-Columbia Music, Inc.
Best-selling record by Jimmy Clanton (Ace).

David and Lisa's Love Song
Words by Edward Heyman, music by Mark Lawrence.
Saunders Publications, Inc., 1962, 1963.
Adapted from a theme from *David and Lisa* (film, 1963).

Daydreaming
Words by Dory Langdon, music by André Previn.
Artists Music, Inc.
Introduced by Doris Day (Columbia).

Days of Wine and Roses
Words by Johnny Mercer, music by Henry Mancini.
M. Witmark & Sons.
Introduced by vocal group in *Days of Wine and Roses* (film).
Academy Award-winning song, 1962. Best-selling records in 1962-
63 by Henry Mancini and his Orchestra (RCA Victor) and Andy
Williams (Columbia). Winner of National Academy of Recording
Arts and Sciences Awards for "Song of the Year," "Record of
the Year" (Mancini version), and "Best Background Arrange-
ment" (Mancini version), 1963.

Dear Lonely Hearts (I'm Writing to You)
Words and music by Bob Halley and Emil Anton.
Sweco Music Corp./Cetra Music Corp.
Best-selling record by Nat "King" Cole (Capitol).

Deep Down Inside
Words by Carolyn Leigh, music by Cy Coleman.
Edwin H. Morris & Co., Inc.
Introduced by Sid Caesar, Virginia Martin, Joey Faye, and chorus
in *Little Me* (musical).

Desafinado (Slightly Out of Tune) (Brazilian)
English words by Jon Hendricks and Jessie Cavanaugh (pseudonym
for Howard S. Richmond), Portuguese words by Newton
Mendonça, music by Antonio Carlos Jobim.
Editora Musical Arapua, São Paulo, Brazil, 1959/Hollis Music, Inc/
Bendig Music Corp.
Best-selling instrumental record by Stan Getz and Charlie Byrd
(Verve). Winner of National Academy of Recording Arts and
Sciences Award for "Best Jazz Performance," 1962. English lyrics
added in 1962; vocal version introduced by Pat Thomas (MGM).

Detroit City
Words and music by Mel Tillis and Danny Dill.
Cedarwood Publishing Co., Inc.
Best-selling record in 1963 by Bobby Bare (RCA Victor). Winner
of National Academy of Recording Arts and Sciences Award for
"Best Country and Western Recording," 1963.

Devil Woman
Words and music by Marty Robbins.
Marty's Music Corp.
Best-selling record by Marty Robbins (Columbia).

Do You Love Me?
Words and music by Berry Gordy, Jr.
Jobete Music Co., Inc.
Best-selling record in 1962 by The Contours (Gordy) and in 1964
by The Dave Clark Five (Epic).

Does He Mean That Much to You?
Words and music by Jack Rollins and Don Robertson.
Ross Jungnickel, Inc.
Best-selling record by Eddy Arnold (RCA Victor).

Don't Ask Me To Be Friends
Words and music by Jack Keller and Gerry Goffin.
Screen Gems-Columbia Music, Inc.
Best-selling record by The Everly Brothers (Warner Bros.).

Don't Be Afraid of Romance
Words and music by Irving Berlin.
Irving Berlin Music Corp.
Introduced by Jack Washburn in *Mr. President* (musical).

Don't Break the Heart That Loves You
Words and music by Benny Davis and Ted Murry.
Francon Music Corp.
Best-selling record by Connie Francis (MGM).

Don't Go Near the Indians
Words and music by Lorene Mann.
Buttercup Music.
Best-selling record by Rex Allen (Mercury).

Don't Let Me Cross Over
Words and music by Penny Jay.
Troy Martin Music, Inc.
Best-selling record by Carl Butler (Columbia).

Don't Let Me Stand in Your Way
Words by Sammy Gallop, music by Arthur Kent.
B. F. Wood Music Co., Inc.
Best-selling record by Frankie Avalon (Chancellor).

Don't Lie
Words and music by Ted Taylor.
Ronnat Music Co.
Best-selling record by Ted Taylor (Okeh).

Don't Make Me Over
Words by Hal David, music by Burt Bacharach.
Jonathan Music Co., Inc.
Best-selling record in 1963 by Dionne Warwick (Scepter).

Don't Play That Song (You Lied)
Words and music by Ahmet M. Ertegun and Betty Nelson.
Progressive Music Publishing Co., Inc.
Best-selling record by Ben E. King (Atco).

Don't Take Away Your Love
Words and music by Bob Goodman.
Arch Music Co., Inc.
Introduced by Johnny Nash (Warner Bros.).

Don't You Believe It
Words by Bob Hilliard, music by Burt F. Bacharach.
Dolfi Music, Inc.
Best-selling record by Andy Williams (Columbia).

Down by the River
Words and music by Jan Crutchfield and Teddy Wilburn.
Sure-Fire Music Co., Inc.
Best-selling record in 1963 by Faron Young (Capitol).

Dream Baby, How Long Must I Dream?
Words and music by Cindy Walker.
Combine Music Corp.
Best-selling record by Roy Orbison (Monument).

Duck, The (O Pato) (Brazilian)
English words by Jon Hendricks, Portuguese words and music by
    Jayme Silva and Neuza Teixeira.
Fermata Do Brasil, São Paulo, Brazil, 1960/Cromwell Music, Inc.

Eager Beaver
Words and music by Richard Rodgers.
Williamson Music, Inc.
Introduced by Bernice Massi and Don Chastain in *No Strings* (musi-
    cal).

(Such an) Easy Question
Words and music by Otis Blackwell and Winfield Scott.
Elvis Presley Music, Inc.
Introduced by Elvis Presley (RCA Victor).

El Watusi
Music by Ray Barretto.
Little Dipper Music Corp., 1962, 1963.
Introduced by Ray Barretto (Tico).

Empty Pockets Filled with Love
Words and music by Irving Berlin.
Irving Berlin Music Corp.
Introduced by Jack Haskell and Anita Gillette in *Mr. President*
    (musical).

End of the World, The
Words by Sylvia Dee, music by Arthur Kent.
Summit Music Corp.
Best-selling record in 1963 by Skeeter Davis (RCA Victor).

Eso Beso (That Kiss)
Words and music by Joe Sherman and Noel Sherman.
Flanka Music Corp.
Best-selling record by Paul Anka (RCA Victor).

Et Maintenant, see What Now My Love.

Everybody Loves Me but You
Words and music by Ronnie Self.
Champion Music Corp.
Best-selling record by Brenda Lee (Decca).

Everybody Ought To Have a Maid
Words and music by Stephen Sondheim.
Burthen Music Co., Inc.
Introduced by David Burns, Zero Mostel, Jack Gilford, and John
    Carradine in *A Funny Thing Happened on the Way to the Forum*
    (musical).

Eve's Theme (Italian)
Music by Mario Nascimbene.
Unart Music Corp.
From *The Happy Thieves* (film).

Family Affair, A
Words and music by James Goldman, John Kander, and William
    Goldman.
Sunbeam Music Corp.
Introduced by chorus and orchestra in *A Family Affair* (musical).

Fingertips
Music by Henry Cosby and Clarence Paul.
Jobete Music Co., Inc.
Best-selling record in 1963 by Little Stevie Wonder (Tamla).

Fingertips (Part II)
Words and music by Henry Cosby and Clarence Paul.
Jobete Music Co., Inc., 1962, 1963.
Best-selling record in 1963 by Little Stevie Wonder (Tamla).

First Lady, The
Words and music by Irving Berlin.
Irving Berlin Music Corp.
Introduced by Nanette Fabray in *Mr. President* (musical).

Fly Me to the Moon, see 1954.

Folk Singer Blues
Words and music by Shel Silverstein.
Hollis Music, Inc.
Introduced by Shel Silverstein.

Follow Me, see **Love Song from *Mutiny on the Bounty.***

Follow the Boys
Words and music by Benny Davis and Ted Murry.
Francon Music Corp.
Title song from *Follow the Boys* (film, 1963). Best-selling record by
    Connie Francis (MGM)

Followed Closely by Teardrops
Words by Fred Tobias, music by Paul Evans.
Northern Music Corp.
Best-selling record by Hank Locklin (RCA Victor).

Fool Never Learns, A
Words and music by Sonny Curtis.
Cricket Music, Inc.
Best-selling record in 1964 by Andy Williams (Columbia).

Fool Too Long, A, see **Poor Fool,** 1960.

Footsteps of a Fool
Words and music by Danny Harrison and Don Carter.
Glad Music Co.
Best-selling record by Judy Lynn (United Artists).

From the Bottom of My Heart (Dammi Dammi Dammi)
Words and music by Danny Di Minno and George Cardini.
Laurel Music Corp.
Best-selling record by Dean Martin (Reprise).

From Way Up Here
Words by Malvina Reynolds, music by Peter Seeger.
Abigail Music Co.
Introduced by Pete Seeger.

Funny Thing Happened, A
Words and music by Harold Rome.
Florence Music Co., Inc.
Introduced by Marilyn Cooper and Elliott Gould in *I Can Get It
    for You Wholesale* (musical).

Funny Way of Laughin'
Words and music by Hank Cochran.
Pamper Music, Inc.
Best-selling record by Burl Ives (Decca). Winner of National Academy of Recording Arts and Sciences Award for "Best Country and Western Recording," 1962.

Gift Today, A
Words and music by Harold Rome.
Florence Music Co., Inc.
Introduced by Steve Curry, Elliott Gould, Lillian Roth, Bambi Linn, Ken Le Roy, and Marilyn Cooper in *I Can Get It for You Wholesale* (musical).

Gina, see 1960.

Girl I Used To Know, A
Words and music by Jack Clement.
Glad Music Co./Jack Music, Inc.
Best-selling record by George Jones and The Jones Boys (United Artists).

Girl Named Tamiko, A
Words by Mack David, music by Elmer Bernstein.
Famous Music Corp.
Adapted from a theme from *A Girl Named Tamiko* (film, 1963).

Girl Shy
Words by Mort Goode, music by Walter Scharf.
Compton Music Corp./Cinema Songs, Inc.
Adaptation of theme from *Harold Lloyd's World of Comedy* (film).

Glad To Be Home
Words and music by Irving Berlin.
Irving Berlin Music Corp.
Introduced by Nanette Fabray and ensemble in *Mr. President* (musical).

Go Away, Little Girl
Words and music by Gerry Goffin and Carole King.
Screen Gems-Columbia Music, Inc.
Introduced and best-selling record in 1963 by Steve Lawrence (Columbia). Revived in 1966 with best-selling record by The Happenings (B.T. Puppy).

Golden Tear
Words and music by Roger Miller.
Tree Publishing Co., Inc.
Introduced by Jimmy Elledge (RCA Victor).

Good Luck Charm
Words and music by Aaron Schroeder and Wally Gold.
Gladys Music, Inc.
Best-selling record by Elvis Presley (RCA Victor).

Gravy
Words by Kal Mann, music by Dave Appell.
Kalmann Music, Inc.
Best-selling record by Dee Dee Sharp (Cameo).

Gravy Waltz
Music by Steve Allen and Ray Brown.
Ray Brown Music.
Best-selling record by Steve Allen (Dot). Winner of National Academy of Recording Arts and Sciences Award for "Best Original Jazz Composition," 1963.

Green Onions
Words and music by Steve Cropper, Al Jackson, Jr., Lewie Steinberg, and Booker T. Jones.
East Publications/Bais Music.
Best selling record by Booker T. and The MG's (Stax).

Greenback Dollar
Words and music by Hoyt Axton and Ken Ramsey.
Davon Music Corp.
Adaptation of traditional American folk song. Best-selling record by The Kingston Trio (Capitol).

Happy Birthday to Me, see 1960.

Happy Thieves Theme (Italian)
Music by Mario Nascimbene.
Unart Music Corp.
From *The Happy Thieves* (film).

Harmony
Words and music by James Goldman, John Kander, and William Goldman.
Sunbeam Music Corp.
Introduced by Bibi Osterwald, Gino Conforti, Linda Lavin, and Jack De Lon in *A Family Affair* (musical).

Have a Dream
Words by Lee Adams, music by Charles Strouse.
Melrose Music Corp.
Introduced by Fritz Weaver in *All American* (musical).

Have I Told You Lately?
Words and music by Harold Rome.
Florence Music Co., Inc.
Introduced by Ken Le Roy and Bambi Linn in *I Can Get It for You Wholesale* (musical).

Have You Looked into Your Heart
Words and music by Teddy Randazzo, Bobby Weinstein, and Billy Barberis.
South Mountain Music Corp., 1962, 1964.
Best-selling record in 1964-65 by Jerry Vale (Columbia).

Having a Party
Words and music by Sam Cooke.
Kags Music.
Best-selling record by Sam Cooke (RCA Victor).

He Is Here (English)
Words and music by Chris Charles and Tolchard Evans.
Dick James Music, Ltd., London, England/Dick James Music, Inc.
Introduced in United States in 1966 by Mahalia Jackson (Columbia).

Heart (I Hear You Beating)
Words and music by Barry Mann and Cynthia Weil.
Screen Gems-Columbia Music, Inc.
Best-selling record by Wayne Newton (Capitol).

Heart in Hand
Words and music by Shari Sheeley and Jackie De Shannon.
Metric Music Co.
Best-selling record by Brenda Lee (Decca).

Heart of Mine, see Song from *Advise and Consent.*

Heartache for a Keepsake, A
Words and music by Roger Miller.
Tree Publishing Co., Inc.
Best-selling record by Kitty Wells (Decca).

Heartbreak, U.S.A., see 1960.

Hello Out There
Words and music by Kent Westbury and Wayne P. Walker.
Cedarwood Publishing Co., Inc.
Best-selling record by Carl Belew (RCA Victor).

Hello Trouble
Words and music by Orville Couch and Eddie McDuff.
Edville Publishing Co.
Best-selling record by Orville Couch (Vee Jay).

Here's to Us
Words by Carolyn Leigh, music by Cy Coleman.
Edwin H. Morris & Co., Inc.
Introduced by Nancy Andrews and chorus in *Little Me* (musical).

He's a Rebel
Words and music by Gene Pitney.
January Music Corp.
Best-selling record by The Crystals (Philles).

He's So Fine
Words and music by Ronnie Mack.
Bright-Tunes Music Corp.
Best-selling record in 1963 by The Chiffons (Laurie).

He's So Heavenly
Words and music by Shari Sheeley and Jackie De Shannon.
Metric Music Co., 1962, 1963.
Best-selling record by Brenda Lee (Decca).

He's Sure the Boy I Love
Words and music by Barry Mann and Cynthia Weil.
Screen Gems-Columbia Music, Inc.
Best-selling record by The Crystals (Philles).

Hey! Baby
Words and music by Margaret Cobb and Bruce Channel.
Le Bill Music, Inc.
Best-selling record by Bruce Channel (Smash).

Hey Little Star
Words and music by Roger Miller.
Tree Publishing Co., Inc.
Introduced by Roger Miller (RCA Victor).

Hey, Paula
Words and music by Ray Hildebrand.
Le Bill Music, Inc./Marbill Music.
Best-selling record in 1963 by Paul and Paula (Philips). "Paul" is
  Ray Hildebrand.

Hitch-Hiker
Words and music by Roger Miller.
Tree Publishing Co., Inc.
Introduced by Roger Miller (RCA Victor).

Holly Jolly Christmas, A
Words and music by Johnny Marks.
St. Nicholas Music, Inc.
From *Rudolph the Red-Nosed Reindeer* (television spectacular).

Honky Tonk Troubles
Words and music by Irene Stanton and Wayne Walker.
Cedarwood Publishing Co., Inc.
Introduced by "Little" Jimmy Dickens (Columbia).

Hopeless
Words and music by Doc Pomus and Alan Jeffreys.
Brenner Music, Inc.
Best-selling record in 1963 by Andy Williams (Columbia).

Hotel Happiness
Words by Earl Shuman, music by Leon Carr.
Mansion Music Corp./Dayben Music Corp.
Best-selling record in 1963 by Brook Benton (Mercury).

How Can I Meet Her?
Words and music by Gerry Goffin and Jack Keller.
Screen Gems-Columbia Music, Inc.
Best-selling record by The Everly Brothers (Warner Bros.).

How Does the Wine Taste?
Words by Matt Dubey, music by Harold Karr.
Chappell & Co., Inc.
Introduced by Kathleen Widdoes in *We Take the Town* (musical, closed before reaching New York). Introduced on records by Carmen McRae (Columbia).

How Sad
Words and music by Richard Rodgers.
Williamson Music, Inc.
Introduced by Richard Kiley in *No Strings* (musical).

How the West Was Won
Words by Ken Darby, music by Alfred Newman.
Robbins Music Corp.
Introduced by voices of The Ken Darby Chorus on soundtrack of *How the West Was Won* (film).

How's My Ex Treating You
Words and music by Vic McAlpin.
Tree Publishing Co., Inc.
Introduced by Jerry Lee Lewis (Sun).

Hum-Drum Blues
Words and music by Oscar Brown, Jr.
Edward B. Marks Music Corp.
Introduced by Oscar Brown, Jr.

Hush, Little Baby, see **Theme from** *The Miracle Worker.*

I Can Mend Your Broken Heart
Words and music by Don Gibson.
Acuff-Rose Publications, Inc.
Best-selling record by Don Gibson (RCA Victor).

I Can't Hang Up the Phone
Words and music by John D. Loudermilk.
Acuff-Rose Publications, Inc.
Best-selling record by Stonewall Jackson (Columbia).

I Can't Stop Loving You, see 1958.

I Catch Myself Crying
Words and music by Roger Miller.
Tree Publishing Co., Inc.
Introduced by Roger Miller (RCA Victor).

I Couldn't Have Done It Alone
Words by Lee Adams, music by Charles Strouse.
Melrose Music Corp.
Introduced by Ron Husmann in *All American* (musical).

I Found a Love
Words and music by Willie Schofield, Wilson Pickett, and Robert
West.
Progressive Music Publishing Co., Inc./Alibri Music Co./Lupine
Music.
Best-selling record by The Falcons (Lupine).

I Go My Merry Way, see Tous Les Chemins.

I Hope, I Think, I Wish
Words and music by Jimmy Day.
Tree Publishing Co., Inc.
Introduced by Conway Twitty (MGM).

I Just Don't Know What To Do with Myself
Words and music by Hal David and Burt Bacharach.
Belinda (Canada) Ltd./Quartet Music, Inc.
Best-selling record in 1966 by Dionne Warwick (Scepter).

I Knew It All the Time (English)
Words and music by Mitch Murray (pseudonym for L. Michael
Stitcher).
Keith Prowse Music Publishing Co., Ltd., London, England/Al
Gallico Music Corp.
Best-selling record in 1964 by The Dave Clark Five (Congress).

I Left My Heart in San Francisco, see 1954.

I Saw Linda Yesterday
Words and music by Dickey Lee and Allen Reynolds.
Jack Music, Inc.
Best-selling record by Dickey Lee (Smash).

I Thank My Lucky Stars
Words and music by Wayne P. Walker.
Cedarwood Publishing Co., Inc.
Best-selling record in 1964 by Eddy Arnold (RCA Victor).

I Want To Love You
Words by Marshall Barer, music by Duke Ellington.
Robbins Music Corp.
Adapted from theme from *The Asphalt Jungle* (television series).

I Want You To Be the First One To Know
Words by June Carroll, music by Arthur Siegel.
'62 Revue Publishers, Inc.
Introduced by Mickey Wayland, Charles Barlow, and Michael Fesco
in *New Faces of '62* (revue).

I Will Live My Life for You (French)
Words by Marcel Stellman, music by Henri Salvador.
Henri Salvador and Marcel Stellman, Paris, France, 1961/Tunetime
Music, Inc./Gil Music Corp.
Introduced by Tony Bennett (Columbia).

I Wish That We Were Married
Words and music by Marion Weiss and Edna Lewis.
Joy Music, Inc.
Best-selling record by Ronnie and The Hi-Lites (Joy).

I Won't Forget You
Words and music by Harlan Howard.
Tuckahoe Music, Inc.
Best-selling record in 1965 by Jim Reeves (RCA Victor).

If a Man Answers
Words and music by Bobby Darin.
T.M. Music, Inc./Champion Music Corp.
Introduced by Bobby Darin in *If a Man Answers* (film).

If a Woman Answers
Words and music by Barry Mann and Cynthia Weil.
Screen Gems-Columbia Music, Inc.
Best-selling record by Leroy Van Dyke (Mercury).

If and When
Words by Sammy Cahn, music by Josef Myrow.
Miller Music Corp.
Introduced by Patti Page (Columbia).

If I Didn't Have a Dime (To Play the Jukebox)
Words and music by Bert Russell and Phil Medley.
January Music Corp.
Best-selling record by Gene Pitney (Musicor).

If I Had a Hammer, see 1958.

If I Were the Man
Words by Ronny Graham, music by Milton Schafer.
Giovanni Music, Inc./Mayfair Music Corp.
Introduced by Cesare Siepi in *Bravo Giovanni* (musical).

If I Were You
Words by Lee Adams, music by Charles Strouse.
Melrose Music Corp.
Introduced by Ray Bolger and Eileen Herlie in *All American* (musical).

If You Wanna Be Happy
Words by Carmela Guida, Frank J. Guida, and Joseph Royster,
    music by Frank J. Guida and Joseph Royster.
Rock Masters, Inc.
Best-selling record in 1963 by Jimmy Soul (S.P.Q.R.).

I'll Never Dance Again
Words and music by Barry Mann and Mike Anthony.
Screen Gems-Columbia Music, Inc.
Best-selling record by Bobby Rydell (Cameo).

I'll Pick up My Heart (And Go Home)
Words and music by Roger Miller.
Tree Publishing Co., Inc.
Introduced by Roger Miller (RCA Victor).

I'll Release You
Words and music by Eddie Miller, Dub Williams, Robert Yount, and
    Ted Taylor.
Four Star Music Co., Inc.
Best-selling record by Ted Taylor (Okeh).

I'm All I've Got
Words by Ronny Graham, music by Milton Schafer.
Giovanni Music, Inc./Mayfair Music Corp.
Introduced by Michèle Lee in *Bravo Giovanni* (musical).

I'm Fascinating
Words by Lee Adams, music by Charles Strouse.
Melrose Music Corp.
Introduced by Ray Bolger in *All American* (musical).

I'm Gonna Be Warm This Winter
Words and music by Hank Hunter and Mark Barkan.
John D. MacArthur Music Corp.
Best-selling record by Connie Francis (MGM).

I'm Gonna Change Everything
Words and music by Alexander Zanetis.
Tuckahoe Music, Inc.
Best-selling record by Jim Reeves (RCA Victor).

I'm Gonna Get Him
Words and music by Irving Berlin.
Irving Berlin Music Corp., 1956, 1962.
Introduced by Nanette Fabray and Anita Gillette in *Mr. President*
    (musical).

I'm Saving My Love
Words and music by Alex Zanetis.
Samos Island Music, Inc.
Best-selling record in 1963 by Skeeter Davis (RCA Victor).

Imagine That
Words and music by Justin Tubb.
Tree Publishing Co., Inc.
Introduced by Patsy Cline (Decca).

In Other Words, see Fly Me to the Moon, 1954.

In Our Hide-Away
Words and music by Irving Berlin.
Irving Berlin Music Corp.
Introduced by Nanette Fabray and Robert Ryan in *Mr. President*
(musical).

**Is He the Only Man in the World, also known as Is She the
Only Girl in the World**
Words and music by Irving Berlin.
Irving Berlin Music Corp., 1956, 1962.
Introduced by Nanette Fabray and Anita Gillette in *Mr. President*
(musical).

**Is She the Only Girl in the World, see Is He the Only Man
in the World.**

Island of Forgotten Lovers, The
Words and music by Dick Manning and Kay Twomey.
Roncom Music Co.
Best-selling record by Perry Como (RCA Victor).

It Ain't Like That No More
Words and music by Pearl Woods, Freddy Johnson, and Leroy
Kirkland.
Figure Music, Inc.
Best-selling record by Ted Taylor (Columbia).

It Gets Lonely in the White House
Words and music by Irving Berlin.
Irving Berlin Music Corp.
Introduced by Robert Ryan in *Mr. President* (musical).

It Is Better To Love
Words by Dusty Negulesco, music by Margueritte Monnot.
Unart Music Corp.
Introduced by Maurice Chevalier in *Jessica* (film).

It Might As Well Rain until September
Words and music by Gerry Goffin and Carole King.
Screen Gems-Columbia Music, Inc.
Introduced and best-selling record by Carole King (Dimension).

It's the Little Things in Texas
Words and music by Richard Rodgers.
Williamson Music, Inc.
Introduced by Tom Ewell and Alice Faye in *State Fair* (film).

It's Up to You
Words and music by Jerry Fuller.
Four Star Music Co., Inc./Hilliard Music Co., 1962, 1963.
Best-selling record in 1963 by Rick Nelson (Imperial).

I've Been Everywhere (Australian)
Words and music by Geoffrey Mack.
Johnny Devlin Music Pty., Ltd., Sydney, Australia/Hill and Range
    Songs, Inc.
Best-selling record by Hank Snow (RCA Victor).

I've Enjoyed As Much of This As I Can Stand
Words and music by Bill Anderson.
Moss Rose Publications, Inc.
Best-selling record in 1963 by Porter Wagoner (RCA Victor).

I've Got Just About Everything
Words and music by Bob Dorough.
Hullabaloo Music Co.
Introduced by Tony Bennett (Columbia).

I've Got To Be Around
Words and music by Irving Berlin.
Irving Berlin Music Corp.
Introduced by Jack Haskell in *Mr. President* (musical).

I've Got Your Number
Words by Carolyn Leigh, music by Cy Coleman.
Edwin H. Morris & Co., Inc.
Introduced by Swen Swenson in *Little Me* (musical).

I've Just Seen Her
Words by Lee Adams, music by Charles Strouse.
Melrose Music Corp.
Introduced by Ron Husmann in *All American* (musical).

Jailer, Bring Me Water
Words and music by Bobby Darin.
T. M. Music, Inc., 1962, 1963.
Introduced by Bobby Darin (Atco).

James Bond Theme, The (English)
Music by Monty Norman.
United Artists Music, Ltd., London, England/Unart Music Corp.
Theme from *Dr. No* (film, 1963). Best-selling record in 1964 by
    Billy Strange (Crescendo).

James, (Hold the Ladder Steady)
Words and music by John D. Loudermilk.
Acuff-Rose Publications, Inc.
Best-selling record by Sue Thompson (Hickory).

Jessica
Words by Dusty Negulesco, music by Margueritte Monnot.
Unart Music Corp.
Introduced by Maurice Chevalier in *Jessica* (film).

Johnny Angel
Words by Lyn Duddy, music by Lee Pockriss.
Post Music, Inc.
Best-selling record by Shelley Fabares (Colpix).

Johnny Get Angry
Words by Hal David, music by Sherman Edwards.
Tod Music, Inc.
Best-selling record by Joanie Sommers (Warner Bros.).

Johnny Loves Me
Words and music by Barry Mann and Cynthia Weil.
Screen Gems-Columbia Music, Inc.
Best-selling record by Shelley Fabares (Colpix).

Johnny's Theme
Words and music by Paul Anka and Johnny Carson.
Spanka Music Corp.
Theme of *Tonight* (television variety show).

Just Say "Auf Wiederseh'n"
Words by Mort Goode, music by Klaus Ogermann.
Glamorous Music, Inc.
Introduced by Pat Thomas (Verve).

Just Tell Her Jim Said Hello
Words and music by Jerry Leiber and Mike Stoller.
Elvis Presley Music, Inc.
Best-selling record by Elvis Presley (RCA Victor).

Keep Your Hands off My Baby
Words and music by Gerry Goffin and Carole King.
Screen Gems-Columbia Music, Inc.
Best-selling record by Little Eva (Dimension).

Kicking Our Hearts Around
Words and music by Wanda Jackson.
Central Songs, Inc.
Best-selling record by Buck Owens (Capitol).

King of Clowns
Words and music by Howard Greenfield and Neil Sedaka.
Screen Gems-Columbia Music, Inc.
Best-selling record by Neil Sedaka (RCA Victor).

King of the Whole Wide World
Words and music by Ruth Batchelor and Bob Roberts.
Elvis Presley Music, Inc.
Introduced by Elvis Presley in *Kid Galahad* (film).

La La La
Words and music by Richard Rodgers.
Williamson Music, Inc.
Introduced by Noelle Adam and Alvin Epstein in *No Strings* (musical).

La Valse à Mille Temps, see Carousels, 1962; **see The Days of the Waltz,** 1964.

Las Vegas
Words by Earl Shuman, music by "Bugs" Bower.
Famous Music Corp.
Introduced and best-selling record by Damita Jo (Mercury).

Le Tourbillon, see The Theme from *Jules and Jim.*

Leavin' on Your Mind
Words and music by Wayne P. Walker and Webb Pierce.
Cedarwood Publishing Co., Inc.
Best-selling record in 1963 by Patsy Cline (Decca).

Leona
Words and music by Cindy Walker.
Cedarwood Publishing Co., Inc.
Best-selling record by Stonewall Jackson (Columbia).

Let Me Do It My Way
Words and music by David Battaglia and Julius Dixon.
Painted Desert Music Corp.
Best-selling record by Jo An Campbell (Cameo).

Let Me Go the Right Way
Words and music by Berry Gordy, Jr.
Jobete Music Co., Inc.
Best-selling record by The Supremes (Motown).

Let's Dance
Words and music by Jim Lee.
Rondell Music/Sherman-De Vorzon Music Corp.
Best-selling record by Chris Montez (Monogram).

Let's Go Back to the Waltz
Words and music by Irving Berlin.
Irving Berlin Music Corp.
Introduced by Nanette Fabray and ensemble in *Mr. President* (musical).

Let's Not Be Sensible
Words by Sammy Cahn, music by James Van Heusen.
Chappell & Co., Inc.
Introduced by Bing Crosby and Dorothy Lamour in *The Road to Hong Kong* (film).

Letter Full of Tears
Words and music by Don Covay.
Betalbin Music Publishing Corp.
Best-selling record by Gladys Knight and The Pips (Fury).

Lie to Me
Words and music by Brook Benton and Margie Singleton.
Benday Music Corp.
Best-selling record by Brook Benton (Mercury).

Limbo Rock
Words and music by Jon Sheldon and William E. Strange.
Four Star Music Co., Inc./Twist Music.
Best-selling record by Chubby Checker (Parkway).

Little Bitty Heart
Words and music by Claude King.
Painted Desert Music Corp.
Introduced by Claude King (Columbia).

Little Bitty Tear, A, see 1960.

Little Black Book
Words and music by Jimmy Dean.
Plainview Music, Inc.
Best-selling record by Jimmy Dean (Columbia).

Little Boat (Brazilian)
English words by Buddy Kaye, Portuguese words by Ronaldo
    Boscoli, music by Roberto Menescal.
Éditions SACHA s.a.r.l., Paris, France, 1962, 1963, 1964/Duchess
    Music Corp.
Original Portuguese title, "O Barquinho."

Little Boxes
Words and music by Malvina Reynolds.
Schroder Music Co., 1962, 1963.
Best-selling record by Pete Seeger (Columbia).

Little Diane
Words and music by Dion Di Mucci.
Marimba Music Corp.
Best-selling record by Dion (Laurie).

Little Heartache, A
Words and music by Wayne P. Walker.
Cedarwood Publishing Co., Inc.
Best-selling record by Eddy Arnold (RCA Victor).

Little Latin Lupe Lu
Words and music by Bill Medley.
Ray Maxwell Music Publishing Co.
Introduced by The Righteous Brothers (Moonglow). Best-selling record in 1966 by Mitch Ryder and The Detroit Wheels (New Voice).

Little Me
Words by Carolyn Leigh, music by Cy Coleman.
Edwin H. Morris & Co., Inc.
Introduced by Nancy Andrews and Virginia Martin in *Little Me* (musical).

Little Town Flirt
Words and music by Marion McKenzie and Del Shannon.
Vicki Music, Inc./Noma Music, Inc.
Best-selling record in 1963 by Del Shannon (Big Top).

Living In the Country
Words and music by Pete Seeger.
Fall River Music, Inc.
Introduced by Pete Seeger.

Loads of Love
Words and music by Richard Rodgers.
Williamson Music, Inc.
Introduced by Diahann Carroll in *No Strings* (musical).

Loco-Motion, The
Words and music by Gerry Goffin and Carole King.
Screen Gems-Columbia Music, Inc.
Best-selling record by Little Eva (Dimension).

Lolita Ya-Ya
Music by Nelson Riddle and Bob Harris.
Chappell & Co., Inc.
From *Lolita* (film). Best-selling record by The Ventures (Dolton).

(Hey There) Lonely Boy
Words by Earl Shuman, music by Leon Carr.
Famous Music Corp.
Best-selling record by Ruby and The Romantics (Kapp).

Lonely Bull, The (El Solo Toro)
Music by Sol Lake.
Almo Music Corp.
Original title, "Twinkle Star." Best-selling record by Herb Alpert and The Tijuana Brass (A&M).

Lonely Teardrops
Words and music by Lee Ross.
Central Songs, Inc.
Best-selling record by Rose Maddox (Capitol).

Lonesome (7-7203)
Words and music by Justin Tubb.
Cedarwood Publishing Co., Inc.
Best-selling record in 1963 by Hawkshaw Hawkins (King).

Long About Now
Words and music by Fred Hellerman and Fran Minkoff.
Appleseed Music, Inc.
Introduced by Harry Belafonte (RCA Victor).

Longest Day, The
Words and music by Paul Anka.
Spanka Music Corp.
Introduced on soundtrack of *The Longest Day* (film) by orchestra
and chorus conducted by Mitch Miller.

Look No Further
Words and music by Richard Rodgers.
Williamson Music, Inc.
Introduced by Diahann Carroll and Richard Kiley in *No Strings*
(musical).

Loop De Loop
Words and music by Teddy Vann (pseudonym for Theodore
Williams) and Joe Dong.
Tobi-Ann Music Publishing Corp.
Best-selling record in 1963 by Johnny Thunder (Diamond).

Lost Someone
Words and music by James Brown, Lloyd Stallworth, and Bobby
Byrd.
Lois Publishing Co.
Best-selling record by James Brown and The Famous Flames (King).

Love Came to Me
Words and music by Dion Di Mucci and John Falbo.
Disal Music Corp./Schwartz Music Co., Inc.
Best-selling record by Dion (Laurie).

Love, I Hear
Words and music by Stephen Sondheim.
Burthen Music Co., Inc.
Introduced by Brian Davies in *A Funny Thing Happened on the
Way to the Forum* (musical).

Love Letters, see 1945.

Love Makes the World Go
Words and music by Richard Rodgers.
Williamson Music, Inc.
Introduced by Polly Rowles and Bernice Massi in *No Strings* (musi-
cal).

Love (Makes the World Go 'Round)
Words and music by Paul Anka.
Spanka Music Corp.
Best-selling record by Paul Anka (RCA Victor).

Love on My Mind
Music by Ray Charles.
Progressive Music Publishing Co., Inc.
Introduced by Ray Charles and Milt Jackson (Atlantic).

Love Song from *Mutiny on the Bounty,* also known as Follow Me
Words by Paul Francis Webster, music by Bronislau Kaper.
Miller Music Corp.
Introduced by chorus in *Mutiny on the Bounty* (film). Nominated for Academy Award, 1962.

Love Theme from *Lolita*
Music by Bob Harris.
Chappell & Co., Inc.
Main theme from *Lolita* (film).

Love Theme from *Phaedra* (Greek)
Music by Mikis Theodorakis.
Unart Music Corp.
From *Phaedra* (film).

Lovely
Words and music by Stephen Sondheim.
Burthen Music Co., Inc.
Introduced by Brian Davies and Preshy Marker, and reprised by Zero Mostel and Jack Gilford, in *A Funny Thing Happened on the Way to the Forum* (musical).

Lovers Who Wander
Words and music by Dion Di Mucci and Ernest Maresca.
Marimba Music Corp./Schwartz Music Co., Inc.
Best-selling record by Dion (Laurie).

Mack the Knife, see 1956.

(Girls, Girls, Girls Were) Made To Love, see 1960.

Magic Fountain, The
Words and music by Steve Allen and Don George.
Rosemeadow Publishing Corp.
From *The Magic Fountain* (film).

Maine
Words and music by Richard Rodgers.
Williamson Music, Inc.
Introduced by Diahann Carroll and Richard Kiley in *No Strings* (musical).

Make It Easy on Yourself
Words by Hal David, music by Burt F. Bacharach.
Famous Music Corp.
Best-selling record by Jerry Butler (Vee Jay).

Mama Didn't Lie
Words and music by Curtis Mayfield.
Curtom Publishing Co., Inc.
Best-selling record in 1963 by Jan Bradley (Chess).

Man of Constant Sorrow
Words and music by Peter Yarrow and Paul Stookey.
Pepamar Music Corp .
Best-selling record by Peter, Paul, and Mary (Warner Bros.).

Man Who Has Everything, The
Words and music by Richard Rodgers.
Williamson Music, Inc.
Introduced by Mitchell Gregg in *No Strings* (musical).

Man Who Robbed the Bank at Santa Fe, The
Words and music by Jerry Leiber, Mike Stoller, and Billy Wheeler.
Trio Music Co., Inc./Butterfield Music Corp.
Best-selling record in 1963 by Hank Snow (RCA Victor).

Man Who Shot Liberty Valance, The
Words by Hal David, music by Burt F. Bacharach.
Famous Music Corp.
"Inspired" by *The Man Who Shot Liberty Valance* (film). Best-selling record by Gene Pitney (Musicor).

Martian Hop
Words and music by John Spirt, Robert Lawrence Rappaport, and Steve Rappaport.
Screen Gems-Columbia Music, Inc.
Best-selling record in 1963 by The Ran-Dells (London).

Mary's Little Lamb
Words and music by Cynthia Weil and Barry Mann.
Screen Gems-Columbia Music, Inc.
Best-selling record by James Darren (Colpix).

Mashed Potato Time
Words and music by Jon Sheldon and Harry Land.
Rice Mill Publishing Co., Inc./Jobete Music Co., Inc.
Best-selling record by Dee Dee Sharp (Cameo).

Meantime
Words by Al Stillman, music by Robert Allen.
Dymor Productions, Inc./Jonathan Music Co., Inc.
Introduced by Carol Burnett in *Julie and Carol at Carnegie Hall* (television spectacular).

Meat and Potatoes
Words and music by Irving Berlin.
Irving Berlin Music Corp.
Introduced by Jack Haskell and Stanley Grover in *Mr. President*
  (musical).

Million Years or So, A
Words and music by Charlie Williams.
Central Songs, Inc.
Best-selling record by Eddy Arnold (RCA Victor).

Miranda
Words by Ronny Graham, music by Milton Schafer.
Giovanni Music, Inc./Mayfair Music Corp.
Introduced by Cesare Siepi in *Bravo Giovanni* (musical).

Miss Marmelstein
Words and music by Harold Rome.
Florence Music Co., Inc.
Introduced by Barbra Streisand in *I Can Get It for You Wholesale*
  (musical).

Mr. Heartache, Move On
Words and music by Coleman O'Neal.
Yonah Music, Inc.
Best-selling record in 1963 by Coleman O'Neal (Chancellor).

Mr. Lonely
Words and music by Bobby Vinton and Gene Allan.
Ripley Music, Inc.
Best-selling record in 1964-65 by Bobby Vinton (Epic).

Mr. Moonlight
Words and music by Roy Lee Johnson.
Lowery Music Co., Inc.
Best-selling record in 1965 by The Beatles (Capitol).

Molly
Words and music by Steve Karliski.
Screen Gems-Columbia Music, Inc.
Best-selling records by Bobby Goldsboro (Laurie), and in 1964 by
  Eddy Arnold (RCA Victor).

Momma, Momma!
Words and music by Harold Rome.
Florence Music Co., Inc.
Introduced by Elliott Gould and Lillian Roth in *I Can Get It for You
  Wholesale* (musical).

Monster Mash
Words and music by Bobby Pickett and Leonard Capizzi.
Garpax Music Publishing Co./Capizzi Music.
Best-selling record by Bobby "Boris" Pickett and The Crypt Kickers
  (Garpax).

Morning After, The
Words by Dory Langdon, music by Harold Arlen.
Harwin Music Corp.
Introduced by Eileen Farrell (Columbia).

My Coloring Book
Words by Fred Ebb, music by John Kander.
Sunbeam Music Corp.
Written for and introduced by Kaye Ballard. Introduced by Sandy
Stewart on television on *The Perry Como Show*. Best-selling
records by Sandy Stewart (Colpix), Kitty Kallen (RCA Victor),
and Barbra Streisand (Columbia).

My Dad
Words and music by Barry Mann and Cynthia Weil.
Screen Gems-Columbia Music, Inc.
Best-selling record in 1963 by Paul Petersen (Colpix).

My Six Loves
Words by Sammy Cahn, music by James Van Heusen.
Famous Music Corp., 1962, 1963.
From *My Six Loves* (film, 1963).

Never Say "No" (To a Man)
Words and music by Richard Rodgers.
Williamson Music, Inc.
Introduced by Alice Faye in *State Fair* (film).

Never Too Late
Words by Sheldon Harnick, music by Jerry Bock.
Sunbeam Music Corp.
Introduced as instrumental cha-cha recording for dance lesson by
Joe Quijano and his Orchestra (Columbia) in *Never Too Late*
(play).

Never-Ending
Words and music by Buddy Kaye and Phil Springer.
Ross Jungnickel, Inc.
Best-selling record by Elvis Presley (RCA Victor).

New *Naked City* Theme
Music by Nelson Riddle.
Gower Music, Inc., 1962, 1963.
Theme of *Naked City* (television series). Introduced and best-selling
record by Nelson Riddle and his Orchestra (Capitol).

Next Door to an Angel
Words and music by Neil Sedaka and Howard Greenfield.
Screen Gems-Columbia Music, Inc.
Best-selling record by Neil Sedaka (RCA Victor).

Niagara Theme (English)
Music by George Martin.
Dick James Music, Ltd., London, England/Tunetime Music, Inc.
Introduced in United States by Roger Williams (Kapp).

Night Has a Thousand Eyes, The
Words and music by Dottie Wayne, Marilyn Garrett, and Ben
    Weisman.
Blen Music, Inc./Mabs Music Co.
Best-selling record in 1963 by Bobby Vee (Liberty).

Nightlife
Words by Lee Adams, music by Charles Strouse.
Melrose Music Corp.
Introduced by Anita Gillette and chorus in *All American* (musical).

No More Blues (Brazilian)
English words by Jon Hendricks and Jessie Cavanaugh, Portuguese
    words by Vinicius De Moraes, music by Antonio Carlos Jobim.
Editora Musical Arapua, São Paulo, Brazil, 1958/Hollis Music, Inc.
Original title, "Chega De Saudade."

No Strings
Words and music by Richard Rodgers.
Williamson Music, Inc.
Introduced by Diahann Carroll and Richard Kiley in *No Strings*
    (musical).

Nobody Told Me
Words and music by Richard Rodgers.
Williamson Music, Inc.
Introduced by Diahann Carroll and Richard Kiley in *No Strings*
    (musical).

Nobody's Fool but Yours
Words and music by Buck Owens.
Blue Book Music Co.
Best-selling record by Buck Owens (Capitol).

O Barquinho, see **Little Boat.**

O Pato, see **The Duck.**

O Willow Waly
Words by Paul Dehn, music by Georges Auric.
Robbins Music Corp.
From *The Innocents* (film).

Oh! Oh! (It Started All Over Again)
Words and music by Gerry Goffin and Jack Keller.
Screen Gems-Columbia Music, Inc.
Best-selling record by Brenda Lee (Decca).

Old Rivers
Words and music by Cliff Crofford.
Glo-Mac Music/Metric Music Co.
Best-selling record by Walter Brennan (Liberty).

Old Showboat
Words and music by Marijohn Wilkin and Fred Burch.
Cedarwood Publishing Co., Inc.
Best-selling record in 1963 by Stonewall Jackson (Columbia).

On Broadway
Words and music by Barry Mann, Cynthia Weil, Jerry Leiber, and
 Mike Stroller.
Screen Gems-Columbia Music, Inc., 1962, 1963.
Best-selling record in 1963 by The Drifters (Atlantic).

Once upon a Summertime (French)
English words by Johnny Mercer, French words by Eddy Marnay,
 music by Michel Legrand and Eddie Barclay.
Compagnie Phonographique Française Éditions Eddie Barclay, 1954,
 1962/Leeds Music Corp.
Original French title, "La Valse des Lilas." Best-selling record by
 Tony Bennett (Columbia).

Once upon a Time
Words by Lee Adams, music by Charles Strouse.
Melrose Music Corp.
Introduced by Ray Bolger and Eileen Herlie in *All American* (musi-
 cal).

One Little World Apart
Words by Ronny Graham, music by Milton Schafer.
Giovanni Music, Inc./Mayfair Music Corp.
Introduced by Michèle Lee in *Bravo Giovanni* (musical).

One Man's Hands
Words by Dr. Alex Comfort, music by Peter Seeger.
Fall River Music, Inc.
Introduced by Pete Seeger.

One Who Really Loves You, The
Words and music by William Robinson.
Jobete Music Co., Inc.
Best-selling record by Mary Wells (Motown).

Only Dance I Know, The, also known as Song for Belly-Dancer
Words and music by Irving Berlin.
Irving Berlin Music Corp.
Introduced by Wisa D'Orso in *Mr. President* (musical).

Only Love Can Break a Heart
Words and music by Burt Bacharach and Hal David.
Arch Music Co., Inc.
Best-selling record by Gene Pitney (Musicor).

Orthodox Fool, An
Words and music by Richard Rodgers.
Williamson Music, Inc.
Introduced by Diahann Carroll in *No Strings* (musical).

Other Side of the Tracks, The
Words by Carolyn Leigh, music by Cy Coleman.
Edwin H. Morris & Co., Inc.
Introduced by Virginia Martin in *Little Me* (musical).

Our Children
Words by Lee Adams, music by Charles Strouse.
Melrose Music Corp.
Introduced by Ray Bolger and Eileen Herlie in *All American* (musical).

Our Day Will Come
Words by Mort Garson, music by Bob Hilliard.
Rosewood Music Corp., 1962, 1963.
Best-selling record in 1963 by Ruby and The Romantics (Kapp).

Palisades Park
Words and music by Chuck Barris.
Claridge Music, Inc.
Best-selling record by Freddy Cannon (Swan).

Papa-Oom-Mow-Mow
Words and music by Al Frazier, Carl White, Turner Wilson, Jr., and
  John Harris.
Beechwood Music Corp.
Best-selling record by The Rivingtons (Liberty).

Paradise
Words and music by Berry Gordy, Jr.
Jobete Music Co., Inc.
Best-selling record by The Temptations (Gordy).

Party Lights
Words and music by Claudine Clark.
Rambed Publishing Co., Inc.
Best-selling record by Claudine Clark (Chancellor).

Patches, see 1960.

Pearl, Pearl, Pearl
Words and music by Paul Henning.
Carolintone Music Co., Inc.
Best-selling record in 1963 by Lester Flatt and Earl Scruggs
  (Columbia.)

Pearly Shells (Pupu O Ewa)
Words and music by Webley Edwards and Leon Pober.
Criterion Music Corp., 1962, 1964.
Featured in *Surf Party* (film, 1964). Best-selling record in 1964 by
  Burl Ives (Decca).

Peel Me a Grape
Words and music by David Frishberg.
Saunders Publications, Inc.

Pepino, the Italian Mouse
Words and music by Ray Allen and Wandra Merrell.
Romance Music, Inc./Ding Dong Music Corp.
Best-selling record in 1963 by Lou Monte (Reprise).

Pigtails and Freckles
Words and music by Irving Berlin.
Irving Berlin Music Corp.
Introduced by Jack Haskell and Anita Gillette in *Mr. President*
  (musical).

Pipeline
Music by Bob Spickard and Brian Carman.
Downey Music Publishing Co., 1962, 1963.
Best-selling record in 1963 by The Chantays (Dot).

Please Mr. Postman
Words and music by Brian Holland and Freddy C. Gorman.
Jobete Music Co., Inc., 1962, 1964.
Best-selling records in 1961 by The Marvelettes (Tamla) and in 1964
  by The Beatles (Capitol).

Please Please Me (English)
Words and music by John Lennon and Paul McCartney.
Dick James Music, Ltd., London, England, 1962, 1964/Concertone
  Songs, Inc.
Best-selling record in 1964 by The Beatles (Vee Jay and Capitol).

Poor Fool, see 1960.

Poor Little Hollywood Star
Words by Carolyn Leigh, music by Cy Coleman.
Edwin H. Morris & Co., Inc.
Introduced by Virginia Martin in *Little Me* (musical).

Popeye (The Hitchhiker)
Words by Kal Mann, music by Dave Appell.
Kalmann Music, Inc.
Best-selling record by Chubby Checker (Parkway).

Pride
Words and music by Wayne P. Walker and Irene Stanton.
Cedarwood Publishing Co., Inc.
Best-selling record by Ray Price (Columbia).

Prince
Words and music by Sharon Sheeley and Jackie De Shannon.
Metric Music Co.
Best-selling record by Jackie De Shannon (Liberty).

Private John Q
Words and music by Roger Miller.
Tree Publishing Co., Inc.
Introduced by Glen Campbell (Capitol).

Proud
Words and music by Barry Mann and Cynthia Weil.
Screen Gems-Columbia Music, Inc., 1962, 1963.
Introduced by Johnny Crawford (Del-Fi).

Quando, Quando, Quando (Tell Me When) (Italian)
English words by Pat Boone, Italian words by Arturo Testa, music
  by Tony Renis (pseudonym for Elio Cesari).
Edizioni Musicali Ritmi e Canzoni, Italy/M. Witmark & Sons.
Introduced in Italy by Tony Renis and Emilio Pericoli. Fourth Place
  Winner of San Remo (Italy) Song Festival, 1962. Best-selling
  record in United States by Pat Boone (Dot).

Quiet Nights of Quiet Stars (Corcovado) (Brazilian)
English words by Gene Lees, Portuguese words and music by
  Antonio Carlos Jobim.
Antonio Carlos Jobim, Brazil, 1962, 1964/Duchess Music Corp.
Original title, "Corcovado," named for mountain near Rio de Janeiro.
  First recording in English by Tony Bennett (Columbia).

Quiet Room
Words and music by Fred Hellerman and Fran Minkoff.
Appleseed Music, Inc.
Introduced by Carol Lawrence (Cameo).

Rain, Rain Go Away
Words and music by Gloria Shayne and Noel Regney.
Regent Music Corp.
Best-selling record by Bobby Vinton (Epic).

Ramblin' Rose
Words and music by Noel Sherman and Joe Sherman.
Sweco Music Corp.
Best-selling record by Nat "King" Cole (Capitol). Not to be confused
  with "Rambling Rose" (see 1948) or "(Love Is Like a) Ramblin'
  Rose" (see 1961).

Real Live Girl
Words by Carolyn Leigh, music by Cy Coleman.
Edwin H. Morris & Co., Inc.
Introduced by Sid Caesar in *Little Me* (musical).

Recado Bossa Nova (Brazilian)
Portuguese words by Luiz Antonio, music by Djalma Ferreira.
Editora Musical Drink, Ltda., São Paulo, Brazil, 1959/Rytvoc, Inc.

Return to Sender
Words and music by Otis Blackwell and Winfield Scott.
Elvis Presley Music, Inc.
Introduced by Elvis Presley in *Girls! Girls! Girls!* (film). Best-
selling record by Elvis Presley (RCA Victor). Lyrics adapted and
title changed to "On Her Majesty's Service" for *Cambridge Circus*
(English revue, 1964).

Reverend Mr. Black, The
Words and music by Billy Wheeler.
Quartet Music, Inc./Butterfield Music Corp.
Best-selling record in 1963 by The Kingston Trio (Capitol).

Rhythm of the Rain
Words and music by John Gummoe.
Sherman-De Vorzon Music Corp., 1962, 1963.
Best-selling record in 1963 by The Cascades (Valiant).

Ring of Fire
Words and music by Merle Kilgore and June Carter.
Painted Desert Music Corp., 1962, 1963.
Best-selling record in 1963 by Johnny Cash (Columbia).

Rinky Dink
Words and music by Paul Winley and David Clowney.
Ben-Ghazi Enterprises, Inc.
Best-selling record by Dave "Baby" Cortez (Chess).

Road to Hong Kong, The
Words by Sammy Cahn, music by James Van Heusen.
Chappell & Co., Inc.
Introduced by Bing Crosby and Bob Hope in *The Road to Hong Kong*
(film).

(Beautiful, Wonderful, Fabulous) Rome
Words by Ronny Graham, music by Milton Schafer.
Giovanni Music, Inc./Mayfair Music Corp.
Introduced by Cesare Siepi in *Bravo Giovanni* (musical).

Ruby Ann
Words and music by Roberta Bellamy.
Marizona Music.
Best-selling record by Marty Robbins (Columbia).

Sealed with a Kiss, see 1960.

Second Chance, A, see **Song from *Two for the Seesaw*.**

Second Hand Love
Words and music by Hank Hunter and Phil Spector.
John D. MacArthur Music Corp.
Best-selling record by Connie Francis (MGM).

Second Hand Rose (Second Hand Heart)
Words and music by Harlan Howard.
Pamper Music, Inc.
Best-selling record in 1963 by Roy Drusky (Decca).

Secret Service, The
Words and music by Irving Berlin.
Irving Berlin Music Corp.
Introduced by Anita Gillette in *Mr. President* (musical).

Seven-Day Weekend
Words and music by Doc Pomus and Mort Shuman.
Hill and Range Songs, Inc.
Best-selling record by Gary "U.S." Bonds (LeGrand).

Shake, Sherrie, see Shake, Sherry.

Shake, Sherry, also known as **Shake, Sherrie**
Words and music by Berry Gordy, Jr.
Jobete Music Co., Inc.
Best-selling record by The Contours (Gordy).

Shame on Me
Words and music by Lawton Williams and Bill Enis.
Western Hills Music, Inc./Saran Music Co./Lois Publishing Co.
Introduced and best-selling record by Lawton Williams (King).

She Cried
Words and music by Ted Daryll and Greg Richards.
Trio Music Co., Inc./Rittenhouse Music.
Introduced by Ted Daryll (Utopia). Best-selling record by Jay and
  The Americans (United Artists).

She Thinks I Still Care
Words and music by Dickey Lee Lipscomb and Steve Duffy.
Glad Music Co./Jack Music, Inc.
Best-selling record by George Jones (United Artists).

Sheila, also known as **Shelia,** also known as **Shiela**
Words and music by Tommy Roe.
Eager Music/Low-Twi Music.
Best-selling record by Tommy Roe (ABC-Paramount).

Shelia, see Sheila.

Sherry
Words and music by Bob Gaudio.
Claridge Music, Inc.
Best-selling record by The Four Seasons (Vee Jay).

She's Not You
Words and music by Doc Pomus, Jerry Leiber, and Mike Stoller.
Elvis Presley Music, Inc.
Best-selling record by Elvis Presley (RCA Victor).

Shiela, see Sheila.

Shoes of a Fool
Words and music by Jimmy Day and Jim Coleman.
Tree Publishing Co., Inc.
Introduced by Bill Goodwin (Vee Jay).

Shout! Shout! Knock Yourself Out!
Words and music by Ernie Maresca and Thomas F. Bogdany.
Broadway Music Corp.
Best-selling record by Ernie Maresca (Seville).

Shutters and Boards
Words and music by Audie Murphy and Scott Turner.
Camp and Canyon Music Co.
Best-selling record by Jerry Wallace (Challenge).

Signifyin' Monkey
Words and music by Oscar Brown, Jr.
Edward B. Marks Music Corp.
Introduced by Oscar Brown, Jr. (Columbia).

Sing a Little Song of Heartaches
Words and music by Del Reeves.
Yonah Music, Inc.
Best-selling record by Rose Maddox (Capitol).

Sinner, The (Mexican)
English words by Mitchell Parish, Spanish words and music by
    Alexandro F. Roth.
Mills Music, de Mexico, Mexico/Mills Music, Inc.
Original Spanish title, "El Pecador."

Slightly Out of Tune, see Desafinado.

Slow Twistin'
Words and music by Jon Sheldon.
Woodcrest Music, Inc.
Best-selling record by Chubby Checker (Parkway).

Smoky Places
Words and music by Abner Spector.
Arc Music Corp./Winlyn Music, Inc.
Best-selling record by The Corsairs and Jay "Bird" Uzzell (Tuff).

Snap Your Fingers
Words and music by Grady Martin and Alex Zanetis.
Cigma Music Co., Inc.
Best-selling record by Joe Henderson (Todd).

So This Is Love
Words and music by Herbert Newman.
Pattern Music, Inc.
Best-selling record by The Castells (Era).

Something's Got a Hold on Me
Words and music by Pearl Woods, Etta James, and Leroy Kirkland.
Figure Music, Inc.
Best-selling record by Etta James (Argo).

Somewhere in the Night, see *Naked City* Theme, 1961.

Song from *Advise and Consent* (Heart of Mine)
Words by Ned Washington, music by Jerry Fielding.
Chappell & Co., Inc.
Adapted from theme from *Advise and Consent* (film).

Song from *Two for the Seesaw* (A Second Chance)
Words by Dory Langdon, music by André Previn.
United Artists Music Co., Inc.
From *Two for the Seesaw* (film). Nominated for Academy Award,
1962.

Soul Twist
Music by Curtis Ousley.
Bob-Dan Music Co./Kilynn Music Publishing, Inc.
Best-selling record by King Curtis (Enjoy).

Sound of Money, The
Words and music by Harold Rome.
Florence Music Co., Inc.
Introduced by Elliott Gould, Sheree North, Barbara Monte, William
Reilly, and Edward Verso in *I Can Get It for You Wholesale*
(musical).

Steady, Steady
Words by Ronny Graham, music by Milton Schafer.
Giovanni Music, Inc./Mayfair Music Corp.
Introduced by Michèle Lee in *Bravo Giovanni* (musical).

Steel Men
Words and music by David Martins.
Southside Music Corp.
Best-selling record by Jimmy Dean (Columbia).

(I Love You) Still
Words and music by Bill Anderson.
Moss Rose Publications, Inc.
Best-selling rceord in 1963 by Bill Anderson (Decca).

Stoney Burke Theme, The
Music by Dominic Frontiere.
Esteem Music Corp., 1962, 1963.
Theme from *Stoney Burke* (television series).

Stormy Monday Blues
Words and music by Earl Hines, Billy Eckstine, and Bob Crowder.
Advanced Music Corp.
Best-selling record in 1942 by Earl Hines and his Orchestra, vocal
by Billy Eckstine (Bluebird). Not copyrighted until 1962.

Straight, No Chaser
Music by Thelonious Monk.
Bar-Thel Music Corp.
Introduced by Thelonious Monk.

Strange I Know
Words and music by Brian Holland, Freddy Gorman, and Lamont
Dozier.
Jobete Music Co., Inc.
Best-selling record by The Marvelettes (Tamla).

Stubborn Kind of Fellow
Words and music by William Stevenson, Marvin Gaye, and George
Gordy.
Jobete Music Co., Inc.
Best-selling record by Marvin Gaye (Tamla).

Sugar Shack
Words and music by Keith McCormack and Faye Voss.
Dundee Music.
Best-selling record in 1963 by Jimmy Gilmer and The Fireballs (Dot).

Surfer Girl
Words and music by Brian Wilson.
Guild Music Co.
Best-selling record in 1963 by The Beach Boys (Capitol).

Surfin' Safari
Words and music by Mike Love and Brian Wilson.
Guild Music Co.
Best-selling record by The Beach Boys (Capitol).

Suspicion
Words and music by Doc Pomus and Mort Shuman.
Elvis Presley Music, Inc.
Best-selling record in 1964 by Terry Stafford (Crusader).

Sweet September (English)
Words and music by Bill McGuffie, Lorraine Philips, and Peter
Stanley.
B.F. Wood Music Co., Ltd., London, England, 1962, 1963/B.F.
Wood Music Co., Inc.
Original title, "Sweet Tuesday." From *The Boys* (British film).
First recording in United States by Bill Evans with Orchestra
(Verve); first vocal version by Sylvia Syms (Columbia).

Sweetest Sounds, The
Words and music by Richard Rodgers.
Williamson Music, Inc.
Introduced by Diahann Carroll and Richard Kiley in *No Strings*
(musical).

Swingin' Safari, A
Music by Bert Kaempfert.
Roosevelt Music Co., Inc.
Best-selling record by Billy Vaughn and his Orchestra (Dot).

Take a Letter, Miss Gray
Words and music by Justin Tubb.
Tree Publishing Co., Inc.
Best-selling record in 1963 by Justin Tubb (Groove).

Take Five, see 1960.

Taste of Honey, A, see 1960.

Teamwork
Words by Sammy Cahn, music by James Van Heusen.
Chappell & Co., Inc.
Introduced by Bing Crosby and Bob Hope in *The Road to Hong Kong*
(film).

Teenage Idol, A
Words and music by Jack Lewis.
Nelson Music Publishing Co.
Best-selling record by Ricky Nelson (Imperial).

Tell Me
Words and music by Dick St. John.
Odin Music Co.
Best-selling record by Dick and Dee Dee (Liberty).

Tell Me When, see **Quando, Quando, Quando.**

Tell the World, see **Wheels,** 1960.

Telstar (English)
Music by Joe Meek.
Ivy Music, Ltd., London, England/Campbell-Connelly, Inc.
Best-selling record by The Tornadoes (London). Lyrics by Joe Meek
added in 1963 under title, "Magic Star"; vocal version introduced
by Margie Singleton (Mercury).

That Happy Feeling
Words and music by Guy Warren.
Northern Music Corp.
Originally copyrighted in 1956 under title, "Eyi Wala Dong (Thank
Him)," also known as "An African's Prayer." Best-selling record
under present title by Bert Kaempfert and his Orchestra (Decca).

That Old Song and Dance
Words by Marilyn Keith and Alan Bergman, music by Lew Spence.
Empress Music, Inc.

That'll Show Him
Words and music by Stephen Sondheim.
Burthen Music Co., Inc.
Introduced by Preshy Marker in *A Funny Thing Happened on the Way to the Forum* (musical).

That's Old Fashioned (That's the Way Love Should Be)
Words and music by Bill Giant, Bernie Baum, and Florence Kaye.
Hill and Range Songs, Inc.
Best-selling record by The Everly Brothers (Warner Bros.).

That's the Way Love Is
Words and music by Deadric Malone.
Lion Publishing Co., Inc.
Best-selling record in 1963 by Bobby Bland (Duke).

Theme from *A Majority of One*
Music by Max Steiner.
M. Witmark & Sons.
From *A Majority of One* (film).

Theme from *David and Lisa*
Music by Mark Lawrence.
Saunders Publications, Inc., 1962, 1963.
Theme from *David and Lisa* (film, 1963).

Theme from *Jules and Jim,* The, also known as Le Tourbillon (French)
Words and music by Georges Delerue and Cyrus Bassiak.
Société Nouvelle des Éditions Musicales Tutti, Paris, France/ B.F. Wood Music Co., Inc.
Introduced by Jeanne Moreau in *Jules and Jim* (French film).

Theme from *Lawrence of Arabia*
Music by Maurice Jarre.
Gower Music, Inc.
Theme from *Lawrence of Arabia* (film).

Theme from *Long Day's Journey into Night*
Music by André Previn.
LDJN Music Corp.
From *Long Day's Journey into Night* (film).

Theme from *Mutiny on the Bounty*
Music by Bronislau Kaper.
Miller Music Corp.
From *Mutiny on the Bounty* (film).

Theme from *Sodom and Gomorrah*
Music by Miklos Rozsa.
Titanus Edizioni Musicali, Rome, Italy/Robbins Music Corp.
Theme from *Sodom and Gomorrah* (film, 1963).

Theme from *Taras Bulba,* also known as The Wishing Star
Words by Mack David, music by Franz Waxman.
United Artists Music Co., Inc.
Adapted from a theme from *Taras Bulba* (film).

Theme from *The Eleventh Hour*
Music by Harry Sukman.
Miller Music Corp.
From *The Eleventh Hour* (television series).

**Theme from *The Miracle Worker,* also known as
    Hush, Little Baby**
Adaptation of words and music by Don Costa and Arthur Siegel.
United Artists Music Co., Inc.
Based on traditional song. Introduced by Anne Bancroft in *The
    Miracle Worker* (film).

**Theme from *The Wonderful World of the Brothers Grimm,*
    The**
Music by Bob Merrill.
Robbins Music Corp.
Main theme from *The Wonderful World of the Brothers Grimm*
    (film).

Then a Tear Fell
Words and music by Warner McPherson.
Valley Publishers, Inc.
Best-selling record by Earl Scott (Kapp).

There's a Room in My House
Words and music by James Goldman, John Kander, and William
    Goldman.
Sunbeam Music Corp.
Introduced by Larry Kert and Rita Gardner in *A Family Affair*
    (musical).

They Love Me
Words and music by Irving Berlin.
Irving Berlin Music Corp.
Introduced by Nanette Fabray in *Mr. President* (musical).

This Is a Great Country
Words and music by Irving Berlin.
Irving Berlin Music Corp.
Introduced by Robert Ryan in *Mr. President* (musical).

This Isn't Heaven
Words and music by Richard Rodgers.
Williamson Music, Inc.
Introduced by Bobby Darin in *State Fair* (film).

Thou Shalt Not Steal
Words and music by John D. Loudermilk.
Acuff-Rose Publications, Inc.
Best-selling record in 1964-65 by Dick and Deedee (Warner Bros.).

Time Is Now, The (French)
English words by Bud McCreery, French words and music by
Charles Aznavour.
Breton & Cie, Paris, France, 1956, 1961, 1962/MCA, Inc.
Original French title, "Sa Jeunesse . . . Entre Ses Mains." Intro-
duced by Charles Aznavour.

Torture
Words and music by John D. Loudermilk.
Acuff-Rose Publications, Inc.
Best-selling record by Kris Jones (Hickory).

Tous Les Chemins, also known as I Go My Merry Way (Belgian)
English words by Noel Regney, French words and music by Soeur
Sourire, O.P.
Éditions Primavera, s.a., Brussels, Belgium/General Music
Publishing Co., Inc.
Best-selling record in 1963-64 by "The Singing Nun," Soeur Sourire,
O.P. (Philips).

Truck Driving Man
Words and music by Terry Fell.
American Music, Inc.
Best-selling record in 1965 by George Hamilton IV (RCA Victor).

True, True Love, A
Words and music by Bobby Darin.
T.M. Music, Inc./Champion Music Corp.
Love theme from *If a Man Answers* (film). Introduced by Bobby
Darin (Capitol).

Turn! Turn! Turn! (To Everything There Is a Season)
Words from the book of *Ecclesiastes*, adaptation and music by Pete
Seeger.
Melody Trails, Inc.
Introduced by Pete Seeger (Columbia). Best-selling record in 1965-
66 by The Byrds (Columbia).

Twelve Days of Christmas, The
Words and adaptation of music by Eric Blau.
Cherry Lane Music, Inc.
Topical parody of traditional Christmas song. Introduced by William
  Heyer in *O, Oysters!* (off-Broadway revue). Best-selling record
  by The Chad Mitchell Trio (Mercury).

25 Minutes To Go
Words and music by Shel Silverstein.
Hollis Music, Inc.
Introduced by Shel Silverstein.

Twist and Shout, see 1960.

Twist, Twist Senora
Words and music by Frank J. Guida, Gene Barge, and Joseph
  Royster.
Rock Masters, Inc.
Best-selling record by Gary "U.S." Bonds (LeGrand).

Twistin' the Night Away
Words and music by Sam Cooke.
Kags Music.
Best-selling record by Sam Cooke (RCA Victor).

Two Lovers
Words and music by William Robinson, Jr.
Jobete Music Co., Inc.
Best-selling record in 1963 by Mary Wells (Motown).

Two of Us
Words and music by Anthony Velona.
Chesnick Music, Inc .
Introduced by Robert Goulet (Columbia).

Unloved, Unwanted
Words and music by Wayne P. Walker and Irene Stanton.
Cedarwood Publishing Co., Inc.
Best-selling record by Kitty Wells (Decca).

Up on the Roof
Words and music by Gerry Goffin and Carole King.
Screen Gems-Columbia Music, Inc.
Best-selling record in 1963 by The Drifters (Atlantic).

Uptown
Words and music by Barry Mann and Cynthia Weil.
Screen Gems-Columbia Music, Inc.
Best-selling record by The Crystals (Philles).

V-A-C-A-T-I-O-N
Words and music by Gary Weston, Hank Hunter, and Connie
    Francis.
John D. MacArthur Music Corp.
Best-selling record by Connie Francis (MGM).

Vespa Song, The
Words by Dusty Negulesco, music by Mario Nascimbene.
Unart Music Corp.
Introduced by Maurice Chevalier in *Jessica* (film).

Wah-Watusi, The
Words by Kal Mann, music by Dave Appell.
Kalmann Music, Inc./Lowe Music Corp.
Best-selling record by The Orlons (Cameo).

Walk in the Black Forest, A (German)
Music by Horst Jankowski.
Blackwood Music, Inc. or M.R.C. Music, Inc. (in litigation).
Original German title, "Eine Schwarzwaldfahrt." Best-selling record
    in 1965 by Horst Jankowski and his Orchestra (Mercury).

Walk Me to the Door
Words and music by Conway Twitty.
Pamper Music, Inc.
Best-selling record in 1963 by Ray Price (Columbia).

Walking Happy
Words by Sammy Cahn, music by James Van Heusen.
Shapiro, Bernstein & Co., Inc., 1962, 1966.
Introduced by Louise Troy, Norman Wisdom, and chorus in *Walking
    Happy* (musical, 1966).

Wall to Wall Love
Words and music by Helen Carter and June Carter.
Acuff-Rose Publications, Inc.
Best-selling record by Bob Gallion (Hickory).

Wanderer, The, see 1960.

Warmer Than a Whisper
Words by Sammy Cahn, music by James Van Heusen.
Chappell & Co., Inc.
Introduced by Dorothy Lamour in *The Road to Hong Kong* (film).

Washington Twist, The
Words and music by Irving Berlin.
Irving Berlin Music Corp.
Introduced by Anita Gillette in *Mr. President* (musical). Introduced
    on records by André Kostelanetz (Columbia).

Watermelon Man
Words and music by Oscar Brown, Jr.
Edward B. Marks Music Corp.
Introduced by Oscar Brown, Jr.

Watermelon Man
Music by Herb Hancock.
Hancock Music Co.
Best-selling record, instrumental, in 1963 by Mongo Santamaria
(Battle).

We Missed You
Words and music by Bill Anderson.
Tree Publishing Co., Inc./Champion Music Corp.
Best-selling record by Kitty Wells (Decca).

What a Country!
Words by Lee Adams, music by Charles Strouse.
Melrose Music Corp.
Introduced by Ray Bolger and chorus in *All American* (musical).

What Are They Doing to Us Now?
Words and music by Harold Rome.
Florence Music Co., Inc.
Introduced by Barbra Streisand, Kelly Brown, James Hickman, Luba
Lisa, Wilma Curley, Pat Turner, and chorus in *I Can Get It for
You Wholesale* (musical).

What Did You Learn in School Today?
Words and music by Tom Paxton.
Teena Music Corp.
Introduced by Tom Paxton.

What Have They Done to the Rain?
Words and music by Malvina Reynolds.
Schroder Music Co., 1962, 1964.
Introduced by Malvina Reynolds. Best-selling record in 1964 by
The Searchers (Kapp).

What Kind of Love Is This?
Words and music by Johnny Nash.
Planetary Music Publishing Corp.
Best-selling record by Joey Dee (Roulette).

What Now My Love (French)
English words by Carl Sigman, French words by P. Dalanoe, music
by Gilbert Becaud.
Éditions Le Rideau Rouge, Paris, France/Remick Music Corp.
Original French title, "Et Maintenant." Introduced in France by
Gilbert Becaud. Best-selling records by Jane Morgan (Kapp) and
in 1966 by Sonny and Cher (Atco) and Herb Alpert and The
Tijuana Brass (A&M).

What's in It for Me?

Words and music by Harold Rome.
Florence Music Co., Inc.
Introduced by Harold Lang and Sheree North in *I Can Get It for You Wholesale* (musical).

Wheels, see 1960.

When I Fall in Love, see 1952.

When I Get Thru with You, You'll Love Me Too

Words and music by Harlan Howard.
Pamper Music, Inc.
Best-selling record by Patsy Cline (Decca).

Where Do You Come From?

Words and music by Ruth Batchelor and Bob Roberts.
Elvis Presley Music, Inc.
Introduced by Elvis Presley in *Girls! Girls! Girls!* (film).

Where I Oughta Be

Words and music by Harlan Howard.
Red River Songs, Inc.
Best-selling record by Skeeter Davis (RCA Victor).

Who Knows?

Words and music by Harold Rome.
Florence Music Co., Inc.
Introduced by Marilyn Cooper in *I Can Get It for You Wholesale* (musical).

Who's Been Cheatin' Who

Words and music by Ned Miller and Sue Miller.
Central Songs, Inc.
Best-selling record by Johnny and Jonie Mosley (Columbia).

Why Do Lovers Break Each Other's Hearts?

Words and music by Ellie Greenwich, Tony Powers, and Phil Spector.
January Music Corp.
Best-selling record by Bob B. Soxx and The Blue Jeans (Philles).

Will You Remember

Words by Dusty Negulesco, music by Marqueritte Monnot.
Unart Music Corp.
Introduced by Maurice Chevalier in *Jessica* (film).

Willie the Weeper

Words and music by Billy Walker and Freddie Hart.
Pamper Music, Inc.
Best-selling record by Billy Walker (Decca).

Willing and Eager
Words and music by Richard Rodgers.
Williamson Music, Inc.
Introduced by Pat Boone and Ann-Margret in *State Fair* (film).

Wishing Star, The, see **Theme from *Taras Bulba*.**

Wolverton Mountain
Words and music by Merle Kilgore and Claude King.
Painted Desert Music Corp.
Adapted from traditional American mountain song. Best-selling
record by Claude King (Columbia).

Wonderful To Be Young
Words by Hal David, music by Burt F. Bacharach.
Famous Music Corp.
Introduced by Cliff Richard in *Wonderful To Be Young* (film).

Wonderful World of the Young, The
Words and music by Sid Tepper and Roy C. Bennett.
Leeds Music Corp.
Best-selling record by Andy Williams (Columbia).

Working for the Man
Words and music by Roy Orbison.
Acuff-Rose Publications, Inc.
Best-selling record by Roy Orbison (Monument).

X-Ray Blues
Music by Ray Charles.
Progressive Music Publishing Co., Inc.
Introduced by Ray Charles and Milt Jackson (Atlantic).

Yesterday's Memories
Words and music by Hank Cochran.
Pamper Music, Inc.
Best-selling record by Eddy Arnold (RCA Victor).

You Beat Me to the Punch
Words and music by William Robinson and Ronald White.
Jobete Music Co., Inc.
Best-selling record by Mary Wells (Motown).

You Belong to Me, see 1952.

You Don't Know Me, see 1955.

You'll Lose a Good Thing
Words and music by Barbara Lynn Ozen.
Jamie Music Publishing Co./Crazy Cajun Music Co.
Best-selling record by Barbara Lynn (Jamie).

You'll Never Get a Better Chance Than This
Words and music by Justin Tubb.
Tree Publishing Co., Inc.
Introduced by Johnny and Jack (Decca).

Young Emotions
Words by Mack David, music by Jerry Livingston.
Nelson Music Publishing Co.
Best-selling record in 1960 by Ricky Nelson (Imperial).

Young World
Words and music by Jerry Fuller.
Four Star Music Co., Inc./Hilliard Music Co.
Best-selling record by Ricky Nelson (Imperial).

Your Used To Be
Words and music by Howard Greenfield and Jack Keller.
Screen Gems-Columbia Music, Inc., 1962, 1963.
Best-selling record by Brenda Lee (Decca).

You're the Reason I'm Living
Words and music by Bobby Darin.
Adaris Music, Inc., 1962, 1963.
Best-selling record in 1963 by Bobby Darin (Capitol).

1963

Abilene
Words and adaptation of music by John Loudermilk, Lester Brown, Bob Gibson, and Albert Stanton.
Acuff-Rose Publications, Inc.
Based on traditional song. Best-selling record by George Hamilton IV (RCA Victor).

Act Naturally
Words by Vonie Morrison, music by Johnny Russell.
Blue Book Music Co.
Best-selling records by Buck Owens (Capitol) and in 1965 by The Beatles (Capitol).

Afrikaan Beat, see 1961.

Ain't Got Time for Nothin'
Words and music by Harlan Howard.
Acuff-Rose Publications, Inc.
Best-selling record by Bob Gallion (Hickory).

Ain't Nothing You Can Do
Words and music by Deadric Malone and Joseph W. Scott.
Don Music Co.
Best-selling record in 1964 by Bobby Bland (Duke).

Ain't That Love?
Words and music by Fred Smith.
Kags Music/Keymen Music.
Best-selling record by Billy Preston (Derby).

Airegin
Music by Sonny Rollins.
Prestige Music Co., Inc., 1963, 1964.
Airegin is "Nigeria" spelled backwards. Jazz instrumental first recorded by Miles Davis, Rollins, Horace Silver, Percy Heath, and Kenny Clarke in 1954 (Prestige).

152

Alice in Wonderland
Words and music by Howard Greenfield and Neil Sedaka.
Screen Gems-Columbia Music, Inc.
Introduced and best-selling record by Neil Sedaka (RCA Victor).

All Cried Out
Words by Buddy Kaye, music by Philip Springer.
Kingsley Music, Inc.
Best-selling record by Dusty Springfield (Philips).

All for You
Words by Anne Croswell, music by Lee Pockriss.
Piedmont Music Co., Inc.
Introduced by Vivien Leigh and Jean Pierre Aumont in *Tovarich*
　(musical).

All I've Got To Do (English)
Words and music by John Lennon and Paul McCartney.
Northern Songs, Ltd., London, England, 1963, 1964/Maclen Music,
　Inc.
Best-selling record by The Beatles (Capitol).

All My Loving (English)
Words and music by John Lennon and Paul McCartney.
Northern Songs, Ltd., London, England, 1963, 1964/Maclen Music,
　Inc.
Introduced and best-selling record in England and United States by
　The Beatles (Capitol).

All the Way Home
Words by Stanley Styne, music by Jule Styne.
Famous Music Corp./Chappell-Styne, Inc.
From *All the Way Home* (film).

Ally, Ally Oxen Free
Words and music by Rod McKuen, Tom Drake, and Steven Yates.
In Music Co.
Introduced by The Kingston Trio (Capitol).

Amen, see Theme from *Lilies of the Field.*

Amy
Words and music by Cynthia Weil and Barry Mann.
Screen Gems-Columbia Music, Inc.
Introduced by Paul Petersen (Colpix).

Anonymous Phone Call
Words by Hal David, music by Burt F. Bacharach.
Famous Music Corp.
Best-selling record by Bobby Vee (Liberty).

Another Bridge To Burn
Words and music by Harlan Howard.
Pamper Music, Inc.
Introduced by Little Jimmy Dickens (Columbia).

Another Saturday Night
Words and music by Sam Cooke.
Kags Music.
Best-selling record by Sam Cooke (RCA Victor).

Antony and Cleopatra Theme
Music by Alex North.
Robbins Music Corp.
Love theme from *Cleopatra* (film).

Anyone Who Had a Heart
Words by Hal David, music by Burt Bacharach.
U. S. Songs, Inc.
Best-selling records in 1964 by Dionne Warwick (Scepter) and in
    England by Cilla Black.

Arm in Arm
Words and music by Meredith Willson.
Frank Music Corp./Rinimer Corp.
Introduced by Janis Paige in *Here's Love* (musical).

As Long As He Needs Me, see 1960.

As Long As There's a Sunday
Words and music by Justin Tubb.
Tree Publishing Co., Inc.
Introduced by Justin Tubb (Groove).

As Usual
Words and music by Alex Zanetis.
Samos Island Music, Inc.
Introduced by Brenda Lee (Decca).

Ask Me Why (English)
Words and music by John Lennon and Paul McCartney.
Dick James Music, Ltd., London, England, 1963, 1964/Concertone
    Songs, Inc.
Best-selling record by The Beatles (Vee Jay and Capitol).

B. J., the D. J.
Words and music by Hugh Lewis.
Cedarwood Publishing Co., Inc.
Best-selling record in 1964 by Stonewall Jackson (Columbia).

Baby, I Love You
Words and music by Phil Spector, Ellie Greenwich, and Jeff Barry.
Mother Bertha Music, Inc./Trio Music Co., Inc.
Introduced and best-selling record by The Ronettes (Philles).

Baby, I'm Gone Again
Words by Shel Silverstein, music by Bob Gibson.
Melody Trials, Inc.

Baby, Workout
Words and music by Alonzo Tucker and Jackie Wilson.
Merrimac Music Corp.
Best-selling record by Jackie Wilson (Brunswick).

Bad Girl
Words and music by Neil Sedaka and Howard Greenfield.
Screen Gems-Columbia Music, Inc.
Best-selling record by Neil Sedaka (RCA Victor).

Bad News
Words and music by John D. Loudermilk.
Acuff-Rose Publications, Inc.
Best-selling record in 1964 by Johnny Cash (Columbia).

Bad to Me (English)
Words and music by John Lennon and Paul McCartney.
Northern Songs, Ltd., London, England/Metric Music Co.
Best-selling record in 1964 by Billy J. Kramer and The Dakotas
(Imperial).

Ballad of Hollis Brown
Words and music by Bob Dylan.
M. Witmark & Sons.
Introduced by Bob Dylan (Columbia).

Be My Baby
Words and music by Jeff Barry, Ellie Greenwich, and Phil Spector.
Trio Music Co., Inc./Mother Bertha Music, Inc.
Best-selling record by The Ronettes (Philles).

Be True to Your School
Words and music by Brian Wilson.
Sea of Tunes Publishing Co.
Introduced by The Beach Boys (Capitol).

Before I Kiss the World Goodbye
Words and music by Howard Dietz and Arthur Schwartz.
Harms, Inc.
Introduced by Mary Martin in *Jennie* (musical).

Before the Parade Passes By
Words and music by Jerry Herman.
Edwin H. Morris & Co., Inc.
Introduced by Carol Channing and company in *Hello, Dolly!* (musi-
cal, 1964).

Begging to You
Words and music by Marty Robbins.
Marty's Music Corp.
Best-selling record by Marty Robbins (Columbia).

Bells, The
Words by Edgar Allen Poe adapted by Phil Ochs, music by Phil Ochs.
Appleseed Music, Inc.
Introduced by Phil Ochs.

Big City Girls
Words and music by Baker Knight.
Four Star Music Co., Inc.
Best-selling record by Carl Belew (RCA Victor).

Big Clown Balloons, The
Words and music by Meredith Willson.
Frank Music Corp./Rinimer Corp.
Introduced by The Paradesters in *Here's Love* (musical).

Bird Is the Word, The
Words and music by Al Frazier, Carl White, Turner Wilson, Jr., and
    John E. Harris.
Beechwood Music Corp.
Best-selling record by The Rivingtons (Liberty).

Blue on Blue
Words by Hal David, music by Burt Bacharach.
Famous Music Corp.
Best-selling record by Bobby Vinton (Epic).

Blue Velvet, see 1951.

Blue Winter
Words and music by Ben Raleigh and John Gluck, Jr.
January Music Corp., 1963, 1964.
Best-selling record by Connie Francis (MGM).

Bluesette
Words by Norman Gimbel, music by Jean Thielemans.
Duchess Music Corp.
Introduced and best-selling record by Jean "Toots" Thielemans (ABC-
    Paramount). Vocal version introduced by Sarah Vaughan (Mer-
    cury).

Boots of Spanish Leather
Words and music by Bob Dylan.
M. Witmark & Sons.
Introduced by Bob Dylan (Columbia).

Born Again
Words and music by Howard Dietz and Arthur Schwartz.
Harms, Inc.
Introduced by Mary Martin, Jack De Lon, and company in *Jennie*
(musical).

Borning Day, The
Words and music by Fred Hellerman and Fran Minkoff.
Appleseed Music, Inc.
Introduced by Harry Belafonte (RCA Victor).

Boss Guitar
Words and music by Duane Eddy and Lee Hazlewood.
Linduane Corp.
Best-selling record by Duane Eddy (RCA Victor).

Bossa Nova Baby
Words and music by Jerry Leiber and Mike Stroller.
Elvis Presley Music, Inc.
From *Fun in Acapulco* (film). Best-selling record by Elvis Presley
(RCA Victor).

Bottle of Wine
Words and music by Tom Paxton.
Deep Fork Music, Inc.
Introduced by Tom Paxton.

Bound for Glory
Words and music by Phil Ochs.
Appleseed Music, Inc.
Song about Woody Guthrie. Introduced by Phil Ochs.

(I Didn't Have To) Break Up Someone's Home
Words and music by Justin Tubb.
Tree Publishing Co., Inc.
Introduced by Kitty Wells (Decca).

Breakfast with the Blues
Words by Martin David, music by Vic McAlpin.
Maricana Music, Inc.
Best-selling record by Hank Snow (RCA Victor).

Burning Memories
Words and music by Mel Tillis and Wayne P. Walker.
Cedarwood Publishing Co., Inc.
Best-selling record in 1964 by Ray Price (Columbia).

Caesar and Cleopatra Theme, see A World of Love.

Cajun Stripper
Words and music by Doug Kershaw and Rusty Kershaw.
Acuff-Rose Publications, Inc.
Introduced by Rusty and Doug Kershaw (RCA Victor).

Call Me Mister Brown
Words and music by Barbara Miller.
Le Jean Music.
Best-selling record by Skeets McDonald (Columbia).

Candy Girl
Words and music by Larry Santos.
Claridge Music, Inc.
Best-selling record by The Four Seasons (Vee Jay).

Canto D'Amore (Song of Love) (Italian)
Italian words by Deni', music by Carlo Rustichelli.
Edizioni CAM, Rome, Italy, 1962/Embassy Music Corp.
From *Divorce—Italian Style* (Italian film).

Charade
Words by Johnny Mercer, music by Henry Mancini.
Southdale Music Corp./Northern Music Corp.
Title song from *Charade* (film). Nominated for Academy Award,
  1963. Best-selling records by Andy Williams (Columbia) and
  Henry Mancini and his Orchestra (RCA Victor).

Chariot, see I Will Follow Him.

Charms
Words and music by Howard Greenfield and Helen Miller.
Screen Gems-Columbia Music, Inc.
Best-selling record by Bobby Vee (Liberty).

Chim Chim Cher-ee
Words and music by Richard M. Sherman and Robert B. Sherman.
Wonderland Music Co., Inc.
Introduced by Dick Van Dyke, Julie Andrews, Karen Dotrice, and
  Matthew Garber in *Mary Poppins* (film). Academy Award-winning
  song, 1964. Best-selling record by The New Christy Minstrels
  (Columbia).

Circumstances
Words and music by Ronnie Self.
Champion Music Corp.
Best-selling record in 1964 by Billy Walker (Columbia).

Ciumachella de Trastevere (Italian)
English words by Carl Sigman, Italian words by Pietro Garinei and
  Sandro Giovannini, music by Armando Trovajoli.
Edizioni Musicali C.A.M., Rome, Italy, 1962/Harms, Inc.
Translation of title, "Ciumachella," "Tender Flower." Original
  Italian version introduced in Italy and, in 1964, in United States
  by Lando Fiorini in *Rugantino* (musical). English version en-
  titled "Tender Flower."

Closing Credits, The
Words and music by Jack Wolf and "Bugs" Bower.
Integrity Music Corp./Nancy Music Co.
Introduced by Robert Goulet (Columbia).

Cold and Lonely (Is the Forecast for Tonight)
Words and music by Roy Botkin.
Forrest Hills Music, Inc./Kitty Wells Publications.
Best-selling record by Kitty Wells (Decca).

Consider Yourself, see 1960.

Cousins, see **The Patty Duke Theme.**

Cowboy Boots
Words and music by Baker Knight.
Four Star Music Co., Inc.
Best-selling record by Dave Dudley (Golden Wing).

Cowboy in the Continental Suit, The
Words and music by Marty Robbins.
Marizona Music.
Best-selling record in 1964 by Marty Robbins (Columbia).

Coyote, My Little Brother
Words and music by Peter La Farge.
United International Copyright Representatives, Ltd.
Introduced by Peter La Farge.

Crabs Walk Sideways
Words and music by Jeff Barry and Art Resnick.
T. M. Music, Inc., 1963, 1964.
Best-selling record by The Wayfarers (RCA Victor).

Cry Baby
Words and music by Norman Meade and Bert Russell.
Robert Mellin, Inc./Rittenhouse Music.
Best-selling record by Garnett Mimms and The Enchanters (United
  Artists).

D. J. for a Day
Words and music by Tom Hall.
Newkeys Music, Inc.
Best-selling record by Jimmy "C" Newman (Decca).

Da Doo Ron Ron (When He Walked Me Home)
Words and music by Jeff Barry, Ellie Greenwich, and Phil Spector.
Trio Music Co., Inc./Mother Bertha Music, Inc.
Best-selling record by The Crystals (Philles).

Dancing
Words and music by Jerry Herman.
Edwin H. Morris & Co., Inc.
Introduced by Carol Channing, Charles Nelson Reilly, Jerry Dodge,
 Sondra Lee, Eileen Brennan, and company in *Hello, Dolly!* (musi-
 cal, 1964).

Danke Schoen (German)
English words by Kurt Schwabach and Milt Gabler, music by Bert
 Kaempfert.
Tonika-Verlag Horst Bussow, Hamburg, Germany, 1962/Roosevelt
 Music Co., Inc.
Best-selling instrumental recording by Bert Kaempfert and his
 Orchestra (Decca); best-selling vocal recording by Wayne Newton
 (Capitol).

Dawn (Go Away)
Words and music by Bob Gaudio and Sandy Linzer
Saturday Music, Inc./Gavadima Music, Inc.
Best-selling record in 1964 by The Four Seasons (Philips).

Days Gone By
Words by Sheldon Harnick, music by Jerry Bock.
Sunbeam Music Corp.
Introduced by Ludwig Donath in *She Loves Me* (musical).

Dead Man's Curve
Words and music by Roger Christian, Jan Berry, Artie Kornfeld,
 and Brian Wilson.
Screen Gems-Columbia Music, Inc.
Best-selling record in 1964 by Jan and Dean (Liberty).

Dear Friend
Words by Sheldon Harnick, music by Jerry Bock.
Sunbeam Music Corp.
Introduced by Barbara Cook in *She Loves Me* (musical).

Denise
Words and music by Neil Levenson.
Bright-Tunes Music Corp.
Best-selling record by Randy and The Rainbows (Rust).

Devil in Disguise, see You're the Devil in Disguise.

Did You Have a Happy Birthday?
Words and music by Paul Anka and Howard Greenfield.
Screen Gems-Columbia Music, Inc.
Introduced by Paul Anka (ABC-Paramount).

Distant Drums
Words and music by Cindy Walker.
Combine Music Corp.
Best-selling record in 1966 by Jim Reeves (RCA Victor).

Do the Bird
Words by Kal Mann, music by Dave Appell.
Kalmann Music, Inc.
Best-selling record by Dee Dee Sharp (Cameo).

Do Wah Diddy Diddy
Words and music by Jeff Barry and Ellie Greenwich.
Trio Music Co., Inc.
Best-selling record in 1964 in England and United States by Manfred Mann (Ascot).

Do You Want To Know a Secret? (English)
Words and music by John Lennon and Paul McCartney.
Northern Songs, Ltd., London, England/Metric Music Co.
Best-selling record in England and in 1964 in United States by The Beatles (Vee Jay and Capitol).

Does Goodnight Mean Goodbye
Words and music by Howard Greenfield, Gerry Goffin, and Jack Keller.
Screen Gems-Columbia Music, Inc.
From *The Victors* (film). Best-selling record by Jane Morgan (Kapp).

Dominique (Belgian)
English words by Noel Regney, French words and music by Soeur Sourire, O.P.
Éditions Primavera, s.a., Brussels, Belgium, 1962/General Music Publishing Co., Inc.
Introduced and best-selling record, in French, by "The Singing Nun," Soeur Sourire, O.P. (Philips). Winner of National Academy of Recording Arts and Sciences Award for "Best Gospel or Other Religious Recording (Musical)," 1963.

Donna the Prima Donna
Words and music by Dion Di Mucci and Ernie Maresca.
Marimba Music Corp.
Introduced and best-selling record by Dion Di Mucci (Columbia).

Don't Be Afraid, Little Darlin'
Words and music by Cynthia Weil and Barry Mann.
Screen Gems-Columbia Music, Inc.
Best-selling record by Steve Lawrence (Columbia).

Don't Bother Me (English)
Words and music by George Harrison.
Jaep Music, Ltd., London, England, 1963, 1964/Jaep Music, Inc.
Best-selling record by The Beatles (Capitol).

Don't Call Me from a Honky Tonk, see 1961.

Don't Hang Up
Words by Kal Mann, music by Dave Appell.
Kalmann Music, Inc.
Best-selling record in 1962 by The Orlons (Cameo).

Don't Make My Baby Blue
Words and music by Cynthia Weil and Barry Mann.
Screen Gems-Columbia Music, Inc.
Introduced by Frankie Laine.

Don't Say Nothin' Bad (About My Baby)
Words and music by Gerry Goffin and Carole King.
Screen Gems-Columbia Music, Inc.
Best-selling record by The Cookies (Dimension).

Don't Take Our Charlie for the Army
Words and music by Noël Coward.
Chappell & Co., Inc.
Introduced by Tessie O'Shea, Sean Scully, and ensemble in *The Girl
Who Came to Supper* (musical).

Don't Think Twice, It's All Right
Words and music by Bob Dylan.
M. Witmark & Sons.
Introduced by Bob Dylan (Columbia). Best-selling record by Peter,
Paul, and Mary (Warner Bros.).

Don't Try To Fight It, Baby
Words and music by Gerry Goffin and Jack Keller.
Screen Gems-Columbia Music, Inc.
Best-selling record by Eydie Gormé (Columbia).

Don't Wait Too Long
Words and music by Sunny Skylar.
Panther Music Corp.
Introduced by Tony Bennett (Columbia).

Don't You Forget It
Words by Al Stillman, music by Henry Mancini.
Northridge Music, Inc.
Adapted from a 1961 instrumental composition by Mancini, entitled
"Tinpanola." Best-selling record by Perry Como (RCA Victor).

Drag City
Words and music by Roger Christian, Jan Berry, and Brian Wilson.
Screen Gems-Columbia Music, Inc.
Introduced by Jan and Dean (Liberty).

Drownin' My Sorrows
Words and music by Hunter Vincent and Bill Justis.
John D. MacArthur Music Corp.
Best-selling record by Connie Francis (MGM).

Dum-De-Da
Words and music by Merle Kilgore and Margie Singleton.
Al Gallico Music Corp.
Best-selling record by Bobby Vinton (Epic).

Easier Said Than Done
Words and music by William Linton and Larry Huff.
Nom Music, Inc.
Best-selling record by The Essex (Roulette).

East Side/West Side, see Theme from *East Side/West Side*.

Easy Come, Easy Go
Words and music by Bill Anderson.
Moss Rose Publications, Inc.
Best-selling record by Bill Anderson (Decca).

Eight Years
Words and music by Don Wayne.
Tree Publishing Co., Inc.
Introduced by Claude Gray (Mercury).

Eight-by-Ten
Words by Bill Anderson, music by Walter Haynes.
Moss Rose Publications, Inc.
Best-selling record by Bill Anderson (Decca).

Eighteen Yellow Roses
Words and music by Bobby Darin.
T. M. Music, Inc.
Best-selling record by Bobby Darin (Capitol).

Elegance
Words and music by Jerry Herman.
Edwin H. Morris & Co., Inc.
Introduced by Eileen Brennan, Charles Nelson Reilly, Sondra Lee, and Jerry Dodge in *Hello, Dolly!* (musical, 1964).

Et Pourtant, see Yet . . . I Know, 1963.

Everybody
Words and music by Tommy Roe.
Low-Twi Music.
Best-selling record by Tommy Roe (ABC-Paramount).

Everything Beautiful Happens at Night
Words by Tom Jones, music by Harvey Schmidt.
Chappell & Co., Inc.
Introduced by George Church, Scooter Teague, Lesley Warren, and Townspeople in *110 in the Shade* (musical).

Expect Things To Happen
Words and music by Meredith Willson.
Frank Music Corp./Rinimer Corp.
Introduced by Laurence Naismith in *Here's Love* (musical).

Farmer's Daughter, The
Words and music by Barry Mann and Cynthia Weil.
Screen Gems-Columbia Music, Inc., 1963, 1964.
From *The Farmer's Daughter* (television series).

Feed the Birds (Tuppence a Bag)
Words and music by Richard M. Sherman and Robert B. Sherman.
Wonderland Music Co., Inc.
Introduced by Julie Andrews and chorus in *Mary Poppins* (film).

Fiesta (German)
Music by Heino Gaze
Ufaton Vorlagsgesellschaft GmbH , Berlin, Germany, 1958/Gil Music
 Corp.
Best-selling record by Lawrence Welk and his Orchestra (Dot).

Fine, Fine Boy, A
Words and music by Phil Spector, Ellie Greenwich, and Jeff Barry.
Mother Bertha Music, Inc./Trio Music Co., Inc.
Introduced and best-selling record by Darlene Love (Philles).

500 Miles Away from Home
Words by Bobby Bare and Hedy West, music by Charlie Williams
 and Hedy West.
Atzal Music, Inc./Central Songs, Inc.
Best-selling record by Bobby Bare (RCA Victor).

Five Little Fingers
Words and music by Bill Anderson.
Moss Rose Publications, Inc.
Best-selling record in 1964 by Bill Anderson (Decca).

Flipper
Words by By Dunham, music by Henry Vars.
Leo Feist, Inc.
From *Flipper's New Adventure* (film, 1964).

Food, Glorious Food, see 1960.

Foolish Little Girl
Words and music by Howard Greenfield and Helen Miller.
Screen Gems-Columbia Music, Inc.
Best-selling record by The Shirelles (Scepter).

Fools Rush In (Where Angels Fear To Tread), see 1940.

For Mama (French)

English words by Don Black, French words by Robert Gall, music by
Charles Aznavour,

Éditions Musicales Charles Aznavour, Paris, France, 1963, 1964/
Ludlow Music, Inc.

Original French title, "La Mamma." Introduced in France by
Charles Aznavour.

For Your Precious Love

Words and music by Arthur Brooks, Richard Brooks, and Jerry
Butler.

Gladstone Music, Inc.

Best-selling record by Garnett Mimms and The Enchanters (United
Artists).

Forget Him (English)

Words and music by Mark Anthony (pseudonym for Tony Hatch).

Welbeck Music, Ltd., London, England/Leeds Music Corp.

Best-selling record by Bobby Rydell (Cameo).

Fort Worth, Dallas or Houston

Words and music by John D. Loudermilk.

Acuff-Rose Publications, Inc.

Best-selling record in 1964 by George Hamilton IV (RCA Victor).

Four Strong Winds

Words and music by Ian Tyson.

M. Witmark & Sons.

Introduced by Ian and Sylvia. Best-selling record in 1964 by Bobby
Bare (RCA Victor).

Frankie and Johnnie

Adaptation of words and music by Sam Cooke.

Kags Music.

Based on traditional song. Best-selling record by Sam Cooke (RCA
Victor).

Friendliest Thing (Two People Can Do), The

Words and music by Ervin Drake.

Harms, Inc.

Introduced by Bernice Massi in *What Makes Sammy Run?* (musical,
1964). First recording by Eydie Gormé (Columbia).

From Me to You (English)

Words and music by John Lennon and Paul McCartney.

Northern Songs, Ltd., London, England/Gil Music Corp.

Best-selling record by The Beatles (Vee Jay).

From Russia with Love (English)

Words and music by Lionel Bart.

United Artists Music, Ltd., London, England/Unart Music Corp.

Title song, introduced by voice of Matt Monro, in *From Russia with
Love* (film).

Gather Your Dreams
Words by Bart Howard, music by Michel Legrand.
United Artists Music Co., Inc.
Adapted from a theme from *Love Is a Ball* (film).

Gegetta
Words and music by George David Weiss and Al Kasha.
Screen Gems-Columbia Music, Inc.
Introduced by James Darren in *Gidget Goes to Rome* (film).

Girl from Ipanema, The (Brazilian)
English words by Norman Gimbel, Portuguese words by Vinicius De
    Moraes, music by Antonio Carlos Jobim.
Antonio Carlos Jobim and Vinicius De Moraes, Brazil/Duchess
    Music Corp.
Original Portuguese title, "Garota de Ipanema." Ipanema is a
    suburb of Rio do Janeiro. First recorded by João Gilberto. Best-
    selling record in 1964 by Stan Getz (saxophone), João Gilberto
    (Portuguese vocal), and Astrud Gilberto (English vocal) (Verve).
    Winner of National Academy of Recording Arts and Sciences
    Award for "Record of the Year," 1964.

Girl from Spanish Town, The
Words and music by Marty Robbins.
Marty's Music Corp.
Best-selling record by Marty Robbins (Columbia).

Give Us Your Blessing
Words and music by Jeff Barry and Ellie Greenwich.
Trio Music Co., Inc.
Best-selling record in 1965 by The Shangri-Las (Red Bird).

Glad All Over (English)
Words and music by Dave Clark and Mike Smith.
Ivy Music, Ltd., London, England/Campbell-Connelly, Inc.
Best-selling record in 1964 in England and United States by The
    Dave Clark Five (Epic).

Go Now
Words and music by Larry Banks and Milton Bennett.
Trio Music Co., Inc.
First recording by Bessie Banks (Red Bird). Best-selling record in
    1964-65 by The Moody Blues (London).

Going through the Motions of Living
Words and music by Jean Chapel and Bob Tubert.
Regent Music Corp.
Best-selling record by Sonny James (Capitol).

Gonna Be Another Hot Day
Words by Tom Jones, music by Harvey Schmidt.
Chappell & Co., Inc.
Introduced by Stephen Douglass and Townspeople in *110 in the Shade*
(musical).

Gonna Send You Back to Georgia (A City Slick), also known as
Gonna Send You Back to Walker
Words and music by Johnnie Mathews and Jake Hammonds, Jr.
Zann Music, Inc.
Best-selling record by The Animals (MGM).

Gonna Send You Back to Walker, see **Gonna Send You Back to
Georgia (A City Slick)**.

Good Life, The (French)
Words by Jack Reardon, music by Sacha Distel.
Diffusion Musicales Française, Paris, France, 1962/Paris Music
Co., Inc.
Melody introduced on soundtrack of *The Seven Capital Sins* (French
film). First recording by Kathy Keegan (Malibu); best-selling
record by Tony Bennett (Columbia).

Goodbye My Lover, Goodbye
Words and music by Robert Mosley, Lamar Simington, and Leroy
Swearingen.
Sea-Lark Enterprises, Inc.
Best-selling record in 1965 by The Searchers (Kapp).

Gotta Move
Words and music by Peter Matz.
Columbine Music Corp.
Introduced by Barbra Streisand (Columbia).

Grand Knowing You
Words by Sheldon Harnick, music by Jerry Bock.
Sunbeam Music Corp.
Introduced by Jack Cassidy in *She Loves Me* (musical).

Grande Luna Italiana (Gidget's Roman Moon)
Words and music by George David Weiss and Al Kasha.
Screen Gems-Columbia Music, Inc.
Introduced by James Darren in *Gidget Goes to Rome* (film).

Grass Is Greener, The
Words and music by Barry Mann and Mike Anthony.
Screen Gems-Columbia Music, Inc.
Best-selling record by Brenda Lee (Decca).

Great Escape March, The
Words by Al Stillman, music by Elmer Bernstein.
United Artists Music Co., Inc.
From *The Great Escape* (film).

Green, Green
Words and music by Barry McGuire and Randy Sparks.
New Christy Music Publishing Co.
Based on fragments of traditional material. Introduced and best-selling record by The New Christy Minstrels (Columbia).

Guantanamera (Cuban)
Spanish words by José Marti, adaptation of music by Pete Seeger and Hector Angulo.
Fall River Music, Inc.
From poem by Cuban revolutionary writer, José Marti. Introduced by Pete Seeger. Best-selling record in 1966 by The Sandpipers (A&M).

Guilty, also known as Guilty of Loving You
Words and music by Alex Zanetis.
Samos Island Music, Inc./Tuckahoe Music, Inc.
Best-selling record by Jim Reeves (RCA Victor).

Guilty of Loving You, see Guilty.

Half a Sixpence (English)
Words and music by David Heneker.
Britannia Music Co., Ltd., London, England/Chappell & Co., Inc.
Introduced by Tommy Steele and Polly James in New York production (1965) of *Half a Sixpence* (musical).

Half the Battle
Words by Sidney Michaels, music by Mark Sandrich, Jr.
Morley Music Co., Inc., 1963, 1964.
Introduced by Robert Preston, Jerry Schaefer, Franklin Kiser, and Bob Kaliban in *Ben Franklin in Paris* (musical, 1964).

Hallelujah! (Alleluia!) (Belgian)
English words by Noel Regney, French words and music by Soeur Sourire, O.P.
Éditions Primavera, s.a., Brussels, Belgium, 1962/General Music Publishing Co., Inc.
Introduced by "The Singing Nun," Soeur Sourire, O.P. (Philips).

Happy To Be Unhappy, see 1961.

Hard Rain's A-Gonna Fall
Words and music by Bob Dylan.
M. Witmark & Sons.
Introduced by Bob Dylan (Columbia).

Haunting
Music by Lalo Schifrin.
Hastings Music Corp.
"Inspired" by *The Haunting* (film).

He Was My Brother
Words and music by Paul Simon.
Edward B. Marks Music Corp.
Introduced in 1964 by Simon and Garfunkel (Columbia).

Heart, Be Careful
Words and music by Jay Bovington and Billy Walker.
Cedarwood Publishing Co., Inc.
Best-selling record by Billy Walker (Columbia).

Heat Wave
Words and music by Eddie Holland, Brian Holland, and Lamont
    Dozier.
Jobete Music Co., Inc.
Best-selling record by Martha and The Vandellas (Gordy).

Hello, Dolly!
Words and music by Jerry Herman.
Edwin H. Morris & Co., Inc.
Introduced by Carol Channing and company in *Hello, Dolly!* (musical, 1964). Best-selling record in 1964-65 by Louis Armstrong (Kapp). Winner of National Academy of Recording Arts and Sciences Awards for "Best Song of the Year" and "Best Male Vocal Performance," 1964. Subject of legal dispute in which the writer and publishers of the song, "Sunflower" (see 1948) claimed that the "Hello, Dolly!" melody was an infringement of their copyright. Case settled out of court.

Hello Heartache, Goodbye, Love
Words and music by Hugo Peretti, Luigi Creatore, and George
    David Weiss.
Atrium Music Corp.
Introduced by Little Peggy March (RCA Victor).

Hello Little Girl (English)
Words and music by John Lennon and Paul McCartney.
Northern Songs, Ltd., London, England/Maclen Music, Inc.
Introduced by The Beatles.

Hello Mudduh, Hello Fadduh (A Letter from Camp)
Words by Allan Sherman, musical adaptation by Lou Busch.
Curtain Call Productions, Inc.
Music based on "Dance of the Hours," by Ponchielli. Best-selling record by Allan Sherman (Warner Bros.). Winner of National Academy of Recording Arts and Sciences Award for "Best Comedy Performance," 1963.

Hello Stranger
Words and music by Barbara Lewis.
McLaughlin Publishing Co./Cotillion Music, Inc.
Best-selling record by Barbara Lewis (Atlantic).

Here and Now
Words and music by Noël Coward.
Chappell & Co., Inc.
Introduced by Florence Henderson in *The Girl Who Came to Supper* (musical).

Here's Love
Words and music by Meredith Willson.
Frank Music Corp./Rinimer Corp.
Introduced by Laurence Naismith, Craig Stevens, and chorus in *Here's Love* (musical).

He's a Bad Boy
Words and music by Gerry Goffin and Carole King.
Screen Gems-Columbia Music, Inc.
Introduced by Carole King (Dimension).

He's My Friend
Words and music by Meredith Willson.
Frank Music Corp./Rinimer Corp.
Introduced by Harve Presnell in *The Unsinkable Molly Brown* (film, 1964).

Hey, Girl
Words and music by Gerry Goffin and Carole King.
Screen Gems-Columbia Music, Inc.
Best-selling record by Freddie Scott (Colpix).

Hey Little Cobra
Words and music by Marshal Howard Connors (pseudonym for Marshal Kleinbard) and Carol Connors (pseudonym for Annette Kleinbard).
T.M. Music, Inc./Daywin Music, Inc., 1963, 1964.
Best-selling record in 1964 by The Rip Chords (Columbia).

Hey Little Girl
Words and music by Curtis Mayfield.
Curtom Publishing Co., Inc./Jalynne Corp.
Best-selling record by Major Lance (Okeh).

Hey Nelly Nelly
Words and music by Shel Silverstein and Jim Friedman.
Hollis Music, Inc.
Introduced by Shel Silverstein.

Hey There, Lonely Boy
Words by Earl Shuman, music by Leon Carr.
Famous Music Corp.
Best-selling record by Ruby and The Romantics (Kapp).

Hobo Flats
Words and music by Oliver Nelson.
Noslen Music Co.
Best-selling record, instrumental, by Jimmy Smith (Verve).

Hold Me Tight (English)
Words and music by John Lennon and Paul McCartney.
Northern Songs, Ltd., London, England, 1963, 1964/Maclen Music,
   Inc.
Best-selling record by The Beatles (Capitol).

Honolulu Lulu
Words and music by Jan Berry, Roger Christian, and Spunky.
Screen Gems-Columbia Music, Inc.
Best-selling record by Jan and Dean (Liberty).

Hootenanny Saturday Night
Words by Alfred Uhry, music by Richard Lewine.
Saunders Publications, Inc.
Theme from *Hootenanny* (television series).

Hot Pastrami
Words and music by Dessie Rozier.
Sherlyn Publishing Co.
Best-selling record by The Dartells (Dot).

How Insensitive (Insensatez) (Brazilian)
English words by Norman Gimbel, Portuguese words by Vinicius
   de Moraes, music by Antonio Carlos Jobim.
Antonio Carlos Jobim and Vinicius de Moraes, Brazil, 1963, 1964/
   Duchess Music Corp.
Best-selling record by Astrud Gilberto (Verve).

How Much Can a Lonely Heart Stand
Words and music by Sandra Rhodes.
Tree Publishing Co., Inc.
Introduced by Skeeter Davis (RCA Victor).

I Adore Him
Words and music by Jan Berry and Art Kornfeld.
Screen Gems-Columbia Music, Inc.
Best-selling record by The Angels (Smash).

I Call Your Name (English)
Words and music by John Lennon and Paul McCartney.
Northern Songs, Ltd., London, England/Maclen Music, Inc.
Best-selling record by The Beatles (Capitol).

I Can't Stay Mad at You
Words and music by Gerry Goffin and Carole King.
Screen Gems-Columbia Music, Inc.
Best-selling record by Skeeter Davis (RCA Victor).

I Could Go On Singing
Words by E.Y. Harburg, music by Harold Arlen.
Harwin Music Corp.
Introduced by Judy Garland in *I Could Go On Singing* (film).

I Don't Care Much
Words by Fred Ebb, music by John Kander.
Sunbeam Music Corp.
Introduced by Barbra Streisand (Columbia).

I Go to Bed
Words by Anne Croswell, music by Lee Pockriss.
Piedmont Music Co., Inc.
Introduced by Jean Pierre Aumont in *Tovarich* (musical).

I Know the Feeling
Words by Anne Croswell, music by Lee Pockriss.
Piedmont Music Co., Inc.
Introduced by Vivien Leigh in *Tovarich* (musical).

I Love To Laugh
Words and music by Richard M. Sherman and Robert B. Sherman.
Wonderland Music Co., Inc.
Introduced by Ed Wynn, Julie Andrews, and Dick Van Dyke in *Mary Poppins* (film).

(P.S.) I Love You (English)
Words and music by John Lennon and Paul McCartney.
Ardmore and Beechwood, Ltd., London, England/Beechwood Music Corp.
Best-selling record by The Beatles (Capitol).

I Love You More and More Every Day
Words and music by Don Robertson.
Don Robertson Music Corp.
Best-selling record in 1964 by Al Martino (Capitol).

I Only Want To Be With You (English)
Words and music by Mike Hawker and Ivor Raymonde.
Springfield Music, Ltd., London, England/Chappell & Co., Inc.
Best-selling record in 1964 by Dusty Springfield (Philips).

I Put My Hand In
Words and music by Jerry Herman.
Edwin H. Morris & Co., Inc.
Introduced by Carol Channing and company in *Hello, Dolly!* (musical, 1964).

I Saw Her Standing There (English)
Words and music by John Lennon and Paul McCartney.
Northern Songs, Ltd., London, England/Gil Music Corp.
Best-selling record in 1964 by The Beatles (Capitol and Vee Jay).

I Saw Me
Words and music by June Davis.
Mixer Music/Glad Music Co.
Best-selling record by George Jones (United Artists).

I Stayed Too Long at the Fair, see 1957.

I Still Look at You That Way
Words and music by Howard Dietz and Arthur Schwartz.
Harms, Inc.
Introduced by Mary Martin in *Jennie* (musical).

I Wanna Be Around, see 1959.

I Wanna Be Your Man (English)
Words and music by John Lennon and Paul McCartney.
Northern Songs, Ltd., London, England/Gil Music Corp.
Best-selling record by The Rolling Stones (London).

I Want To Hold Your Hand (English)
Words and music by John Lennon and Paul McCartney.
Northern Songs, Ltd., London, England/Duchess Music Corp.
Introduced and best-selling record in England and in 1964 in United
   States by The Beatles (Capitol).

I Want To Stay Here
Words and music by Gerry Goffin and Carole King.
Screen Gems-Columbia Music, Inc.
Best-selling record by Steve Lawrence and Eydie Gormé (Columbia).

I Will Follow Him, also known as **I Will Follow You** (French)
English words by Norman Gimbel and Arthur Altman, French words
   by Jacques Plante, music by J. W. Stole and Del Roma.
Les Éditions Jacques Plante, Paris, France, 1962, 1963/Leeds Music
   Corp.
Best-selling record by Little Peggy March (RCA Victor). Original
   French title, "Chariot."

I Will Follow You, see **I Will Follow Him.**

I Will Love You
Words and music by Shelby Flint and Barry De Vorzon.
Sherman-De Vorzon Music Corp.
Best-selling record in 1962 by Richard Chamberlain (MGM).

I'd Do Anything, see 1960.

If I Had a Hammer, see 1958.

If I Ruled the World (English)
Words by Leslie Bricusse, music by Cyril Ornadel.
Delfont Music, London, England/Chappell & Co., Ltd., London,
   England/Chappell & Co., Inc.
Introduced by Harry Secombe in London and United States (1964-
   65) productions of *Pickwick* (musical). Best-selling record by
   Tony Bennett (Columbia).

If It Pleases You
Words and music by Wayne P. Walker.
Cedarwood Publishing Co., Inc.
Best-selling record in 1965 by Billy Walker (Columbia).

If the Rain's Got To Fall (English)
Words and music by David Heneker.
Britannia Music Co., Ltd., London, England/Chappell & Co., Inc.
  1963, 1965.
Introduced by Tommy Steele, Grover Dale, Will Mackenzie, Norman
  Allen, and Shopgirls in New York production (1965) of *Half a
  Sixpence* (musical).

If You Need Me
Words and music by Wilson Pickett, Robert Bateman, and Sonny
  Sanders.
Cotillion Music, Inc./Lupine Music.
Best-selling record by Solomon Burke (Atlantic).

I'll Be on My Way (English)
Words and music by John Lennon and Paul McCartney.
Northern Songs, Ltd., London, England/Metric Music Co.
Best-selling record by Billy J. Kramer and The Dakotas (Liberty).

I'll Get You (English)
Words and music by John Lennon and Paul McCartney.
Northern Songs, Ltd., London, England/Maclen Music, Inc.
Best-selling record by The Beatles (Capitol).

I'll Keep You Satisfied (English)
Words and music by John Lennon and Paul McCartney.
Northern Songs, Ltd., London, England/Metric Music Co.
Best-selling record in 1964 by Billy J. Kramer (Imperial).

I'll Remember Her
Words and music by Noël Coward.
Chappell & Co., Inc.
Introduced by José Ferrer in *The Girl Who Came to Supper* (musi-
  cal).

I'll Take You Home
Words and music by Cynthia Weil and Barry Mann.
Screen Gems-Columbia Music, Inc.
Best-selling record by The Drifters (Atlantic).

Ilona
Words by Sheldon Harnick, music by Jerry Bock.
Sunbeam Music Corp.
Introduced by Jack Cassidy in *She Loves Me* (musical).

I'm a Woman, see 1961.

I'm Gonna Be Strong
Words and music by Barry Mann and Cynthia Weil.
Screen Gems-Columbia Music, Inc.
Best-selling record by Gene Pitney (Musicor).

I'm the Lonely One (English)
Words and music by Gordon Mills.
Eugene Music, Ltd., London, England/Duchess Music Corp.
Best-selling record in 1964 in England and United States by Cliff
   Richard (Epic).

In Dreams
Words and music by Roy Orbison.
Acuff-Rose Publications, Inc.
Best-selling record by Roy Orbison (Monument).

In the Summer of His Years (English)
Words by Herbert Kretzmer, music by David Lee.
Leeds Music, Ltd., London, England/Leeds Music Corp.
Written as a tribute to the late President John F. Kennedy. In-
   troduced by Millicent Martin on *That Was the Week That Was*
   (BBC television series). Best-selling record by Millicent Martin
   (ABC-Paramount).

Is It Really Me?
Words by Tom Jones, music by Harvey Schmidt.
Chappell & Co., Inc.
Introduced by Inga Swenson and Robert Horton in *110 in the Shade*
   (musical).

Is It Really Over
Words and music by Jim Reeves.
Tuckahoe Music, Inc.
Best-selling record in 1965 by Jim Reeves (RCA Victor).

Is This Me?
Words and music by Bill West and Dottie West.
Window Music Publishers/Open Road Music, Inc.
Best-selling record by Jim Reeves (RCA Victor).

It Only Takes a Moment
Words and music by Jerry Herman.
Edwin H. Morris & Co., Inc.
Introduced by Charles Nelson Reilly, Eileen Brennan, and company
   in *Hello, Dolly!* (musical, 1964).

It Takes a Woman
Words and music by Jerry Herman.
Edwin H. Morris & Co., Inc.
Introduced by David Burns and company in *Hello, Dolly!* (musical,
   1964).

It Won't Be Long (English)
Words and music by John Lennon and Paul McCartney.
Northern Songs, Ltd., London, England, 1963, 1964/Maclen Music,
    Inc.
Best-selling record by The Beatles (Capitol).

It's a Mad, Mad, Mad, Mad World
Words by Mack David, music by Ernest Gold.
United Artists Music Co., Inc.
From *It's a Mad, Mad, Mad, Mad World* (film). Nominated for
    Academy Award, 1963.

It's All in the Game, see 1951.

It's All Right!
Words and music by Curtis Mayfield.
Curtom Publishing Co., Inc.
Best-selling record by The Impressions (ABC-Paramount).

It's in His Kiss, see **The Shoop, Shoop Song.**

It's My Party
Words and music by Herb Wiener, Wally Gold, and John Gluck, Jr.
Arch Music Co., Inc.
Best-selling record by Lesley Gore (Mercury).

It's Too Late
Words and music by Wilson Pickett.
Correct-Tone Publishing Co.
Best-selling record by Wilson Pickett (Double L).

I've Been Invited to a Party
Words and music by Noël Coward.
Chappell & Co., Inc.
Introduced by Florence Henderson in *The Girl Who Came to Supper*
    (musical).

Jazz 'n' Samba (So Danco Samba), also known as **Jazz Samba**
    (Brazilian)
English words by Norman Gimbel, Portuguese words and music by
    Antonio Carlos Jobim and Vinicius de Moraes.
Edizioni Suvini Zerboni, Milan, Italy/Ludlow Music, Inc.
Featured in *Copacabana Palace* (Italian film).

Jazz Samba, see **Jazz 'n' Samba.**

Jolly Holiday
Words and music by Richard M. Sherman and Robert B. Sherman.
Wonderland Music Co., Inc.
Introduced by Dick Van Dyke and Julie Andrews in *Mary Poppins*
    (film).

Judy's Turn To Cry
Words by Edna Lewis, music by Beverly Ross.
Glamorous Music, Inc.
Best-selling record by Lesley Gore (Mercury).

Just One Look
Words and music by Gregory Carroll and Doris Payne.
Premier Music Publishing Co.
Best-selling record by Doris Troy (Atlantic).

Keeping Up with the Joneses
Words and music by Justin Tubb.
Tree Publishing Co., Inc.
Best-selling record in 1964 by Margie Singleton and Faron Young
  (Mercury).

Kentucky Bluebird, see **Message to Michael.**

Kind of Boy You Can't Forget, The
Words and music by Jeff Barry and Ellie Greenwich.
Trio Music Co., Inc.
Best-selling record by The Raindrops (Jubilee). "The Raindrops" is
  pseudonym for multiply-recorded voices of Jeff Barry and Ellie
  Greenwich.

Kiss Me No Kisses
Words and music by Ervin Drake.
Harms, Inc.
Introduced by Sally Ann Howes in *What Makes Sammy Run?*
  (musical, 1964).

La Donna nel Mondo (Italian)
Music by Riz Ortolani.
Ed. Mus. C.A.M., Rome, Italy/Edward B. Marks Music Corp.
From *Women of the World* (Italian film).

Land of a Thousand Dances
Words and music by Chris Kenner.
Tune-Kel Publishing Co., Inc.
Best-selling records in 1963 by Kris Kenner (Instant) and in 1965
  by Round Robin (Domain) and Cannibal and The Headhunters
  (Rampart).

Last Day in the Mines
Words and music by Jimmy Key.
Newkeys Music, Inc.
Best-selling record in 1964 by Dave Dudley (Mercury).

Laughing Boy
Words and music by William Robinson.
Jobete Music Co., Inc.
Best-selling record by Mary Wells (Motown).

Let's Go Fly a Kite
Words and music by Richard M. Sherman and Robert B. Sherman.
Wonderland Music Co., Inc.
Introduced by Dick Van Dyke and David Tomlinson in *Mary Poppins* (film).

Let's Go Steady Again
Words and music by Howard Greenfield and Neil Sedaka.
Screen Gems-Columbia Music, Inc.
Best-selling record by Neil Sedaka (RCA Victor).

Let's Invite Them Over
Words and music by Onie Wheeler.
Glad Music Co.
Best-selling record by George Jones and Melba Montgomery (United Artists).

Let's Turkey Trot
Words and music by Gerry Goffin and Jack Keller.
Screen Gems-Columbia Music, Inc.
Best-selling record by Little Eva (Dimension).

Life I Lead, The
Words and music by Richard M. Sherman and Robert B. Sherman.
Wonderland Music Co., Inc.
Introduced by David Tomlinson in *Mary Poppins* (film).

Lights of Roma, The, see Roma, Nun Fa' la Stupida Stasera.

Little Bird
Words by Tommy Wolf, music by Dick Grove and Pete Jolly.
Wolf-Mills Music, Inc.
Introduced by The Pete Jolly Trio (Ava).

Little Boy, The
Words by Al Stillman, music by Guy Wood.
Edwin H. Morris & Co., Inc.
Introduced by Tony Bennett (Columbia).

Little Child (English)
Words and music by John Lennon and Paul McCartney.
Northern Songs, Ltd., London, England, 1963, 1964/Maclen Music, Inc.
Introduced and best-selling record by The Beatles (Capitol).

Lock, Stock and Teardrops
Words and music by Roger Miller.
Tree Publishing Co., Inc.
Introduced by Roger Miller (RCA Victor).

Locking Up My Heart
Words and music by Brian Holland, Lamont Dozier, and Eddie Holland.
Jobete Music Co., Inc.
Best-selling record by The Marvelettes (Tamla).

London (Is a Little Bit of All Right)
Words and music by Noël Coward.
Chappell & Co., Inc.
Introduced by Tessie O'Shea, Sean Scully, and ensemble in *The Girl Who Came to Supper* (musical).

Look Again, see Theme from *Irma la Douce.*

Look for Small Pleasures
Words by Sidney Michaels, music by Mark Sandrich, Jr.
Morley Music Co., Inc., 1963, 1964.
Introduced by Robert Preston and Ulla Sallert in *Ben Franklin in Paris* (musical, 1964).

Look, Little Girl
Words and music by Meredith Willson.
Frank Music Corp./Rinimer Corp.
Introduced by Craig Stevens, and reprised by Janis Paige, in *Here's Love* (musical).

Losing You (French)
English words by Carl Sigman, French words by Pierre Havet, music by Jean Renard.
Romantic Music Corp., Paris, France, 1961, 1963/BNP Music Publishing Co.
Best-selling record by Brenda Lee (Decca). Original French title, "Un Ange Est Venu."

Louie Louie
Words and music by Richard Berry.
Limax Music, Inc.
Best-selling records in 1963-64 by The Kingsmen (Wand) and in 1964 by Paul Revere and The Raiders (Columbia).

Love, Don't Turn Away
Words by Tom Jones, music by Harvey Schmidt.
Chappell & Co., Inc., 1963, 1964.
Introduced by Inga Swenson in *110 in the Shade* (musical).

Love in the Country, see McLintock's Theme.

Love Is a Ball
Words by Richard Adler, music by Michel Legrand.
United Artists Music Co., Inc.
Adapted from title theme from *Love Is a Ball* (film).

Love Is Like a Heat Wave
Words and music by Lamont Dozier, Brian Holland, and Eddie
    Holland.
Jobete Music Co., Inc.
Best-selling record by Martha and The Vandellas (Gordy).

Love Looks Good on You
Words and music by Jerry Shook.
Sure-Fire Music Co., Inc.
Best-selling record in 1965 by Lefty Frizzell (Columbia).

Love Me Do (English)
Words and music by John Lennon and Paul McCartney.
Ardmore and Beechwood, Ltd., London, England, 1962/Beechwood
    Music Corp.
Introduced and best-selling record in England and in 1964 in United
    States by The Beatles (Tollie).

Love Me Tender, see 1956.

Love of My Man, The
Words and music by Ed Townsend.
Sylvia Music Publishing Co., Inc.
Best-selling record by Theola Kilgore (Serock).

Love of the Loved (English)
Words and music by John Lennon and Paul McCartney.
Northern Songs, Ltd., London, England/Maclen Music, Inc.
Introduced in England by Cilla Black (Parlaphone).

Love She Can Count On, A
Words and music by William Robinson.
Jobete Music Co., Inc.
Best-selling record by The Miracles (Tamla).

Love with the Proper Stranger
Words by Johnny Mercer, music by Elmer Bernstein.
Paramount Music Corp.
Introduced by Jack Jones on soundtrack of *Love with the Proper
    Stranger* (film, 1964). Best-selling record by Jack Jones (Kapp).

Love's Gonna Live Here Again
Words and music by Buck Owens.
Blue Book Music Co.
Best-selling record by Buck Owens (Capitol).

Lucky Lips, see 1957.

McLintock's Theme (Love in the Country)
Words and music by Frank De Vol and By Dunham.
Unart Music Corp.
From *McLintock!* (film).

Magda's Song
Words by Freddy Douglass, music by Sol Kaplan.
Screen Gems-Columbia Music, Inc.
From *The Victors* (film).

Magic Star, see **Telstar,** 1962.

Make the World Go Away
Words and music by Hank Cochran.
Pamper Music, Inc.
Best-selling records by Timi Yuro (Liberty), Ray Price (Columbia),
    and in 1965 by Eddy Arnold (RCA Victor).

Man and a Woman, A
Words by Tom Jones, music by Harvey Schmidt.
Chappell & Co., Inc.
Introduced by Inga Swenson and Stephen Douglass in *110 in the
    Shade* (musical).

Man from the Diners' Club, The
Words by Johnny Lehmann, music by Steve Lawrence.
Gower Music, Inc.
Introduced by voice of Steve Lawrence on soundtrack of *The Man
    from the Diners' Club* (film).

March of the Victors
Words by Freddy Douglass, music by Sol Kaplan.
Screen Gems-Columbia Music, Inc.
From *The Victors* (film).

Maria Elena, see 1941.

Marlena
Words and music by Bob Gaudio.
Claridge Music, Inc.
Best-selling record by The Four Seasons (Vee Jay).

Masters of War
Words and music by Bob Dylan.
M. Witmark & Sons.
Introduced by Bob Dylan (Columbia).

Matador, The
Words and music by Johnny Cash and June Carter.
Johnny Cash Music, Inc.
Best-selling record by Johnny Cash (Columbia).

May Each Day
Words and music by Mort Green and George Wyle.
Barnaby Music Corp.
Introduced by Andy Williams (Columbia).

Maybe He'll Come Back to Me
Words and music by Larry Kolber and Jack Keller.
Screen Gems-Columbia Music, Inc.
Introduced by Patti Page.

Maybe Some Other Time
Words and music by Ervin Drake.
Harms, Inc.
Introduced by Robert Alda and Sally Ann Howes in *What Makes Sammy Run?* (musical, 1964).

Me
Words and music by Alex Zanetis.
Acclaim Music, Inc./Samos Island Music, Inc.
Best-selling record in 1964 by Bill Anderson (Decca).

Mean Woman Blues
Words and music by Jerry West and Whispering Smith.
Excellorec Music Co.
Best-selling record by Roy Orbison (Monument).

Mecca
Words and music by Neval Nader and John Gluck, Jr.
January Music Corp.
Best-selling record by Gene Pitney (Musicor).

Meditation (Meditacão) (Brazilian)
English words by Norman Gimbel, Portuguese words by Newton Mendonca, music by Antonio Carlos Jobim.
Antonio Carlos Jobim and Mrs. Newton Mendonca, Brazil, 1962, 1963/Duchess Music Corp.
First recording in English by Pat Boone (Dot).

Message to Michael, also known as Kentucky Bluebird
Words and music by Burt Bacharach and Hal David.
U.S. Songs, Inc.
Best-selling record in 1966 by Dionne Warwick (Scepter).

Mexican Pearls
Words and music by Don Randi and Joe Mikolas.
Englewood Publications, Inc.
Best-selling record, instrumental, in 1965 by Billy Vaughn and his Orchestra (Dot).

Mickey's Monkey
Words and music by Lamont Dozier, Brian Holland, and Eddie Holland.
Jobete Music Co., Inc.
Best-selling record by The Miracles (Tamla).

Midnight Mary
Words and music by Art Wayne and Ben Raleigh.
Jimskip Music, Inc.
Best-selling record by Jerry Cole (Capitol).

Mighty Sons of Hercules, The
Words and music by Leonard Whitcup, Ted Lehrman, and Peter
  Reiner.
Luristan Music, Inc.
Theme from *Sons of Hercules* (television series).

Millie's Theme
Music by Michel Legrand.
United Artists Music Co., Inc.
A theme from *Love Is a Ball* (film).

Minute You're Gone, The
Words and music by Jimmy Gateley.
Regent Music Corp.
Best-selling record by Sonny James (Capitol).

Misery (English)
Words and music by John Lennon and Paul McCartney.
Northern Songs, Ltd., London, England/Gil Music Corp.
Best-selling record by The Beatles (Vee Jay).

Mr. Wishing Well
Words and music by Laurence Weiss and Lockie Edwards, Jr.
Screen Gems-Columbia Music, Inc.
Introduced by Nat "King" Cole.

Mockingbird
Words and music by Inez Foxx and Charlie Foxx.
Saturn Music, Inc.
Best-selling record by Inez Foxx (Symbol).

Money To Burn (English)
Words and music by David Heneker.
Britannia Music Co., Ltd., London, England/Chappell & Co., Inc.
Introduced by Tommy Steele, Eleanore Treiber, and The Men in
  New York production (1965) of *Half a Sixpence* (musical).

Monkey Time, The
Words and music by Curtis Mayfield.
Curtom Publishing Co., Inc./Nicolet Music.
Best-selling record by Major Lance (Okeh).

More (Theme from *Mondo Cane*) (Italian)
English words by Norman Newell, Italian words by M. Ciorciolini,
  music by Riz Ortolani and N. Oliviero.
Ed. C.A.M., Rome, Italy, 1962/Ardmore and Beechwood, Ltd.,
  London, England/Edward B. Marks Music Corp.
Adapted from a theme from *Mondo Cane* (Italian documentary film)
  and interpolated by Kathina Ortolani on soundtrack of film after
  its release in United States. Nominated for Academy Award, 1963.
  First recording and best-selling vocal recording by Danny Williams
  (United Artists). Best-selling instrumental recording by Kai
  Winding (Verve). Winner of National Academy of Recording
  Arts and Sciences Award for "Best Instrumental Theme," 1963.

Motherhood March, The
Words and music by Jerry Herman.
Edwin H. Morris & Co., Inc.
Introduced by Carol Channing, Eileen Brennan, and Sondra Lee in
  Hello, Dolly! (musical, 1964).

Mountain of Love
Words and music by Laura Martin and Venita Del Rio.
Al Gallico Music Corp.
Best-selling record by David Houston (Epic).

Move Over, Darling
Words and music by Joe Lubin, Hal Kanter, and Terry Melcher.
Daywin Music, Inc.
Introduced by Doris Day in *Move Over, Darling* (film).

My Boyfriend's Back
Words and music by Robert Feldman, Gerald Goldstein, and Richard
  Gottehrer.
Blackwood Music, Inc.
Best-selling record by The Angels (Smash).

My First Lonely Night, see Sukiyaki.

My Heart Skips a Beat
Words and music by Buck Owens.
Blue Book Music Co.
Best-selling record in 1964 by Buck Owens (Capitol).

My Home Town
Words and music by Ervin Drake.
Harms, Inc.
Introduced by Steve Lawrence in *What Makes Sammy Run?* (musi-
  cal, 1964).

My Special Dream, see Theme from *The Victors*.

My State, My Kansas, My Home, see 1961.

My Summer Love
Words by Bob Hilliard, music by Mort Garson.
Rosewood Music Corp./Day Music Co./Bob Hilliard Music Co.
Best-selling record by Ruby and The Romantics (Kapp).

My Tears Are Overdue
Words and music by Freddie Hart.
Central Songs, Inc.
Best-selling record by George Jones (United Artists).

My Whole World Is Falling Down
Words and music by Bill Anderson and Jerry Crutchfield.
Moss Rose Publications, Inc./Champion Music Corp.
Best-selling record by Brenda Lee (Decca).

My Wish
Words and music by Meredith Willson.
Frank Music Corp./Rinimer Corp.
Introduced by Craig Stevens and Valerie Lee in *Here's Love* (musical).

Navy Blue
Words and music by Bob Crewe, Eddie Rambeau (pseudonym for Edward Fluri), and Bud Rehak (pseudonym for Andrew Racheck).
Saturday Music, Inc.
Best-selling record in 1964 by Diane Renay (20th Century-Fox).

Needles and Pins
Words and music by Sonny Bono and Jack Nitzsche.
Metric Music Co.
Best-selling records by Jackie De Shannon (Liberty) and in 1964 in England and United States by The Searchers (Kapp).

Nester, The
Words and music by Don Wayne.
Tree Publishing Co., Inc.
Introduced by Lefty Frizzell (Columbia).

New Pair of Shoes, A
Words and music by Ervin Drake.
Harms, Inc.
Introduced by Steve Lawrence, Robert Alda, and ensemble in *What Makes Sammy Run?* (musical, 1964).

Ninety Miles an Hour down a Dead-End Street
Words by Hal Blair and Don Robertson, music by Don Robertson.
Don Robertson Music Corp.
Best-selling record by Hank Snow (RCA Victor).

Nitchevo
Words by Anne Croswell, music by Lee Pockriss.
Piedmont Music Co., Inc.
Introduced by Jean Pierre Aumont, Michael Kermoyan, Gene Varrone, Rita Metzger, and ensemble in *Tovarich* (musical).

Nitty Gritty, The
Words and music by Lincoln Chase.
Al Gallico Music Corp.
Best-selling record by Shirley Ellis (Congress).

Noelle
Words and music by George Wyle and Eddie Pola.
Barnaby Music Corp.
Introduced by Andy Williams (Columbia).

Not So Long Ago
Words and music by Marty Robbins.
Marty's Music Corp.
Best-selling record by Marty Robbins (Columbia).

Not What I Had in Mind
Words and music by Jack Clement.
Glad Music Co./Jack Music, Inc.
Best-selling record by George Jones (United Artists).

Now!
Words by Betty Comden and Adolph Green, adaptation of music by
    Jule Styne.
Stratford Music Corp.
Civil rights song set to music of Israeli song, "Hava Nagila." In-
    troduced by Lena Horne.

Old Records
Words and music by Arthur Thomas and Merle Kilgore.
Al Gallico Music Corp.
Best-selling record by Margie Singleton (Mercury).

Old Smokey Locomotion
New words and music adaptation by Gerry Goffin and Carole King.
Screen Gems-Columbia Music, Inc.
Based on folk song, "On Top of Old Smoky." Best-selling record by
    Little Eva (Dimension).

On Top of Spaghetti
Words and music adapted by Tom Glazer.
Songs Music, Inc.
Adaptation of the American folk song, "On Top of Old Smoky."
    Introduced by Tom Glazer (Kapp). Best-selling record by Burl
    Ives (Decca).

One Broken Heart for Sale
Words and music by Otis Blackwell and Winfield Scott.
Elvis Presley Music, Inc.
From *It Happened at the World's Fair* (film). Best-selling record by
    Elvis Presley (RCA Victor).

One Fine Day
Words and music by Gerry Goffin and Carole King.
Screen Gems-Columbia Music, Inc.
Best-selling record by The Chiffons (Laurie).

One More Mountain (One More River)
Words and music by Paul Vance and Eddie Snyder.
Roncom Music Co.
Introduced by Perry Como (RCA Victor).

Only a Pawn in Their Game
Words and music by Bob Dylan.
M. Witmark & Sons.
Introduced by Bob Dylan (Columbia).

Only in America
Words and music by Jerry Leiber, Cynthia Weil, Mike Stoller, and
    Barry Mann.
Screen Gems-Columbia Music, Inc.
Introduced by Jay and The Americans (United Artists).

Only One, The
Words by Anne Croswell, music by Lee Pockriss.
Piedmont Music Co., Inc.
Introduced by Vivien Leigh in *Tovarich* (musical).

007 (English)
Music by John Barry.
United Artists Music, Ltd., London, England/Unart Music Corp.
A theme from *From Russia with Love* (film).

Open Highway, see Theme from *Route 66*, 1960.

Our Winter Love (Canadian)
Words by Bob Tubert, music by John Cowell.
BMI Canada, Ltd., 1962, 1963/Cramart Music, Inc.
Originally copyrighted without lyrics under title, "Long Island
    Sound." Best-selling instrumental recording by Bill Purcell (Co-
    lumbia).

Out of Limits
Words and music by Michael Z. Gordon.
Wrist Music Co.
Best-selling record in 1963-64 by The Marketts (Warner Bros.).

P.S. I Love You, see (P.S.) I Love You.

Painted, Tainted Rose
Words and music by Peter De Angelis and Jean Sawyer.
Damian Music Publishing Co.
Best-selling record by Al Martino (Capitol).

(Down at) Papa Joe's
Words and music by Jerry Dean Smith.
Tuneville Music, Inc.
Best-selling record by The Dixiebelles (Sound Stage 7).

Paris Mist
Music by Erroll Garner.
Famous Music Corp.
From *A New Kind of Love* (film).

Part Time Love
Words and music by Clay Hammond.
Cireco Music, Inc./Escort Music Co.
Best-selling record by Little Johnny Taylor (Galaxy).

Password
Words and music by Herman Phillips.
Kitty Wells Publications.
Best-selling record in 1964 by Kitty Wells (Decca).

Patty Duke Theme, The (Cousins)
Words by Bob Wells, music by Sid Ramin.
United Artists Music Co., Inc.
Theme from *The Patty Duke Show* (television series).

Peel Me a 'Nanner
Words and music by Bill Anderson.
Moss Rose Publications, Inc.
Best-selling record in 1964 by Roy Drusky (Mercury).

Peking Theme, The, see So Little Time.

Perfect Nanny, The
Words and music by Richard M. Sherman and Robert B. Sherman.
Wonderland Music Co., Inc.
Introduced by Karen Dotrice and Matthew Garber in *Mary Poppins*
    (film).

Petticoat Junction
Words and music by Paul Henning and Curt Massey.
Carolintone Music Co., Inc.
Theme from *Petticoat Junction* (television series). Introduced and
    best-selling record in 1964 by Lester Flatt and Earl Scruggs
    (Columbia).

Pillow That Whispers, The
Words and music by Cal Veale.
Yonah Music, Inc.
Best-selling record by Carl Smith (Columbia).

Pine Cones and Holly Berries
Words and music by Meredith Willson.
Frank Music Corp./Rinimer Corp.
Introduced by Laurence Naismith, Janis Paige, and Fred Gwynne,
    and reprised by Laurence Naismith and Valerie Lee, in *Here's
    Love* (musical).

Pink Panther Theme
English words by Johnny Mercer, Italian words by Franco Migliacci,
    music by Henry Mancini.
Northridge Music, Inc./United Artists Music Co., Inc.
Theme song from *The Pink Panther* (film, 1964). Best-selling in-
    strumental recording by Henry Mancini and his Orchestra (RCA
    Victor). Winner of National Academy of Recording Arts and
    Sciences Awards for "Best Instrumental Composition (Non-Jazz),"
    "Best Instrumental Performance (Non-Jazz)," and "Best Instru-
    mental Arrangement," 1964.

Pirogue (Pero)
Words and music by Doug Kershaw and Jimmy Newman.
Acuff-Rose Publications, Inc.
Best-selling record by Rusty and Doug Kershaw (RCA Victor).

Please Make Him Love Me
Words by Hal David, music by Burt Bacharach.
U. S. Songs, Inc./Purchase Music, Inc.
Introduced by Dionne Warwick (Scepter).

Please Say You're Foolin'
Words and music by Bobby Stevenson.
Eden Music, Inc.
Best-selling record in 1966 by Ray Charles (ABC-Paramount).

Please Talk to My Heart
Words and music by Jimmy Fautheree and Johnny Mathis.
Glad Music Co.
Best-selling records in 1964 by Ray Price (Columbia) and Country
  Johnny Mathis (United Artists).

Poor Little Rich Girl
Words and music by Gerry Goffin and Carole King.
Screen Gems-Columbia Music, Inc.
Best-selling record by Steve Lawrence (Columbia).

Popsicles and Icicles
Words and music by David Gates.
Dragonwyck Music.
Best-selling record by The Murmaids (Chattahoochee).

Power and the Glory, The
Words and music by Phil Ochs.
Appleseed Music, Inc.
Introduced by Phil Ochs.

Pride and Joy
Words and music by Marvin Gaye, William Stevenson, and Norman
  Whitfield.
Jobete Music Co., Inc.
Best-selling record by Marvin Gaye (Tamla).

Puff (The Magic Dragon)
Words and music by Peter Yarrow and Leonard Lipton.
Pepamar Music Corp.
Best-selling record by Peter, Paul, and Mary (Warner Bros.).

Puppy Love
Words and music by Barbara Lewis.
McLaughlin Publishing Co.
Best-selling record by Barbara Lewis (Atlantic).

Pushover
Words and music by Roquel Davis and Tony Clarke.
Chevis Publishing Corp./Salaam Music Co.
Best-selling record by Etta James (Argo).

Put On Your Sunday Clothes
Words and music by Jerry Herman.
Edwin H. Morris & Co., Inc.
Introduced by Charles Nelson Reilly, Jerry Dodge, Carol Channing,
    and Igors Gavon in *Hello, Dolly!* (musical, 1964).

Quicksand
Words and music by Eddie Holland, Brian Holland, and Lamont
    Dozier.
Jobete Music Co., Inc.
Best-selling record by Martha and The Vandellas (Gordy).

Ramblin' Boy
Words and music by Tom Paxton.
Cherry Lane Music, Inc.
Introduced by Tom Paxton.

Raunchy
Words by Tom Jones, music by Harvey Schmidt.
Chappell & Co., Inc.
Introduced by Inga Swenson and Will Geer in *110 in the Shade*
    (musical).

Ribbons Down My Back
Words and music by Jerry Herman.
Edwin H. Morris & Co., Inc.
Introduced by Eileen Brennan in *Hello, Dolly!* (musical, 1964).

Ride
Words and music by John Sheldon and David Leon.
Kalmann Music, Inc./C.C. Publishing Co., Inc.
Best-selling record in 1962 by Dee Dee Sharp (Cameo).

Ringo
Words by Hal Blair and Don Robertson, music by Don Robertson.
Don Robertson Music Corp.
Best-selling record in 1964 by Lorne Green (RCA Victor).

Ringo's Theme, see This Boy.

Roll Muddy River, see 1960.

Roma, Nun Fa' la Stupida Stasera (Italian)
English words by Carl Sigman, Italian words by Pietro Garinei and
    Sandro Giovannini, music by Armando Trovajoli.
Edizioni Musicali C.A.M., Rome, Italy, 1962/Harms, Inc.
Original Italian version introduced in Italy and, in 1964, in United
    States by Nino Manfredi, Ornella Vanoni, Bice Valori, Aldo
    Fabrizi, Lando Fiorini, and chorus in *Rugantino* (musical). Eng-
    lish version entitled "The Lights of Roma."

Ronnie, Call Me When You Get a Chance
Words and music by Mike Anthony and Ted Cooper.
Screen Gems-Columbia Music, Inc.
Best-selling record by Shelley Fabares (Colpix).

Room without Windows, A
Words and music by Ervin Drake.
Harms, Inc.
Introduced by Steve Lawrence and Sally Ann Howes in *What Makes
    Sammy Run?* (musical, 1964).

Saginaw, Michigan
Words and music by Don Wayne and Bill Anderson.
Tree Publishing Co., Inc.
Best-selling record in 1964 by Lefty Frizzell (Columbia).

St. Thomas
Music by Sonny Rollins.
Prestige Music Co., Inc.
Introduced by Sonny Rollins. Best-selling record by Herbie Mann
    (United Artists).

Sally Go 'Round the Roses
Words and music by Zell Sanders and Lona Stevens (pseudonym for
    Lona Spector).
Winlyn Music, Inc.
Best-selling record by The Jaynettes (Tuff).

Samba do Avião, see Song of the Jet.

Save Your Heart for Me
Words and music by Gary Geld and Peter Udell.
Geld-Udell Music Corp.
Best-selling record in 1965 by Gary Lewis and The Playboys
    (Liberty).

Say Wonderful Things (English)
Words and music by Norman Newell and Phil Green.
Ardmore and Beechwood, Ltd., London, England/Hill and Range
    Songs, Inc./Valley Publishers, Inc.
Introduced in England by Ronnie Carroll (Philips). Best-selling
    record in United States by Patti Page (Columbia).

Scarlett O'Hara (English)
Music by Jerry Lordan.
Francis, Day & Hunter, Ltd., London, England/Regent Music Corp.
Best-selling records by Jet Harris and Tony Meehan (London) and
    Lawrence Welk and his Orchestra (Dot).

See the Funny Little Clown
Words and music by Bobby Goldsboro.
Unart Music Corp., 1963, 1964.
Introduced and best-selling record in 1964 by Bobby Goldsboro
    (United Artists).

Shake Me I Rattle (Squeeze Me I Cry), see 1957.

She Looks Good to the Crowd
Words and music by Joe Poovey.
English Music, Inc.
Best-selling record by Bobby Barnett (Sims).

She Loves Me
Words by Sheldon Harnick, music by Jerry Bock.
Sunbeam Music Corp.
Introduced by Daniel Massey in *She Loves Me* (musical).

She Loves You (English)
Words and music by John Lennon and Paul McCartney.
Northern Songs, Ltd., London, England/Gil Music Corp.
Best-selling record in 1964 by The Beatles (Swan and Capitol).

Shelter of Your Arms, The
Words and music by Jerry Samuels.
Print Music Co., Inc.
Best-selling record in 1964 by Sammy Davis, Jr. (Reprise).

She's a Fool
Words and music by Ben Raleigh and Mark Barkan.
Helios Music Corp./M.R.C. Music, Inc.
Best-selling record by Lesley Gore (Mercury).

Shoop, Shoop Song, The, also known as **It's in His Kiss**
Words and music by Rudy Clark.
T.M. Music, Inc./Old Lyne Music.
Best-selling record in 1964 by Betty Everett (Vee Jay).

Shut Down
Words by Roger Christian, music by Brian Wilson.
Sea of Tunes Publishing Co.
Best-selling record by The Beach Boys (Capitol).

Silver Threads and Golden Needles, see 1956.

Simple Little Things
Words by Tom Jones, music by Harvey Schmidt.
Chappell & Co., Inc.
Introduced by Inga Swenson in *110 in the Shade* (musical).

Sing a Sad Song
Words and music by Wynn Stewart.
Owen Publications.
Best-selling record by Buddy Cagle (Capitol).

Single Girl Again
Words and music by Harlan Howard.
Pamper Music, Inc.
Best-selling record in 1965 by Molly Bee (Liberty).

Sister Suffragette
Words and music by Richard M. Sherman and Robert B. Sherman.
Wonderland Music Co., Inc.
Introduced by Glynis Johns in *Mary Poppins* (film).

Six Days on the Road
Words and music by Earl Green and Carl Montgomery.
Newkeys Music, Inc./Tune Publishers, Inc.
Best-selling record by Dave Dudley (Golden Wing).

Small Cartel, A
Words by Anne Croswell, music by Lee Pockriss.
Piedmont Music Co., Inc.
Introduced by Louise Kirtland, George S. Irving, and ensemble in
    Tovarich (musical).

Snowflakes, see 1951.

So Little Time, also known as **The Peking Theme**
Words by Paul Francis Webster, music by Dimitri Tiomkin.
Samuel Bronston Music Publishing, Inc.
Introduced by voice of Andy Williams behind end titles on sound-
    track of *55 Days at Peking* (film). Nominated for Academy Award,
    1963. Best-selling record by Andy Williams (Columbia).

So Long, Dearie
Words and music by Jerry Herman.
Edwin H. Morris & Co., Inc.
Introduced by Carol Channing in *Hello, Dolly!* (musical, 1964).

So Much in Love
Words by William Jackson and George Williams, music by Roy
    Straigis.
Cameo-Parkway Publishing Co., Inc.
Best-selling record by The Tymes (Parkway).

Some Days Everything Goes Wrong
Words and music by Ervin Drake.
Harms, Inc.
Introduced by Steve Lawrence in *What Makes Sammy Run?* (musi-
    cal, 1964).

Someone To Take Your Place
Words and music by Joe Tex.
Tree Publishing Co., Inc.
Introduced by Joe Tex (Dial).

Something To Live For
Words and music by Ervin Drake.
Harms, Inc.
Introduced by Sally Ann Howes in *What Makes Sammy Run?*
    (musical, 1964).

Song of Love, see **Canto D'Amore.**

Song of the Jet (Brazilian)
English words by Gene Lees, Portuguese words and music by
  Antonio Carlos Jobim.
Edizioni Suvini Zerboni, S.p.A., Milan, Italy/Hollis Music, Inc.
Original title, "Samba do Avião." Introduced in *Copacabana Palace*
  (Italian film). First recording in English by Tony Bennett (Co-
  lumbia).

Soon (I'll Be Home Again)
Words and music by Bob Crewe and Bob Gaudio.
Claridge Music, Inc.
Best-selling record by The Four Seasons (Vee Jay).

Sorrow on the Rocks
Words and music by Tony Moon.
Screen Gems-Columbia Music, Inc.
Best-selling record in 1964 by Porter Wagoner (RCA Victor).

Sound of Surf, The
Music by Charles Albertine.
Screen Gems-Columbia Music, Inc.
Introduced by Percy Faith and his Orchestra (Columbia).

South Street
Words by Kal Mann, music by Dave Appell.
Kalmann Music, Inc.
Best-selling record by The Orlons (Cameo).

Southtown, U.S.A.
Words and music by Billy Sherrill.
Al Gallico Music Corp.
Best-selling record in 1964 by The Dixiebelles (Sound Stage 7).

Spoonful of Sugar, A
Words and music by Richard M. Sherman and Robert B. Sherman.
Wonderland Music Co., Inc.
Introduced by Julie Andrews in *Mary Poppins* (film).

Stay Awake
Words and music by Richard M. Sherman and Robert B. Sherman.
Wonderland Music Co., Inc.
Introduced by Julie Andrews in *Mary Poppins* (film).

Stay with Me
Words by Carolyn Leigh, music by Jerome Moross.
Chappell & Co., Inc.
Adapted from the theme from *The Cardinal* (film). First recording
  by Frank Sinatra (Reprise).

Steal Away
Words and music by Jimmy Hughes.
Fame Publishing Co.
Best-selling record in 1964 by Jimmy Hughes (Fame).

Step in Time
Words and music by Richard M. Sherman and Robert B. Sherman.
Wonderland Music Co., Inc.
Introduced by Dick Van Dyke and Chimney Sweeps in *Mary Poppins* (film).

Stolen Hours, The
Words by Marilyn Keith and Alan Bergman, music by Mort Lindsay.
United Artists Music Co., Inc.
Introduced in *Stolen Hours* (film).

Stuck with Each Other
Words by Anne Croswell, music by Lee Pockriss.
Piedmont Music Co., Inc.
Introduced by Margery Gray and Byron Mitchell in *Tovarich* (musical).

Sugar and Spice (English)
Words and music by Fred Nightingale.
Welbeck Music, Ltd., London, England/Duchess Music Corp.
Best-selling record in 1964 by The Searchers (Liberty).

Sukiyaka, see Sukiyaki.

Sukiyaki (My First Lonely Night), also known as Sukiyaka (Japanese)
English words by Tom Leslie and Buzz Cason, Japanese words and music by Hachidai Nakamura and Rokusuke Ei.
Toshiba Music Publishing Co., Ltd., Tokyo, Japan, 1961/Beechwood Music Corp.
Original Japanese title, "Ueo Muite Arukuo" ("Walk with Your Chin Up"). Introduced in England in 1962 as an instrumental, under the title "Sukiyaki," by Kenny Ball and his Band (Pye). Best-selling record in Japan and United States by Kyu Sakamoto (Capitol).

Summer Green and Winter White
Words and music by Charles Tobias and Nat Simon.
Skidmore Music Co., Inc.

Sun A-Rise (Australian)
Words and music by Rolf Harris and Harry Butler.
Castle Music Pty., Ltd., Australia, 1960/Beechwood Music Corp.
Best-selling record by Rolf Harris (Epic).

Sunday in New York
Words by Carroll Coates, music by Peter Nero.
Hastings Music Corp.
From *Sunday in New York* (film, 1964). Introduced by Peter Nero
and Orchestra (RCA Victor).

Supercalifragilisticexpialidocious
Words and music by Richard M. Sherman and Robert B. Sherman.
Wonderland Music Co., Inc.
Introduced by Julie Andrews, Dick Van Dyke, and The Pearlies in
Mary Poppins (film).

Surf City
Words and music by Jan Berry and Brian Wilson.
Screen Gems-Columbia Music, Inc.
Best-selling record by Jan and Dean (Liberty).

Surfer Joe
Words and music by Ron Wilson.
Robin Hood Music Co./Miraleste Music.
Best-selling record by The Surfaris (Dot).

Surfin' U.S.A.
Words by Brian Wilson, music by Chuck Berry.
Arc Music Corp.
Revised version of Chuck Berry's "Sweet Little Sixteen" (see 1958).
Best-selling record by The Beach Boys (Capitol).

Take Ten
Music by Paul Desmond.
Desmond Music Co.
Jazz instrumental introduced by Paul Desmond (RCA Victor).

Talk Back Trembling Lips
Words and music by John Loudermilk.
Acuff-Rose Publications, Inc.
Best-selling records by Debbie Stuart (Philips), Ernest Ashworth
(Hickory), and Johnny Tillotson (MGM).

Talk to Me Baby
Words by Johnny Mercer, music by Robert Emmett Dolan.
Commander Publications.
Introduced by John Davidson and Julienne Marie in *Foxy* (musical,
1964). First recording by Frank Sinatra (Reprise).

Tandy
Words by Harold Adamson, music by George Stoll and Robert Van
Eps.
Leo Feist, Inc.
From *A Ticklish Affair* (film).

Teen Scene
Words and music by Jerry Reed and Chet Atkins.
Lowery Music Co., Inc.
Best-selling record by Chet Atkins (RCA Victor).

Tell Her So
Words and music by Glenn Douglas Tubb.
Combine Music Corp.
Best-selling records by The Wilburn Brothers (Decca) and in 1965
   by Ernest Tubb (Decca).

Tell Him
Words and music by Bert Russell.
Robert Mellin, Inc.
Best-selling record by The Exciters (United Artists).

Tell Me the Truth
Words and music by George Harold Jackson and Dimple Marcene
   Jackson.
Harold and Dimple Publishing Co.
Introduced by Nancy Wilson (Capitol).

Tender Flower, see Ciumachella de Trastevere.

Thank You Girl (English)
Words and music by John Lennon and Paul McCartney.
Northern Songs, Ltd., London, England/Conrad Publishing Co., Inc.
Best-selling record by The Beatles (Vee Jay).

Thanks a Lot
Words and music by Eddie Miller and Don Sessions.
Hotpoint Music, Inc.
Best-selling record by Ernest Tubb (Decca).

That Man Over There
Words and music by Meredith Willson.
Frank Music Corp./Rinimer Corp.
Introduced by Paul Reed in *Here's Love* (musical).

That Sunday (That Summer)
Words by George David Weiss, music by Joe Sherman.
Comet Music Corp.
Best-selling record by Nat "King" Cole (Capitol).

That's All That Matters
Words and music by Hank Cochran.
Pamper Music, Inc.
Best-selling record by Ray Price (Columbia).

Theme from *A New Kind of Love*
Music by Erroll Garner.
Famous Music Corp.
From *A New Kind of Love* (film).

Theme from *East Side/West Side*
Music by Kenyon Hopkins.
Groton Music, Inc.
Theme from *East Side/West Side* (television series).

Theme from *8½* (Italian)
Italian words by Tino Fornai, music by Nino Rota.
Ed. Mus. C.A.M., Rome, Italy/Edward B. Marks Music Corp.
Theme from *8½* (Italian film)

Theme from *Harry's Girls*
Words by Joseph Stein, music by Stu Phillips.
Hastings Music Corp.
Theme from *Harry's Girls* (television series).

Theme from *Irma la Douce* (**Look Again**)
Words by Dory Langdon, music by André Previn.
United Artists Music Co., Inc./Fairlane Music Corp.
Adapted from a theme from *Irma la Douce* (film).

Theme from *Lilies of the Field,* also known as **Amen**
Music by Jerry Goldsmith.
Unart Music Corp.
Introduced by orchestra conducted by Jerry Goldsmith on soundtrack
    of *Lilies of the Field* (film).

Theme from *Lord of the Flies*
Words and music by Raymond Leppard.
Saunders Publications, Inc.
Theme from *Lord of the Flies* (film).

Theme from *Mr. Novak*
Music by Lyn Murray.
Miller Music Corp.
Theme from *Mr. Novak* (television series).

Theme from *Mondo Cane,* see **More.**

Theme from *The Lieutenant* (**Like March**)
Music by Jeff Alexander.
Miller Music Corp.
Theme from *The Lieutenant* (television series).

Theme from *The Prize*
Music by Jerry Goldsmith.
Hastings Music Corp.
Theme from *The Prize* (film).

Theme from *The Travels of Jaimie McPheeters*
Words by Jerry Winn, music by Leigh Harline.
Miller Music Corp.
Theme from *The Travels of Jaimie McPheeters* (television series).

Theme from *The V.I.P.'s* (The Willow)
Words by Mack David, music by Miklos Rozsa.
Robbins Music Corp.
Adapted from a theme from *The V.I.P.'s* (film).

Theme from *The Victors* (My Special Dream)
Words by Freddy Douglass and Howard Greenfield, music by Sol
    Kaplan.
Screen Gems-Columbia Music, Inc.
Adapted from a theme from *The Victors* (film).

Then He Kissed Me
Words and music by Jeff Barry, Ellie Greenwich, and Phil Spector.
Trio Music Co., Inc./Mother Bertha Music, Inc.
Best-selling record by The Crystals (Philles).

There but for Fortune
Words and music by Phil Ochs.
Appleseed Music, Inc.
Best-selling record in 1965 by Joan Baez (Vanguard).

There's a Place (English)
Words and music by John Lennon and Paul McCartney.
Northern Songs, Ltd., London, England/Gil Music Corp.
Best-selling record by The Beatles (Vee Jay).

There's Something about You (English)
Words by Leslie Bricusse, music by Cyril Ornadel.
Chappell & Co., Ltd., London, England/Chappell & Co., Inc.
Introduced by Anton Rodgers and Hilda Braid in London production
    (1964) and by Anton Rodgers and Helena Carroll in New York
    production (1965) of *Pickwick* (musical).

Thieving Stranger, The
Words and music by Ervin Drake.
Empress Music, Inc.
Introduced by Walter Brennan (Dot).

Thirty One Flavors
Words by Mack David, music by Ernest Gold.
United Artists Music Co., Inc.
Introduced by voices of The Shirelles on soundtrack of *It's a Mad,
    Mad, Mad, Mad World* (film).

This Boy, also known as Ringo's Theme (English)
Words and music by John Lennon and Paul McCartney.
Northern Songs, Ltd., London, England/Maclen Music, Inc.
Introduced by The Beatles in *A Hard Day's Night* (film). Best-
    selling record by The Beatles (United Artists).

This Day of Days
Words and adaptation of music by Hy Gilbert.
Ritvale Music Corp.
Adapted from Chopin's "Etude, No. 3." Introduced by Jerry Vale
 (Columbia).

This Is All I Ask, see 1958.

This Land Is Your Land, see 1956.

This Little Girl
Words and music by Gerry Goffin and Carole King.
Screen Gems-Columbia Music, Inc.
Best-selling record by Dion (Columbia).

This Time It's True Love
Words and music by Noël Coward.
Chappell & Co., Inc.
Introduced by Florence Henderson and José Ferrer in *The Girl
 Who Came to Supper* (musical).

Those Lazy-Hazy-Crazy Days of Summer (German)
Words by Charles Tobias, music by Hans Carste.
Editions Primus Rolf Budde KG, Berlin, Germany, 1962/Comet
 Music Corp.
Original German title, "Du Spielst 'ne Tolle Rolle." Best-selling
 record by Nat "King" Cole (Capitol).

Those Wonderful Years
Words and music by Webb Pierce and Don Schroeder.
Cedarwood Publishing Co., Inc.
Best-selling record by Webb Pierce (Decca).

(Love Is) A Ticklish Affair
Words by Harold Adamson, music by George Stoll and Robert Van
 Eps.
Leo Feist, Inc.
Introduced by voice of Jack Jones under titles of *A Ticklish Affair*
 (film).

Tie Me Kangaroo Down, Sport, see 1961.

Timber, I'm Falling
Words by Dalton Timbur, music by Ferlin Husky.
Husky Music Co., Inc.
Best-selling record by Ferlin Husky (Capitol).

Time Is on My Side
Words and music by Jerry Ragovoy.
Rittenhouse Music/Maygar Publishing Co.
Best-selling record by The Rolling Stones (London).

Times, They Are A-Changin', The
Words and music by Bob Dylan.
M. Witmark & Sons.
Best-selling record by Bob Dylan (Columbia).

Tip of My Fingers, The, see 1960.

Tip of My Tongue (English)
Words and music by John Lennon and Paul McCartney.
Northern Songs, Ltd., London, England/Maclen Music, Inc.
Introduced in England by Tommy Quickly.

To Be Alone with You
Words by Sidney Michaels, music by Mark Sandrich, Jr.
Morley Music Co., Inc., 1963, 1964.
Introduced by Robert Preston and Ulla Sallert in *Ben Franklin in
    Paris* (musical, 1964).

To Kill a Mockingbird
Words by Mack David, music by Elmer Bernstein.
Northern Music Corp.
Adapted from a theme from *To Kill a Mockingbird* (film). Introduced
    by Vincent Edwards (Decca).

Together Again
Words and music by Buck Owens.
Central Songs, Inc.
Introduced by Buck Owens (Capitol). Best-selling record in 1966 by
    Ray Charles (ABC-Paramount).

Tonight at Eight
Words by Sheldon Harnick, music by Jerry Bock.
Sunbeam Music Corp.
Introduced by Daniel Massey in *She Loves Me* (musical).

Too Late To Try Again
Words and music by Carl Butler.
Pearl Dee Publishing Co.
Best-selling record in 1964 by Carl Butler and Pearl (Columbia).

Toys in the Attic
Words and music by George Duning, Joe Sherman, and George D.
    Weiss.
United Artists Music Co., Inc.
Adapted from a theme from *Toys in the Attic* (film).

Treat Him Nicely
Words and music by Guy Hemric and Jim Styner.
Dijon Music.
Best-selling record by Annette (Vista).

Triangle
Words and music by Jean Chapel.
Regent Music Corp.
Best-selling record by Carl Smith (Columbia).

Tribute (English)
Words and music by Anthony Newley.
Concord Music, Ltd., London, England/Melody Trials, Inc.
A "tribute" to the late President John F. Kennedy, introduced by
    Anthony Newley (Acappella).

20 Miles
Words by Kal Mann, music by Bernie Lowe.
Lowe Music Corp./Kalmann Music, Inc.
Best-selling record by Chubby Checker (Parkway).

Twenty-four Hours from Tulsa
Words by Hal David, music by Burt Bacharach.
Arch Music Co., Inc.
Best-selling record by Gene Pitney (Musicor).

Twinkle Lullaby
Words and music by Joe Lubin.
Daywin Music, Inc.
From *Move Over, Darling* (film). Introduced by Doris Day (Co-
    lumbia).

Twisting Matilda
Words and music by Norman Span.
General Music Publishing Co., Inc./Pickwick Music Corp.
Based on "Matilda, Matilda," published in 1953. Best-selling record
    in 1963 by Jimmy Soul (SPQR).

Two Faces Have I
Words and music by Twyla Herbert and Lou Sacco.
Painted Desert Music Corp./RTD Music.
Best-selling record by Lou Christie (Roulette).

Uh-Oh!
Words by Anne Croswell, music by Lee Pockriss.
Piedmont Music Co., Inc.
Introduced by Margery Gray and Byron Mitchell in *Tovarich* (musi-
    cal).

Um Um Um Um Um Um, also known as **Unh Unh Unh**
Words and music by Curtis Mayfield.
Curtom Publishing Co., Inc./Jalynne Corp.
Best-selling record in 1964 by Major Lance (Okeh).

Under the Yum-Yum Tree
Words by Sammy Cahn, music by James Van Heusen.
Colgems Music Corp.
From *Under the Yum-Yum Tree* (film). Introduced on records by
    Robert Goulet (Columbia).

Unh Unh Unh, see **Um Um Um Um Um Um.**

Universal Soldier, The
Words and music by Buffy Sainte-Marie.
Woodmere Music.
Introduced by Buffy Sainte-Marie (Vanguard).

Volunteer, The
Words and music by Autry Inman.
Big Bopper Music Co.
Best-selling record by Autry Inman (Sims).

Wait Till My Bobby Gets Home
Words and music by Phil Spector, Ellie Greenwich, and Jeff Barry.
Mother Bertha Music, Inc./Trio Music Co., Inc.
Best-selling record by Darlene Love (Philles).

Waitin' for the Evening Train
Words and music by Howard Dietz and Arthur Schwartz.
Harms, Inc.
Introduced by Mary Martin and George Wallace in *Jennie* (musical).

Walk Like a Man
Words and music by Bob Crewe and Bob Gaudio.
Saturday Music, Inc.
Best-selling record by The Four Seasons (Vee Jay).

Walk On By
Words by Hal David, music by Burt F. Bacharach.
Blue Seas Music, Inc./Jac Music Co., Inc.
Best-selling record in 1964 by Dionne Warwick (Scepter).

Walkin', Talkin', Cryin', Barely Beatin' Broken Heart
Words and music by Justin Tubb and Roger Miller.
Tree Publishing Co., Inc.
Introduced by Johnny Wright (Decca).

Walking Proud
Words and music by Gerry Goffin and Carole King.
Screen Gems-Columbia Music, Inc.
Best-selling record by Steve Lawrence (Columbia).

Walking the Dog
Words and music by Rufus Thomas.
East Publications.
Best-selling record by Rufus Thomas (Stax).

Waltz from *The Cardinal*
Music by Jerome Moross.
Chappell & Co., Inc.
From *The Cardinal* (film).

Washington Square
Words and music by Bob Goldstein and David Shire.
Showboat Songs, Inc./Chappell & Co., Inc.
Best-selling instrumental recording by The Village Stompers (Epic).
First vocal version by Marilyn May (RCA Victor).

Waves Roll Out, The
Words and music by Shel Silverstein and Bob Gibson.
Hollis Music, Inc.
Introduced by Shel Silverstein.

We Must Have Been Out of Our Minds
Words and music by Melba Montgomery.
Glad Music Co.
Best-selling record by George Jones and Melba Montgomery (United Artists).

Week in the Country, A
Words and music by Baker Knight.
Four Star Music Co., Inc.
Best-selling record in 1964 by Ernest Ashworth (Hickory).

We'll Sing in the Sunshine
Words and music by Gale Garnett.
Lupercalia Music Publishing Co.
Best-selling record in 1964-65 by Gale Garnett (RCA Victor). Winner of National Academy of Recording Arts and Sciences Award for "Best Folk Recording," 1964.

We're the Talk of the Town
Words by Buck Owens, music by Rollie Weber.
Blue Book Music Co.
Best-selling record by Buck Owens and Rose Maddox (Capitol).

What Kind of Fool Do You Think I Am?
Words and music by Ray Whitley.
Low-Twi Music.
Best-selling record in 1964 by The Tams (ABC-Paramount).

What Will My Mary Say?, see 1961.

Whatever Happened to Baby Jane?
Words and music by Lukas Heller and Frank De Vol.
Seven Arts Music Corp.
Introduced by Debbie Burton, with narration by Bette Davis (MGM).

What's Easy for Two Is So Hard for One
Words and music by William Robinson.
Jobete Music Co., Inc.
Best-selling record by Mary Wells (Motown).

What's That I Hear
Words and music by Phil Ochs.
Appleseed Music, Inc.
Introduced by Phil Ochs (Elektra).

Wheeler Dealers, The
Words and music by Randy Sparks.
Miller Music Corp.
From *The Wheeler Dealers* (film). Introduced by The New Christy
Minstrels.

When the Ship Comes In
Words and music by Bob Dylan.
M. Witmark & Sons.
Introduced by Bob Dylan (Columbia).

Where Is Love?, see 1960.

White on White
Words by Bernice Ross, music by Lor Crane.
Painted Desert Music Corp., 1963, 1964.
Best-selling record in 1964 by Danny Williams (United Artists).

Who Killed Norma Jean?
Words by Norman Rosten, music by Pete Seeger.
Ludlow Music, Inc.
Dedicated to Marilyn Monroe. Introduced by Pete Seeger.

Who Will Buy?, see 1960.

Who's Been Sleeping in My Bed?
Words by Hal David, music by Burt F. Bacharach.
Famous Music Corp.
"Inspired" by *Who's Been Sleeping in My Bed?* (film, 1964).

Wild Weekend, see 1960.

Wild Weekend Cha Cha, see **Wild Weekend,** 1960.

Wildwood Days
Words by Kal Mann, music by Dave Appell.
Kalmann Music, Inc.
Best-selling record by Bobby Rydell (Cameo).

Wilkes-Barre, Pa.
Words by Anne Croswell, music by Lee Pockriss.
Piedmont Music Co., Inc.
Introduced by Vivien Leigh and Byron Mitchell in *Tovarich* (musical).

Will He Like Me?
Words by Sheldon Harnick, music by Jerry Bock.
Sunbeam Music Corp.
Introduced by Barbara Cook in *She Loves Me* (musical).

Willow, The, see **Theme from *The V.I.P.'s.***

Wine, Women, and Song
Words and music by Betty Sue Perry.
Sure-Fire Music Co., Inc.
Best-selling record in 1964 by Loretta Lynn (Decca).

Wipe Out
Music by Robert Berryhill, Patrick Connolly, James Fuller, and
    Ron Wilson.
Miraleste Music/Robin Hood Music Co.
Best-selling instrumental by The Surfaris (Dot).

Wishin' and Hopin'
Words by Hal David, music by Burt Bacharach.
Jonathan Music Co., Inc.
Best-selling record in 1964 by Dusty Springfield (Philips).

With God on Our Side
Words and music by Bob Dylan.
M. Witmark & Sons.
Music based on melody of "Patriot Game," by Dominic Behan. In-
    troduced by Bob Dylan (Columbia).

Wives and Lovers
Words by Hal David, music by Burt F. Bacharach.
Famous Music Corp.
"Inspired" by *Wives and Lovers* (film). Best-selling record by Jack
    Jones (Kapp). Winner of National Academy of Recording Arts
    and Sciences Award for "Best Solo Vocal Performance—Male,"
    1963.

Wonderful Summer
Words and music by Gil Garfield and Perry Botkin, Jr.
Rock Music Co.
Introduced by Robin Ward (Dot).

Wonderful! Wonderful!, see 1956.

Wonderful World of Love
Words and music by Jack Brooks and Sid Ramin.
Chesnick Music, Inc.
Introduced by Robert Goulet (Columbia).

World I Used To Know, The
Words and music by Rod McKuen.
In Music Co., 1963, 1964.
Introduced by Rod McKuen. Best-selling record in 1964 by Jimmie
    Rodgers (Dot).

World of Love, A, also known as **Caesar and Cleopatra Theme**
Words by Sid Wayne, music by Alex North.
Robbins Music Corp.
Adapted from a theme from *Cleopatra* (film).

Worlds Apart
Words by Sheldon Harnick, music by Jerry Bock.
Sunbeam Music Corp.
From *Man in the Moon* (Bil and Cora Baird marionette play with
music).

Yakety Axe, see **Yakety Sax.**

Yakety Sax, also known as **Yakety Axe**
Words and music by Randy Randolph and James Rich.
Tree Publishing Co., Inc.
Introduced, as "Yakety Sax," by Boots Randolph (Monument). Best-
selling record, as "Yakety Axe," in 1965 by Chet Atkins (RCA
Victor).

Yeh Yeh
Words and music by Rodgers Grant, Pat Patrick, and Jon Hendricks.
Mongo Music.
Introduced instrumentally by Mongo Santamaria (Battle). Best-
selling rcord in England in 1964 by Georgie Fame with The Blue
Flames (Imperial).

Yellow Bandana, The, see 1960.

Yet . . . I Know (French)
English words by Don Raye, French words by Charles Aznavour,
music by Georges Garvarentz.
Les Éditions French Music, Paris, France, 1963, 1964/Éditions
Musicales Charles Aznavour, Paris, France, 1963, 1964/Leeds
Music Corp.
Original French title, "Et Pourtant." Introduced by Charles Azna-
vour. Introduced in English by Steve Lawrence (Columbia).

You Can't Sit Down, see 1960.

You Comb Her Hair
Words and music by Harlan Howard and Hank Cochran.
Pamper Music, Inc.
Best-selling record by George Jones (United Artists).

You Don't Know
Words and music by Meredith Willson.
Frank Music Corp./Rinimer Corp.
Introduced by Janis Paige in *Here's Love* (musical).

You Don't Own Me
Words and music by John Madara and David White.
Merjoda Music, Inc.
Best-selling record in 1964 by Lesley Gore (Mercury).

You Love Me
Words by Anne Croswell, music by Lee Pockriss.
Piedmont Music Co., Inc.
Introduced by Vivien Leigh and Jean Pierre Aumont in *Tovarich* (musical).

You Were Made for Me (English)
Words and music by Mitch Murray.
B. Feldman & Sons, Ltd., London, England/Edward B. Marks Music Corp.
Best-selling record in 1965 by Freddie and The Dreamers (Tower).

You'll Drive Me Back (Into Her Arms Again)
Words and music by Merle Kilgore and Miriam Lewis.
Al Gallico Music Corp.
Best-selling record in 1964 by Faron Young (Mercury).

Young Lovers
Words and music by Ray Hildebrand and Jill Jackson.
Le Bill Music, Inc./Marbill Music.
Best-selling record by Paul and Paula (Philips).

Young Only Yesterday
Words and music by Bob Perper and Yvette Ball.
Gil Music Corp.

Your Old Standby
Words and music by Janie Bradford and William Robinson, Jr.
Jobete Music Co., Inc.
Best-selling record by Mary Wells (Motown).

Your Other Love
Words by Ben Raleigh, music by Claus Ogerman.
Helios Music Corp./John D. MacArthur Music Corp.
Introduced by Connie Francis (MGM).

You're the Devil in Disguise
Words and music by Bill Giant, Bernie Baum, and Florence Kaye.
Elvis Presley Music, Inc.
Best-selling record by Elvis Presley (RCA Victor).

You've Really Got a Hold on Me
Words and music by William Robinson.
Jobete Music Co., Inc.
Best-selling record by The Miracles (Tamla).

1964

Absent Minded Me
Words by Bob Merrill, music by Jule Styne.
Chappell & Co., Inc.
Introduced and best-selling record by Barbra Streisand (Columbia).

Ain't That Just Like Me, see 1961.

All Day and All of the Night
Words and music by Ray Davies.
Jay-Boy Music Corp.
Best-selling record in 1964-65 in England and United States by The
Kinks (Reprise).

All Grown Up
Words and music by Phil Spector, Ellie Greenwich, and Jeff Barry.
Mother Bertha Music, Inc./Trio Music Co., Inc.
Introduced and best-selling record by The Crystals (Philles).

All I Really Want To Do
Words and music by Bob Dylan.
M. Witmark & Sons.
Introduced by Bob Dylan (Columbia). Best-selling records in 1965 by
Cher (Imperial) and The Byrds (Columbia).

All Summer Long
Words and music by Brian Wilson.
Sea of Tunes Publishing Co.
Best-selling record by The Beach Boys (Capitol).

Almost There
Words and music by Jack Keller and Gloria Shayne.
Northern Music Corp./Barnaby Music Corp.
From *I'd Rather Be Rich* (film). Best-selling record by Andy
Williams (Columbia).

Always Something There To Remind Me
Words by Hal David, music by Burt Bacharach.
Ross Jungnickel, Inc./Blue Seas Music, Inc./Jac Music Co., Inc.
Best-selling record by Sandi Shaw (Reprise).

Amen
Words and music by John W. Pate, Sr. and Curtis Mayfield.
Pamco Music, Inc.
Best-selling record by The Impressions (ABC-Paramount).

Amore, Scusami, see My Love, Forgive Me.

Anaheim, Azusa and Cucamonga Sewing Circle, Book Review and Timing Association, The
Words and music by Jan Berry, Roger Christian, and Don Altfeld.
Screen Gems-Columbia Music, Inc.
Best-selling record by Jan and Dean (Liberty).

And I Love Her, also known as And I Love Him (English)
Words and music by Paul McCartney and John Lennon.
Northern Songs, Ltd., London, England/Maclen Music, Inc./Unart Music Corp.
Introduced by The Beatles in *A Hard Day's Night* (film). Best-selling record by The Beatles (Capitol). Best-selling record of female version, "And I Love Him," in 1965 by Esther Phillips (Atlantic).

And I Love Him, see And I Love Her.

... And Roses and Roses
Words and music by Ray Gilbert and Darival Caymmi.
Ipanema Music Co.
Best-selling record by Andy Williams (Columbia).

Angelito
English and Spanish words and music by Rene Herrera and Rene Ornellos.
Gil Music Corp./Epps Music Co.
Introduced by Rene and Rene (Columbia).

Anna (Go to Him), see 1962.

Another Cup of Coffee
Words by Earl Shuman, music by Leon Carr.
The Peter Maurice Music Co., Ltd.
Best-selling record by Brook Benton (Mercury).

Any Old Time of Day
Words and music by Hal David and Burt Bacharach.
U.S. Songs, Inc.
Best-selling record by Dionne Warwick (Scepter).

Any Time at All (English)
Words and music by John Lennon and Paul McCartney.
Northern Songs, Ltd., London, England/Maclen Music, Inc.
Best-selling record by The Beatles (Capitol).

Any Way You Want It (English)
Words and music by Dave Clark.
Sphere Music Co., Ltd., London, England/Branston Music, Inc.
Best-selling record by The Dave Clark Five (Epic).

Anyone Can Whistle
Words and music by Stephen Sondheim.
Burthen Music Co., Inc.
Introduced by Lee Remick in *Anyone Can Whistle* (musical).

As Long As There's a Shadow
Words and music by Roger Miller.
Tree Publishing Co., Inc.
Introduced by Roger Miller (Smash).

As Tears Go By (English)
Words and music by Milt Jagger, Keith Richards, and Andrew
  Oldham.
Forward, Ltd., England/Essex Music, Inc.
Best-selling record by Marianne Faithfull (London).

Ask Me (Italian)
English words by Bill Giant, Florence Kaye, and Bernie Baum,
  Italian words and music by Domenico Modugno.
Accordo Edizioni Musicali, Milan, Italy, 1958/Elvis Presley Music,
  Inc.
Best-selling record by Elvis Presley (RCA Victor).

Autumn
Words and music by Richard Maltby, Jr. and David Shire.
Emanuel Music Corp.
Introduced by Barbra Streisand (Columbia).

Baby, I Need Your Loving
Words and music by Eddie Holland, Brian Holland, and Lamont
  Dozier.
Jobete Music Co., Inc.
Best-selling record by The Four Tops (Motown).

Baby I'm Yours
Words and music by Van McCoy.
Blackwood Music, Inc.
Best-selling record in 1965 by Barbara Lewis (Atlantic).

Baby Love
Words and music by Brian Holland, Eddie Holland, and Lamont
  Dozier.
Jobete Music Co., Inc.
Best-selling record in 1964-65 by The Supremes (Motown).

Baby, the Rain Must Fall
Words by Ernie Sheldon, music by Elmer Bernstein.
Colgems Music Corp.
Introduced by The We Three in *Baby, the Rain Must Fall* (film, 1965).
  Best-selling record in 1965 by Glenn Yarbrough (RCA Victor).

Baby, You Been on My Mind, also known as Mama, You Been on My Mind
Words and music by Bob Dylan.
M. Witmark & Sons.
Introduced by Bob Dylan (Columbia).

Baby's in Black (English)
Words and music by John Lennon and Paul McCartney.
Northern Songs, Ltd., London, England/Maclen Music, Inc.
Best-selling record in 1965 by The Beatles (Capitol).

Ballad in Plain D
Words and music by Bob Dylan.
M. Witmark & Sons.
Introduced by Bob Dylan (Columbia).

Ballad of Gilligan's Isle, The
Words and music by Sherwood Schwartz and George Wyle.
United Artists Music Co., Inc.
Theme from *Gilligan's Island* (television series).

Ballad of Ira Hayes, see 1962.

Baltimore
Words and music by Felice Bryant and Boudleaux Bryant.
Acuff-Rose Publications, Inc.
Best-selling record by Sonny James (Capitol).

Barry's Boys
Words and music by June Reizner.
B. F. Wood Music Co., Inc.
Introduced by Gerry Matthews, Jamie Ross, and Nagle Jackson in
  Baker's Dozen (cabaret revue). Best-selling record by The Chad
  Mitchell Trio (Mercury).

Beach Girl
Words and music by Terry Melcher and Bruce Johnson.
T. M. Music, Inc./Blackwood Music, Inc.
Best-selling record by Pat Boone (Dot).

Beans in My Ears
Words and music by Len H. Chandler, Jr.
Fall River Music, Inc.
Best-selling record by The Serendipity Singers (Philips).

Beautiful Land, The (English)
Words and music by Leslie Bricusse and Anthony Newley.
Concord Music, Ltd., London, England/Musical Comedy Productions, Inc.
Introduced by The Urchins in *The Roar of the Greasepaint—The Smell of the Crowd* (musical).

Because (English)
Words and music by Dave Clark.
Ivy Music, Ltd., London, England/Campbell-Connelly, Inc.
Best-selling record by The Dave Clark Five (Epic).

Before and After
Words and music by Van McCoy.
Blackwood Music, Inc., 1964, 1965.
First recording by The Fleetwoods (Dolton). Best-selling record in 1965 by Chad and Jeremy (Columbia).

Big Man in Town
Words and music by Bob Gaudio.
Saturday Music, Inc./Gavadima Music, Inc.
Best-selling record by The Four Seasons (Philips).

Birds and the Bees, The
Words and music by Herb Newman.
Pattern Music, Inc.
Best-selling record in 1965 by Jewel Akens (Era).

Birmingham Sunday
Words by Richard Fariña, music, traditional.
Ryerson Music Publishers, Inc.
Music adapted from old English folk song, "I Loved a Lass." Lyrics about bombing of Negro church in Birmingham, Alabama. Introduced by Richard and Mimi Fariña.

Bits and Pieces (English)
Words and music by Dave Clark and Mike Smith.
Ardmore and Beechwood, Ltd., London, England/Beechwood Music Corp.
Introduced and best-selling record in England and United States by The Dave Clark Five (Epic).

Black Crow Blues
Words and music by Bob Dylan.
M. Witmark & Sons.
Introduced by Bob Dylan (Columbia).

Bleecker Street
Words and music by Paul Simon.
Edward B. Marks Music Corp.
Introduced by Simon and Garfunkel (Columbia).

Blind Man
Words and music by Deadric Malone and Joseph Scott.
Don Music Co.
Best-selling record by Bobby Bland (Wand).

Born To Wander, see 1961.

Boy from New York City, The
Words and music by John Taylor.
Trio Music Co., Inc.
Best-selling record in 1965 by The Ad Libs (Blue Cat).

Boy Ten Feet Tall, A
Words by Ned Washington, music by Les Baxter.
Arch Music Co., Inc.
Adapted from a theme from *A Boy Ten Feet Tall* (film).

Boys, see 1960.

Bread and Butter
Words and music by Larry Parks and Jay Turnbow.
Acuff-Rose Publications, Inc.
Best-selling record by The Newbeats (Hickory).

Bucket "T"
Words and music by Don Altfeld, Roger Christian, and Dean
    Torrence.
Screen Gems-Columbia Music, Inc.
Best-selling record by Ronnie and The Daytonas (Mala).

Bye Bye Baby (Baby Goodbye)
Words and music by Bob Crewe and Bob Gaudio.
Saturday Music, Inc./Seasons Four Music Corp.
Best-selling record in 1965 by The Four Seasons (Philips).

California Sun, see 1961.

Can You Jerk Like Me
Words and music by William Stevenson and Ivy Hunter.
Jobete Music Co., Inc.
Best-selling record by The Contours (Gordy).

Can't Buy Me Love (English)
Words and music by John Lennon and Paul McCartney.
Northern Songs, Ltd., London, England/Maclen Music, Inc.
Introduced by The Beatles in *A Hard Day's Night* (film). Best-
    selling record by The Beatles (Capitol).

Can't Get Over (The Bossa Nova)
Words and music by Steve Lawrence, Eydie Gormé, and Marilyn
    Gins.
April Music, Inc./Maxana Music Corp.
Best-selling record by Eydie Gormé (Columbia).

214

Can't You See It?
Words by Lee Adams, music by Charles Strouse.
Morley Music Co., Inc.
Introduced by Sammy Davis, Jr. in *Golden Boy* (musical).

Can't You See That She's Mine? (English)
Words and music by Dave Clark and Mike Smith.
Ardmore and Beechwood, Ltd., London, England/Beechwood Music
  Corp.
Best-selling record by The Dave Clark Five (Epic).

Cat, The
Music by Lalo Schifrin.
Hastings Music Corp., 1964, 1965.
From *Joy House* (film). Lyrics added by Rick Ward in 1965. Best-
  selling records by Lalo Schifrin and Orchestra (Verve) and Jimmy
  Smith (Verve). Winner of National Academy of Recording Arts
  and Sciences Award for "Best Original Jazz Composition," 1964.

Cement Octopus
Words and music by Malvina Reynolds.
Schroder Music Co.
Introduced by Malvina Reynolds.

Chains, see 1962.

Chapel of Love
Words and music by Phil Spector, Ellie Greenwich, and Jeff Barry.
Trio Music Co., Inc.
Best-selling record by The Dixie Cups (Red Bird).

Charlemagne (French)
English words by Sydney Lee, French words by Robert Gall, music
  by Georges Liferman.
Éditions Bagatelle, Paris, France/Gil Music Corp.
Adapted from traditional French children's song. Introduced in
  France by France Gall (Philips). Introduced in United States by
  Frank D'Rone with The Quinto Sisters (Columbia).

Chimes of Freedom
Words and music by Bob Dylan.
M. Witmark & Sons.
Introduced by Bob Dylan (Columbia).

Chug-A-Lug
Words and music by Roger Miller.
Tree Publishing Co., Inc.
Best-selling record by Roger Miller (Smash).

Circus World
Words by Ned Washington, music by Dimitri Tiomkin.
Leo Feist, Inc.
From *Circus World* (film).

Clinging Vine, see 1962.

Close Harmony
Words by Betty Comden and Adolph Green, music by Jule Styne.
Stratford Music Corp./Chappell & Co., Inc.
Introduced by Jack Cassidy, Lou Jacobi, Tina Louise, and Nephews
in *Fade Out—Fade In* (musical).

Closest Thing to Heaven, The
Words and music by Howard Greenfield and Neil Sedaka.
Screen Gems-Columbia Music, Inc.
Introduced by Neil Sedaka (RCA Victor).

C'mon and Swim
Words by Thomas Coman, music by Sylvester Stewart.
Taracrest Music, Inc.
Best-selling record by Bobby Freeman (Autumn).

Cod'ine
Words and music by Buffy Sainte-Marie.
Gypsy Boy Music, Inc.
Introduced by Buffy Sainte-Marie (Vanguard).

Colorful
Words by Lee Adams, music by Charles Strouse.
Morley Music Co., Inc.
Introduced by Sammy Davis, Jr. in *Golden Boy* (musical).

Come a Little Bit Closer
Words and music by Tommy Boyce, Bobby Hart, and Wes Farrell.
Picturetone Music Publishing Corp.
Best-selling record by Jay and The Americans (United Artists).

Come Home (English)
Words and music by Dave Clark and Mike Smith.
Sphere Music Co., Ltd., London, England/Branston Music, Inc.
Best-selling record in 1965 by The Dave Clark Five (Epic).

Come On, Do the Jerk
Words and music by Donald Whited, Warren Moore, Robert Rogers,
and William Robinson.
Jobete Music Co., Inc.
Best-selling record by The Miracles (Tamla).

Come On, Let Yourself Go
Words and music by Jan Berry and Art Kornfeld.
Screen Gems-Columbia Music, Inc.
From *The New Interns* (film).

Come See about Me
Words and music by Brian Holland, Eddie Holland, and Lamont
Dozier.
Jobete Music Co., Inc.
Best-selling record by The Supremes (Motown).

Confidence
Words by Earl Shuman, music by Leon Carr.
April Music, Inc.
Introduced by Rudy Tronto, Cathryn Damon, and Marc London in
The Secret Life of Walter Mitty (musical). First recording by
The Kirby Stone Four (Columbia).

Cornet Man
Words by Bob Merrill, music by Jule Styne.
Chappell & Co., Inc.
Introduced by Barbra Streisand in *Funny Girl* (musical).

Cotton Candy
Music by Russ Damon.
Al Gallico Music Corp.
Introduced and best-selling record by Al Hirt (RCA Victor).

Cotton Mill Man
Words and music by Joe Langston.
Screen Gems-Columbia Music, Inc.
Introduced by Jim and Jesse (Epic).

Crooked Little Man, see Don't Let the Rain Come Down.

Cross the Brazos at Waco
Words and music by Kay Arnold.
Painted Desert Music Corp.
Best-selling record by Billy Walker (Columbia).

Cuando Caliente El Sol, see 1961.

Dance, Dance, Dance
Words and music by Brian Wilson and Carl Wilson.
Sea of Tunes Publishing Co.
Best-selling record by The Beach Boys (Capitol).

Dancing in the Street
Words and music by William Stevenson and Marvin Gaye.
Jobete Music Co., Inc.
Best-selling record by Martha and The Vandellas (Gordy).

Dang Me
Words and music by Roger Miller.
Tree Publishing Co., Inc.
Best-selling record by Roger Miller (Smash). Winner of National
Academy of Recording Arts and Sciences Awards for "Best
Country and Western Song," "Best Country and Western Single,"
and "Best Country and Western Vocal Performance—Male," 1964.

Daniel Boone
Words by Vera Matson, music by Lionel Newman.
Hastings Music Corp.
Theme from *Daniel Boone* (television series).

Days of the Waltz, The (French-Belgian)
English words by Will Holt, French words and music by Jacques Brel.
Les Éditions Musicales Tutti, Paris, France, 1959, 1962, 1964/ Leeds Music Corp.
Original French title, "La Valse à Mille Temps." Introduced in France by Jacques Brel (Philips). First English-language version introduced in United States in 1962 by Elly Stone in *O, Oysters!* (off-Broadway revue) under title, "Carousels," with lyrics by Eric Blau. Holt adaptation introduced by Felicia Sanders; first recording by Patti Page (Columbia). See "Carousels," 1962.

Dear Heart
Words by Jay Livingston and Ray Evans, music by Henry Mancini.
Northridge Music, Inc./M. Witmark & Sons.
Introduced by orchestra and chorus in *Dear Heart* (film). Nominated for Academy Award, 1964. Best-selling records by Andy Williams (Columbia) and Jack Jones (Kapp).

Dern Ya
Words and music by Roger Miller and Justin Tubb.
Tree Publishing Co., Inc.
Introduced by Ruby Wright (Rik).

Disorderly Orderly, The
Words by Earl Shuman, music by Leon Carr.
Paramount Music Corp.
Introduced by Sammy Davis, Jr. in *The Disorderly Orderly* (film).

Do It Right
Words and music by Rudy Clark.
T. M. Music, Inc.
Best-selling record by Brook Benton (Mercury).

Do What You Do, Do Well
Words and music by Ned Miller and Sue Miller.
Central Songs, Inc., 1964, 1965.
Best-selling record in 1965 by Ned Miller (Fabor).

Do You Love Me?
Words by Sheldon Harnick, music by Jerry Bock.
Sunbeam Music Corp.
Introduced by Zero Mostel and Maria Karnilova in *Fiddler on the Roof* (musical).

Do You Love Me?, see 1962.

Dodo, The
Words and music by Milton Addington, Allen Reynolds, and Dickey Lee.
Screen Gems-Columbia Music, Inc.
Introduced by Gene Simmons (London).

Don't Come Running Back to Me
Words and music by Sid Tepper and Roy C. Bennett.
MCA, Inc.
Introduced by Nancy Wilson (Capitol).

Don't Forget I Still Love You
Words and music by Guy Louis.
South Mountain Music Corp.
Best-selling record by Bobbi Martin (Coral).

Don't Forget 127th Street
Words by Lee Adams, music by Charles Strouse.
Morley Music Co., Inc.
Introduced by Johnny Brown, Sammy Davis, Jr. and company in
    Golden Boy (musical).

Don't Let Me Be Misunderstood
Words and music by Bennie Benjamin, Sol Marcus, and Gloria
    Caldwell.
Bennie Benjamin Music, Inc.
Best-selling record by Nina Simone (Philips).

Don't Let the Rain Come Down (Crooked Little Man)
Words and music by Ersel Hickey and Ed. E. Miller.
Serendipity Publishing Corp./Robert Mellin, Inc.
Best-selling record by The Serendipity Singers (Philips).

Don't Let the Sun Catch You Crying (English)
Words and music by Gerrard Marsden.
Pacermusic, Ltd., London, England/Pacemaker Music Co., Inc.
Best-selling record in England and United States by Gerry and The
    Pacemakers (Laurie).

Don't Rain on My Parade
Words by Bob Merrill, music by Jule Styne.
Chappell & Co., Inc.
Introduced by Barbra Streisand in *Funny Girl* (musical).

Don't Throw Your Love Away
Words and music by Billy Jackson and Jim Wisner.
Wyncote Music Publishing Co., Inc.
Best-selling record by The Searchers (Kapp).

Don't Worry Baby
Words and music by Brian Wilson and Roger Christian.
Sea of Tunes Publishing Co.
Best-selling record by The Beach Boys (Capitol).

Do-Wacka-Do
Words and music by Roger Miller.
Tree Publishing Co., Inc.
Introduced and best-selling record by Roger Miller (Smash).

Downtown (English)
Words and music by Tony Hatch.
Welbeck Music, Ltd., London, England/Leeds Music Corp.
Best-selling record in England and United States in 1964-65 by Petula
  Clark (Warner Bros.). Winner of National Academy of Recording
  Arts and Sciences Award for "Best Rock and Roll Recording,"
  1964.

Draft Dodger Rag
Words and music by Phil Ochs.
Appleseed Music, Inc.
Introduced by Phil Ochs (Elektra).

Dream On Little Dreamer
Words and music by Jan Crutchfield and Fred Burch.
Cedarwood Publishing Co., Inc./Forrest Hills Music, Inc.
Best-selling record by Perry Como (RCA Victor).

Early Mornin' Rain
Words and music by Gordon Lightfoot.
M. Witmark & Sons.
Best-selling records in 1965 by Peter, Paul, and Mary (Warner
  Bros.) and in 1966 by Chad and Jeremy (Columbia).

Ebb Tide, see 1953.

Eight Days a Week (English)
Words and music by John Lennon and Paul McCartney.
Northern Songs, Ltd., London, England/Maclen Music, Inc.
Introduced and best-selling record in 1965 by The Beatles (Capitol).

Emily
Words by Johnny Mercer, music by Johnny Mandel.
Miller Music Corp.
Adapted from a theme from *The Americanization of Emily* (film).
  Best-selling record by Andy Williams (Columbia).

Every Little Thing (English)
Words and music by John Lennon and Paul McCartney.
Northern Songs, Ltd., London, England/Maclen Music, Inc.
Best-selling record by The Beatles (Capitol).

Everybody Knows (English)
Words and music by Jimmy Duncan and Les Reed.
Francis, Day & Hunter, Ltd., London, England/Gil Music Corp.
Best-selling record by Steve Lawrence (Columbia).

Everybody Knows (I Still Love You) (English)
Words and music by Dave Clark and Lenny Davidson.
Sphere Music Co., Ltd., London, England/Branston Music, Inc.
Introduced and best-selling record by The Dave Clark Five (Epic).

Everybody Loves Somebody, see 1948.

Everybody Says Don't
Words and music by Stephen Sondheim.
Burthen Music Co., Inc.
Introduced by Harry Guardino in *Anyone Can Whistle* (musical).

Everything Makes Music When You're in Love
Words by Sammy Cahn, music by James Van Heusen.
Miller Music Corp.
Introduced by Ann-Margret in *The Pleasure Seekers* (film, 1965).

Everything's Great
Words by Lee Adams, music by Charles Strouse.
Morley Music Co., Inc.
Introduced by Kenneth Tobey and Paula Wayne in *Golden Boy*
    (musical).

Fade Out—Fade In
Words by Betty Comden and Adolph Green, music by Jule Styne.
Stratford Music Corp./Chappell & Co., Inc.
Introduced by Carol Burnett and Dick Patterson in *Fade Out—Fade
    In* (musical).

Faith
Words and music by Jack Lawrence and Stan Freeman.
Mesquite Music Corp.
Introduced by Richard Kiley, The Alley Gang, and ensemble in
    I Had a Ball (musical).

Fall of Love, The
Words by Ned Washington, music by Dimitri Tiomkin.
Leo Feist, Inc.
Adapted from a theme from *The Fall of the Roman Empire* (film).

Fan the Flame
Words by Earl Shuman, music by Leon Carr.
April Music, Inc.
Introduced by Cathryn Damon in *The Secret Life of Walter Mitty*
    (musical).

Far from the Home I Love
Words by Sheldon Harnick, music by Jerry Bock.
Sunbeam Music Corp.
Introduced by Julia Migenes and Zero Mostel in *Fiddler on the Roof*
    (musical).

Farewell
Words and music by Bob Dylan.
M. Witmark & Sons.
Introduced by Bob Dylan (Columbia).

Feeling Good (English)

Words and music by Leslie Bricusse and Anthony Newley.

Concord Music, Ltd., London, England/Musical Comedy Productions, Inc.

Introduced by Gilbert Price and The Urchins in *The Roar of the Greasepaint—The Smell of the Crowd* (musical).

Ferry cross the Mersey (English)

Words and music by Gerrard Marsden.

Pacermusic, Ltd., London, England/Pacemaker Music Co., Inc.

Introduced by Gerry and the Pacemakers in *Ferry cross the Mersey* (British film). Best-selling record in 1965 by Gerry and The Pacemakers (Laurie).

Fiddler on the Roof

Music by Sheldon Harnick and Jerry Bock.

Sunbeam Music Corp.

Theme from *Fiddler on the Roof* (musical).

Find Yourself a Man

Words by Bob Merrill, music by Jule Styne.

Chappell & Co., Inc.

Introduced by Danny Meehan, Kay Medford, and Jean Stapleton in *Funny Girl* (musical).

Finding Words for Spring

Words and music by Marian Grudeff and Raymond Jessel.

Edward B. Marks Music Corp.

Introduced by Inga Swenson in *Baker Street* (musical, 1965).

Fireball

Words and music by B. H. Graves, Lester Flatt, and Earl Scruggs.

Flatt and Scruggs Publishing Co.

Introduced by Lester Flatt and Earl Scruggs (Columbia).

Fool Killer, The

Words by Hal David, music by Burt Bacharach.

Arch Music Co., Inc.

"Inspired" by *The Fool Killer* (film). Introduced by Gene Pitney (Musicor).

Fool Never Learns, A, see 1962.

For Lovin' Me

Words and music by Gordon Lightfoot.

M. Witmark & Sons.

Best-selling record by Peter, Paul, and Mary (Warner Bros.).

Forever and a Day

Words and music by Hugh Martin and Timothy Gray.

Cromwell Music, Inc.

Introduced by Tammy Grimes and Edward Woodward in *High Spirits* (musical).

Freedom Is the Word
Words by E. Y. Harburg, music by Burton Lane.
The Players Music Corp.
Civil rights song introduced by Robert Preston and children's chorus
on closed circuit television show, sponsored by National Associa-
tion for the Advancement of Colored People.

From a Window (English)
Words and music by John Lennon and Paul McCartney.
Northern Songs, Ltd., London, England/Maclen Music, Inc.
Best-selling record by Billy J. Kramer and The Dakotas (Imperial).

Fun, Fun, Fun
Words and music by Brian Wilson.
Sea of Tunes Publishing Co.
Best-selling record by The Beach Boys (Capitol).

Funny, see 1961.

Funny Girl
Words by Bob Merrill, music by Jule Styne.
Chappell & Co., Inc.
Written as "promotion" song for *Funny Girl* (musical), but not in
show. Introduced by Barbra Streisand (Columbia).

Funny How Time Slips Away, see Funny, 1961.

Funny World (Italian)
English words by Alan Brandt, Italian words by Francesco Torti and
Guido Castaldo, music by Ennio Morricone.
Ed. Mus. C.A.M., Rome, Italy/Edward B. Marks Music Corp.
Original Italian title, "Questi Vent 'anni Miei." Introduced by Jane
Morgan in English, behind titles, on soundtrack of *Malamondo*
(film).

G. T. O.
Words and music by John Wilkin.
Buckhorn Music Publishers.
Best-selling record by Ronny and The Daytonas (Mala).

Game of Love, The
Words and music by Clint Ballard.
Skidmore Music Co., Inc.
Best-selling record in 1965 by Wayne Fontana and The Mindbenders
(Fontana).

Gimme Some
Words by Lee Adams, music by Charles Strouse.
Morley Music Co., Inc.
Introduced by Terrin Miles and Sammy Davis, Jr. in *Golden Boy*
(musical).

Girl on the Billboard
Words and music by Hank Mills and Walter Haynes.
Moss Rose Publications, Inc.
Best-selling record in 1965 by Del Reeves (United Artists).

Give Him a Great Big Kiss
Words and music by George Morton.
Trio Music Co., Inc.
Best-selling record by The Shangri-Las (Red Bird).

Give Me 40 Acres (To Turn This Rig Around)
Words and music by Earl Green and John Green.
Starday Music.
Best-selling record by The Willis Brothers (Starday).

Giving Up
Words and music by Van McCoy.
Trio Music Co., Inc.
Best-selling record by Gladys Knight and The Pips (Maxx).

Go, Cat Go
Words and music by Harlan Howard.
Wilderness Music Publishing Co.
Best-selling record by Norma Jean (RCA Victor).

God Bless the Grass
Words and music by Malvina Reynolds.
Schroder Music Co.
Best-selling record in 1965 by Pete Seeger (Columbia).

Goin' Out of My Head
Words and music by Teddy Randazzo and Bobby Weinstein.
South Mountain Music Corp.
Best-selling record by Little Anthony and The Imperials (DCP).

Golden Boy
Words by Lee Adams, music by Charles Strouse.
Morley Music Co., Inc.
Introduced by Paula Wayne in *Golden Boy* (musical).

Goldfinger (English)
Words by Leslie Bricusse and Anthony Newley, music by John Barry.
United Artists Music, Ltd., London, England/Unart Music Corp.
Title song, introduced by voice of Shirley Bassey, in *Goldfinger* (film). Best-selling record in 1965 by Shirley Bassey (United Artists).

Gonna Get Along without You Now, see 1951.

Good News
Words and music by Sam Cooke.
Kags Music.
Best-selling record by Sam Cooke (RCA Victor).

Goodbye Charlie
Words by Dory Langdon, music by André Previn.
Miller Music Corp.
Title song from *Goodbye Charlie* (film).

Half-Way Loved
Words and music by Max Powell and Wayne P. Walker.
Cedarwood Publishing Co., Inc.
Introduced by "Little" Jimmy Dickens (Columbia).

Hang on Sloopy (My Girl Sloopy)
Words and music by Bert Russell and Wes Farrell.
Picturetone Music Publishing Corp./Robert Mellin, Inc.
First introduced in Canada by Little Caesar and The Consuls. Best-
selling records by The Vibrations (Atlantic) and in 1965 by The
McCoys (Bang).

Happy Birthday
Words and music by Ron Kitson.
Sure-Fire Music Co., Inc.
Best-selling record in 1965 by Loretta Lynn (Decca).

Hard Day's Night, A (English)
Words and music by John Lennon and Paul McCartney.
Northern Songs, Ltd., London, England/Maclen Music, Inc./Unart
Music Corp.
Title song from *A Hard Day's Night* (film). Introduced and best-
selling record by The Beatles (United Artists). Winner of Na-
tional Academy of Recording Arts and Sciences Award for "Best
Performance by a Vocal Group," 1964.

Have I the Right (English)
Words and music by Alan Blaikley and Howard Blaikley.
Ivy Music, Ltd., London, England/Duchess Music Corp.
Best-selling record in England and United States by The Honey-
combs (Interphon).

Have You Looked into Your Heart, see 1962.

He Ain't No Angel
Words and music by Jeff Barry and Ellie Greenwich.
Trio Music Co., Inc.
Best-selling record by The Ad Libs (Blue Cat).

He Says the Same Things to Me
Words by Peter Udell, music by Gary Geld.
Geld-Udell Music Corp.
Best-selling record by Skeeter Davis (RCA Victor).

He Won't Ask Me (English)
Words and music by Bobby Willis.
Jaep Music, Ltd., London, England/Jaep Music, Inc.
Best-selling record by Cilla Black (Capitol).

Healing Hands of Time
Words and music by Willie Nelson.
Pamper Music, Inc.
Introduced by Willie Nelson (RCA Victor).

Heart Must Learn To Cry, A, see **Theme from** *36 Hours.*

Hello, I Love You, Goodbye
Words by Earl Shuman, music by Leon Carr.
April Music, Inc.
Introduced by Eugene Roche, Marc London, and Rudy Tronto in *The
    Secret Life of Walter Mitty* (musical).

Here Comes My Baby Back Again
Words and music by Dottie West and Bill West.
Tree Publishing Co., Inc.
Best-selling record by Dottie West (RCA Victor). Winner of Na-
    tional Academy of Recording Arts and Sciences Award for "Best
    Country and Western Vocal Performance—Female," 1964.

Hey Bobba Needle
Words and music by Kal Mann and Dave Appell.
Kalmann Music, Inc./C.C. Publishing Co., Inc.
Best-selling record by Chubby Checker (Parkway).

Hi-Heel Sneakers
Words and music by Robert Higgenbotham.
Medal Music, Inc.
Best-selling records by Tommy Tucker (Checker) and in 1965 by
    Stevie Wonder (Tamla).

Hold What You've Got
Words and music by Joe Tex.
Tree Publishing Co., Inc.
Best-selling record in 1964-65 by Joe Tex (Dial).

Honey-Wind Blows
Words and music by Fred Hellerman and Fran Minkoff.
Appleseed Music, Inc.
Best-selling record by Glen Yarbrough (RCA Victor).

Honky Tonk Happy
Words and music by Curly Putman.
Tree Publishing Co., Inc.
Best-selling record in 1966 by Billy Ranger (Cameo Parkway).

House of the Rising Sun, The
Words and adaptation of music by Alan Price.
Keith Prowse Music Publishing Co., Ltd., London, England/Al
    Gallico Music Corp.
Adapted from traditional American song. Best-selling record in
    England and United States by The Animals (MGM).

How Do You Do It (English)
Words and music by Mitch Murray.
Dick James Music, Ltd., London, England, 1962/Just Music, Inc.
Best-selling record by Gerry and The Pacemakers (Laurie).

How D'Ya Talk to a Girl
Words by Sammy Cahn, music by James Van Heusen.
Shapiro, Bernstein & Co., Inc., 1964, 1966.
Introduced by Norman Wisdom and Gordon Dilworth in *Walking Happy* (musical, 1966).

(You Don't Know) How Glad I Am
Words and music by Jimmy Williams and Larry Harrison.
Roosevelt Music Co., Inc.
Introduced and best-selling record by Nancy Wilson (Capitol). Winner of National Academy of Recording Arts and Sciences Award for "Best Rhythm and Blues Recording," 1964.

How Sweet It Is (To Be Loved by You)
Words and music by Eddie Holland, Brian Holland, and Lamont Dozier.
Jobete Music Co., Inc.
Best-selling record in 1965 by Marvin Gaye (Tamla).

How To Murder Your Wife
Words by Neal Hefti and Lil Mattis, music by Neal Hefti.
United Artists Music Co., Inc., 1964, 1965.
Adapted from a theme from *How To Murder Your Wife* (film, 1965).

Hudson River Song, The, see **My Dirty Stream.**

Hush . . . Hush, Sweet Charlotte
Words by Mack David, music by Frank De Vol.
Miller Music Corp., 1964, 1965.
Title song, introduced by voice of Al Martino, in *Hush . . . Hush, Sweet Charlotte* (film). Nominated for Academy Award, 1964. Best-selling record in 1965 by Patti Page (Columbia).

I Ain't Marchin' Anymore
Words and music by Phil Ochs.
Appleseed Music, Inc.
Introduced by Phil Ochs.

I Am a Rock
Words and music by Paul Simon.
Eclectic Music Co.
Best-selling record in 1966 by Simon and Garfunkel (Columbia).

I Am Woman, You Are Man, see **You Are Woman, I Am Man.**

I Can
Words and music by Walter Marks.
Mesquite Music Corp.
Introduced by Chita Rivera and Nancy Dussault in *Bajour* (musical).

I Can't Get Over Me (Not Gettin' Over You)
Words and music by Wayne P. Walker and Chuck Reed.
Cedarwood Publishing Co., Inc.
Introduced by "Little" Jimmy Dickens (Columbia).

I Don't Believe You (She Acts Like We Never Have Met)
Words and music by Bob Dylan.
M. Witmark & Sons.
Introduced by Bob Dylan (Columbia).

I Don't Care
Words and music by Buck Owens.
Blue Book Music Co.
Best-selling record by Buck Owens (Capitol).

I Don't Love You Any More
Words and music by Bill Anderson.
Moss Rose Publications, Inc.
Best-selling record by Charlie Louvin (Capitol).

I Don't Think I'm in Love
Words by Sammy Cahn, music by James Van Heusen.
Shapiro, Bernstein & Co., Inc., 1964, 1966.
Introduced by Norman Wisdom and Louise Troy in *Walking Happy*
  (musical, 1966).

I Don't Want To See You Again (English)
Words and music by John Lennon and Paul McCartney.
Northern Songs, Ltd., London, England/Maclen Music, Inc.
Introduced and best-selling record by Peter and Gordon (Capitol).

I Don't Want To Spoil the Party (English)
Words and music by John Lennon and Paul McCartney.
Northern Songs, Ltd., London, England/Maclen Music, Inc.
Introduced and best-selling record by The Beatles (Capitol).

I Feel Fine (English)
Words and music by John Lennon and Paul McCartney.
Northern Songs, Ltd., London, England/Maclen Music, Inc.
Introduced and best-selling record in 1964-65 by The Beatles (Capi-
  tol.)

I Get Around
Words and music by Brian Wilson.
Sea of Tunes Publishing Co.
Best-selling record by The Beach Boys (Capitol).

I Go to Pieces
Words and music by Del Shannon.
Vicki Music, Inc./Noma Music, Inc.
Best-selling record in 1965 by Peter and Gordon (Capitol).

I Got a Thing Going On
Words and music by Bobby Marchan.
Tree Publishing Co., Inc.
Introduced by Bobby Marchan (Dial).

I Got Everything I Want
Words and music by Jack Lawrence and Stan Freeman.
Mesquite Music Corp.
Introduced by Karen Morrow in *I Had a Ball* (musical).

I Had a Ball
Words and music by Jack Lawrence and Stan Freeman.
Mesquite Music Corp.
Introduced by Karen Morrow, The Alley Gang, and ensemble in
    I Had a Ball (musical).

I Knew It All the Time, see 1962.

I Know Your Heart
Words and music by Hugh Martin and Timothy Gray.
Cromwell Music, Inc.
Introduced by Edward Woodward and Tammy Grimes in *High
    Spirits* (musical).

I Like It Like That, see 1961.

I Love To Dance with Annie
Words and music by Felice Bryant and Boudleaux Bryant.
Acuff-Rose Publications, Inc.
Best-selling record by Ernest Ashworth (Hickory).

I Should Have Known Better (English)
Words and music by John Lennon and Paul McCartney.
Northern Songs, Ltd., London, England/Maclen Music, Inc./Unart
    Music Corp.
Introduced by The Beatles in *A Hard Day's Night* (film). Best-
    selling record by The Beatles (United Artists).

I Thank My Lucky Stars, see 1962.

I Wanna Be in Love Again
Words and music by Johnny Mercer.
Cromwell Music, Inc. 1964, 1965.
First recording by Jackie Cain and Roy Kral (Roulette).

I Wanna Love Him So Bad
Words and music by Jeff Barry and Ellie Greenwich.
Trio Music Co., Inc.
Best-selling record by The Jelly Beans (Red Bird).

I Want To Be with You
Words by Lee Adams, music by Charles Strouse.
Morley Music Co., Inc.
Introduced by Sammy Davis, Jr. and Paula Wayne in *Golden Boy* (musical).

I Want You To Meet My Baby
Words and music by Barry Mann and Cynthia Weil.
Screen Gems-Columbia Music, Inc.
Best-selling record by Eydie Gormé (Columbia).

I Washed My Hands in Muddy Water
Words and music by Joe Babcock.
Maricana Music, Inc.
Best-selling record in 1966 by Johnny Rivers (Imperial).

I Will Wait for You (French)
English words by Norman Gimbel, French words by Jacques Demy, music by Michel Legrand.
Productions Michel Legrand, Paris, France/Productions Francis Lemarque, La Verne (Seine), France/South Mountain Music Corp./Jonware Music Corp.
Originally introduced in French by voices of Danielle Licari (dubbed for Catherine Deneuve) and José Bartel (dubbed for Nino Castelnuovo) in *The Umbrellas of Cherbourg* (French film). Nominated for Academy Award, 1965. Introduced in English by Steve Lawrence (Columbia).

I Wish You Love, see 1955.

I Wouldn't Trade You for the World
Words and music by Bill Smith, Curtis Kirk, and Bill Taylor.
Le Bill Music, Inc./Tyler Publishing Co.
Best-selling record by The Bachelors (London).

I'd Do It Again
Words and music by Marian Grudeff and Raymond Jessel.
Edward B. Marks Music Corp.
Introduced by Inga Swenson in *Baker Street* (musical, 1965).

If I Fell (English)
Words and music by John Lennon and Paul McCartney.
Northern Songs, Ltd., London, England/Maclen Music, Inc.
Introduced by The Beatles in *A Hard Day's Night* (film). Best-selling record by The Beatles (United Artists).

If I Gave You ...
Words and music by Hugh Martin and Timothy Gray.
Cromwell Music, Inc.
Introduced by Edward Woodward and Louise Troy in *High Spirits* (musical).

If I Were a Rich Man
Words by Sheldon Harnick, music by Jerry Bock.
Sunbeam Music Corp.
Introduced by Zero Mostel in *Fiddler on the Roof* (musical).

If You Love Him
Words and music by Bobby Darin.
T. M. Music, Inc./Champion Music Corp.
Introduced in *The Lively Set* (film).

I'll Be Back (English)
Words and music by John Lennon and Paul McCartney.
Northern Songs, Ltd., London, England/Maclen Music, Inc.
Best-selling record in 1965 by The Beatles (Capitol).

I'll Be There, see 1960.

I'll Cry Instead (English)
Words and music by John Lennon and Paul McCartney.
Northern Songs, Ltd., London, England/Maclen Music, Inc.
Introduced by The Beatles in *A Hard Day's Night* (film). Best-
selling record by The Beatles (United Artists).

I'll Follow the Sun (English)
Words and music by John Lennon and Paul McCartney.
Northern Songs, Ltd., London, England/Maclen Music, Inc.
Best-selling record in 1965 by The Beatles (Capitol).

I'll Go Down Swinging
Words and music by Bill Anderson.
Moss Rose Publications, Inc.
Best-selling record by Porter Wagoner (RCA Victor).

I'll Make a Man of the Man
Words by Sammy Cahn, music by James Van Heusen.
Shapiro, Bernstein & Co., Inc., 1964, 1966.
Introduced by Louise Troy in *Walking Happy* (musical, 1966).

I'll Never Go There Anymore
Words by Eddie Lawrence, music by Moose Charlap.
Chappell & Co., Inc.
Introduced by Don Francks and Anita Gillette in *Kelly* (musical,
1965).

I'll Repossess My Heart
Words and music by Paul Yandell.
Kitty Wells Publications.
Best-selling record in 1965 by Kitty Wells (Decca).

I'm a Loser (English)
Words and music by John Lennon and Paul McCartney.
Northern Songs, Ltd., London, England/Maclen Music, Inc.
Best-selling record in 1965 by The Beatles (Capitol).

I'm All Smiles
Words by Herbert Martin, music by Michael Leonard.
Mayfair Music Corp./Emanuel Music Corp.
Introduced by Barbra Streisand. Sung by Carmen Alvarez in *The Yearling* (musical, 1965).

I'm Crying (English)
Words and music by Eric Burdon and Alan Price.
Ivy Music Ltd., London, England/Al Gallico Music Corp.
Best-selling record in England and United States by The Animals (MGM).

I'm Happy Just To Dance with You (English)
Words and music by John Lennon and Paul McCartney.
Northern Songs, Ltd., London, England/Maclen Music, Inc.
Introduced by The Beatles in *A Hard Day's Night* (film). Best-selling record by The Beatles (United Artists).

I'm Into Something Good
Words and music by Gerry Goffin and Carole King.
Screen Gems-Columbia Music, Inc.
Best-selling record in England and United States by Herman's Hermits (MGM).

I'm Not Crazy Yet
Words and music by Don Rollins.
Pamper Music, Inc.
Best-selling record in 1966 by Ray Price (Columbia).

I'm Not Talking
Words and music by Mose Allison.
Audre Mae Music.
Introduced by Mose Allison.

I'm on the Outside (Looking In)
Words and music by Teddy Randazzo and Bobby Weinstein.
South Mountain Music Corp.
Best-selling record by Little Anthony and The Imperials (DCP).

I'm So Miserable without You
Words and music by Eugene Strasser and George Winters.
Regent Music Corp.
Introduced in 1960 by Billy Walker (Columbia).

I'm So Proud
Words and music by Curtis Mayfield.
Curtom Publishing Co., Inc.
Best-selling record by The Impressions (ABC-Paramount).

I'm the Greatest Star
Words by Bob Merrill, music by Jule Styne.
Chappell & Co., Inc.
Introduced by Barbra Streisand in *Funny Girl* (musical).

I'm with You
Words by Betty Comden and Adolph Green, music by Jule Styne.
Stratford Music Corp./Chappell & Co., Inc.
Introduced by Carol Burnett and Jack Cassidy in *Fade Out—Fade In* (musical).

"In" Crowd, The
Words and music by Billy Page.
American Music, Inc.
First vocal record by Dobie Gray (Charger). Best-selling instrumental record in 1965 by The Ramsey Lewis Trio (Cadet). Winner of National Academy of Recording Arts and Sciences Award for "Best Instrumental Jazz Performance—Small Group," 1965.

In My Lonely Room
Words and music by Eddie Holland, Brian Holland, and Lamont Dozier.
Jobete Music Co., Inc.
Best-selling record by Martha and The Vandellas (Gordy).

In My Room
Words and music by Brian Wilson and Gary Usher.
Sea of Tunes Publishing Co.
Best-selling record by The Beach Boys (Capitol).

In the Name of Love
Words and music by Ken Rankin and Estelle Levitt.
Blackwood Music, Inc.
Introduced by Peggy Lee (Capitol).

Invisible Tears
Words and music by Ned Miller and Sue Miller.
Central Songs, Inc.
Best-selling records by The Ray Conniff Singers (Columbia) and Ned Miller (Fabor).

It Ain't Me, Babe
Words and music by Bob Dylan.
M. Witmark & Sons.
Introduced by Bob Dylan. Best-selling records by Bob Dylan (Columbia), Johnny Cash (Columbia), and in 1965 by The Turtles (White Whale).

It Happened Just That Way
Words and music by Roger Miller.
Tree Publishing Co., Inc.
Introduced by Roger Miller (Smash).

It Hurts To Be in Love
Words and music by Howard Greenfield and Helen Miller.
Screen Gems-Columbia Music, Inc.
Best-selling record by Gene Pitney (Musicor).

It's All in the Game, see 1951.

It's All Over
Words and music by Curtis Mayfield.
Curtom Publishing Co., Inc./Jalynne Corp.
Best-selling record by Walter Jackson (Okeh).

It's for You (English)
Words and music by John Lennon and Paul McCartney.
Northern Songs, Ltd., London, England/Maclen Music, Inc.
Best-selling record by Cilla Black (Capitol).

It's Gonna Be All Right (English)
Words and music by Gerrard Marsden.
Pacermusic, Ltd., London, England/Pacemaker Music Co., Inc.
Best-selling record in 1965 by Gerry and The Pacemakers (Laurie).

It's Got the Whole World Shakin'
Words and music by Sam Cooke.
Kags Music.
Best-selling record by Sam Cooke (RCA Victor).

It's Over
Words and music by Roy Orbison and Bill Dees.
Acuff-Rose Publications, Inc.
Best-selling record by Roy Orbison (Monument).

I've Got a Tiger by the Tail
Words and music by Buck Owens and Harlan Howard.
Blue Book Music Co.
Best-selling record in 1965 by Buck Owens (Capitol).

I've Got Everything I Want
Words and music by Jack Lawrence and Stan Freeman.
Mesquite Music Corp.
Introduced by Karen Morrow in *I Had a Ball* (musical).

I've Got Sand in My Shoes
Words and music by Artie Resnick and Kenny Young.
T. M. Music, Inc.
Best-selling record by The Drifters (Atlantic).

I've Got You To Lean On
Words and music by Stephen Sondheim.
Burthen Music Co., Inc.
Introduced by Angela Lansbury, Gabriel Dell, Arnold Soboloff, James
  Frawley, Sterling Clark, Harvey Evans, Larry Roquemore, and
  Tucker Smith in *Anyone Can Whistle* (musical).

Jamaica Ska (Jamaican)
Words and music by Byron Lee.
Benders Music, Inc.
Best-selling record by The Ska Kings (Atlantic).

James Bond Theme, The, see 1962.

Java, see 1958.

Jenny Rebecca
Words and music by Carol Hall.
Musical Comedy Productions, Inc.
Introduced by Barbra Streisand.

Jerk, The
Words and music by Don Julian.
Cash Songs.
Best-selling record by The Larks (Money).

Joker, The (English)
Words and music by Leslie Bricusse and Anthony Newley.
Concord Music, Ltd., London, England/Musical Comedy Productions,
    Inc.
Introduced by Anthony Newley in *The Roar of the Greasepaint—
    The Smell of the Crowd* (musical).

Joy in the Morning
Words by Paul Francis Webster, music by Sammy Fain.
Miller Music Corp., 1964, 1965.
From *Joy in the Morning* (film).

Julie Knows
Words and music by Leon Carr and Paul Vance.
Apt Music Corp.
Best-selling record by Randy Sparks (Columbia).

Just a Little Bit Better
Words and music by Kenny Young.
T. M. Music, Inc., 1964, 1965.
Best-selling record in 1965 by Herman's Hermits (MGM).

Keep On Pushing
Words and music by Curtis Mayfield.
Curtom Publishing Co., Inc.
Best-selling record by The Impressions (ABC-Paramount).

Keep Searchin' (We'll Follow the Sun)
Words and music by Del Shannon.
Vicki Music, Inc./Noma Music, Inc.
Best-selling record in 1964-65 by Del Shannon (Amy).

Kid Again, A
Words and music by Johnny Melfi and Roger Perry.
Screen Gems-Columbia Music, Inc.
Introduced in 1965 by Barbra Streisand in *My Name Is Barbra*
    (television spectacular).

King of the Road
Words and music by Roger Miller.
Tree Publishing Co., Inc., 1964, 1965.
Introduced and best-selling record in 1965 by Roger Miller (Smash).
   Winner of National Academy of Recording Arts and Sciences
   Awards for "Best Contemporary Single Record," "Best Contem-
   porary Vocal Performance—Male," "Best Country and Western
   Single," "Best Country and Western Vocal Performance—Male,"
   and "Best Country and Western Song," 1965. New lyrics by Mary
   Taylor added in 1965; this version entitled "Queen of the House."
   Introduced and best-selling record by Jody Miller (Capitol). Winner
   of National Academy of Recording Arts and Sciences Award for
   "Best Country and Western Vocal Performance—Female," 1965.

Kiss Me, Sailor
Words and music by Eddie Rambeau and Bud Rehak.
Saturday Music, Inc.
Best-selling record by Diane Renay (20th Century-Fox).

Kissin' Cousins
Words and music by Fred Wise and Randy Starr.
Gladys Music, Inc.
Introduced by Elvis Presley in *Kissin' Cousins* (film).

La La La La La
Words and music by Brian Holland, Eddie Holland, and Lamont
   Dozier.
Jobete Music Co., Inc.
Best-selling record by The Blendells (Reprise).

La Novia, see The Wedding, 1961.

La Valse à Mille Temps, see Carousels, 1962; see The
   Days of the Waltz, 1964.

Lady Bird
Words and music by Buddy Killen and Billy Sherrill.
Tree Publishing Co., Inc.
Best-selling record by The Dawnbusters (Cameo Parkway).

Last Kiss, see 1961.

Last Thing on My Mind, The
Words and music by Tom Paxton.
Deep Fork Music, Inc.
Introduced by Tom Paxton (Elektra).

Laugh, Laugh
Words and music by Ronald C. Elliott.
Taracrest Music, Inc.
Best-selling record in 1965 by The Beau Brummels (Autumn).

Lay Down Your Weary Tune
Words and music by Bob Dylan.
M. Witmark & Sons.
Introduced by Bob Dylan (Columbia).

Leader of the Laundromat
Words and music by Paul Vance and Lee Pockriss.
Apt Music Corp./Quartet Music, Inc./Sherwin Music, Inc.
Best-selling record in 1964-65 by The Detergents (Roulette).

Leader of the Pack
Words and music by George Morton, Jeff Barry, and Ellie Greenwich.
Tender Tunes Music/Elmwin Music, Inc.
Best-selling record by The Shangri-Las (Red Bird).

Lemon Tree, see 1960.

Less and Less
Words and music by Roger Miller.
Tree Publishing Co., Inc.
Introduced by Charlie Louvin (Capitol).

Let's Lock the Door (And Throw Away the Key)
Words and music by Roy Alfred and Wes Farrell.
Picturetone Music Publishing Corp.
Best-selling record by Jay and The Americans (United Artists).

Lifetime of Loneliness, A
Words and music by Burt Bacharach and Hal David.
Blue Seas Music, Inc./Jac Music Co., Inc.
Best-selling record by Jackie De Shannon (Imperial).

Like Dreamers Do (English)
Words and music by John Lennon and Paul McCartney.
Northern Songs, Ltd., London, England/Maclen Music, Inc.

Little Boy
Words and music by Phil Spector, Ellie Greenwich, and Jeff Barry.
Mother Bertha Music, Inc./Trio Music Co., Inc.
Best-selling record by The Crystals (Philles).

Little Children
Words and music by Mort Shuman and J. Leslie McFarland.
Rumbalero Music, Inc.
Best-selling record by Billy J. Kramer and The Dakotas (Imperial).

Little Honda
Words and music by Brian Wilson.
Sea of Tunes Publishing Co.
Best-selling records by The Hondells (Mercury) and The Beach
  Boys (Capitol).

Little Old Lady (From Pasadena), The
Words and music by Roger Christian and Don Altfeld.
Screen Gems-Columbia Music, Inc.
Best-selling record by Jan and Dean (Liberty).

Little Things
Words and music by Bobby Goldsboro.
Unart Music Corp.
Best-selling record in 1965 by Bobby Goldsboro (United Artists).

Little Things Like That
Words and music by Russ Titelman and Larry Kolber.
Screen Gems-Columbia Music, Inc.
Introduced in 1966 by Linda Lloyd (Columbia).

Live Wire
Words and music by Eddie Holland, Brian Holland, and Lamont
    Dozier.
Jobete Music Co., Inc.
Best-selling record by Martha and The Vandellas (Gordy).

Living Simply
Words and music by Walter Marks.
Mesquite Music Corp.
Introduced by Robert Burr, Nancy Dussault, and trio in *Bajour*
    (musical).

Lonesome Death of Hattie Carroll
Words and music by Bob Dylan.
M. Witmark & Sons.
Introduced by Bob Dylan (Columbia).

Long Ships, The (Yugoslavian)
Music by Dusan Radic.
ZAMP, Belgrade, Yugoslavia/Screen Gems-Columbia Music, Inc.
Theme from *The Long Ships* (film).

Look at That Face (English)
Words and music by Leslie Bricusse and Anthony Newley.
Concord Music, Ltd., London, England/Musical Comedy Productions,
    Inc.
Introduced by Cyril Ritchard, Sally Smith, and The Urchins in *The
    Roar of the Greasepaint—The Smell of the Crowd* (musical).

Look of Love
Words and music by Jeff Barry and Ellie Greenwich.
Trio Music Co., Inc.
Best-selling record in 1965 by Lesley Gore (Mercury).

Looking for Love
Words and music by Hank Hunter and Stan Vincent.
John D. MacArthur Music Corp.
Introduced by Connie Francis in *Looking for Love* (film).

Looking for More in '64
Words and music by B. Moore.
Peach Music.
Best-selling record by Jim Nesbitt (Chart).

Lorna's Here
Words by Lee Adams, music by Charles Strouse.
Morley Music Co., Inc.
Introduced by Paula Wayne in *Golden Boy* (musical).

Louisa's Theme
Music by Nelson Riddle.
Hastings Music Corp.
From *What a Way To Go* (film).

Love
Words and music by Bert Kaempfert and Milt Gabler.
Roosevelt Music Co., Inc.
Best-selling record by Nat "King" Cole (Capitol).

Love Goddess, The
Words by Mack David, music by Percy Faith.
Famous Music Corp.
Adapted from theme from *The Love Goddesses* (film, 1965). First vocal recording by Jerry Vale (Columbia).

Love Is a Bore
Words by Sammy Cahn, music by Jimmy Van Heusen.
Van Heusen Music Corp./Glorste, Inc.
Introduced by Barbra Streisand (Columbia).

Love Is a Chance
Words and music by Walter Marks.
Mesquite Music Corp.
Introduced by Nancy Dussault in *Bajour* (musical).

Love Is No Excuse
Words and music by Justin Tubb.
Tree Publishing Co., Inc.
Best-selling record by Jim Reeves and Dottie West (RCA Victor).

Love Me with All Your Heart, see **Cuando Caliente El Sol,** 1961.

Love Song of Tom Jones, The (English)
Words by Mack David, music by John Addison.
United Artists Music, Ltd., London, England/United Artists Music Co., Inc.
Adapted from a theme from *Tom Jones* (British film).

Love-Line
Words and music by Walter Marks.
Mesquite Music Corp.
Introduced by Chita Rivera in *Bajour* (musical).

Luck of Ginger Coffey, The (Watching the World Go By)
Words by Will Holt, music by Bernardo Segáll.
Walter Reade-Sterling Music Corp.
Adapted from the theme from *The Luck of Ginger Coffey* (film).

Lumberjack, The
Words and music by Hal Willis and Ginger Willis.
English Music, Inc.
Best-selling record by Hal Willis (Sims).

Mad
Words and music by Thomas Hall.
Newkeys Music, Inc.
Best-selling record by Dave Dudley (Mercury).

Madrigal (English)
Words and music by Mack David and Malcolm Arnold.
Henrees Music, Ltd., London, England/Northern Music Corp.
From *The Chalk Garden* (film). Best-selling record by Andy Williams (Columbia).

Make Me an Offer
Words and music by Benny Joy and Hugh X. Lewis.
Cedarwood Publishing Co., Inc.
Introduced by Carl and Pearl Butler (Columbia).

Mallory (French)
Words and music by André Popp, Sydney Lee, and Pierre Cour.
Éditions Bagatelle, Paris, France/Gil Music Corp.
Winner of Grand Prix Eurovision, 1964.

Mama, You Been on My Mind, see Baby, You Been on My Mind.

March from *Guns at Batasi*
Music by John Addison.
Miller Music Corp.
From *Guns at Batasi* (film).

Marriage Is for Old Folks
Words by Earl Shuman, music by Leon Carr.
April Music, Inc.
Introduced by Cathryn Damon, Marc London, and Rudy Tronto in *The Secret Life of Walter Mitty* (musical).

Married Man, A
Words and music by Marian Grudeff and Raymond Jessel.
Edward B. Marks Music Corp.
Introduced by Peter Sallis in *Baker Street* (musical, 1965). Introduced on records by Richard Burton (MGM).

Matador, The
Words and music by Carl Davis, William B. Butler, and Major Lance.
Curtom Publishing Co., Inc./Jalynne Corp.
Best-selling record by Major Lance (Okeh).

Matchmaker, Matchmaker
Words by Sheldon Harnick, music by Jerry Bock.
Sunbeam Music Corp.
Introduced by Joanna Merlin, Julia Migenes, and Tanya Everett in
Fiddler on the Roof (musical).

Maybe I Know
Words and music by Ellie Greenwich and Jeff Barry.
Trio Music Co., Inc.
Best-selling record by Lesley Gore (Mercury).

Meadowgreen
Words and music by Roger Miller.
Tree Publishing Co., Inc.
Introduced by The Browns (RCA Victor).

Memory Number One
Words and music by Wayne P. Walker and Max Powell.
Cedarwood Publishing Co., Inc.
Best-selling record by Webb Pierce (Decca).

Mercy, Mercy
Words and music by Don Covay and Ronnie Miller.
Cotillion Music, Inc./Vonglo Music Co.
Best-selling record by Don Covay (Rosemart).

Mexican Shuffle
Words and music by Sol Lake.
Almo Music Corp.
Introduced by Herb Alpert and The Tijuana Brass (A&M).

Midnight Special
Words and adaptation of music by Johnny Rivers.
Trousdale Music Publishers, Inc., 1964, 1965.
Adapted from traditional American folk song. Best-selling record in
1965 by Johnny Rivers (Imperial).

Minute Waltz, The
Words and adaptation of music by Lan O'Kun.
Arch Music Co., Inc.
Based on "The Minute Waltz," by Chopin. Introduced in 1966 by
Barbra Streisand in *Color Me Barbra* (television spectacular).

Miracle of Miracles
Words by Sheldon Harnick, music by Jerry Bock.
Sunbeam Music Corp.
Introduced by Austin Pendleton in *Fiddler on the Roof* (musical).

Mississippi Goddam
Words and music by Nina Simone.
Sam Fox Publishing Co., Inc.
Introduced by Nina Simone (Philips).

Mr. and Mrs. Used To Be
Words and music by Joe Deaton.
Sure-Fire Music Co., Inc.
Best-selling record by Ernest Tubb and Loretta Lynn (Decca).

Mr. Lonely, see 1962.

Mr. Tambourine Man
Words and music by Bob Dylan.
M. Witmark & Sons.
Introduced by Bob Dylan (Columbia). Best-selling record in 1965 by
  The Byrds (Columbia).

Mrs. Brown, You've Got a Lovely Daughter (English)
Words and music by Trevor Peacock.
Jack Good Music Publishing Co., Ltd., London, England/Brakenbury
  Music, Inc./Big Top Records, Inc.
Introduced by Tom Courtenay in British television play. Best-selling
  record in 1965 by Herman's Hermits (MGM).

Molly, see 1962.

Monica
Words by Earl Shuman, music by Elmer Bernstein.
Famous Music Corp.
Adapted from a theme from *The Carpetbaggers* (film).

Motel
Words and music by Jean Surrey.
Fred Burch Music.
Introduced in 1966 by Sherry Dinning (Alpine).

Motorpsycho Nightmare
Words and music by Bob Dylan.
M. Witmark & Sons.
Introduced by Bob Dylan (Columbia).

Muleskinner
Words and music by Stuart Gotz.
Frigate Music Corp.
Introduced by The Brothers Four (Columbia).

Munster's Theme
Music by Jack Marshall and Bob Mosher.
Hawaii Music Co., Inc.
Theme from *The Munsters* (television series).

Music That Makes Me Dance, The
Words by Bob Merrill, music by Jule Styne.
Chappell & Co., Inc.
Introduced by Barbra Streisand in *Funny Girl* (musical).

Must It Be Love?
Words and music by Walter Marks.
Mesquite Music Corp.
Introduced by Nancy Dussault in *Bajour* (musical).

My Baby Walks All over Me
Words and music by Billy Mize.
Owen Publications.
Best-selling record by Johnny Sea (Philips).

My Back Pages (I'm Younger Than That Now)
Words and music by Bob Dylan.
M. Witmark & Sons.
Introduced by Bob Dylan (Columbia).

My Dirty Stream (The Hudson River Song)
Words and music by Pete Seeger.
Fall River Music, Inc.
Introduced by Pete Seeger.

My First Love Song (English)
Words and music by Leslie Bricusse and Anthony Newley.
Concord Music, Ltd., London, England/Musical Comedy Productions,
    Inc.
Introduced by Anthony Newley and Joyce Jillson in *The Roar of the
    Greasepaint—The Smell of the Crowd* (musical).

My Friend on the Right
Words and music by Red Lane and Faron Young.
Tree Publishing Co., Inc.
Introduced by Faron Young (Mercury).

My Girl
Words and music by William Robinson and Ronald White.
Jobete Music Co., Inc., 1964, 1965.
Best-selling record in 1964-65 by The Temptations (Gordy).

My Girl Sloopy, see **Hang on Sloopy (My Girl Sloopy).**

My Guy
Words and music by William Robinson.
Jobete Music Co., Inc.
Best-selling record by Mary Wells (Motown).

My Heart Belongs to Only You, see 1952.

My Kind of Town
Words by Sammy Cahn, music by James Van Heusen.
Sergeant Music Co./Glorste, Inc./Van Heusen Music Corp.
Introduced by Frank Sinatra in *Robin and the 7 Hoods* (film). Nominated for Academy Award, 1964. Best-selling record by Frank
    Sinatra (Reprise).

My Land Is a Good Land
Words and music by Eric Anderson.
Deep Fork Music, Inc.

My Love (Roses Are Red)
Words and music by Robert Esposito.
Ashland Music Corp.
Best-selling record by "You Know Who" Group (4 Corners).

My Love, Forgive Me (Amore, Scusami) (Italian)
English words by Sydney Lee, Italian words by Vito Pallavicini,
    music by Gino Mescoli.
Edizioni Leonardi, S.r.l., Milan, Italy/Gil Music Corp.
Introduced in United States and best-selling record by Robert Goulet
    (Columbia).

Nadine (Is It You?)
Words and music by Chuck Berry.
Arc Music Corp.
Introduced by Chuck Berry (Chess).

Name Game, The
Words and music by Shirley Elliston and Lincoln Chase.
Al Gallico Music Corp.
Best-selling record in 1964-65 by Shirley Ellis (Congress).

Natural Man
Words and music by Randy Sparks and Nick Woods.
Cherrybell Music Co.
Introduced by The Back Porch Majority (Epic).

Need You Home
Words and music by Ted Taylor.
Ronnat Music Co.
Best-selling record by Ted Taylor (Epic).

Needle in a Haystack
Words and music by Norman Whitfield and William Stevenson.
Jobete Music Co., Inc.
Best-selling record by The Velvelettes (V.I.P.).

Night Song
Words by Lee Adams, music by Charles Strouse.
Morley Music Co., Inc.
Introduced by Sammy Davis, Jr. in *Golden Boy* (musical).

No More
Words by Lee Adams, music by Charles Strouse.
Morley Music Co., Inc.
Introduced by Sammy Davis, Jr. and company in *Golden Boy* (musi-
    cal).

No More Songs for Me
Words by Richard Maltby, Jr., music by David Shire.
Chappell & Co., Inc.
Introduced by Barbra Streisand (Columbia).

No Particular Place To Go
Words and music by Chuck Berry.
Arc Music Corp.
Best-selling record by Chuck Berry (Chess).

No Reply (English)
Words and music by John Lennon and Paul McCartney.
Northern Songs, Ltd., London, England/Maclen Music, Inc.
Best-selling record in 1965 by The Beatles (Capitol).

Nobody I Know (English)
Words and music by John Lennon and Paul McCartney.
Northern Songs, Ltd., London, England/Maclen Music, Inc.
Best-selling record by Peter and Gordon (Capitol).

Not a Second Time (English)
Words and music by John Lennon and Paul McCartney.
Northern Songs, Ltd., London, England, 1963, 1964/Maclen Music,
    Inc.
Best-selling record by The Beatles (Capitol).

Now I Have Everything
Words by Sheldon Harnick, music by Jerry Bock.
Sunbeam Music Corp.
Introduced by Bert Convy and Julia Migenes in *Fiddler on the Roof*
    (musical).

Ode to the Little Brown Shack Out Back
Words and music by Billy Edd Wheeler.
Bexhill Music Corp./Quartet Music, Inc.
Best-selling record in 1965 by Billy Edd Wheeler (Kapp).

Oh! No, Not My Baby
Words and music by Gerry Goffin and Carole King.
Screen Gems-Columbia Music, Inc.
Best-selling record by Maxine Brown (Wand).

Oh, Pretty Woman
Words and music by Roy Orbison and Bill Dees.
Acuff-Rose Publications, Inc.
Best-selling record by Roy Orbison (Monument).

Once a Day
Words and music by Bill Anderson.
Moss Rose Publications, Inc.
Best-selling record by Connie Smith (RCA Victor).

One More Time
Words and music by Buz Kohan and Bill Angelos.
January Music Corp.
Best-selling record by The Ray Charles Singers (Command).

One of These Days
Words and music by Marty Robbins.
Mariposa Music, Inc.
Best-selling record by Marty Robbins (Columbia).

One Potato, Two Potato
Words and music by Gerald Fried.
Arch Music Co., Inc.
Main theme from *One Potato, Two Potato* (film).

Other Half of Me, The
Words and music by Jack Lawrence and Stan Freeman.
Mesquite Music Corp.
Introduced by Richard Kiley in *I Had a Ball* (musical).

Our Everlasting Love
Words by Earl Shuman, music by Leon Carr.
Mansion Music Corp.
Best-selling record by Ruby and The Romantics (Kapp).

Pack Up Your Sorrows
Words and music by Pauline Marden and Richard Fariña.
Ryerson Music Publishers, Inc.
Best-selling record by Joan Baez (Vanguard).

Parade in Town, A
Words and music by Stephen Sondheim.
Burthen Music Co., Inc.
Introduced by Angela Lansbury in *Anyone Can Whistle* (musical).

Party Girl
Words and music by Buddy Buie and William Gilmore.
Unart Music Corp.
Best-selling record by Tommy Roe (ABC-Paramount).

Pass Me By
Words by Carolyn Leigh, music by Cy Coleman.
Edwin H. Morris & Co., Inc./Northern Music Corp.
Introduced by Digby Wolfe on soundtrack of *Father Goose* (film,
    1965). First recording by Peggy Lee (Capitol).

Pass the Booze
Words and music by Gene Northington and Ray Butts.
Lonzo & Oscar Music Publishing Co., Inc.
Best-selling record by Ernest Tubb (Decca).

Pearly Shells, see 1962.

People
Words by Bob Merrill, music by Jule Styne.
Chappell & Co., Inc.
Introduced by Barbra Streisand in *Funny Girl* (musical). Best-selling record by Barbra Streisand (Columbia). Winner of National Academy of Recording Arts and Sciences Awards for "Best Female Vocal Performance" and "Best Accompaniment Arrangement" (by Peter Matz), 1964.

People Say
Words and music by Jeff Barry and Ellie Greenwich.
Trio Music Co., Inc.
Best-selling record by The Dixie Cups (Red Bird).

Phoenix Love Theme, The, also known as Senza Fine (Italian)
English words by Alec Wilder, Italian words and music by Gino Paoli.
Edizioni Musicali Fama, S.R.L., 1961/Ludlow Music, Inc., 1964, 1965.
Instrumental versions introduced in United States in 1961 under Italian title, "Senza Fine." Reintroduced under new title on soundtrack of *The Flight of the Phoenix* (film, 1965). First vocal recording in English by Peggy Lee (Capitol).

Pick of the Week
Words and music by Liz Anderson.
Yonah Music, Inc.
Best-selling record by Roy Drusky (Mercury).

Playboys and Playgirls
Words and music by Bob Dylan.
M. Witmark & Sons.
Introduced by Bob Dylan (Columbia).

Please Mr. Postman, see 1962.

Please Please Me, see 1962.

Pleasure Seekers, The
Words by Sammy Cahn, music by James Van Heusen.
Miller Music Corp., 1964, 1965.
Introduced by Ann-Margret in *The Pleasure Seekers* (film, 1965).

Popsicles in Paris
Words by Sheldon Harnick, music by Jerry Bock.
Sunbeam Music Corp.
Introduced by the company in *To Broadway with Love* (musical at New York World's Fair).

Promised Land, The
Words and music by Chuck Berry.
Arc Music Corp.
Best-selling record in 1964-65 by Chuck Berry (Chess).

Queen of the House, see **King of the Road.**

Quiet Joys of Brotherhood, The
Words and music by Richard Fariña.
Ryerson Music Publishers, Inc.
Introduced by Richard and Mimi Fariña.

Race Is On, The
Words and music by Don Rollins.
Acclaim Music, Inc./Glad Music Co.
Best-selling records by George Jones (United Artists) and in 1965
    by Jack Jones (Kapp).

Rag Doll
Words and music by Bob Crewe and Bob Gaudio.
Saturday Music, Inc./Gavadima Music, Inc.
Best-selling record by The Four Seasons (Philips).

Remember (Walking in the Sand)
Words and music by George F. Morton.
Tender Tunes Music/Trio Music Co., Inc.
Best-selling record by The Shangri-Las (Red Bird) and Dean
    Martin (Reprise).

Rhythm
Words and music by Curtis Mayfield.
Curtom Publishing Co., Inc./Jalynne Corp.
Best-selling record by Major Lance (Okeh).

Rio Conchos
Words by Bernie Wayne, music by Jerry Goldsmith.
Hastings Music Corp.
From *Rio Conchos* (film).

Roll Over Beethoven, see 1956.

(Just Like) Romeo and Juliet
Words and music by Bob Hamilton and Freddy Gorman.
Myto Music, Inc.
Best-selling record by The Reflections (Golden World).

Ronnie
Words and music by Bob Crewe and Bob Gaudio.
Saturday Music, Inc.
Best-selling record by The Four Seasons (Philips).

Runnin' Out of Fools
Words and music by Kay Rogers and Richard Ahlert.
Roosevelt Music Co., Inc.
Best-selling record by Aretha Franklin (Columbia).

Sabbath Prayer
Words by Sheldon Harnick, music by Jerry Bock.
Sunbeam Music Corp.
Introduced by Zero Mostel, Maria Karnilova, and chorus in *Fiddler on the Roof* (musical).

Sad Tomorrows
Words and music by Gerald Marcellino and John Greenbach.
Cornerstone Publishing Co., 1964, 1965.
Introduced in 1965 by Trini Lopez (Reprise).

Sadie, Sadie
Words by Bob Merrill, music by Jule Styne.
Chappell & Co., Inc.
Introduced by Barbra Streisand and ensemble in *Funny Girl* (musical).

Sailor Boy
Words and music by Gerry Goffin and Russ Titelman.
Screen Gems-Columbia Music, Inc.
Best-selling record by The Chiffons (Laurie).

Sam Hill
Words and music by Tommy Collins.
Central Songs, Inc.
Best-selling record by Claude King (Columbia).

Saturday Night at the Movies
Words and music by Barry Mann and Cynthia Weil.
Screen Gems-Columbia Music, Inc.
Best-selling record by The Drifters (Atlantic).

Save It For Me
Words and music by Bob Crewe and Bob Gaudio.
Saturday Music, Inc./Gavadima Music, Inc.
Best-selling record by The Four Seasons (Philips).

Say You, see 1960.

Seasons in the Sun (French)
English words by Rod McKuen, French words and music by Jacques Brel.
Société Nouvelle des Éditions Musicales Tutti, Paris, France, 1961, 1964/Edward B. Marks Music Corp.
Original French title, "Le Moribond." Introduced in France by Belgian composer-singer Jacques Brel. English-language version introduced in United States by The Kingston Trio (Capitol).

Second Fiddle (To an Old Guitar)
Words and music by Betty Amos.
Starday Music.
Best-selling record by Jean Shepard (Capitol).

Secret Life, The
Words by Earl Shuman, music by Leon Carr.
April Music, Inc.
Introduced by the company in *The Secret Life of Walter Mitty* (musical). First recording by Teri Thornton (Columbia).

See What It Gets You
Words and music by Stephen Sondheim.
Burthen Music Co., Inc.
Introduced by Lee Remick in *Anyone Can Whistle* (musical).

Send Me No Flowers
Words and music by Burt Bacharach and Hal David.
Artists Music, Inc.
Introduced by Doris Day in *Send Me No Flowers* (film).

Senza Fine, see The Phoenix Love Theme.

Seventh Dawn, The
Words by Paul Francis Webster, music by Riz Ortolani.
United Artists Music Co., Inc.
Adapted from a theme from *The Seventh Dawn* (film). Best-selling record by Danny Williams (United Artists).

Shake
Words and music by Sam Cooke.
Kags Music.
Best-selling record in 1965 by Sam Cooke (RCA Victor).

Sha-La-La
Words by Robert Mosley, music by Robert Taylor.
Flomar Music Publishing, Inc./Ludix Publishing Co., Inc.
Best-selling records by The Shirelles (Scepter) and Manfred Mann and The Manfreds (Ascot).

Shangri-La, see 1946.

She Understands Me
Words and music by Merle Kilgore and Margie Singleton.
Al Gallico Music Corp.
Best-selling record by Johnny Tillotson (MGM).

She's a Woman (English)
Words and music by John Lennon and Paul McCartney.
Northern Songs, Ltd., London, England/Maclen Music, Inc.
Introduced and best-selling record by The Beatles (Capitol).

She's Gone Gone Gone
Words and music by Harlan Howard.
Wilderness Music Publishing Co.
Best-selling record by Lefty Frizzell (Columbia).

She's My Girl (English)
Words and music by Len Beadle and Robin Conrad.
Sydney Bron Music Co., Ltd., London, England/Spectorious Music
 Corp.
Best-selling record by Bobby Shafto (Rust).

She's Not There (English)
Words and music by Rod Argent.
Marquis Music, Ltd., London, England/Al Gallico Music Corp.
Best-selling record by The Zombies (Parrot).

Sin and Silver
Words and music by Scott Holtzman and Vivian Holtzman.
Central Songs, Inc.
Introduced by George Morgan and Marion Worth (Columbia).

Sittin' in an All Nite Cafe
Words and music by James W. Glaser.
Glaser Publications.
Best-selling record in 1965 by Warner Mack (Decca).

So Long, Big Time
Words by Dory Langdon, music by Harold Arlen.
Harwin Music Corp.
Introduced by Tony Bennett in *20th Century* television documentary
 on Harold Arlen.

Sole, Sole, Sole (Italian)
English words by Hal David, Italian words by Laura Zanin, music
 by Arturo Casadei.
Edizioni Musicali, Italy/M.R.C. Music, Inc.
Best-selling record by Siw Maimkvist and Umberto Marcato (Jubi-
 lee). English-language version introduced by Sarah Vaughan
 (Mercury).

Some Day We're Gonna Love Again
Words and music by Sharon McMahan.
McLaughlin Publishing Co.
First recording by Barbara Lewis (Atlantic). Best-selling record
 by The Searchers (Kapp).

Something Tells Me
Words and music by Hugh Martin and Timothy Gray.
Cromwell Music, Inc.
Introduced by Tammy Grimes in *High Spirits* (musical).

Soul Hootenanny
Words and music by Eugene Dixon (pseudonym for Gene Chandler).
Aba, Inc.
Best-selling record by Gene Chandler (Constellation).

Sounds of Silence, The
Words and music by Paul Simon.
Eclectic Music Co.
Best-selling record in 1965-66 by Simon and Garfunkel (Columbia).

Spanish Harlem Incident
Words and music by Bob Dylan.
M. Witmark & Sons.
Introduced by Bob Dylan (Columbia).

Stampede
Words and music by Peter La Farge.
Piedmont Music Co., Inc.
Introduced by Peter La Farge.

Stay Away from My Baby
Words and music by Ray Pennington.
Lois Publishing Co., Inc.
Best-selling record by Ted Taylor (Okeh).

Stay Awhile (English)
Words by Mike Hawker, music by Ivor Raymonde.
Flamingo Music, Ltd., London, England/M.R.C. Music, Inc.
Best-selling record by Dusty Springfield (Philips).

Stick Around
Words by Lee Adams, music by Charles Strouse.
Morley Music Co., Inc.
Introduced by Sammy Davis, Jr. in *Golden Boy* (musical).

Stop
Words and music by Joy Byers.
Valley Publishers, Inc.
Introduced in 1966 by Sherry Dinning (Alpine).

Stop and Think It Over
Words and music by Jake Graffagnino.
Crazy Cajun Music Co./Red Stick Publishing Co.
Best-selling record by Dale and Grace (Montel).

Suddenly I'm All Alone
Words and music by Van McCoy.
Blackwood Music, Inc.
Best-selling record by Walter Jackson (Okeh).

Sugar Lips
Words and music by Buddy Killen and Billy Sherrill.
Tree Publishing Co., Inc.
Best-selling record by Al Hirt (RCA Victor).

Summer Song, A (English)
Words and music by Clive Metcalfe, Keith Noble, and David Stuart.
Rogers Music, Ltd., England/Unart Music Corp.
Best-selling record by Chad Stuart and Jeremy Clyde (World Artists).

Sunrise, Sunset
Words by Sheldon Harnick, music by Jerry Bock.
Sunbeam Music Corp.
Introduced by Zero Mostel, Maria Karnilova, and chorus in *Fiddler on the Roof* (musical).

Sunshine, Lollipops and Rainbows
Words by Howard Liebling, music by Marvin Hamlisch.
Charles H. Hansen Music Corp.
Best-selling record in 1965 by Lesley Gore (Mercury).

Surfin' Bird
Words and music by Al Frazier, Carl White, John Earl Harris, and Turner Wilson.
Beechwood Music Corp.
Best-selling record by The Trashmen (Garrett).

Suspicion, see 1962.

Sweet Beginning (English)
Words and music by Leslie Bricusse and Anthony Newley.
Concord Music, Ltd., London, England/Musical Comedy Productions, Inc.
Introduced by Anthony Newley, Cyril Ritchard, and The Urchins in *The Roar of the Greasepaint—The Smell of the Crowd* (musical).

Sweet William
Words and music by Buddy Kaye and Philip Springer.
Budd Music Corp.
Best-selling record by Millie Small (Smash).

Sylvia
Words by Paul Francis Webster, music by David Raksin.
Famous Music Corp.
Introduced by Paul Anka on soundtrack of *Sylvia* (film, 1965).

Take My Ring off Your Finger
Words and music by Benny Joy and Hugh X. Lewis.
Cedarwood Publishing Co., Inc.
Best-selling record by Carl Smith (Columbia).

Tear Down the Walls
Words and music by Fred Neil.
Folkways Music Publishers, Inc.
Introduced by Judy Collins (Elektra).

Tell Her No (English)
Words and music by Rod Argent.
Zerulam Music Co., Ltd., London, England/Mainstay Music, Inc.
Best-selling record in England and United States in 1964-65 by The Zombies (Parrot).

Tell Me (English)
Words and music by Michael Jagger and Keith Richards.
Southern Music Publishing Co., Ltd., London, England/Southern
  Music Publishing Co., Inc.
Best-selling record by The Rolling Stones (London).

Tell Me Why (English)
Words and music by John Lennon and Paul McCartney.
Northern Songs, Ltd., London, England/Maclen Music, Inc.
Introduced by The Beatles in *A Hard Day's Night* (film). Best-
  selling record by The Beatles (United Artists).

That's Life
Words and music by Dean Kay and Kelly Gordon.
Four Star Television Music Co., Inc.
First recording by Ocie Smith (Columbia). Best-selling record in
  1966 by Frank Sinatra (Reprise).

That's the Way It's Gonna Be
Words and music by Bob Gibson and Phil Ochs.
M. Witmark & Sons.
Introduced by The Mitchell Trio (Mercury).

Theme from *Golden Boy*
Music by Charles Strouse and Lee Adams.
Morley Music Co., Inc.
Best-selling record by Quincy Jones (Mercury).

Theme from *Mr. Broadway*
Music by Dave Brubeck.
Groton Music, Inc./Edward B. Marks Music Corp.
Theme from *Mr. Broadway* (television series).

Theme from *Of Human Bondage* (English)
Music by Ron Goodwin.
Miller Music Corp.
Theme from *Of Human Bondage* (film).

Theme from *The Man from U.N.C.L.E.*
Music by Jerry Goldsmith.
Hastings Music Corp.
Theme from *The Man from U.N.C.L.E.* (television series).

Theme from *36 Hours* (A Heart Must Learn To Cry)
Words by Paul Francis Webster, music by Dimitri Tiomkin.
Leo Feist, Inc.
From *36 Hours* (film, 1965).

Theme from *Valentine's Day*
Music by Lionel Newman.
Hastings Music Corp.
Theme from *Valentine's Day* (television series).

Theme from *Voyage to the Bottom of the Sea*
Music by Paul Sawtell.
Miller Music Corp.
Theme from *Voyage to the Bottom of the Sea* (television series).

Theme from *Zorba the Greek*
Music by Mikis Theodorakis.
Miller Music Corp., 1964, 1965.
Theme from *Zorba the Greek* (film, 1965).

Then and Only Then
Words and music by Bill Anderson.
Moss Rose Publications, Inc.
Best-selling record in 1965 by Connie Smith (RCA Victor).

There, I've Said It Again, see 1941.

There Won't Be Trumpets
Words and music by Stephen Sondheim.
Burthen Music Co., Inc.
Introduced by Lee Remick in *Anyone Can Whistle* (musical).

They Gotta Quit Kickin' My Dog Around
Words and music by Vivian Holtzman, Scott Holtzman, and Nick
    Woods.
Blackwood Music, Inc.
Introduced by The New Christy Minstrels (Columbia).

Things Have Gone to Pieces
Words and music by Leon Payne.
Glad Music Co.
Introduced by Leon Payne (D Records). Best-selling record in 1965
    by George Jones (Musicor).

Things We Said Today (English)
Words and music by John Lennon and Paul McCartney.
Northern Songs, Ltd., London, England/Maclen Music, Inc.
Best-selling record by The Beatles (Capitol).

Think Nothing about It
Words and music by Curtis Mayfield.
Curtom Publishing Co., Inc.
Best-selling record by Gene Chandler (Constellation).

This Diamond Ring
Words and music by Al Kooper, Irwin Levine, and Bob Brass.
Sea-Lark Enterprises, Inc.
Best-selling record in 1964-65 by Gary Lewis and The Playboys
    (Liberty).

This Dream (English)
Words and music by Leslie Bricusse and Anthony Newley.
Concord Music, Ltd., London, England/Musical Comedy Productions, Inc.
Introduced by Anthony Newley and The Urchins in *The Roar of the Greasepaint—The Smell of the Crowd* (musical).

This Is It
Words and music by Cindy Walker.
Acclaim Music, Inc.
Best-selling record in 1965 by Jim Reeves (RCA Victor).

This Is the Life
Words by Lee Adams, music by Charles Strouse.
Morley Music Co., Inc.
Introduced by Billy Daniels, Sammy Davis, Jr., and company in *Golden Boy* (musical).

This White Circle on My Finger, see 1961.

Thou Shalt Not Steal, see 1962.

Three Window Coupe
Words and music by Jan Berry and Roger Christian.
Screen Gems-Columbia Music, Inc.
Best-selling record by The Rip Chords (Columbia).

Tired of Waiting for You (English)
Words and music by Roy Davies.
Edward Kassner Music Co., Ltd., London, England/Jay-Boy Music Corp.
Best-selling record in 1965 by The Kinks (Reprise).

To Life
Words by Sheldon Harnick, music by Jerry Bock.
Sunbeam Music Corp.
Introduced by Zero Mostel, Michael Granger, and Men in *Fiddler on the Roof* (musical).

To Ramona
Words and music by Bob Dylan.
M. Witmark & Sons.
Introduced by Bob Dylan (Columbia).

Tobacco Road, see 1960.

Today
Words and music by Randy Sparks.
Miller Music Corp.
Introduced on soundtrack of *Advance to the Rear* (film). Best-selling record by The New Christy Minstrels (Columbia).

Toki's Theme
Music by Dave Brubeck.
Groton Music, Inc./Edward B. Marks Music Corp.
From *Mr. Broadway* (television series).

Too Busy Saying Goodbye
Words and music by Johnny Colmus.
Window Music Publishers.
Introduced by George Morgan and Marion Worth (Columbia).

Too Many Fish in the Sea
Words and music by Eddie Holland and Norman Whitfield.
Jobete Music Co., Inc.
Best-selling record by The Marvelettes (Tamla).

Too Many Rivers
Words and music by Harlan Howard.
Combine Music Corp.
Best-selling record in 1965 by Brenda Lee (Decca).

Topkapi (Greek)
Words by Noel Sherman, music by Manos Hadjidakis.
United Artists Music Co., Inc.
Adapted from a theme from *Topkapi* (film).

Tradition
Words by Sheldon Harnick, music by Jerry Bock.
Sunbeam Music Corp.
Introduced by Zero Mostel and chorus in *Fiddler on the Roof* (musical).

Try It Baby
Words and music by Berry Gordy, Jr.
Jobete Music Co., Inc.
Best-selling record by Marvin Gaye (Tamla).

12 O'Clock High
Music by Dominic Frontiere.
Hastings Music Corp.
Theme from *12 O'Clock High* (television series).

Twist and Shout, see 1960.

Under the Boardwalk
Words and music by Artie Resnick and Kenny Young.
T. M. Music, Inc.
Best-selling record by The Drifters (Atlantic).

Understand Your Man
Words and music by Johnny Cash.
Johnny Cash Music, Inc.
Best-selling record by Johnny Cash (Columbia).

Unless You Care
Words and music by Philip Sloan and Steve Barri.
Trousdale Music Publishers, Inc.
Best-selling record by Terry Black (Tollie).

Use Your Head
Words and music by Wade Flemons, Chuck Barksdale, and Barrett
    Strong.
Conrad Publishing Co., Inc./Shake-Well Music, Inc.
Best-selling record by Mary Wells (20th Century-Fox).

Use Your Noggin'
Words by Sammy Cahn, music by James Van Heusen.
Shapiro, Bernstein & Co., Inc., 1964, 1966.
Introduced by Louise Troy, Sharon Dierking, and Gretchen Van
    Aken in *Walking Happy* (musical, 1966).

Venice Blue (French)
English words by Gene Lees, French words by Françoise Dorin,
    music by Charles Aznavour.
Éditions Musicales Charles Aznavour, Paris, France, 1964, 1965/
    Ludlow Music, Inc.
Original French title, "Que C'est Triste Venise." Introduced in
    French and English by Charles Aznavour.

Viva Las Vegas
Words and music by Doc Pomus and Mort Shuman.
Elvis Presley Music, Inc.
Introduced by Elvis Presley in *Viva Las Vegas* (film).

Walk—Don't Run '64, see **Walk, Don't Run,** 1960.

Walkin' with Peninnah
Words by Earl Shuman, music by Leon Carr.
April Music, Inc.
Introduced by Marc London and Christopher Norris in *The Secret
    Life of Walter Mitty* (musical).

Walking in the Rain
Words and music by Barry Mann, Cynthia Weil, and Phil Spector.
Screen Gems-Columbia Music, Inc.
Best-selling record by The Ronettes (Philles).

Waltz for Debby
Words by Gene Lees, music by Bill Evans.
Acorn Music Corp., 1964, 1965.
Adapted from jazz composition by Evans. First vocal recording by
    Tony Bennett (Columbia).

Was She Prettier Than I?
Words and music by Hugh Martin and Timothy Gray.
Cromwell Music, Inc.
Introduced by Louise Troy in *High Spirits* (musical).

Watch What Happens (French)
English words by Norman Gimbel, French words by Jacques Demy, music by Michel Legrand.
Productions Michel Legrand, Paris, France/Productions Francis Lemarque, La Verne (Seine), France/South Mountain Music Corp./Jonware Music Corp., 1964, 1965.
"Lola's Theme," introduced in French by voice of Georges Blanès (dubbed for Marc Michel) in *The Umbrellas of Cherbourg* (French film). Used earlier as a theme in Jacques Demy's *Lola* (French film, 1960). Introduced in English by Jean-Paul Vignon (Columbia).

Watching the World Go By, see The Luck of Ginger Coffey.

Way You Do the Things You Do, The
Words and music by William Robinson and Bobby Rogers.
Jobete Music Co., Inc.
Best-selling record by The Temptations (Gordy).

We Love You Beatles
Words by Lee Adams, music by Charles Strouse.
Edwin H. Morris & Co., Inc.
Based on "We Love You Conrad" from *Bye Bye Birdie* (musical, 1960). Best-selling record by The Carefrees (London International).

Wedding, The, see 1961.

Week-End, The
Words and music by Lou Stallman, Bobby Weinstein, and Teddy Randazzo.
South Mountain Music Corp.
Introduced in 1966 by Jack Jones (Kapp) and Steve Lawrence (Columbia).

Welcome to My World, see 1961.

What a Night This Is Going To Be!
Words and music by Marian Grudeff and Raymond Jessel.
Edward B. Marks Music Corp., 1964, 1965.
Introduced by Fritz Weaver, Inga Swenson, Peter Sallis, and Virginia Vestoff in *Baker Street* (musical, 1965).

What a Way To Go
Words by Betty Comden and Adolph Green, music by Jule Styne.
Miller Music Corp.
"Inspired" by *What a Way To Go!* (film).

What Do You Want with Me
Words and music by Chad Stuart and Jeremy Clyde.
Chad & Jeremy Music, Inc.
Best-selling record by Chad and Jeremy (World Artists).

What Have They Done to the Rain?, see 1962.

What I Need Most
Words and music by Hugh X. Lewis.
Cedarwood Publishing Co., Inc.
Best-selling record by Hugh X. Lewis (Kapp).

What Makes a Man Wander?
Words and music by Harlan Howard.
Bramble Music Publishing Co., Inc.
Best-selling record by Jan Howard (Decca).

What You're Doing (English)
Words and music by John Lennon and Paul McCartney.
Northern Songs, Ltd., London, England/Maclen Music, Inc.
Best-selling record by The Beatles (Capitol).

When Everything Was Green
Words by Robert Colby, music by Ettore Stratta.
April Music, Inc.
Introduced in 1965 by The Brothers Four (Columbia).

When I Get Home (English)
Words and music by John Lennon and Paul McCartney.
Northern Songs, Ltd., London, England/Maclen Music, Inc.
Best-selling record by The Beatles (Capitol).

When I Grow Up To Be a Man
Words and music by Brian Wilson.
Sea of Tunes Publishing Co.
Best-selling record by The Beach Boys (Capitol).

When I'm Gone
Words and music by William Robinson, Jr.
Jobete Music Co., Inc., 1964, 1965.
Best-selling record in 1965 by Brenda Holloway (Tamla).

When in Rome (I Do As the Romans Do)
Words by Carolyn Leigh, music by Cy Coleman.
Edwin H. Morris & Co., Inc.
Introduced by Barbra Streisand (Columbia).

When You're Young and in Love
Words and music by Van McCoy.
Picturetone Music Publishing Corp.
Introduced by Ruby and The Romantics (Kapp).

Whenever a Teenager Cries
Words and music by Ernie Maresca.
S & J Music Publishing Co., 1964, 1965.
Best-selling record by Reparata and The Delrons (World Artists).

Whenever He Holds You
Words and music by Bobby Goldsboro.
Unart Music Corp.
Introduced by Bobby Goldsboro (United Artists).

Where Did Our Love Go
Words and music by Eddie Holland, Lamont Dozier, and Brian Holland.
Jobete Music Co., Inc.
Best-selling record by The Supremes (Motown).

Where Does a Little Tear Come From
Words and music by Marge Barton and Fred A. MacRae.
Mimosa Publishing Co.
Best-selling record by George Jones (United Artists).

Where Love Has Gone
Words by Sammy Cahn, music by James Van Heusen.
Famous Music Corp.
Introduced by Jack Jones in *Where Love Has Gone* (film). Nominated for Academy Award, 1964.

While the City Sleeps
Words by Lee Adams, music by Charles Strouse.
Morley Music Co., Inc.
Introduced by Billy Daniels in *Golden Boy* (musical).

Whipped Cream
Music by Naomi Neville.
Jarb Publishing Co., 1964, 1965.
Introduced in 1965 by Herb Alpert's Tijuana Brass (A&M).

Who Are You Now?
Words by Bob Merrill, music by Jule Styne.
Chappell & Co., Inc.
Introduced by Barbra Streisand in *Funny Girl* (musical).

Who Can I Turn To (When Nobody Needs Me) (English)
Words and music by Leslie Bricusse and Anthony Newley.
Concord Music, Ltd., London, England/Musical Comedy Productions, Inc.
Introduced by Anthony Newley in *The Roar of the Greasepaint— The Smell of the Crowd* (musical). First and best-selling record by Tony Bennett (Columbia).

Why (English)
Words and music by Bill Crompton and Tony Sheridan.
Pan-Musik, Ltd., London, England/Al Gallico Music Corp.
Best-selling record by The Beatles with Tony Sheridan (MGM).

Why
Words and music by Cindy Walker.
Tree Publishing Co., Inc.
Introduced by Eddy Arnold (RCA Victor).

Why Can't You Feel Sorry for Me
Words and music by Merle Kilgore and Marvin Rainwater.
Al Gallico Music Corp.
Introduced by Carl Smith (Columbia).

Wild One
Words and music by William Stevenson and Ivy Hunter.
Jobete Music Co., Inc.
Best-selling record by Martha and The Vandellas (Gordy).

Willa, Willa
Words by Earl Shuman, music by Leon Carr.
April Music, Inc.
Introduced by Charles Rydell in *The Secret Life of Walter Mitty*
    (musical).

With So Little To Be Sure Of
Words and music by Stephen Sondheim.
Burthen Music Co., Inc.
Introduced by Lee Remick and Harry Guardino in *Anyone Can
    Whistle* (musical).

Wonderful Day Like Today, A (English)
Words and music by Leslie Bricusse and Anthony Newley.
Concord Music, Ltd., London, England/Musical Comedy Productions,
    Inc.
Introduced by Cyril Ritchard and The Urchins in *The Roar of the
    Greasepaint—The Smell of the Crowd* (musical).

Wooly Bully
Words and music by Domingo Samudio.
Beckie Publishing Co., Inc.
Best-selling record in 1965 by Sam the Sham and The Pharoahs
    (MGM).

World without Love (English)
Words and music by John Lennon and Paul McCartney.
Northern Songs, Ltd., London, England/Maclen Music, Inc.
Best-selling records by Peter and Gordon (Capitol) and Bobby
    Rydell (Cameo).

Worried Guy
Words and music by Jack Reardon and Paul Evans.
B. F. Wood Music Co., Inc.
Best-selling record by Johnny Tillotson (MGM).

Wrong for Each Other
Words and music by Doc Pomus and Mort Shuman.
Valley Publishers, Inc.
Best-selling record by Andy Williams (Columbia).

You Are Woman, I am Man, also known as **I Am Woman, You Are Man**
Words by Bob Merrill, music by Jule Styne.
Chappell & Co., Inc.
Introduced by Barbra Streisand and Sydney Chaplin in *Funny Girl* (musical).

You Can't Do That (English)
Words and music by John Lennon and Paul McCartney.
Northern Songs, Ltd., London, England/Maclen Music, Inc.
Best-selling record by The Beatles (Capitol).

You Can't Roller Skate in a Buffalo Herd
Words and music by Roger Miller.
Tree Publishing Co., Inc.
Introduced by Roger Miller (Smash).

You Mustn't Feel Discouraged
Words by Betty Comden and Adolph Green, music by Jule Styne.
Stratford Music Corp./Chappell & Co., Inc.
Introduced by Carol Burnett and Tiger Haynes in *Fade Out—Fade In* (musical).

You Really Got Me (English)
Words and music by Ray Davies.
Kassner Music Co., Ltd., London, England/Jay-Boy Music Corp.
Best-selling record in England and United States by The Kinks (Reprise).

You Were on My Mind
Words and music by Sylvia Fricker.
M. Witmark & Sons, 1964, 1965.
Introduced by Ian and Sylvia (Vanguard). Best-selling record in 1965 by We Five (A&M).

You'd Better Go
Words and music by Art Kornfield and Ted Daryll.
Big Seven Music Corp.
Best-selling record by Chance Eden (Roulette).

You'd Better Love Me
Words and music by Hugh Martin and Timothy Gray.
Cromwell Music, Inc.
Introduced by Tammy Grimes in *High Spirits* (musical).

Your Heart Turned Left (And I Was on the Right)
Words and music by Harlan Howard.
Glad Music Co.
Best-selling record by George Jones (United Artists).

You're a Wonderful One
Words and music by Eddie Holland, Brian Holland, and Lamont Dozier.
Jobete Music Co., Inc.
Best-selling record by Marvin Gaye (Tamla).

You're My World (Italian)
English words by Carl Sigman, Italian words by Gino Paoli, music by Umberto Bindi.
Edizioni Musicali M.E.C., Italy, 1963, 1964/Plan Two Music, Inc.
Original title, "Il Mio Mondo." Best-selling record by Cilla Black (Capitol).

You're the Only World I Know
Words and music by Sonny Jones and Robert F. Tubert.
Marson Music Co.
Best-selling record by Sonny James (Capitol).

You've Lost That Lovin' Feelin'
Words and music by Phil Spector, Barry Mann, and Cynthia Weil.
Screen Gems-Columbia Music, Inc.
Best-selling record in 1964-65 by The Righteous Brothers (Philles).

Supplement

Songs Copyrighted Before 1960
That Became Significant in 1960-1964

This Supplement includes information about songs copyrighted before 1960 that became significant in 1960-1964.

For songs copyrighted in the 1940's and 1950's, for which there was no significant development up to the time of the preparation of Volumes 1 and 2 of *Popular Music,* complete information is listed.

For songs copyrighted in the 1940's and 1950's, for which the basic data appear in Volume 1 or 2, the subsequent information is listed in this Supplement, with a reference to the year in Volume 1 or 2 under which the basic information appears.

For songs copyrighted before 1940, the facts relating to 1960-1964 are given, with a reference to the copyright year under which the basic information will be listed in subsequent volumes of *Popular Music* covering the years before 1940. While there may be some temporary inconvenience until this material is published, it seemed cumbersome and inconsistent to duplicate full listings for such songs.

Songs copyrighted in the 1940's and 1950's, for which complete data, including that for 1960-1964, appear in Volume 1 or 2, are not listed in this Supplement but under the year in 1960-1964 in which the development occurred, with a reference to the year in Volume 1 or 2 in which all the information appears. They may be located by consulting the List of Titles.

Supplement

Above and Beyond (The Call of Love)
Words and music by Harlan Howard.
Jat Music, Inc.
Copyright, 1959. Best-selling record in 1960 by Buck Owens (Capitol).

Adam and Eve
Words and music by Paul Anka.
Spanka Music Corp.
Copyright, 1959. Best-selling record in 1960 by Paul Anka (ABC-Paramount).

All in My Mind, also known as Maybe It's All in My Mind
Words and music by Leroy Kirkland, Maxine Brown, and Fred Johnson.
Figure Music, Inc.
Copyright, 1959. Best-selling record in 1961 by Maxine Brown (Nomar).

Am I Losing You?, see 1956.
Best-selling record in 1960 by Jim Reeves (RCA Victor).

Am I That Easy To Forget?
Words and music by Carl Belew and W.S. Stevenson.
Four Star Music Co., Inc.
Copyright, 1958, 1963. Best-selling record in 1963 by Jerry Wallace (Challenge).

Among My Souvenirs, see 1927.
Best-selling record in 1960 by Connie Francis (MGM).

Another
Words by Vic McAlpin, music by Roy Drusky.
Moss Rose Publications, Inc.
Copyright, 1959. Best-selling record in 1960 by Roy Drusky (Decca).

Are You Lonesome Tonight, see 1926.
Best-selling record in 1960 by Elvis Presley (RCA Victor).

Are You Willing Willie
Words and music by Marion Worth.
Travis Music Co./Jamie Music Publishing Co.
Copyright, 1959. Best-selling record in 1960 by Marion Worth (Columbia).

At Last, see 1942.
Best-selling record in 1961 by Etta James (Argo).

Bells of Rhymney
Words by Idris Davies, music by Pete Seeger.
Ludlow Music, Inc.
Copyright, 1959. Popularized in early 1960's by Pete Seeger.

Beyond the Sea, see 1947.
Best-selling record in 1960 by Bobby Darin (Atco).

Big Boy Pete
Words and music by Don Harris and Dewey Terry.
Venice Music, Inc.
Copyright, 1959. Best-selling record in 1960 by The Olympics
  (Arvee).

Big Iron
Words and music by Marty Robbins.
Marty's Music Corp.
Copyright, 1959. Best-selling record in 1960 by Marty Robbins
  (Columbia).

Blue Hawaii, see 1936.
Title song, sung by Elvis Presley, in *Blue Hawaii* (film, 1961). Best-
  selling record in 1962 by Elvis Presley (RCA Victor).

Blue Moon, see 1934.
Best-selling record in 1961 by The Marcels (Colpix).

Blue Yodel No. 1, see **T for Texas.**

Cherry Pie
Words and music by Joe Josea and Marvin Phillips.
Modern Music Publishing Co.
Copyright, 1954. Best-selling record in 1960 by Skip and Flip
  (Brent).

Cherry Pink and Apple Blossom White, see 1951.
Best-selling record in 1961 by Jerry Murad and his Harmonicats
  (Columbia).

Copper Kettle (The Pale Moonlight)
Words and music by Albert F. Beddoe.
Melody Trials, Inc.
Copyright, 1953, 1961. Introduced by Oscar Brand. Best-selling
  record in 1964 by Joan Baez (Vanguard).

Corrina, Corrina, see 1932.
Best-selling record in 1960 by Ray Peterson (Dunes).

Cow Town
Words and music by Jack Padgett.
Le Bill Music, Inc.
Copyright, 1949. Best-selling record in 1962-63 by Webb Pierce
  (Decca).

Cruel Love
Words and music by Arthur Smiley.
Lois Publishing Co.
Copyright, 1955. Best-selling record in 1960 by Lou Smith (KRCO).

Supplement

Dedicated to the One I Love
Words and music by Lowman Pauling and Ralph Bass.
Lois Publishing Co.
Copyright, 1957. Best-selling record in 1961 by The Shirelles
(Scepter).

Deep Purple, see 1934.
Best-selling record in 1963 by Nino Tempo and April Stevens (Atco).
Winner of National Academy of Recording Arts and Sciences
Award for "Best Rock and Roll Recording," 1963.

Devil or Angel, see 1955.
Best-selling record in 1960 by Bobby Vee (Liberty).

Diane, see 1927.
Best-selling record in 1964 by The Bachelors (London).

**Does Your Chewing Gum Lose Its Flavor on the Bedpost
Overnight?,** see 1924.
Best-selling record in 1961 by Lonnie Donegan (Dot).

Don't Be Angry
Words and music by Wade Jackson.
Acuff-Rose Publications, Inc.
Copyright, 1957. Best-selling record in 1964 by Stonewall Jackson
(Columbia).

Don't Cry Baby, see 1929.
Best-selling record in 1961 by Etta James (Argo).

Door Is Still Open to My Heart, The, see 1955.
Best-selling record in 1964 by Dean Martin (Reprise).

Drip Drop
Words and music by Jerry Leiber and Mike Stroller.
Tiger Music, Inc.
Copyright, 1954, 1963. Best-selling record in 1963 by Dion Di Mucci
(Columbia).

Everlovin'
Words and music by Dave Burgess.
Jat Music, Inc.
Copyright, 1959, 1961. Best-selling record in 1961 by Dave Burgess
(Challenge).

Every Beat of My Heart
Words and music by Johnny Otis.
Valjo Publishing Co.
Copyright, 1952. Best-selling record in 1961 by The Pips (Vee Jay).

268

Every Step of the Way
Words by Al Stillman, music by Robert Allen.
International Pauline Corp.
Copyright, 1959. Best-selling record in 1962 by Johnny Mathis
(Columbia).

Everybody but Me
Words and music by Dave Burgess.
Jat Music, Inc.
Copyright, 1959. Best-selling record in 1962-63 by Ernest Ashworth
(Hickory).

Faded Love
Words and music by John Wills and Bob Wills.
Hill and Range Songs, Inc.
Copyright, 1950. Best-selling record in 1963 by Patsy Cline (Decca).

For My Baby
Words and music by Clyde Otis and Brook Benton.
Play Music, Inc.
Copyright, 1958. Best-selling record in 1961 by Brook Benton
(Mercury).

For You, see 1930.
Best-selling record in 1964 by Rick Nelson (Decca).

Forever
Words and music by Buddy Killen.
Tree Publishing Co., Inc.
Copyright, 1959. Best-selling record in 1960-61 by The Little Dippers
(University).

From a Jack to a King
Words and music by Ned Miller.
Jamie Music Publishing Co.
Copyright, 1957. Best-selling record in 1963 by Ned Miller (Fabor).

Georgia on My Mind, see 1930.
Best-selling record in 1960-61 by Ray Charles (ABC-Paramount).
Winner of National Academy of Recording Arts and Sciences
Awards for "Best Rock and Roll Recording" and "Best Solo Vocal
Performance—Male," 1960.

Happy Days Are Here Again, see 1929.
Best-selling record in 1963 by Barbra Streisand (Columbia).

Harbor Lights, see 1937.
Best-selling record in 1960 by The Platters (Mercury).

Haunted House
Words and music by Robert Geddins.
Venice Music, Inc./B-Flat Publishing Co.
Copyright, 1958. Best-selling record in 1964 by Gene Simmons (Hi).

Heartaches, see 1931.
Best-selling record in 1961 by The Marcels (Colpix).

Hillbilly Heaven, see **I Dreamed of a Hillbilly Heaven.**

Hurt, see 1953.
Best-selling record in 1961 by Timi Yuro (Liberty).

I Dreamed of a Hillbilly Heaven
Words by Hal Sothern, music by Eddie Dean.
Sage and Sand Music Publishers.
Copyright, 1954, 1961. New lyrics and arrangement written by Floyd
   Bartlett in 1961; introduced and best-selling record in 1961 by Tex
   Ritter (Capitol).

I Feel So Bad
Words and music by Chuck Willis.
Berkshire Music, Inc./Elvis Presley Music, Inc.
Copyright, 1954, 1961. Best-selling record in 1961 by Elvis Presley
   (RCA Victor).

I Got a Woman (I Got a Sweetie), see 1954.
Best-selling record in 1963 by Jimmy McGriff (Sue).

I Gotta Know
Words and music by Paul Evans and Matt Williams.
Gladys Music, Inc.
Copyright, 1959. Best-selling record in 1960 by Elvis Presley (RCA
   Victor).

I Guess I'm Crazy for Loving You
Words and music by Werly Fairburn.
Mallory Music Publications.
Copyright, 1955. Best-selling record in 1964 by Jim Reeves (RCA
   Victor).

I Love You Because, see 1949.
Best-selling record in 1963 by Al Martino (Capitol).

I Need Your Lovin'
Words and music by Clarence Paul, Sonny Woods, and Willie
   Jennings.
Walnut Music Corp./Peer International Corp./Lion Publishing
   Co., Inc.
Copyright, 1958. Best-selling record in 1962 by Don Gardner and
   Dee Dee Ford (Fire).

I Remember You, see 1942.
Best-selling record in 1962-63 by Frank Ifield (Vee Jay).

I Said Good Morning
Words by Betty Comden and Adolph Green, music by André Previn.
Stratford Music Corp.
Copyright, 1959. Introduced by Betty Comden and Adolph Green.
  Featured by Elly Stone in 1966.

I Take the Chance, see 1956.
Best-selling record in 1963 by Ernest Ashworth (Hickory).

If You Don't Know I Ain't Gonna Tell You
Words and music by George Hamilton IV.
Bentley Music Co.
Copyright, 1956. Best-selling record in 1962 by George Hamilton IV
  (RCA Victor).

I'll Take Care of You
Words and music by Brook Benton.
Lion Publishing Co., Inc./B-Flat Publishing Co.
Copyright, 1959. Best-selling record in 1960 by Bobby "Blue" Bland
  (Duke).

I'm Gonna Go Fishin'
Words by Peggy Lee, music by Duke Ellington.
Chappell & Co., Inc.
Copyright, 1959. An extension and adaptation of a theme from
  Anatomy of a Murder (film). Introduced in 1960 by Peggy Lee.

I'm Leaving It All Up to You, see **I'm Leaving It Up to You.**

I'm Leaving It Up to You, also known as **I'm Leaving It All Up
  to You,** also known as **Leavin' It All Up to You**
Words and music by Dewey Terry and Don F. Harris.
Venice Music, Inc.
Copyright, 1957. Best-selling record in 1963 by Dale and Grace
  (Montel-Michele).

In the Jailhouse Now, see 1928.
Best-selling record in 1962 by Johnny Cash (Columbia).

I've Told Every Little Star, see 1932.
Best-selling record in 1961 by Linda Scott (Canadian-American).

Just a Little Bit
Words and music by Del Gordon.
Conrad Publishing Co., Inc.
Copyright, 1959. Best-selling record in 1960 by Roscoe Gordon (Vee
  Jay).

Kiddio
Words and music by Brook Benton and Clyde Otis.
Eden Music, Inc./Brookville Music, Inc.
Copyright, 1957. Best-selling record in 1960 by Brook Benton
  (Mercury).

271

Lazy River, see 1931.
Best-selling record in 1961 by Si Zentner (RCA Victor). Winner
of National Academy of Recording Arts and Sciences Award for
"Best Performance by an Orchestra," 1961.

Leavin' It All Up to You, see I'm Leaving It Up to You.

Left to Right
Words and music by Lorene Mann.
Sure-Fire Music Co., Inc.
Copyright, 1958, 1959. Best-selling record in 1960 by Kitty Wells
(Decca).

Let Forgiveness In
Words and music by Webb Pierce and Rex Griffin.
Cedarwood Publishing Co., Inc./Valley Publishers, Inc.
Copyright, 1954. Best-selling record in 1961 by Webb Pierce (Decca).

Let Her Dance
Words and music by Carl Spencer, Bert Lawrence, and Henry Glover.
Belmar Music Publishing Co./Maureen Music, Inc.
Copyright, 1959. Original title, "Let the Little Girl Dance." Best-
selling record in 1960 by Billy Bland (Old Town).

Let It Be Me, see 1957.
Best-selling records in 1960 by The Everly Brothers (Cadence) and
in 1964 by Betty Everett and Jerry Butler (Vee Jay).

Let the Good Times Roll, see 1946.
Best-selling record in 1960 by Ray Charles (Atlantic). Winner of
National Academy of Recording Arts and Sciences Award for
"Best Rhythm and Blues Recording," 1960.

Let the Little Girl Dance, see Let Her Dance.

Little Ole You
Words by Wayne P. Walker and Mel Tillis, music by Wayne P.
Walker.
Cedarwood Publishing Co., Inc.
Copyright, 1959. Best-selling record in 1963 by Jim Reeves (RCA
Victor).

Long Gone Lonesome Blues, see 1950.
Best-selling record in 1964 by Hank Williams, Jr. (MGM)

Loose Talk, see 1954.
Best-selling record in 1961 by Buck Owens and Rose Maddox
(Capitol).

Love You So
Words and music by Ron Holden.
Maravilla Music, Inc.
Copyright, 1959. Best-selling record in 1960 by Ron Holden (Donna).

Mama, see 1946.
Best-selling record in 1960 by Connie Francis (MGM).

Maria, see 1957.
Best-selling record in 1962 by Roger Williams (Kapp).

Matchbox
Words and music by Carl Perkins.
Knox Music, Inc.
Copyright, 1957. Best-selling record in 1964 by The Beatles (Capitol).

Maybe It's All in My Mind, see **All in My Mind.**

Memphis
Words and music by Chuck Berry.
Arc Music Corp.
Copyright, 1959, 1963. Best-selling records in 1963 by Lonnie Mack
    (Fraternity) and in 1964 by Johnny Rivers (Imperial).

Miller's Cave
Words and music by Jack Clement.
Jack Music, Inc.
Copyright, 1959. Best-selling records in 1960-61 by Hank Snow
    (RCA Victor) and in 1964 by Bobby Bare (RCA Victor).

Missing You, see 1955.
Best-selling record in 1961 by Ray Peterson (MGM and Dune).

Misty, see 1955.
Best-selling record in 1962 by Johnny Mathis (Columbia).

Money, That's What I Want
Words and music by Berry Gordy, Jr. and Janie Bradford.
Jobete Music Co., Inc.
Copyright, 1959. Best-selling records in 1960 by Barrett Strong
    (Anna) and in 1964 by The Kingsmen (Wand).

Mountain of Love
Words and music by Harold Dorman.
Vaughn Publishing Co., Inc./Trousdale Music Publishers, Inc.
Copyright, 1959. Best-selling record in 1964-65 by Johnny Rivers
    (Imperial).

Mule Skinner Blues, also known as **New Mule Skinner Blues,**
    see 1931.
Best-selling record in 1960 by The Fendermen (Soma).

My Boy Lollipop
Words and music by Johnny Roberts and Morris Levy.
Nom Music, Inc.
Copyright, 1956. Best-selling record in 1964 by Millie Small (Smash).

New Mule Skinner Blues, see **Mule Skinner Blues.**

Night
Words and music by Johnny Lehman and Herb Miller.
Merrimac Music Corp.
Copyright, 1959. Best-selling record in 1960 by Jackie Wilson
(Brunswick).

Night Train, see 1952.
Best-selling record in 1962 by James Brown and The Famous Flames
(King.)

No Love Have I
Words and music by Tommy Collins.
Central Songs, Inc.
Copyright, 1954. Best-selling record in 1960 by Webb Pierce (Decca).

Not Fade Away
Words and music by Charles Hardin and Norman Petty.
Nor Va Jak Music, Inc.
Copyright, 1957. Revived and best-selling record in England and
United States in 1964 by The Rolling Stones (London).

Oklahoma Hills, see 1945.
Best-selling record in 1961 by Hank Thompson (Capitol).

Old Lamp-Lighter, The, see 1946.
Best-selling record in 1960 by The Browns (RCA Victor).

One You Slip Around With, The
Words and music by Harlan Howard and Fuzzy Owen.
Jat Music, Inc.
Copyright, 1959. Best-selling record in 1960 by Jan Howard (Challenge).

Over and Over
Words and music by Robert Byrd.
Recordo Music Publishers.
Copyright, 1958. First recording in 1959 by Bobby Day (Class).
Best-selling record in 1964 by The Dave Clark Five (Epic).

Please Love Me Forever
Words and music by Johnny Malone and Ollie Blanchard.
Selma Music Corp.
Copyright, 1959. Best-selling record in 1961 by Cathy Jean (Valmor).

Prisoner of Love, see 1931.
Best-selling record in 1963 by James Brown and The Famous Flames
(King).

Release Me, see 1954.
Best-selling record in 1962 by "Little Esther" Phillips (Lenox).

274

Rockin' Good Way (To Mess Around and Fall in Love), A
Words and music by Brook Benton, Clyde Otis, and Luchi De Jesus.
Eden Music, Inc./Conrad Publishing Co., Inc.
Copyright, 1958, 1960. Best-selling record in 1960 by Brook Benton
and Dinah Washington (Mercury).

Ruby Baby
Words and music by Jerry Leiber and Mike Stoller.
Tiger Music, Inc.
Copyright, 1955, 1963. Best-selling record in 1963 by Dion Di Mucci
(Columbia).

Running Scared
Words and music by Roy Orbison and Joe Melson.
Acuff-Rose Publications, Inc.
Copyright, 1952. Best-selling record in 1961 by Roy Orbison (Monument).

San Antonio Rose, see 1940.
Best-selling record in 1961 by Floyd Cramer (RCA Victor).

Sands of Gold
Words and music by Webb Pierce, Hal Eddy, and Cliff Parman.
Cedarwood Publishing Co., Inc.
Copyright, 1956. Best-selling record in 1963 by Webb Pierce (Decca).

Sawmill
Words and music by Horace Whatley and Melvin Tillis.
Cedarwood Publishing Co., Inc.
Copyright, 1959. Best-selling record in 1963 by Webb Pierce (Decca).

Scarlet Ribbons (For Her Hair), see 1949.
Best-selling record in 1960 by The Browns (RCA Victor).

Scotch and Soda
Adaptation of words and music by Dave Guard.
Beechwood Music Corp.
Copyright, 1959, 1961. Based on traditional song. Best-selling record
in 1961 by The Kingston Trio (Capitol).

Seasons of My Heart, see 1955.
Best-selling record in 1960 by Johnny Cash (Columbia).

Send Me Some Lovin', see 1957.
Best-selling record in 1963 by Sam Cooke (RCA Victor).

Shout (Part 1 and 2)
Words and music by O'Kelly Isley, Ronald Isley, and Rudolph Isley.
Wemar Music Corp./Nom Music, Inc.
Copyright, 1959. Best-selling records in 1962 by Joey Dee and The
Starliters (Roulette) and in 1964 by Lulu and The Luvers (Parrot).

Signed, Sealed and Delivered, see 1947.
Best-selling record in 1961 by Cowboy Copas (Starday).

Since I Fell for You, see 1948.
Best-selling record in 1963 by Lenny Welch (Cadence).

Sixteen Reasons (Why I Love You)
Words and music by Bill Post and Doree Post.
American Music, Inc.
Copyright, 1959. Best-selling record in 1960 by Connie Stevens
  (Warner Bros.).

Sleepy-Eyed John
Words and music by Tex Atcheson.
Vanguard Songs.
Copyright, 1950. Best-selling record in 1961 by Johnny Horton
  (Columbia).

Slow Down
Words and music by Lawrence E. Williams.
Venice Music, Inc.
Copyright, 1957, 1964. Best-selling record in 1964 by The Beatles
  (Capitol).

Somebody Loves You, see 1932.
Best-selling record in 1961 by Skeeter Davis (RCA Victor).

Someone, Someone (English)
Words and music by Edwin Greines Cohen and Violet Ann Petty.
Burlington Music, England/Nep Music, Inc.
Copyright, 1958. Best-selling record in England and United States
  in 1964 by Brian Poole and The Tremeloes (Monument).

Sweet Dreams, see 1955.
Best-selling records in 1961 by Don Gibson (RCA Victor) and in
  1963 by Patsy Cline (Decca).

Sweet Sixteen
Words and music by Riley King and Joe Josea.
Modern Music Publishing Co.
Copyright, 1959. Best-selling record in 1960 by B.B. King (Kent).

T for Texas, also known as **Blue Yodel No. 1**
Words and music by Jimmie Rodgers.
Peer International Corp.
Copyright, 1953. Best-selling record in 1963 by Grandpa Jones
  (Monument).

Take These Chains from My Heart, see 1952.
Best-selling record in 1963 by Ray Charles (ABC-Paramount).

Talk to Me, also known as **Talk to Me, Talk to Me,** see
  Talk to Me, Talk to Me, 1958.
Best-selling record in 1963 by Sunny and The Sunglows (Tear Drop).

Tell Me Why, see 1951.
Best-selling record in 1964 by Bobby Vinton (Epic).

That's All You Gotta Do
Words and music by Jerry Reed.
Lowery Music Co., Inc.
Copyright, 1958. Best-selling record in 1960-61 by Brenda Lee
(Decca).

Then I'll Stop Loving You
Words and music by Jim Reeves.
American Music, Inc.
Copyright, 1954. Best-selling record in 1964 by The Browns (RCA
Victor).

There's Something on Your Mind
Words and music by C. Jay McNeely.
Mercedes Music Co.
Copyright, 1959. Best-selling record in 1960 by Bobby Marchan
(Fire).

Think
Words and music by Lowman Pauling.
Armo Music Corp.
Copyright, 1957. Best-selling record in 1960 by James Brown and
The Famous Flames (Federal).

This Time
Words and music by Chips Moman.
Tree Publishing Co., Inc.
Copyright, 1958. Best-selling record in 1961 by Troy Shondell
(Liberty).

Timbrook
Words and music by James A. Howell and Don Pierce.
Ralph's Radio Music.
Copyright, 1959. Best-selling record in 1960 by Lewis Pruitt (Decca).

Together, see 1928.
Best-selling record in 1961 by Connie Francis (MGM).

Tragedy, see 1958.
Best-selling record in 1961 by The Fleetwoods (Dolton).

True Love Ways
Words and music by Norman Petty and Buddy Holly.
Nor Va Jak Music, Inc.
Copyright, 1958. Best-selling record in 1965 by Peter and Gordon
(Capitol).

Trust in Me, see 1934.
Best-selling record in 1961 by Etta James (Argo).

Turn Around
Words and music by Alan Greene, Harry Belafonte, and Malvina
    Reynolds.
Clara Music Publishing Corp.
Copyright, 1958. Best-selling record in 1964 by Dick and Dee Dee
    (Warner Bros.).

Twist, The
Words and music by Hank Ballard.
Lois Publishing Co.
Copyright, 1959. Introduced by Hank Ballard and The Midnighters
    (King). Best-selling record in 1960-62 by Chubby Checker (Park-
    way).

Violet and a Rose, The
Words and music by Mel Tillis, Bud Augue, and John Reinfield.
Cedarwood Publishing Co., Inc.
Copyright, 1958. Best-selling record in 1962 by "Little" Jimmy
    Dickens (Columbia).

Walk Right In, see 1930.
Best-selling record in 1963 by The Rooftop Singers (Vanguard).

Walking the Streets
Words and music by Gene Evans, Jimmy Fields, and Jimmy
    Littlejohn.
Buna Music Corp.
Copyright, 1955. Best-selling record in 1961 by Webb Pierce (Decca).

Way Down Yonder in New Orleans, see 1922.
Best-selling record in 1960 by Freddie Cannon (Swan).

Where or When, see 1937.
Best-selling record in 1960 by Dion and The Belmonts (Laurie).

Wings of a Dove, also known as (On the) Wings of a Dove
Words and music by Robert B. Ferguson.
Larrick Music Co./Husky Music Co., Inc.
Copyright, 1959. Best-selling record in 1960 by Ferlin Husky
    (Capitol).

Wishful Thinking
Words and music by Wynn Stewart.
Jat Music, Inc.
Copyright, 1959. Best-selling record in 1960 by Wynn Stewart (Chal-
    lenge).

Woman, a Lover, a Friend, A
Words and music by Sid Wyche.
Merrimac Music Corp.
Copyright, 1959. Best-selling record in 1960 by Jackie Wilson
    (Brunswick).

Woman's Intuition, A
Words and music by Madeline Burroughs.
Sure-Fire Music Co., Inc.
Copyright, 1959. Best-selling record by The Wilburn Brothers
(Decca).

Wonder of You
Words and music by Baker Knight.
Duchess Music Corp.
Copyright, 1958. Best-selling record in 1964 by Ray Peterson (RCA
Victor).

Words
Words and music by Johnny Horton.
American Music, Inc.
Copyright, 1952, 1957, 1962. Best-selling record in 1962 by Johnny
Horton (Columbia), released posthumously.

Wound Time Can't Erase, A
Words and music by William D. Johnson.
Buna Music Corp.
Copyright, 1957. Best-selling record in 1962 by Stonewall Jackson
(Columbia).

Wreck on the Highway, see 1946.
Best-selling record in 1961 by Wilma Lee and Stoney Cooper
(Hickory).

You Are My Flower, see 1939.
Best-selling record in 1964 by Lester Flatt and Earl Scruggs
(Columbia).

You Are My Sunshine, see 1940.
Best-selling record in 1962 by Ray Charles (ABC-Paramount).

You Can Depend on Me, see 1932.
Best-selling record in 1961 by Brenda Lee (Decca).

You Can't Pick a Rose in December
Words and music by Leon Payne.
Fred Rose Music, Inc.
Copyright, 1949. Best-selling record in 1960 by Ernest Ashworth
(Decca).

You Got What It Takes, also known as You've Got What It Takes
Words and music by Berry Gordy, Jr., Gwen Gordy, and Tyran
Carlo.
Fidelity Music Co.
Copyright, 1959. Best-selling record in 1960 by Marv Johnson
(United Artists).

You Must Have Been a Beautiful Baby, see 1938.
Best-selling record in 1961 by Bobby Darin (Atco).

You Took Her off My Hands (Now Please Take Her off My Mind)
Words and music by Wynn Stewart, Skeets McDonald, and Harlan Howard.
Central Songs, Inc.
Copyright, 1956. Best-selling record in 1963 by Ray Price (Columbia).

You'll Always Be the One I Love, see 1947.
Best-selling record in 1964 by Dean Martin (Reprise).

Your Old Love Letters
Words and music by Johnny Bond.
Red River Songs, Inc.
Copyright, 1955. Best-selling record in 1961 by Porter Wagoner (RCA Victor).

You're for Me
Words and music by Tommy Collins and E. A. Owens, Jr.
Central Songs, Inc.
Copyright, 1954. Best-selling record in 1963 by Buck Owens (Capitol).

You're the Only Good Thing (That's Happened to Me)
Words and music by Chuck Gregory.
Golden West Melodies, Inc.
Copyright, 1954, 1959. Introduced in 1954 by Gene Autry. Best-selling record in 1960 by George Morgan (Columbia).

You've Got What It Takes, see **You Got What It Takes.**

Zip-a-Dee-Doo-Dah, see 1945.
Best-selling record in 1962 by Bob B. Soxx and The Blue Jeans (Philles).

List of Titles

A

Abilene, 1963.
Above and Beyond (The Call of Love), Supplement.
Above the Stars, 1961.
Absent Minded Me, 1964.
Aching, Breaking Heart, 1960.
Act Naturally, 1963.
Ada, 1961.
Adam and Eve, Supplement.
Addio, Addio, 1962.
Adios Amigo, 1962.
Adios, My Love (The Song of Athens), 1961.
African Waltz, The 1961.
Afrikaan Beat, 1961.
After Loving You, 1962.
Ah! Camminare, 1962.
Ahab the Arab, 1962.
Ain't Got Time for Nothin', 1963.
Ain't Nothing but a Man, 1962.
Ain't Nothing You Can Do, 1963.
Ain't That Just Like Me, 1961.
Ain't That Love?, 1963.
Ain't That Loving You, 1961.
Air Mail to Heaven, 1961.
Airegin, 1963.
Al Di Là, 1961.
Alabam, 1960.
Aladdin, 1962.
Alice in Wonderland, 1963.
All Alone Am I, 1962.
All Cried Out, 1963.
All Day and All of the Night, 1964.
All for You, 1963.
All Grown Up, 1964.
All I Could Do Was Cry, 1960.
All I Really Want To Do, 1964.

All in My Mind, Supplement.
All I've Got To Do, 1963.
(You Were Made for) All My Love, 1960.
All My Loving, 1963.
All Night Long, 1961.
All Over the World, 1962.
All Summer Long, 1964.
All the Way Home, 1963.
All You Need Is a Quarter, 1960.
Alla My Love, 1962.
Alley Cat, 1962.
Alley Cat Song, The, see Alley Cat, 1962.
Alley Oop, 1960.
Allison's Theme from *Parrish*, 1961.
Ally, Ally Oxen Free, 1963.
Almost There, 1964.
Alone at Last, 1960.
Alvin's Orchestra, 1960.
Always Something There To Remind Me, 1964.
Am I Losing You?, Supplement.
Am I That Easy To Forget?, Supplement.
Amen, 1964.
Amen, see Theme from *Lilies of the Field*, 1963.
Amigo's Guitar, 1960.
Among My Souvenirs, Supplement.
Amore, Scusami, see My Love, Forgive Me, 1964.
Amy, 1963.
Anaheim, Azusa and Cucamonga Sewing Circle, Book Review and Timing Association, The, 1964.
And I Love Her, 1964.
And I Love Him, see And I Love Her, 1964.
.... And Roses and Roses, 1964.

Titles

Angel Baby, 1960.
Angel or Devil, 1961.
Angelito, 1964.
Anna (Go to Him), 1962.
Annie Get Your Yo Yo, 1961.
Anonymous Phone Call, 1963.
Another, Supplement.
Another Bridge To Burn, 1963.
Another Cup of Coffee, 1964.
Another Saturday Night, 1963.
Another Time, Another Place, 1961.
Antony and Cleopatra Theme, 1963.
Any Day Now, 1962.
Any Old Time of Day, 1964.
Any Time at All, 1964.
Any Way the Wind Blows, 1960.
Any Way You Want It, 1964.
Anybody but Me, 1960.
Anymore, 1960.
Anyone Can Whistle, 1964.
Anyone Who Had a Heart, 1963.
Anything That's Part of You, 1962.
Anytime at All, 1961.
Apache, 1960.
Apple Green, 1960.
Are You Lonesome Tonight,
    Supplement.
Are You Sure, 1960.
Are You Sure?, 1961.
Are You Willing Willie, .
    Supplement.
Arm in Arm, 1963.
Artificial Flowers, 1960.
As If I Didn't Know, 1961.
As Long As He Needs Me, 1960.
As Long As There's a Shadow,
    1964.
As Long As There's a Sunday, 1963.
As Simple As That, 1961.
As Tears Go By, 1964.
As Usual, 1963.
Asia Minor, 1961.
Ask Anyone in Love, 1960.
Ask Me, 1964.
Ask Me Nice, 1961.
Ask Me Why, 1963.
Asking for You, 1960.
At Last, Supplement.
Athina (White Rose of Athens),
    1961.
Autumn, 1964.

B

B.J., the D.J., 1963.
Baby Elephant Walk, 1961.

Baby, I Love You, 1963.
Baby, I Need Your Loving, 1964.
Baby, I'm Gone Again, 1963.
Baby I'm Yours, 1964.
Baby, It's You, 1961.
Baby Love, 1964.
Baby Sittin' Boogie, 1960.
Baby, Talk to Me, 1960.
Baby, the Rain Must Fall, 1964.
Baby, Workout, 1963.
Baby, You Been on My Mind, 1964.
Baby, You're Right, 1961.
Baby (You've Got What It Takes),
    1960.
Baby's in Black, 1964.
Bachelor Boy, 1962.
Bachelor in Paradise, 1961.
Back on the Corner, 1961.
Back Street, 1961.
Back-Track, 1961.
Bad and the Beautiful, The, 1960.
Bad Girl, 1963.
Bad News, 1963.
Bad to Me, 1963.
Badman's Blunder, 1960.
Bag's Groove, 1962.
Bald Headed Lena, 1962.
Ballad in Plain D, 1964.
Ballad of Gilligan's Isle, The, 1964.
Ballad of Hollis Brown, 1963.
Ballad of Ira Hayes, 1962.
Ballad of Jed Clampett, 1962.
Ballad of Lady Jane, The, see My
    Love Doesn't Love Me at All,
    1960.
Ballad of the Alamo, 1960.
Ballad of Wild River, The, 1960.
Baltimore, 1964.
Banjo-Boy, 1960.
Barabbas, 1962.
Barbara Ann, 1961.
Barry's Boys, 1964.
Bayou Talk, 1962.
Be a Performer, 1962.
Be a Santa, 1961.
Be My Baby, 1963.
Be My Host, 1962.
Be Quiet, Mind, 1961.
Be True to Your School, 1963.
Beach Girl, 1964.
Beans in My Ears, 1964.
Beatnik Fly, 1960.
Beautiful, 1962.
Beautiful Candy, 1961.
Beautiful Land, The, 1964.

Because, 1964.
Because They're Young, 1960.
Beechwood 4-5789, 1962.
Before and After, 1964.
Before I Gaze at You Again, 1960.
Before I Kiss the World Goodbye, 1963.
Before I'm Over You, 1962.
Before the Parade Passes By, 1963.
Before This Day Ends, 1960.
Beggar to a King, 1960.
Begging to You, 1963.
Being in Love, 1961.
Bells, The, 1963.
Bells of Rhymney, Supplement.
Belly Up to the Bar, Boys, 1960.
Berlin Melody, The, 1961.
Best Dressed Beggar in Town, The, 1962.
Beyond the Sea, Supplement.
Big Bad John, 1961.
Big Boy Pete, Supplement.
Big City Girls, 1963.
Big Clown Balloons, The, 1963.
Big, Cold Wind, 1961.
Big Daddy, 1961.
Big Girls Don't Cry, 1962.
Big Hurt, The, 1960.
Big Iron, Supplement.
Big John (Ain't You Gonna Marry Me?), 1961.
Big Man in Town, 1964.
Big River, Big Man, 1961.
Big Wide World, 1962.
Bilbao Song, The, 1961.
Bird is the Word, The, 1963.
Bird Man, The, 1962.
Birds and the Bees, The, 1964.
Birmingham Sunday, 1964.
Bit of Soul, A, 1961.
Bits and Pieces, 1964.
Black Crow Blues, 1964.
Blame It on the Bossa Nova, 1962.
Blanket Roll Blues, see Not a Soul, 1960.
Bleecker Street, 1964.
Bless You, 1961.
Blind Man, 1964.
Blizzard, The, 1961.
Blowin' in the Wind, 1962.
Blue Angel, 1960.
Blue Genius, 1962.
Blue Hawaii, Supplement.
Blue Moon, Supplement.
Blue on Blue, 1963.

Blue Rondo a la Turk, 1960.
Blue Train, The, 1960.
Blue Velvet, 1963.
Blue Winter, 1963.
Blue Yodel No. 1, see T for Texas, Supplement.
Blues I Got Comin' Tomorrow, The, 1961.
Bluesette, 1963.
Boa Constrictor, 1962.
Bobby's Girl, 1962.
Boll Weevil Song, 1960.
Bom Di Di Bom, 1961.
Bonanza, 1960.
Boots of Spanish Leather, 1963.
Born Again, 1963.
Born To Wander, 1961.
Borning Day, The, 1963.
Boss Guitar, 1963.
Bossa Nova Baby, 1963.
Bossa Nova U.S.A., 1962.
Bottle of Wine, 1963.
Bound for Glory, 1963.
Boy from New York City, The, 1964.
Boy Ten Feet Tall, A, 1964.
Boys, 1960.
Boys' Night Out, The, 1962.
Bread and Butter, 1964.
Break It to Me Gently, 1961.
(I Didn't Have To) Break Up Someone's Home, 1963.
Breakfast with the Blues, 1963.
Breaking In a Brand New Broken Heart, 1961.
Breaking Up Is Hard To Do, 1962.
Bright Lights, Big City, 1961.
Bring It On Home to Me, 1962.
Bristol Stomp, The, 1961.
Broken Heart and a Pillow Filled with Tears, A, 1960.
Brotherhood of Man, 1961.
Brown Baby, 1962.
Bucket "T", 1964.
Burning Bridges, 1960.
Burning Memories, 1963.
Burning of Atlanta, The, 1961.
Busted, 1962.
But I Do, 1960.
By Love Possessed, 1961.
Bye Bye Baby (Baby Goodbye), 1964.
Bye Bye Birdie, 1962.
Bye Bye Johnny, 1960.

Titles

C

Caesar and Cleopatra Theme, see A World of Love, 1963.
Cajun Queen, The, 1962.
Cajun Stripper, 1963.
Calcutta, 1960.
Calendar Girl, 1961.
California Sun, 1961.
Call Me Irresponsible, 1962.
Call Me Mister Brown, 1963.
Call Me Mr. In-Between, 1962.
Call on Me, 1962.
Camelot, 1960.
Can You Jerk Like Me, 1964.
Candy Girl, 1963.
Candy Man, 1961.
Can't Buy Me Love, 1964.
Can't Get Over (The Bossa Nova), 1964.
Can't Get Used To Losing You, 1962.
Can't Help Falling in Love, 1961.
Can't Take No More, 1962.
Can't You See It?, 1964.
Can't You See That She's Mine?, 1964.
Canto D'Amore (Song of Love), 1963.
Captain Buffalo, 1960.
Carina Marie, 1962.
Carousels, 1962.
Cast Your Fate to the Wind, 1960.
Cat, The, 1964.
Caterina, 1962.
Cathy's Clown, 1960.
Cement Octopus, 1964.
Cha Cha Cha, The, 1962.
Chain Gang, 1960.
Chains, 1962.
Chapel by the Sea, The, 1961.
Chapel of Love, 1964.
Charade, 1963.
Chariot, see I Will Follow Him, 1963.
Charlemagne, 1964.
Charlesville, 1961.
Charlie's Shoes, 1961.
Charms, 1963.
Cherie, 1961.
Cherry Pie, Supplement.
Cherry Pink and Apple Blossom White, Supplement.
Chim Chim Cher-ee, 1963.
Chime In!, 1961.

Chimes of Freedom, 1964.
China Doll, 1960.
Ching Ching, see Ding, Ding, 1960.
Chip Chip, 1961.
Chug-A-Lug, 1964.
Cindy's Birthday, 1962.
Cinnamon Cinder (It's a Very Nice Dance), 1962.
Circumstances, 1963.
Circus World, 1964.
Ciumachella de Trastevere, 1963.
Clementine, 1960.
Cleo's Mood, 1962.
Clinging Vine, 1962.
Close Harmony, 1964.
Close to Cathy, 1962.
Closest Thing to Heaven, The, 1964.
Closing Credits, The, 1963.
Cloud Song, The, see Suzie Wong, 1960.
C'mon and Swim, 1964.
Cod'ine, 1964.
Cold and Lonely (Is the Forecast for Tonight), 1963.
Cold Dark Waters Below, 1962.
Colorado, My Home, 1960.
Colorful, 1964.
Comancheros, The, 1961.
Come a Little Bit Closer, 1964.
Come and Get These Memories, 1962.
Come Away Melinda, 1962.
Come Home, 1964.
Come On, Do the Jerk, 1964.
Come On, Let Yourself Go, 1964.
Come See about Me, 1964.
Comeback, The, 1962.
Comedy Tonight, 1962.
Comes Once in a Lifetime!, 1961.
Comin' Home Baby, 1962.
Company Way, The, 1961.
Confidence, 1964.
Conscience, 1961.
Consider Yourself, 1960.
Control Yourself, 1962.
Copper Kettle (The Pale Moonlight), Supplement.
Corcovado, see Quiet Nights of Quiet Stars, 1962.
Cornet Man, 1964.
Corrina, Corrina, Supplement.
Cotton Candy, 1964.
Cotton Fields, 1962.
Cotton Mill Man, 1964.
Country Girl, 1960.

Cousins, see The Patty Duke Theme, 1963.
Cow Town, Supplement.
Cowboy Boots, 1963.
Cowboy in the Continental Suit, The, 1963.
Coyote, My Little Brother, 1963.
Crabs Walk Sideways, 1963.
Cradle of Love, 1960.
Crazy, 1961.
Crazy Wild Desire, 1962.
Criss-Cross, 1962.
Crooked Little Man, see Don't Let the Rain Come Down, 1964.
Cross the Brazos at Waco, 1964.
Crowd, The, 1962.
Cruel Love, Supplement.
Cry Baby, 1963.
Cry Like the Wind, 1960.
Cry to Me, 1961.
Crying, 1961.
Crying in the Rain, 1961.
Cuando Caliente El Sol, 1961.
Cupid, 1961.
Cuttin' In, 1962.

D

D.J. for a Day, 1963.
Da Doo Ron Ron (When He Walked Me Home), 1963.
Daddy's Home, 1961.
Dance, Dance, Dance, 1964.
Dance On, Little Girl, 1960.
Dancin' Party, 1962.
Dancing, 1963.
Dancing in the Street, 1964.
Dang Me, 1964.
Daniel Boone, 1964.
Danke Schoen, 1963.
Darkest Street in Town, The, 1962.
Darling (Gonna Work Out Fine), see It's Gonna Work Out Fine, 1961.
David and Lisa's Love Song, 1962.
Dawn (Go Away), 1963.
Dawn Ray, 1961.
Day into Night, 1961.
Daydreaming, 1962.
Daydreams, 1961.
Days Gone By, 1963.
Days of the Waltz, The, 1964.
Days of Wine and Roses, 1962.
Dead Man's Curve, 1963.
Dear Friend, 1963.

Dear Heart, 1964.
Dear Ivan, 1961.
Dear Lady, 1961.
Dear Lonely Hearts (I'm Writing to You), 1962.
Dear One, 1961.
Dedicated to the One I Love, Supplement.
Deep Down Inside, 1962.
Deep Purple, Supplement.
Delaware, 1960.
Denise, 1963.
Deportee, see Plane Wreck at Los Gatos, 1961.
Dern Ya, 1964.
Desafinado (Slightly Out of Tune), 1962.
Detroit City, 1962.
Devil in Disguise, see You're the Devil in Disguise, 1963.
Devil or Angel, Supplement.
Devil Woman, 1962.
Diamond Head, 1961.
Diane, Supplement.
Did You Have a Happy Birthday?, 1963.
Ding Ding, 1960.
Ding-a-Ling, 1960.
Dis-Donc, Dis-Donc, 1960.
Disorderly Orderly, The, 1964.
Distant Drums, 1963.
Do It Right, 1964.
Do the Bird, 1963.
Do Wah Diddy Diddy, 1963.
Do What You Do, Do Well, 1964.
Do You Ever Dream of Vienna?, 1960.
Do You Love Me?, 1962, 1964.
Do You Mind?, 1960.
Do You Want To Know a Secret?, 1963.
Dodo, The, 1964.
Does Goodnight Mean Goodbye, 1963.
Does He Mean That Much to You?, 1962.
Does Your Chewing Gum Lose Its Flavor on the Bedpost Overnight?, Supplement.
Doggin' Around, 1960.
Dolce Far Niente, 1960.
Dollar Down, A, 1960.
Dominique, 1963.
Dondi, 1960.
Donna the Prima Donna, 1963.

Titles

Don't Ask Me To Be Friends, 1962.
Don't Be Afraid, Little Darlin',
   1963.
Don't Be Afraid of Romance, 1962.
Don't Be Angry, Supplement.
Don't Bet Money, Honey, 1961.
Don't Bother Me, 1963.
Don't Break the Heart That Loves
   You, 1962.
Don't Call Me from a Honky Tonk,
   1961.
Don't Come Knockin', 1960.
Don't Come Running Back to Me,
   1964.
Don't Cry Baby, Supplement.
Don't Cry No More, 1960.
Don't Forget I Still Love You, 1964.
Don't Forget 127th Street, 1964.
Don't Go Near the Indians, 1962.
Don't Hang Up, 1963.
Don't Let Me Be Misunderstood,
   1964.
Don't Let Me Cross Over, 1962.
Don't Let Me Stand in Your Way,
   1962.
Don't Let the Rain Come Down
   (Crooked Little Man), 1964.
Don't Let the Sun Catch You
   Crying, 1964.
Don't Lie, 1962.
Don't Make Me Over, 1962.
Don't Make My Baby Blue, 1963.
Don't Play That Song (You Lied),
   1962.
Don't Rain on My Parade, 1964.
Don't Read the Letter, 1961.
Don't Say Nothin' Bad (About My
   Baby), 1963.
Don't Take Away Your Love, 1962.
Don't Take Our Charlie for the
   Army, 1963.
Don't Think Twice, It's All Right,
   1963.
Don't Throw Your Love Away, 1964.
Don't Try To Fight It, Baby, 1963.
Don't Wait Too Long, 1963.
Don't Worry, 1960.
Don't Worry Baby, 1964.
Don't You Believe It, 1962.
Don't You Forget It, 1963.
Door Is Still Open to My Heart,
   The, Supplement.
Do-Wacka-Do, 1964.
Down by the River, 1962.

Down by the Station, see Early in
   the Morning, 1960.
Downtown, 1964.
Draft Dodger Rag, 1964.
Drag City, 1963.
Dream Baby, How Long Must I
   Dream?, 1962.
Dream On Little Dreamer, 1964.
(He's My) Dreamboat, 1961.
Dreamin', 1960.
Dreamstreet, 1961.
Dreamy, 1960.
Drip Drop, Supplement.
Driving Wheel, 1961.
Drownin' My Sorrows, 1963.
Duck, The (O Pato), 1962.
Duke of Earl, 1961.
Dum Dum, 1961.
Dum-De-Da, 1963.

E

Each Moment Spent with You,
   1960.
Eager Beaver, 1962.
Early in the Morning, 1960.
Early Mornin' Rain, 1964.
Easier Said Than Done, 1963.
East Side/West Side, see Theme
   from *East Side/West Side*, 1963.
Easy Come, Easy Go, 1963.
(Such an) Easy Question, 1962.
Ebb Tide, 1964.
Ebony Eyes, 1961.
Eddie, My Darling, 1960.
Eight Days a Week, 1964.
Eight Years, 1963.
Eight-by-Ten, 1963.
Eighteen Yellow Roses, 1963.
El Paso, 1960.
El Watusi, 1962.
Elegance, 1963.
Elena, 1961.
Emily, 1964.
Emotions, 1960.
Empty Pockets Filled with Love,
   1962.
Enchanted Melody, The, 1960.
End of the World, The, 1962.
English Teacher, An, 1960.
Eso Beso (That Kiss), 1962.
Especially for the Young, 1960.
Et Maintenant, see What Now My
   Love, 1962.

Et Pourtant, see Yet . . . I Know, 1963.
Eventually, 1961.
Everlovin', Supplement.
Every Beat of My Heart, Supplement.
Every Breath I Take, 1961.
Every Little Thing, 1964.
Every Step of the Way, Supplement.
Every Which-a-Way, 1961.
Everybody, 1963.
Everybody but Me, Supplement.
Everybody Knows, 1964.
Everybody Knows (I Still Love You), 1964.
Everybody Loves Me but You, 1962.
Everybody Loves Somebody, 1964.
Everybody Ought To Have a Maid, 1962.
Everybody Says Don't, 1964.
Everything Beautiful Happens at Night, 1963.
Everything Makes Music When You're in Love, 1964.
Everything's Great, 1964.
Eve's Theme, 1962.
Ev'rybody's Somebody's Fool, 1960.
Ev'rything Beautiful, 1961.
Excuse Me (I Think I've Got a Heartache), 1960.
Exodus, 1960.
Exodus Song, The (This Land Is Mine), see Exodus, 1960.
Expect Things To Happen, 1963.

F

Face to the Wall, 1960.
Facts of Life, The, 1960.
Fade Out — Fade In, 1964.
Faded Love, Supplement.
Fair Swiss Maiden, 1961.
Faith, 1964.
Falcon and the Dove, The, see Love Theme from *El Cid*, 1961.
Fall of Love, The, 1964.
Fallen Angel, 1960.
Fame and Fortune, 1960.
Familiar, 1961.
Family Affair, A, 1962.
Family Bible, 1960.
Fan the Flame, 1964.
Fannie Mae, 1960.
Fanny, 1961.

Far from the Home I Love, **1964.**
Faraway Boy, 1960.
Faraway Part of Town, The, 1960.
Farewell, 1964.
Farmer's Daughter, The, 1963.
Faucets Are Dripping, The, 1960.
Feed the Birds (Tuppence a Bag), 1963.
Feel So Fine (Feel So Good), 1960.
Feeling Good, 1964.
Ferry cross the Mersey, 1964.
Fiddler on the Roof, 1964.
Fie on Goodness!, 1960.
Fiesta, 1963.
Find Another Girl, 1961.
Find Yourself a Man, 1964.
Finding Words for Spring, 1964.
Fine, Fine Boy, A, 1963.
Finger Poppin' Time, 1960.
Fingertips, 1962.
Fingertips (Part II), 1962.
Fings Ain't Wot They Used T'Be, 1960.
Fireball, 1964.
Fireworks, 1960.
First Lady, The, 1962.
First Lady Waltz, The, 1961.
Fish, The, 1961.
Fishin' Hole, The, 1961.
500 Miles Away from Home, 1963.
Five Little Fingers, 1963.
Flat Top, 1961.
Flipper, 1963.
Fly, The, 1961.
Fly by Night, 1961.
Fly Me to the Moon, 1962.
Fog and the Grog, The, 1961.
Folk Singer Blues, 1962.
Follow Me, 1960.
Follow Me, see Love Song from *Mutiny on the Bounty*, 1962.
Follow the Boys, 1962.
Followed Closely by Teardrops, 1962.
Food, Glorious Food, 1960.
Fool in Love (Tell Me What's Wrong), A, 1960.
Fool Killer, The, 1964.
Fool Never Learns, A, 1962.
Fool Number One, 1961.
Fool Too Long, A, see Poor Fool, 1960.
Foolin' 'Round, 1961.
Foolish Little Girl, 1963.
Fools Rush In (Where Angels Fear To Tread), 1963.

Footsteps, 1960.
Footsteps of a Fool, 1962.
For Lovin' Me, 1964.
For Mama, 1963.
For My Baby, Supplement.
For the First Time, 1961.
For You, Supplement.
For Your Precious Love, 1963.
Forever, Supplement.
Forever and a Day, 1964.
Forever My Love, 1961.
Forget Him, 1963.
Fort Worth, Dallas or Houston, 1963.
Fortune Teller, 1961.
Forty Winks Away, 1960.
Four Strong Winds, 1963.
Frankie and Johnnie, 1963.
Freedom Is the Word, 1964.
Friendliest Thing (Two People Can Do), The, 1963.
From a Beggar to a King, see Beggar to a King, 1960.
From a Jack to a King, Supplement.
From a Window, 1964.
From Me to You, 1963.
From Russia with Love, 1963.
From the Bottom of My Heart (Dammi Dammi Dammi), 1962.
From the Terrace (Love Theme), 1960.
From Way Up Here, 1962.
Fun, Fun, Fun, 1964.
Funny, 1961.
Funny Girl, 1964.
Funny How Time Slips Away, see Funny, 1961.
Funny Thing Happened, A, 1962.
Funny Way of Laughin', 1962.
Funny World, 1964.

G

G.T.O., 1964.
Game of Love, The, 1964.
Gather Your Dreams, 1963.
Gee Whiz! (Look at His Eyes), 1960.
Gegetta, 1963.
Genius after Hours, The, 1961.
Georgia on My Mind, Supplement.
Get a Little Dirt on Your Hands, 1961.
Gift Today, A, 1962.
Gimme Some, 1964.

Gimme That Wine, 1960.
Gina, 1960.
Ginny Come Lately, 1961.
Girl from Ipanema, The, 1963.
Girl from Spanish Town, The, 1963.
Girl I Used To Know, A, 1962.
Girl Named Tamiko, A, 1962.
Girl on the Billboard, 1964.
Girl Shy, 1962.
Girls Like Me, 1961.
Give a Little Whistle, 1960.
Give Him a Great Big Kiss, 1964.
Give Me 40 Acres (To Turn This Rig Around), 1964.
Give Us Your Blessing, 1963.
Giving Up, 1964.
Glad All Over, 1963.
Glad To Be Home, 1962.
Gloria, 1960.
Go Away, Little Girl, 1962.
Go, Cat Go, 1964.
Go Home, 1961.
Go, Jimmy, Go, 1960.
Go Now, 1963.
Go Slow, Johnny, 1961.
God Bless the Grass, 1964.
Goin' Out of My Head, 1964.
Going through the Motions of Living, 1963.
Golden Boy, 1964.
Golden Tear, 1962.
Goldfinger, 1964.
Gone Is My Love, 1960.
Gonna Be Another Hot Day, 1963.
Gonna Build a Mountain, 1961.
Gonna Get Along without You Now, 1964.
Gonna Send You Back to Georgia (A City Slick), 1963.
Gonna Send You Back to Walker, see Gonna Send You Back to Georgia (A City Slick), 1963.
Good Clean Fun, 1960.
Good Life, The, 1963.
Good Luck Charm, 1962.
Good News, 1964.
Good Time Baby, 1961.
Good Timin', 1960.
Goodbye Charlie, 1964.
Goodbye Cruel World, 1961.
Goodbye Is a Lonesome Sound, 1961.
Goodbye, Juan, see Plane Wreck at Los Gatos, 1961.
Goodbye My Lover, Goodbye, 1963.

Got My Mojo Working, 1960.
Gotta Move, 1963.
Grand Knowing You, 1963.
Grand Old Ivy, 1961.
Grande Luna Italiana (Gidget's Roman Moon), 1963.
Grass Is Greener, The, 1963.
Gravy, 1962.
Gravy Waltz, 1962.
Great Escape March, The, 1963.
Green Fields, 1960.
Green, Green, 1963.
Green Leaves of Summer, The, 1960.
Green Onions, 1962.
Greenback Dollar, 1962.
Greener Pastures, 1960.
Guantanamera, 1963.
Guenevere, 1960.
Guilty, 1963.
Guilty of Loving You, 1961.
Guilty of Loving You, see Guilty, 1963.
Guns of Navarone, The, 1961.
G'Won Train, 1960.
Gypsy Woman, 1961.

H

Half a Sixpence, 1963.
Half the Battle, 1963.
Half-Way Loved, 1964.
Halfway to Paradise, 1961.
Hallelujah! (Alleluia!), 1963.
Handbag Is Not a Proper Mother, A, 1960.
Handy Man, 1960.
Hang On Sloopy (My Girl Sloopy), 1964.
Happiness, 1960.
Happy Birthday, 1964.
Happy Birthday, Sweet Sixteen, 1961.
Happy Birthday to Me, 1960.
Happy Days Are Here Again, Supplement.
Happy Go Lucky Me, 1960.
Happy Journey, 1961.
Happy Thieves Theme, 1962.
Happy Times (Are Here To Stay), 1961.
Happy To Be Unhappy, 1961.
Happy To Keep His Dinner Warm, 1961.
Harbor Lights, Supplement.

Hard Day's Night, A, 1964.
Hard Rain's A-Gonna Fall, 1963.
Hard Times (No One Knows Better Than I), 1961.
Harmony, 1962.
Hatari!, 1961.
Hats Off to Larry, 1961.
Haunted House, Supplement.
Haunting, 1963.
Have a Dream, 1962.
Have I the Right, 1964.
Have I Told You Lately?, 1962.
Have You Looked into Your Heart, 1962.
Having a Party, 1962.
Hawaii Tattoo, 1961.
He Ain't No Angel, 1964.
He Cried, 1961.
He Is Here, 1962.
He Says the Same Things to Me, 1964.
He Was My Brother, 1963.
He Will Break Your Heart, 1960.
He Won't Ask Me, 1964.
Healing Hands of Time, 1964.
Heart, Be Careful, 1963.
Heart (I Hear You Beating), 1962.
Heart in Hand, 1962.
Heart Must Learn To Cry, A, see Theme from *36 Hours*, 1964.
Heart of Mine, see Song from *Advise and Consent*, 1962.
Heart over Mind, 1961.
Heart to Heart Talk, 1960.
Heartache for a Keepsake, A, 1962.
Heartaches, Supplement.
Heartaches by the Number, 1960.
Heartbreak (It's Hurting Me), 1960.
Heartbreak, U.S.A., 1960.
Heat Wave, 1963.
He'll Have To Go, 1960.
He'll Have To Stay, 1960.
Hello, Dolly!, 1963.
Hello Fool, 1961.
Hello Heartache, Goodbye, Love, 1963.
Hello, I Love You, Goodbye, 1964.
Hello Little Girl, 1963.
Hello, Mary Lou, 1961.
Hello Mudduh, Hello Fadduh (A Letter from Camp), 1963.
Hello Out There, 1962.
Hello Stranger, 1963.
Hello Trouble, 1962.
Hello Walls, 1961.
Hennesey, 1960.

Titles

Her Face, 1961.
Her Royal Majesty, 1961.
Here and Now, 1963.
Here Comes My Baby Back Again, 1964.
Here's Love, 1963.
Here's to Us, 1962.
He's a Bad Boy, 1963.
He's a Rebel, 1962.
He's My Friend, 1963.
He's So Fine, 1962.
He's So Heavenly, 1962.
He's Sure the Boy I Love, 1962.
Hey! Baby, 1962.
Hey Bobba Needle, 1964.
Hey, Girl, 1963.
Hey Little Cobra, 1963.
Hey Little Girl, 1963.
Hey Little Star, 1962.
Hey, Look Me Over, 1960.
Hey Nelly Nelly, 1963.
Hey, Paula, 1962.
Hey There, Lonely Boy, 1963.
Hide Away — 1962, 1961.
Hi-Heel Sneakers, 1964.
Hillbilly Heaven, see I Dreamed of a Hillbilly Heaven, Supplement.
His Latest Flame, 1961.
Hit the Road, Jack, 1961.
Hitch-Hiker, 1962.
Hobo Flats, 1963.
Hold Me Tight, 1963.
Hold What You've Got, 1964.
Holly Jolly Christmas, A, 1962.
Hollywood, 1961.
Honestly Sincere, 1960.
Honey-Wind Blows, 1964.
Honky Tonk Happy, 1964.
Honky Tonk Troubles, 1962.
Honolulu Lulu, 1963.
Hootenanny Saturday Night, 1963.
Hop, Skip, Jump, 1960.
Hopeless, 1962.
Hot Pastrami, 1963.
Hotel Happiness, 1962.
House of the Rising Sun, The, 1964.
How Can I Meet Her?, 1962.
How Can I Tell Her It's Over, 1961.
How Can I Write on Paper What I Feel in My Heart, see What I Feel in My Heart, 1961.
How Can You Describe a Face?, 1961.
How Do You Do It, 1964.
How Do You Talk to a Baby?, 1961.
How Does the Wine Taste?, 1962.

How D'Ya Talk to a Girl, 1964.
(You Don't Know) How Glad I Am, 1964.
How Insensitive (Insensatez), 1963.
How Lovely To Be a Woman, 1960.
How Many Tears, 1961.
How Much Can a Lonely Heart Stand, 1963.
How Sad, 1962.
How Sweet It Is (To Be Loved by You), 1964.
How the West Was Won, 1962.
How To Handle a Woman, 1960.
How To Murder Your Wife, 1964.
How To Succeed in Business without Really Trying, 1961.
How Wonderful To Know, 1961.
How's My Ex Treating You, 1962.
Hudson River Song, The, see My Dirty Stream, 1964.
Hum-Drum Blues, 1962.
Humpty Dumpty, 1961.
Hundred Pounds of Clay, A, 1961.
Hurt, Supplement.
Hush . . . Hush, Sweet Charlotte, 1964.
Hush, Little Baby, see Theme from *The Miracle Worker*, 1962.
Hymn for a Sunday Evening, 1960.

I

I Adore Him, 1963.
I Ain't Down Yet, 1960.
I Ain't Marchin' Anymore, 1964.
I Am a Rock, 1964.
I Am Woman, You Are Man, see You Are Woman, I Am Man, 1964.
I Believe in You, 1961.
I Belong to Your Heart, 1960.
I Call Your Name, 1963.
I Can, 1964.
I Can Mend Your Broken Heart, 1962.
I Can See It, 1960.
I Can't Get Over Me (Not Gettin' Over You), 1964.
I Can't Hang Up the Phone, 1962.
I Can't Help You, I'm Falling Too, see Please Help Me, I'm Falling (In Love with You), 1960.
I Can't Stay Mad at You, 1963.
I Can't Stop Loving You, 1962.
I Catch Myself Crying, 1962.

I Could Go On Singing, 1963.
I Couldn't Have Done It Alone, 1962.
I Cry Alone, 1960.
I Don't Believe I'll Fall in Love Today, 1960.
I Don't Believe You (She Acts Like We Never Have Met), 1964.
I Don't Care, 1964.
I Don't Care Much, 1963.
I Don't Love You Any More, 1964.
I Don't Mind, 1961.
I Don't Think I'm in Love, 1964.
I Don't Want To Cry No More, 1961.
I Don't Want To See You Again, 1964.
I Don't Want To Spoil the Party, 1964.
I Dreamed of a Hillbilly Heaven, Supplement.
I Fall to Pieces, 1960.
I Feel Fine, 1964.
I Feel So Bad, Supplement.
I Fought the Law, 1961.
I Found a Love, 1962.
I Get Around, 1964.
I Go My Merry Way, see Tous les Chemins, 1962.
I Go to Bed, 1963.
I Go to Pieces, 1964.
I Got a Thing Going On, 1964.
I Got a Woman (I Got a Sweetie), Supplement.
I Got Everything I Want, 1964.
I Gotta Know, Supplement.
I Guess I'll Never Learn, 1961.
I Guess I'm Crazy for Loving You, Supplement.
I Had a Ball, 1964.
I Hope, I Think, I Wish, 1962.
I Just Don't Know What To Do with Myself, 1962.
I Just Don't Understand, 1961.
I Knew It All the Time, 1962.
I Know about Love, 1960.
I Know One, 1960.
I Know the Feeling, 1963.
I Know (You Don't Want Me No More), 1961.
I Know Your Heart, 1964.
I Left My Heart in San Francisco, 1962.
I Let It Slip Away, 1961.
I Like It Like That, 1961.
I Love How You Love Me, 1961.

I Love the Way You Love, 1960.
I Love To Dance with Annie, 1964.
I Love To Laugh, 1963.
(P.S.) I Love You, 1963.
I Love You Because, Supplement.
I Love You More and More Every Day, 1963.
I Loved You Once in Silence, 1960.
I May Never Get to Heaven, 1960.
I Missed Me, 1960.
I Must Be Dreaming, 1960.
I Need You Lovin', Supplement.
I Only Want To Be with You, 1963.
I Pity the Fool, 1960.
I Put My Hand In, 1963.
I Remember You, Supplement.
I Said Good Morning, Supplement.
I Saw Her Standing There, 1963.
I Saw Linda Yesterday, 1962.
I Saw Me, 1963.
I Should Have Known Better, 1964.
I Stayed Too Long at the Fair, 1963.
I Still Look at You That Way, 1963.
I Take the Chance, Supplement.
I Thank My Lucky Stars, 1962.
I Think I Know, 1960.
I Understand Just How You Feel, 1961.
I Wanna Be Around, 1963.
I Wanna Be in Love Again, 1964.
I Wanna Be Your Man, 1963.
I Wanna Love Him So Bad, 1964.
I Want To Be Wanted, 1960.
I Want To Be with You, 1964.
I Want To Hold Your Hand, 1963.
I Want To Know, 1960.
I Want To Love You, 1962.
I Want To Stay Here, 1963.
I Want You To Be the First One To Know, 1962.
I Want You To Meet My Baby, 1964.
I Washed My Hands in Muddy Water, 1964.
I Went Out of My Way, 1961.
I Will Follow Him, 1963.
I Will Follow You, 1961.
I Will Follow You, see I Will Follow Him, 1963.
I Will Live My Life for You, 1962.
I Will Love You, 1963.
I Will Wait for You, 1964.
I Wish I Could Fall in Love Today, 1960.

I Wish I'd Never Been Born, 1960.
I Wish That We Were Married, 1962.
I Wish You Love, 1964.
I Wonder What It's Like?, 1960.
I Wonder What the King Is Doing Tonight?, 1960.
I Wonder Who, 1961.
I Won't Forget You, 1962.
I Wouldn't Trade You for the World, 1964.
I'd Do Anything, 1960.
I'd Do It Again, 1964.
I'd Rather Loan You Out, 1960.
If a Man Answers, 1962.
If a Woman Answers, 1962.
If and When, 1962.
If Ever I Would Leave You, 1960.
If I Can't Have You, 1960.
If I Didn't Have a Dime (To Play the Jukebox), 1962.
If I Fell, 1964.
If I Gave You . . . , 1964.
If I Had a Girl, 1960.
If I Had a Hammer, 1962.
If I Knew, 1960.
If I Lost Your Love, 1960.
If I Ruled the World, 1963.
If I Were a Rich Man, 1964.
If I Were the Man, 1962.
If I Were You, 1962.
If It Pleases You, 1963.
If Only Tomorrow (Could Be Like Today), 1961.
If She Should Come to You (La Montaña), 1960.
If the Rain's Got To Fall, 1963.
If You Don't Know I Ain't Gonna Tell You, Supplement.
If You Love Him, 1964.
If You Need Me, 1963.
If You Wanna Be Happy, 1962.
I'll Be Back, 1964.
I'll Be on My Way, 1963.
I'll Be There, 1960.
I'll Cry Instead, 1964.
I'll Follow the Sun, 1964.
I'll Get You, 1963.
I'll Go Down Swinging, 1964.
I'll Have Another Cup of Coffee, Then I'll Go, 1960.
I'll Just Have a Cup of Coffee, see I'll Have Another Cup of Coffee, Then I'll Go, 1960.
I'll Keep You Satisfied, 1963.
I'll Make a Man of the Man, 1964.

I'll Never Dance Again, 1962.
I'll Never Go There Anymore, 1964.
I'll Never Say No, 1960.
I'll Pick Up My Heart (And Go Home), 1962.
I'll Release You, 1962.
I'll Remember Her, 1963.
I'll Repossess My Heart, 1964.
I'll Take Care of You, Supplement.
I'll Take You Home, 1963.
Ilona, 1963.
I'm a Fool for Loving You, 1960.
I'm a Loser, 1964.
I'm a Woman, 1961.
I'm All I've Got, 1962.
I'm All Smiles, 1964.
I'm Blue (The Gong Gong Song), 1961.
I'm Crying, 1964.
I'm Fascinating, 1962.
I'm Gettin' Better, 1960.
I'm Gonna Be Strong, 1963.
I'm Gonna Be Warm This Winter, 1962.
I'm Gonna Change Everything, 1962.
I'm Gonna Get Him, 1962.
I'm Gonna Go Fishin', Supplement.
I'm Gonna Knock on Your Door, 1961.
I'm Happy Just To Dance with You, 1964.
I'm Into Something Good, 1964.
I'm Just Taking My Time, 1961.
I'm Leaving It All Up to You, see I'm Leaving It Up to You, Supplement.
I'm Leaving It Up to You, Supplement.
I'm Not Crazy Yet, 1964.
I'm Not Talking, 1964.
I'm on the Outside (Looking In), 1964.
I'm Saving My Love, 1962.
I'm So Miserable without You, 1964.
I'm So Proud, 1964.
I'm Sorry, 1960.
I'm the Greatest Star, 1964.
I'm the Lonely One, 1963.
I'm with You, 1964.
I'm Yours, 1961.
Image of a Girl, 1960.
Imagine That, 1962.
Imitation, 1961.
In All My Wildest Dreams, 1961.

"In" Crowd, The, 1964.
In Dreams, 1963.
In My Lonely Room, 1964.
In My Room, 1964.
In Other Words, see Fly Me to the Moon, 1962.
In Our Hide-Away, 1962.
In the Jailhouse Now, Supplement.
In the Middle of a Heartache, 1961.
In the Name of Love, 1964.
In the Summer of His Years, 1963.
Invisible Tears, 1964.
Irma la Douce, 1960.
Is He the Only Man in the World, 1962.
Is It Really Me?, 1963.
Is It Really Over, 1963.
Is She the Only Girl in the World, see Is He the Only Man in the World, 1962.
Is This Me?, 1963.
Island of Forgotten Lovers, The, 1962.
It Ain't Like That No More, 1962.
It Ain't Me, Babe, 1964.
It Gets Lonely in the White House, 1962.
It Happened Just That Way, 1964.
It Hurts To Be in Love, 1964.
It Is Better To Love, 1962.
It Keeps Right On A-Hurtin' Since I Left, 1961.
It Might As Well Rain until September, 1962.
It Only Takes a Moment, 1963.
It Takes a Woman, 1963.
It Takes All Kinds To Make a World, 1961.
It Was a Very Good Year, 1961.
It Was Always You, 1961.
It Won't Be Long, 1963.
It's a Mad, Mad, Mad, Mad World, 1963.
It's a Raggy Waltz, 1961.
It's All in the Game, 1963.
It's All Over, 1964.
It's All Right!, 1963.
It's for You, 1964.
It's Gonna Be All Right, 1964.
It's Gonna Work Out Fine, 1961.
It's Got the Whole World Shakin', 1964.
It's in His Kiss, see The Shoop, Shoop Song, 1963.
It's My Party, 1963.
It's Now or Never, 1960.

It's Over, 1964.
It's the Little Things in Texas, 1962.
It's Time To Cry, 1960.
It's Too Late, 1963.
It's Up to You, 1962.
It's Your World, 1961.
Itsy Bitsy Teenie Weenie Yellow Polkadot Bikini, 1960.
I've Been Everywhere, 1962.
I've Been Invited to a Party, 1963.
I've Enjoyed As Much of This As I Can Stand, 1962.
I've Got a Tiger by the Tail, 1964.
I've Got Bonnie, 1961.
I've Got Everything I Want, 1964.
I've Got Just About Everything, 1962.
I've Got Sand in My Shoes, 1964.
I've Got To Be Around, 1962.
I've Got You To Lean On, 1964.
I've Got Your Number, 1962.
I've Just Seen Her, 1962.
I've Told Every Little Star, Supplement.

J

Jailer, Bring Me Water, 1962.
Jamaica Ska, 1964.
James Bond Theme, The, 1962.
James, (Hold the Ladder Steady), 1962.
Jamie, 1961.
Java, 1964.
Jazz 'n' Samba (So Danco Samba), 1963.
Jazz Samba, see Jazz 'n' Samba, 1963.
Jenny Rebecca, 1964.
Jeremiah Peabody's Poly-Unsaturated, Quick Dissolving, Fast Acting, Pleasant Tasting, Green and Purple Pills, 1961.
Jerk, The, 1964.
Jessica, 1962.
Jimmy's Girl, 1960.
Joey Baby, 1961.
John Birch Society, The, 1961.
John Riley, 1961.
Johnny Angel, 1962.
Johnny Come Lately, see Ginny Come Lately, 1961.
Johnny Get Angry, 1962.
Johnny Loves Me, 1962.

Johnny's Theme, 1962.
Joker, The, 1964.
Jolly Holiday, 1963.
Jousts, The, 1960.
Joy in the Morning, 1964.
Joy Ride, 1961.
Judy's Turn To Cry, 1963.
Julie Knows, 1964.
Just a Little Bit, Supplement.
Just a Little Bit Better, 1964.
Just an Honest Mistake, 1961.
Just for Old Times' Sake, 1960.
Just One Look, 1963.
Just One Time, 1960.
Just Say "Auf Wiederseh'n," 1962.
Just Tell Her Jim Said Hello, 1962.

K

Keep On Pushing, 1964.
Keep Searchin' (We'll Follow the Sun), 1964.
Keep Your Hands off My Baby, 1962.
Keeping Up with the Joneses, 1963.
Kentucky, Bluebird, see Message to Michael, 1963.
Kicking Our Hearts Around, 1962.
Kid Again, A, 1964.
Kiddio, Supplement.
Kids, 1960.
Kind of Boy You Can't Forget, The, 1963.
King of Clowns, 1962.
King of Holiday Island, The, 1960.
King of Kings Theme, 1961.
King of the Road, 1964.
King of the Whole Wide World, 1962.
Kiss Me No Kisses, 1963.
Kiss Me Quick, 1961.
Kiss Me, Sailor, 1964.
Kissin' Cousins, 1964.
Kissin' on the Phone, 1960.
Kookie Little Paradise, A, 1960.

L

La Dolce Vita (The Sweet Life), 1960.
La Donna nel Mondo, 1963.
La La La, 1962.
La La La La La, 1964.
La Montaña, see If She Should Come to You, 1960.

La Novia, see The Wedding, 1961.
La Valse à Mille Temps, see Carousels, 1962; see The Days of the Waltz, 1964.
Lady Bird, 1964.
Lady Luck, 1960.
Land of a Thousand Dances, 1963.
Las Vegas, 1962.
Last Date, 1960.
Last Day in the Mines, 1963.
Last Kiss, 1961.
Last Night, 1961.
Last Thing on My Mind, The, 1964.
Later Than Spring, 1961.
Laugh, Laugh, 1964.
Laughing Boy, 1963.
Lay Down Your Weary Tune, 1964.
Lazy River, Supplement.
Le Tourbillon, see The Theme from *Jules and Jim*, 1962.
Leader of the Laundromat, 1964.
Leader of the Pack, 1964.
Leavin' It All Up to You, see I'm Leaving It Up to You, Supplement.
Leavin' on Your Mind, 1962.
Left to Right, Supplement.
(I'd Be) A Legend in My Time, 1960.
Lemon Tree, 1960.
Leona, 1962.
Less and Less, 1964.
Let Forgiveness In, Supplement.
Let Her Dance, Supplement.
Let It Be Me, Supplement.
Let Me Belong to You, 1961.
Let Me Do It My Way, 1962.
Let Me Go the Right Way, 1962.
Let Me In, 1961.
Let the Four Winds Blow, 1961.
Let the Good Times Roll, Supplement.
Let the Little Girl Dance, see Let Her Dance, Supplement.
Let There Be Drums, 1961.
Let's Dance, 1962.
Let's Get Together, 1960.
Let's Go Back to the Waltz, 1962.
Let's Go Fly a Kite, 1963.
Let's Go, Let's Go, Let's Go, 1960.
Let's Go Steady Again, 1963.
Let's Invite Them Over, 1963.
Let's Lock the Door (And Throw Away the Key), 1964.
Let's Not Be Sensible, 1962.

Let's Not Waste a Moment (A Short Forever), 1961.
Let's Slip Away, 1960.
Let's Think about Living, 1960.
Let's Turkey Trot, 1963.
Let's Twist Again, 1961.
Letter Full of Tears, 1962.
Lie to Me, 1962.
Life I Lead, The, 1963.
Lifetime of Loneliness, A, 1964.
Lights of Roma, The, see Roma, Nun Fa' la Stupida Stasera, 1963.
Like a Young Man, 1961.
Like Dreamers Do, 1964.
Like Love, 1960.
Limbo Rock, 1962.
Lion Sleeps Tonight, The, 1961.
Little Bird, 1963.
Little Bird, The, 1961.
Little Bit of Soap, A, 1961.
Little Bitty Girl, 1960.
Little Bitty Heart, 1962.
Little Bitty Tear, A, 1960.
Little Black Book, 1962.
Little Boat, 1962.
Little Boxes, 1962.
Little Boy, 1964.
Little Boy, The, 1963.
Little Boy Lost, 1960.
Little Boy Sad, 1960.
Little Child, 1963.
Little Children, 1964.
Little Devil, 1961.
Little Diane, 1962.
Little Drops of Rain, 1961.
Little Heartache, A, 1962.
Little Honda, 1964.
Little Latin Lupe Lu, 1962.
Little Me, 1962.
Little Old Lady (From Pasadena), The, 1964.
Little Old New York, 1960.
Little Ole You, Supplement.
Little Red Rooster, 1961.
Little Sister, 1961.
Little Space Girl, 1960.
Little Susie, 1960.
Little Things, 1964.
Little Things Like That, 1964.
Little Town Flirt, 1962.
Live Wire, 1964.
Living in the Country, 1962.
Living Simply, 1964.
Loads of Love, 1962.
Lock, Stock and Teardrops, 1963.
Locking Up My Heart, 1963.

Loco Weed, 1960.
Loco-Motion, The, 1962.
Lolita Ya-Ya, 1962.
Lollipops and Roses, 1960.
London (Is a Little Bit of All Right), 1963.
Lonely Blue Boy, 1960.
(Hey There) Lonely Boy, 1962.
Lonely Bull, The (El Solo Toro), 1962.
Lonely Teardrops, 1962.
Lonely Teenager, 1960.
Lonely Weekends, 1960.
Lonely Woman, 1960.
Lonesome Death of Hattie Carroll, 1964.
Lonesome Number One, 1961.
Lonesome (7-7203), 1962.
Lonesome Whistle Blues, 1961.
Long About Now, 1962.
Long Gone, 1960.
Long Gone Lonesome Blues, Supplement.
Long Ships, The, 1964.
Longest Day, The, 1962.
Look Again, see Theme from *Irma la Douce*, 1963.
Look at That Face, 1964.
Look for a Sky of Blue, 1960.
Look for a Star, 1960.
Look for Small Pleasures, 1963.
Look in My Eyes, 1961.
Look, Little Girl, 1963.
Look No Further, 1962.
Look of Love, 1964.
Looking for Love, 1964.
Looking for More in '64, 1964.
Loop De Loop, 1962.
Loose Talk, Supplement.
Lorna's Here, 1964.
Losing You, 1963.
Losing Your Love, 1961.
Loss of Innocence, 1961.
Lost Someone, 1962.
Lot of Livin' To Do, A, 1960.
Louie Louie, 1963.
Louisa's Theme, 1964.
Louisiana Man, 1961.
Love, 1964.
Love Came to Me, 1962.
Love, Don't Turn Away, 1963.
Love from a Heart of Gold, 1961.
Love Goddess, The, 1964.
Love Has Laid Her Hands on Me, 1960.

Love Has Made You Beautiful, 1960.
Love, I Hear, 1962.
Love in the Country, see McLintock's Theme, 1963.
Love Is a Ball, 1963.
Love Is a Bore, 1964.
Love Is a Chance, 1964.
Love Is Like a Heat Wave, 1963.
Love Is No Excuse, 1964.
Love Letters, 1962.
Love Looks Good on You, 1963.
Love Makes the World Go, 1962.
Love Makes the World Go 'Round, see Theme from *Carnival!*, 1961.
Love (Makes the World Go 'Round), 1962.
Love Me Do, 1963.
Love Me Some More, 1960.
Love Me Tender, 1963.
Love Me Warm and Tender, 1961.
Love Me with All Your Heart, see Cuando Caliente El Sol, 1961.
(I Wanna) Love My Life Away, 1960.
Love of My Man, The, 1963.
Love of the Loved, 1963.
Love on My Mind, 1962.
Love She Can Count On, A, 1963.
Love Song from *Mutiny on the Bounty*, 1962.
Love Song of Tom Jones, The, 1964.
Love Theme from *El Cid* (The Falcon and the Dove), 1961.
Love Theme from *Lolita*, 1962.
Love Theme from *One-Eyed Jacks*, 1960.
Love Theme from *Phaedra*, 1962.
Love Theme from *The Rat Race*, 1960.
Love Theme from *The World of Suzie Wong*, 1960.
Love with the Proper Stranger, 1963.
Love You So, Supplement.
Love-Line, 1964.
Lovely, 1962.
Lovely Laurie, 1960.
Lovely Work of Art, A, 1960.
Lover Come Back, 1961.
Lover, Please, 1961.
Lovers Who Wander, 1962.
Love's Gonna Live Here Again, 1963.
Loving You (Was Worth This Broken Heart), 1960.

Luck of Ginger Coffey, The (Watching the World Go By), 1964.
Lucky Lips, 1963.
Lucy's Theme from *Parrish*, 1961.
Lumbered, 1961.
Lumberjack, The, 1964.
Lusty Month of May, The, 1960.

M

Mack the Knife, 1962.
McLintock's Theme (Love in the Country), 1963.
Mad, 1964.
(Girls, Girls, Girls Were) Made To Love, 1960.
Madison Time, 1960.
Madrigal, 1964.
Magda's Song, 1963.
Magic Fountain, The, 1962.
Magic Moment, 1961.
Magic Star, see Telstar, 1962.
Magnificent Seven, The, 1960.
Main Title Theme from *The Rat Race*, 1960.
Maine, 1962.
Make It Easy on Yourself, 1962.
Make Me an Offer, 1964.
Make Someone Happy, 1960.
Make the World Go Away, 1963.
Mallory, 1964.
Mama, Supplement.
Mama Didn't Lie, 1962.
Mama Said, see Momma Said, 1961.
Mama Sang a Song, 1961.
Mama, You Been on My Mind, see Baby, You Been on My Mind, 1964.
Man and a Woman, A, 1963.
Man from the Diners' Club, The, 1963.
Man of Constant Sorrow, 1962.
Man Who Has Everything, The, 1962.
Man Who Robbed the Bank at Santa Fe, The, 1962.
Man Who Shot Liberty Valance, The, 1962.
Manhã de Carnaval, 1960.
Many Tears Ago, 1960.
March from *Guns at Batasi*, 1964.
March of the Victors, 1963.
Maria, Supplement.
Maria Elena, 1963.
Maria Ninguem, 1960.
Marlena, 1963.

Marriage Is for Old Folks, 1964.
Marriage-Go-Round, The, 1960.
Married Man, A, 1964.
Martian Hop, 1962.
Marvelous Toy, The, 1961.
Mary's Little Lamb, 1962.
Mashed Potato Time, 1962.
Masters of War, 1963.
Matador, The, 1963, 1964.
Matchbox, Supplement.
Matchmaker, Matchmaker, 1964.
May Each Day, 1963.
Maybe He'll Come Back to Me, 1963.
Maybe I Know, 1964.
Maybe It's All in My Mind, see All in My Mind, Supplement.
Maybe Some Other Time, 1963.
Me, 1963.
Meadowgreen, 1964.
Mean Woman Blues, 1963.
Meantime, 1962.
Meat and Potatoes, 1962.
Mecca, 1963.
Meditation (Meditacão), 1963.
Memory Number One, 1964.
Memphis, Supplement.
Mental Cruelty, 1960.
Mercy, Mercy, 1964.
Mess o' Blues, A, 1960.
Message to Michael, 1963.
Mewsette, 1961.
Mexican Pearls, 1963.
Mexican Shuffle, 1964.
(My Heart's in) Mexico, 1961.
Michael (Row the Boat Ashore), 1961.
Mickey's Monkey, 1963.
Midnight in Moscow, 1961.
Midnight Lace, 1960.
Midnight Mary, 1963.
Midnight Special, 1964.
Mighty Sons of Hercules, The, 1963.
Milk and Honey, 1961.
Miller's Cave, Supplement.
Millie's Theme, 1963.
Million to One, A, 1960.
Million Years or So, A, 1962.
Minute Waltz, The, 1964.
Minute You're Gone, The, 1963.
Mira (Can You Imagine That?), 1961.
Miracle of Miracles, 1964.
Miracles, 1960.
Miranda, 1962.
Misery, 1963.

Misery Loves Company, 1961.
Miss Marmelstein, 1962.
Missing Angel, 1961.
Missing You, Supplement.
Mississippi Goddam, 1964.
Mission Bell, 1960.
Mr. and Mrs. Used To Be, 1964.
Mr. Charles' Blues, 1961.
Mister Custer, 1960.
Mr. Heartache, Move On, 1962.
Mr. Lonely, 1962.
Mr. Lucky, 1960.
Mr. Moonlight, 1962.
Mr. Tambourine Man, 1964.
Mr. Wishing Well, 1963.
Misterioso, 1961.
Mrs. Brown, You've Got a Lovely Daughter, 1964.
Misty, Supplement.
Mockingbird, 1963.
Moliendo Cafe, 1961.
Molly, 1962.
Moment of Fear, 1960.
Momma, Momma!, 1962.
Momma Said, 1961.
Mon Amour Perdu (My Lost Love), 1961.
Money, That's What I Want, Supplement.
Money To Burn, 1963.
Monica, 1964.
Monkey Time, The, 1963.
Monster Mash, 1962.
Moody River, 1961.
Moon Is High and So Am I, The, 1961.
Moon River, 1961.
More (Theme from *Mondo Cane*), 1963.
Morning After, The, 1962.
Moscovian Nights, see Midnight in Moscow, 1961.
Moscow Nights, see Midnight in Moscow, 1961.
Most People Get Married, 1961.
Motel, 1964.
Motherhood March, The, 1963.
Mother-in-Law, 1961.
Motorpsycho Nightmare, 1964.
Mountain of Love, 1963, Supplement.
Mountain's High, The, 1961.
Move Over, Darling, 1963.
Much More, 1960.
Much Too Well, 1960.
Mule Skinner Blues, Supplement.

Muleskinner, **1964.**
Multiplication, 1961.
Munster's Theme, 1964.
Murder, She Said, 1961.
Music of Home, The, 1960.
Music That Makes Me Dance, The, 1964.
Muss I Denn, see Wooden Heart, 1960.
Must Be Santa, 1960.
Must It Be Love?, 1964.
Mustafa, see The Sheik of Chicago, 1960.
My Baby Walks All over Me, 1964.
My Back Pages (I'm Younger Than That Now), 1964.
My Boomerang Won't Come Back, 1961.
My Boy Lollipop, Supplement.
My Boyfriend's Back, 1963.
My Coloring Book, 1962.
My Dad, 1962.
My Dearest Darling, 1960.
My Dirty Stream (The Hudson River Song), 1964.
My Ears Should Burn (When Fools Are Talked About), 1961.
My Empty Arms, 1960.
My First Lonely Night, see Sukiyaki, 1963.
My First Love Song, 1964.
My Friend on the Right, 1964.
My Gentle Young Johnny, 1960.
My Girl, 1964.
My Girl Sloopy, see Hang on Sloopy (My Girl Sloopy), 1964.
My Guy, 1964.
My Heart Belongs to Only You, 1964.
My Heart Has a Mind of Its Own, 1960.
My Heart Skips a Beat, 1963.
My Heart Was an Island, see Swiss Family Theme, 1960.
My Home Town, 1960, 1963.
My Kind of Girl, 1961.
My Kind of Town, 1964.
My Land Is a Good Land, 1964.
My Last Date (With You), 1960.
My Little Corner of the World, 1960.
My Lost Love, see Mon Amour Perdu, 1961.
My Love Doesn't Love Me at All (The Ballad of Lady Jane), 1960.
My Love (Roses Are Red), 1964.

My Love, Forgive Me (Amore, Scusami), 1964.
My Miss Mary, 1960.
My Name Is Mud, 1961.
My Old Man's a Dustman, 1960.
My Six Loves, 1962.
My Special Dream, see Theme from *The Victors*, 1963.
My State, My Kansas, My Home, 1961.
My Summer Love, 1963.
My Tears Are Overdue, 1963.
My True Story, 1961.
My Whole World Is Falling Down, 1963.
My Wish, 1963.

N

Nadine (Is It You?), 1964.
Naked City Theme, 1961.
Name Game, The, 1964.
Natural Man, 1964.
Navy Blue, 1963.
Need for Love, The, see The Unforgiven, 1960.
Need You Home, 1964.
Needle in a Haystack, 1964.
Needles and Pins, 1963.
Nester, The, 1963.
Never on Sunday, 1960.
Never Say "No" (To a Man), 1962.
Never Too Late, 1962.
Never-Ending, 1962.
New Mule Skinner Blues, see Mule Skinner Blues, Supplement.
New *Naked City* Theme, 1962.
(Down in) New Orleans, 1960.
New Pair of Shoes, A, 1963.
Next Door to an Angel, 1962.
Next Time I Love, The, 1960.
Niagara Theme, 1962.
Nice 'n' Easy, 1960.
Nick Teen and Al K. Hall, 1961.
Night, Supplement.
Night Has a Thousand Eyes, The, 1962.
Night Song, 1964.
Night Train, Supplement.
Nightlife, 1962.
Ninety Miles an Hour down a Dead-End Street, 1963.
Nitchevo, 1963.
Nitty Gritty, The, 1963.
No Love Have I, 1960, Supplement.

No More, 1964.
No More Blues, 1962.
No More Songs for Me, 1964.
No One, 1961.
No Particular Place To Go, 1964.
No Regrets, 1961.
No Reply, 1964.
No Strings, 1962.
Nobody Cares, 1961.
Nobody I Know, 1964.
Nobody Told Me, 1962.
Nobody's Fool but Yours, 1962.
Noelle, 1963.
Non, Je Ne Regrette Rien, see
    No Regrets, 1961.
Normal American Boy, 1960.
Norman, 1961.
North to Alaska, 1960.
Not a Second Time, 1964.
Not a Soul (Blanket Roll Blues),
    1960.
Not Fade Away, Supplement.
Not Me, 1960.
No So Long Ago, 1963.
Not What I Had in Mind, 1963.
Nothing More To Look Forward
    To, 1961.
Now!, 1963.
Now and Forever, 1961.
Now I Have Everything, 1964.

O

O Barquinho, see Little Boat, 1962.
O Dio Mio, 1960.
O Pato, see The Duck, 1962.
O Willow Waly, 1962.
Oceans of Love, 1961.
Odds and Ends, Bits and Pieces,
    1961.
Ode to the Little Brown Shack Out
    Back, 1964.
Oh Love, Hast Thou Forsaken Me,
    1961.
Oh! No, Not My Baby, 1964.
Oh! Oh! (It Started All Over
    Again), 1962.
Oh, Oh, Rosie, 1960.
Oh, Pretty Woman, 1964.
Oklahoma Hills, Supplement.
Old Lamp-Lighter, The,
    Supplement.
Old Man Time, 1961.
Old Records, 1963.
Old Rivers, 1962.

Old Showboat, 1962.
Old Smokey Locomotion, 1963.
On Broadway, 1962.
On the Rebound, 1960.
On Top of Spaghetti, 1963.
Once a Day, 1964.
Once in a Blue Moon, 1960.
Once in a Lifetime, 1961.
Once upon a Summertime, 1962.
Once upon a Time, 1962.
One Boy, 1960.
One Broken Heart for Sale, 1963.
One Fine Day, 1963.
One Last Kiss, 1960.
One Little World Apart, 1962.
One Man's Hands, 1962.
One Mint Julep, 1961.
One More Mountain (One More
    River), 1963.
One More Time, 1960, 1964.
One Note Samba (Samba De Uma
    Nota So), 1961.
One of These Days, 1964.
One of Us (Will Weep Tonight),
    1960.
One Potato, Two Potato, 1964.
One Track Mind, 1961.
One, Two, Three Waltz, The, 1961.
One Who Really Loves You, The,
    1962.
One You Slip Around With, The,
    Supplement.
Only a Pawn in Their Game, 1963.
Only Dance I Know, The, 1962.
Only in America, 1963.
Only Love Can Break a Heart,
    1962.
Only One, The, 1963.
Only the Lonely (Know the Way
    I Feel), 1960.
007, 1963.
Open Highway, see Theme from
    Route 66, 1960.
Optimistic, 1961.
Optimistic, see Optimistic, 1961.
Ordinary People, 1961.
Orthodox Fool, An, 1962.
Other Half of Me, The, 1964.
Other Side of the Tracks, The,
    1962.
Our Children, 1962.
Our Concerto, 1960.
Our Day Will Come, 1962.
Our Everlasting Love, 1964.
Our Language of Love, 1960.
Our Winter Love, 1963.

Titles

Out of Limits, 1963.
Over and Over, Supplement.

P

P.S. I Love You, see (P.S.) I Love You, 1963.
P.T. 109, 1961.
Pack Up Your Sorrows, 1964.
Painted, Tainted Rose, 1963.
Palisades Park, 1962.
(Down at) Papa Joe's, 1963.
Papa-Oom-Mow-Mow, 1962.
Paper Roses, 1960.
Parade in Town, A, 1964.
Paradise, 1962.
Paris Blues, 1961.
Paris Is a Lonely Town, 1961.
Paris Mist, 1963.
Paris Original, 1961.
Part Time Love, 1963.
Partin' Time, 1960.
Party Girl, 1964.
Party Lights, 1962.
Pass Me By, 1964.
Pass the Booze, 1964.
Passing Through, 1960.
Password, 1963.
Pastures of Plenty, 1960.
Patches, 1960.
Patty Duke Theme, The (Cousins), 1963.
Peace of Mind, 1961.
Peanut Butter, 1961.
Pearl, Pearl, Pearl, 1962.
Pearly Shells (Pupu O Ewa), 1962.
Peel Me a Grape, 1962.
Peel Me a 'Nanner, 1963.
Peking Theme, The, see So Little Time, 1963.
People, 1964.
People Say, 1964.
Pepe, 1960.
Pepino, the Italian Mouse, 1962.
Peppermint Twist, 1961.
Percolator, 1961.
Perfect Nanny, The, 1963.
Petite Fleur, 1960.
Petticoat Junction, 1963.
Phoenix Love Theme, The, 1964.
Pianissimo, 1961.
Pick of the Week, 1964.
Picture, The, 1960.
Pigtails and Freckles, 1962.
Pillow That Whispers, The, 1963.

Pinball Machine, 1960.
Pine Cones and Holly Berries, 1963.
Pineapple Princess, 1960.
Pink Panther Theme, 1963.
Pipeline, 1962.
Pirogue (Pero), 1963.
Plane Wreck at Los Gatos, 1961.
Playboy, 1961.
Playboys and Playgirls, 1964.
Playboy's Theme, 1960.
Please Don't Ask about Barbara, 1961.
Please Don't Eat the Daisies, 1960.
Please Help Me, I'm Falling (In Love with You), 1960.
Please Love Me Forever, Supplement.
Please Make Him Love Me, 1963.
Please Mr. Postman, 1962.
Please Please Me, 1962.
Please Say You're Foolin', 1963.
(Don't Go) Please Stay, 1961.
Please Talk to My Heart, 1963.
Pleasure of His Company, The, 1961.
Pleasure Seekers, The, 1964.
Po' Folks, 1961.
Pocketful of Miracles, 1961.
Poetry in Motion, 1960.
Point of No Return, 1961.
Pony Time, 1960.
Poor Fool, 1960.
Poor Little Hollywood Star, 1962.
Poor Little Puppet, 1961.
Poor Little Rich Girl, 1963.
Popeye (The Hitchhiker), 1962.
Popsicles and Icicles, 1963.
Popsicles in Paris, 1964.
Portrait of My Love, 1961.
Power and the Glory, The, 1963.
Pretty Blue Eyes, 1960.
Pretty Boy Floyd, 1961.
Pretty Little Angel Eyes, 1961.
Pretty Little Girl in the Yellow Dress, 1961.
Pride, 1962.
Pride and Joy, 1963.
Prince, 1962.
Prisoner of Love, Supplement.
Private John Q, 1962.
Promised Land, The, 1964.
Proud, 1962.
Puff (The Magic Dragon), 1963.
Puppy Love, 1960, 1963.
Pushover, 1963.

Put on a Happy Face, 1960.
Put On Your Sunday Clothes, 1963.

Q

Quando, Quando, Quando (Tell Me When), 1962.
Quarter to Three, 1961.
Queen of the House, see King of the Road, 1964.
Question, 1960.
Quicksand, 1963.
Quien Sabe? (Who Knows? Who Knows?), 1960.
Quiet Joys of Brotherhood, The, 1964.
Quiet Nights of Quiet Stars (Corcovado), 1962.
Quiet Room, 1962.

R

Race Is On, The, 1964.
Rag Doll, 1964.
Rain, Rain Go Away, 1962.
Raindrops, 1961.
Ramblin' Boy, 1963.
(Love Is Like a) Ramblin' Rose, 1961.
Ramblin' Rose, 1962.
Rat Race, The, see Main Title Theme from *The Rat Race*, 1960.
Raunchy, 1963.
Ray's Blues, 1961.
Reach for the Stars, 1961.
Real Live Girl, 1962.
Recado Bossa Nova, 1962.
Release Me, Supplement.
Remember (Walking in the Sand), 1964.
Return to Sender, 1962.
Revenge, 1961.
Reverend Mr. Black, The, 1962.
Rhythm, 1964.
Rhythm of the Rain, 1962.
Ribbons Down My Back, 1963.
Ride, 1963.
Ride through the Night, 1961.
Right or Wrong, I'll Be with You, 1960.
Ring of Fire, 1962.
Ringo, 1963.
Ringo's Theme, see This Boy, 1963.
Rinky Dink, 1962.

Rio Conchos, 1964.
River Boat, 1960.
Road to Hong Kong, The, 1962.
Roaring Twenties, The, 1960.
Rock-A-Hula Baby, 1961.
Rockin' Good Way (To Mess Around and Fall in Love), A, Supplement.
Roll Muddy River, 1960.
Roll Over Beethoven, 1964.
Roma, Nun Fa' la Stupida Stasera, 1963.
(Beautiful, Wonderful, Fabulous) Rome, 1962.
(Just Like) Romeo and Juliet, 1964.
Ronnie, 1964.
Ronnie, Call Me When You Get a Chance, 1963.
Room without Windows, A, 1963.
Roses Are Red (My Love), 1961.
Rosie, 1960.
Rubber Ball, 1960.
Ruby Ann, 1962.
Ruby Baby, Supplement.
Ruby-Duby-Du, 1960.
Rules of the Road, The, 1961.
Run Samson Run, 1960.
Run to Him, 1961.
Runaround Sue, 1961.
Runaway, 1961.
Runnin' Out of Fools, 1964.
Running Bear, 1960.
Running Scared, Supplement.

S

Sabbath Prayer, 1964.
Sacred, 1961.
Sad Movies (Make Me Cry), 1961.
Sad Tomorrows, 1964.
Sadie, Sadie, 1964.
Saginaw, Michigan, 1963.
Sail Away, 1961.
Sailor Boy, 1964.
Sailor (Your Home Is the Sea), 1960.
St. Thomas, 1963.
Sally Go 'Round the Roses, 1963.
Sam Hill, 1964.
Samba de Orfeu, 1960.
Sambo do Avião, see Song of the Jet, 1963.
Same Old Me, 1960.
San Antonio Rose, Supplement.
Sands of Gold, Supplement.
Sandy, 1960.

San-Ho-Zay, 1961.
Satan Never Sleeps, 1961.
Saturday Night at the Movies, 1964.
Save It for Me, 1964.
Save the Last Dance for Me, 1960.
Save Your Heart for Me, 1963.
Sawmill, Supplement.
Say Wonderful Things, 1963.
Say You, 1960.
Scarlet Ribbons (For Her Hair), Supplement.
Scarlett O'Hara, 1963.
School Is Out, 1961.
Scotch and Soda, Supplement.
Sea of Heartbreak, 1960.
Sealed with a Kiss, 1960.
Sea-Shell, 1960.
Seasons in the Sun, 1964.
Seasons of My Heart, Supplement.
Second Chance, A, see Song from *Two for the Seesaw*, 1962.
Second Fiddle (To an Old Guitar), 1964.
Second Hand Love, 1962.
Second Hand Rose (Second Hand Heart), 1962.
Second Time Around, The, 1960.
Secret Life, The, 1964.
Secret Service, The, 1962.
See the Funny Little Clown, 1963.
See What It Gets You, 1964.
Send Me No Flowers, 1964.
Send Me Some Lovin', Supplement.
Senza Fine, see The Phoenix Love Theme, 1964.
Seven Deadly Virtues, The, 1960.
Seven-Day Weekend, 1962.
Seventh Dawn, The, 1964.
Shake, 1964.
Shake Me I Rattle (Squeeze Me I Cry), 1963.
Shake, Sherrie, see Shake, Sherry, 1962.
Shake, Sherry, 1962.
Shake the Hand of a Fool, 1961.
Sha-La-La, 1964.
Shalom, 1961.
Shame on Me, 1962.
Shangri-La, 1964.
She Can't Find Her Keys, 1960.
She Cried, 1962.
She Looks Good to the Crowd, 1963.
She Loves Me, 1963.
She Loves You, 1963.
She Thinks I Still Care, 1962.

She Understands Me, 1964.
Sheik of Chicago (Mustafa), The, 1960.
Sheila, 1962.
Shelia, see Sheila, 1962.
Shelter of Your Arms, The, 1963.
Sherry, 1962.
She's a Fool, 1963.
She's a Woman, 1964.
She's Gone Gone Gone, 1964.
She's Got You, 1961.
She's Just a Whole Lot Like You, 1960.
She's My Girl, 1964.
She's My Love, 1961.
She's Not There, 1964.
She's Not You, 1962.
Shiela, see Sheila, 1962.
Shimmy, Shimmy Ko-Ko Bop, 1960.
Shoes of a Fool, 1962.
Shoop, Shoop Song, The, 1963.
Shop Around, 1961.
Should I Surrender, 1961.
Shout (Part 1 and 2), Supplement.
Shout! Shout! Knock Yourself Out!, 1962.
Show Time, 1960.
Shut Down, 1963.
Shutters and Boards, 1962.
Signed, Sealed and Delivered, Supplement.
Signifyin' Monkey, 1962.
Silver Threads and Golden Needles, 1963.
Simple Joys of Maidenhood, The, 1960.
Simple Little Things, 1963.
Sin and Silver, 1964.
Since I Fell for You, Supplement.
Since I Made You Cry, 1960.
Sing a Little Song of Heartaches, 1962.
Sing a Sad Song, 1963.
Single Girl Again, 1963.
Sink the Bismarck, 1960.
Sinner, The, 1962.
Sister Suffragette, 1963.
Sittin' in an All Nite Cafe, 1964.
Six Days on the Road, 1963.
Six-Pack To Go, A, 1960.
Sixteen Reasons (Why I Love You), Supplement.
Sleepy-Eyed John, Supplement.
Slightly Out of Tune, see Desafinado, 1962.

Slow Down, Supplement.
Slow Twistin', 1962.
Small Cartel, A, 1963.
Smokie, Part II, 1960.
Smoky Places, 1962.
Snap Your Fingers, 1962.
Snowflakes, 1963.
So Little Time, 1963.
So Long, Big Time, 1964.
So Long, Dearie, 1963.
So Much in Love, 1963.
So Sad (To Watch Good Love Go Bad), 1960.
So This Is Love, 1962.
Soft Rain, 1961.
Softly and Tenderly (I'll Hold You in My Arms), 1960.
Softly, As I Leave You, 1960.
Soldier Boy, 1961.
Sole, Sole, Sole, 1964.
Solitaire, 1960.
Some Day Baby, 1961.
Some Day We're Gonna Love Again, 1964.
Some Days Everything Goes Wrong, 1963.
Some Kind-a Wonderful, 1961.
Somebody, 1960.
Somebody Loves You, Supplement.
Someone Nice Like You, 1961.
Someone, Someone, Supplement.
Someone To Take Your Place, 1963.
Something Big, 1961.
Something Special, 1960.
Something Tells Me, 1964.
Something To Live For, 1963.
Something Very Strange, 1961.
Something You Never Had Before, 1961.
Something's Got a Hold on Me, 1962.
Somewhere in the Night, see Naked City Theme, 1961.
Somewhere in the Used To Be, 1961.
Song from Advise and Consent (Heart of Mine), 1962.
Song from Two for the Seesaw (A Second Chance), 1962.
Song of Athens, The, see Adios, My Love, 1961.
Song of Love, see Canto D'Amore, 1963.
Song of the Jet, 1963.
Song without End, 1960.

Soon (I'll Be Home Again), 1963.
Soon It's Gonna Rain, 1960.
Sorrow on the Rocks, 1963.
Sorry Willie, 1961.
Soul Hootenanny, 1964.
Soul Twist, 1962.
Sound of Money, The, 1962.
Sound of Surf, The, 1963.
Sounds of Silence, The, 1964.
South Street, 1963.
Southtown, U.S.A., 1963.
Spanish Harlem, 1960.
Spanish Harlem Incident, 1964.
Spanish Rose, 1960.
Spartacus — Love Theme, 1960.
Speedy Gonzales, 1961.
Spoonful of Sugar, A, 1963.
Stairway to Heaven, 1960.
Stampede, 1964.
Stand by Me, 1961.
Starbright, 1960.
Starry Eyed, 1960.
Stay, 1960.
Stay Awake, 1963.
Stay Away from My Baby, 1964.
Stay Awhile, 1964.
Stay Here with Me, 1960.
Stay with Me, 1963.
Steady, Steady, 1962.
Steal Away, 1963.
Steel Men, 1962.
Step by Step, 1960.
Step in Time, 1963.
Stick Around, 1964.
Stick Shift, 1961.
Sticks and Stones, 1960.
(I Love You) Still, 1962.
Stolen Hours, The, 1963.
Stoney Burke Theme, The, 1962.
Stop, 1964.
Stop and Think It Over, 1964.
Stormy Monday Blues, 1962.
Straight, No Chaser, 1962.
Strange Feeling, 1960.
Strange I Know, 1962.
Stranger on the Shore, 1961.
Strangers When We Meet, 1960.
Stripper, The, 1961.
Stubborn Kind of Fellow, 1962.
Stuck on You, 1960.
Stuck with Each Other, 1963.
Success, 1961.
Suddenly I'm All Alone, 1964.
Sugar and Spice, 1963.
Sugar Lips, 1964.
Sugar Shack, 1962.

Titles

Sukiyaka, see Sukiyaki, 1963.
Sukiyaki (My First Lonely Night), 1963.
Summer Green and Winter White, 1963.
Summer Song, A, 1964.
Summer Sunday, 1961.
Summer's Gone, 1960.
Summertime Lies, 1961.
Summertime Love, 1960.
Sun A-Rise, 1963.
Sunday in New York, 1963.
Sunrise, Sunset, 1964.
Sunshine, Lollipops and Rainbows, 1964.
Supercalifragilisticexpialidocious, 1963.
Surf City, 1963.
Surfer Girl, 1962.
Surfer Joe, 1963.
Surfin' Bird, 1964.
Surfin' Safari, 1962.
Surfin' U.S.A., 1963.
Surfside 6, 1960.
Surrender, 1960.
Suspicion, 1962.
Suzie Wong (The Cloud Song), 1960.
Sweet Beginning, 1964.
Sweet Danger, 1961.
Sweet Dreams, Supplement.
Sweet Life, The, see La Dolce Vita, 1960.
Sweet Lips, 1961.
Sweet Little You, 1961.
Sweet Nothin's, 1960.
Sweet September, 1962.
Sweet Sixteen, Supplement.
Sweet William, 1964.
Sweetest Sounds, The, 1962.
Sweets for My Sweet, 1961.
Swingin' on a Rainbow, 1960.
Swingin' Safari, A, 1962.
Swingin' School, 1960.
Swiss Family Theme (My Heart Was an Island), 1960.
Switcharoo, 1961.
Sylvia, 1964.

T

T for Texas, Supplement.
T.L.C., 1960.
Ta Ta, 1960.
Take a Letter, Miss Gray, 1962.

Take Five, 1960.
Take Good Care of Her, 1961.
Take Good Care of My Baby, 1961.
Take My Hand, Paree, 1961.
Take My Love, I Want To Give It All to You, 1961.
Take My Ring off Your Finger, 1964.
Take Ten, 1963.
Take These Chains from My Heart, Supplement.
Take Time, 1961.
Talk Back Trembling Lips, 1963.
Talk That Talk, 1960.
Talk to Me, Supplement.
Talk to Me Baby, 1963.
Tall Hope, 1960.
Tandy, 1963.
Tarnished Angel, 1960.
Taste of Honey, A, 1960.
Teamwork, 1962.
Tear Down the Walls, 1964.
Tears and Laughter, 1961.
Tears Break Out on Me, 1961.
Teddy, 1960.
Teen Angel, 1960.
Teen Beat, 1960.
Teen Scene, 1963.
Teenage Idol, A, 1962.
Telephone Hour, The, 1960.
Tell Her for Me, 1960.
Tell Her I Said Hello, see Tell Him I Said Hello, 1961.
Tell Her No, 1964.
Tell Her So, 1963.
Tell Him, 1963.
Tell Him I Said Hello, 1961.
Tell Laura I Love Her, 1960.
Tell Me, 1962, 1964.
Tell Me the Truth, 1963.
Tell Me When, see Quando, Quando, Quando, 1962.
Tell Me Why, 1964, Supplement.
Tell the World, see Wheels, 1960.
Telstar, 1962.
Tempo of the Times, The, 1960.
Tender Flower, see Ciumachella de Trastevere, 1963.
Tender Is the Night, 1961.
Tender Love and Care, see T.L.C., 1960.
Tender Years, 1961.
Tennessee Flat-Top Box, 1961.
Thank You Girl, 1963.
Thanks a Lot, 1963.
That Happy Feeling, 1962.

That Man Over There, 1963.
That Old Song and Dance, 1962.
That Sunday (That Summer), 1963.
That Was Yesterday, 1961.
That'll Show Him, 1962.
That's All That Matters, 1963.
That's All You Gotta Do,
Supplement.
That's How It Went, All Right,
1960.
That's Life, 1964.
That's My Kind of Love, 1960.
That's My Pa, 1961.
That's Old Fashioned (That's the
Way Love Should Be), 1962.
That's the Way It's Gonna Be, 1964.
That's the Way Love Is, 1962.
That's What Girls Are Made For,
1961.
Theme for a Dream, 1960.
Theme from *A Majority of One*,
1962.
Theme from *A New Kind of Love*,
1963.
Theme from *A Summer Place*, 1961.
Theme from an Un-filmed Movie,
1960.
Theme from *Ben Casey*, 1961.
Theme from *By Love Possessed*,
1961.
Theme from *Carnival!*, 1961.
Theme from *Come September*, 1961.
Theme from *David and Lisa*, 1962.
Theme from *Dr. Kildare* (Three
Stars Will Shine Tonight), 1961.
Theme from *East Side/West Side*,
1963.
Theme from *8½*, 1963.
Theme from *Golden Boy*, 1964.
Theme from *Goodbye Again*, 1961.
Theme from *Harry's Girls*, 1963.
Theme from *Irma la Douce*
(Look Again), 1963.
Theme from *Jules and Jim*, The,
1962.
Theme from *King of Kings*, see
King of Kings Theme, 1961.
Theme from *Lawrence of Arabia*,
1962.
Theme from *Lilies of the Field*,
1963.
Theme from *Long Day's Journey
into Night*, 1962.
Theme from *Lord of the Flies*, 1963.
Theme from *Mr. Broadway*, 1964.
Theme from *Mr. Novak*, 1963.

Theme from *Mondo Cane*, see
More, 1963.
Theme from *Mutiny on the Bounty*,
1962.
Theme from *My Geisha*, 1961.
Theme from *Of Human Bondage*,
1964.
Theme from *Romanoff and Juliet*,
1961.
Theme from *Route 66*, 1960.
Theme from *Sodom and Gomorrah*,
1962.
Theme from *Sons and Lovers*, 1960.
Theme from *Stowaway in the Sky*,
1960.
Theme from *Summer and Smoke*,
1961.
Theme from *Taras Bulba*, 1962.
Theme from *The Andy Griffith
Show*, see The Fishin' Hole, 1961.
Theme from *The Apartment*, 1960.
Theme from *The Dark at the Top
of the Stairs*, 1960.
Theme from *The Eleventh Hour*,
1962.
Theme from *The Lieutenant* (Like
March), 1963.
Theme from *The Man from
U.N.C.L.E.*, 1964.
Theme from *The Miracle Worker*,
1962.
Theme from *The Misfits*, 1960.
Theme from *The Prize*, 1963.
Theme from *The Sundowners*,
1960.
Theme from *The Travels of Jaimie
McPheeters*, 1963.
Theme from *The V.I.P.'s* (The
Willow), 1963.
Theme from *The Victors* (My
Special Dream), 1963.
Theme from *The Wonderful World
of the Brothers Grimm*, The,
1962.
Theme from *36 Hours* (A Heart
Must Learn To Cry), 1964.
Theme from *Valentine's Day*, 1964.
Theme from *Voyage to the Bottom
of the Sea*, 1964.
Theme from *Zorba the Greek*, 1964.
Then a Tear Fell, 1962.
Then and Only Then, 1964.
Then He Kissed Me, 1963.
Then I'll Stop Loving You,
Supplement.

Titles

Then You May Take Me to the
Fair, 1960.
There but for Fortune, 1963.
There Goes My Baby, 1960.
There, I've Said It Again, 1964.
There Won't Be Trumpets, 1964.
There's a Big Wheel, 1960.
There's a Moon Out Tonight, 1960.
There's a Place, 1963.
There's a Room in My House, 1962.
There's No Other, 1961.
There's No Reason in the World,
1961.
There's Something about You, 1963.
There's Something on Your Mind,
Supplement.
They Gotta Quit Kickin' My Dog
Around, 1964.
They Love Me, 1962.
They Were You, 1960.
Thieving Stranger, The, 1963.
Things, 1961.
Things Have Gone to Pieces, 1964.
Things We Said Today, 1964.
Think, Supplement.
Think Nothing about It, 1964.
Think Twice, 1960.
Thirty One Flavors, 1963.
This Bitter Earth, 1960.
This Boy, 1963.
This Day of Days, 1963.
This Diamond Ring, 1964.
This Dream, 1964.
This Is a Great Country, 1962.
This Is All I Ask, 1963.
This Is It, 1964.
This Is the Life, 1964.
This Isn't Heaven, 1962.
This Land Is Mine, see Exodus,
1960.
This Land Is Your Land, 1963.
This Little Girl, 1963.
This Magic Moment, 1960.
This Time, Supplement.
This Time It's True Love, 1963.
This White Circle on My Finger,
1961.
Those Lazy-Hazy-Crazy Days of
Summer, 1963.
Those Oldies but Goodies Remind
Me of You, 1961.
Those Wonderful Years, 1963.
Thou Shalt Not Steal, 1962.
Thousand Stars, A, 1960.
Three Days, 1961.
Three Hearts in a Tangle, 1960.

Three Nights a Week, 1960.
Three Stars Will Shine Tonight, see
Theme from *Dr. Kildare*, 1961.
Three Steps to the Phone, 1961.
Three Window Coupe, 1964.
(Love Is) A Ticklish Affair, 1963.
Tie Me Kangaroo Down, Sport,
1961.
Timber, I'm Falling, 1963.
Timbrook, Supplement.
Time and the River, 1960.
Time and Time Again, 1960.
Time Is Now, The, 1962.
Time Is on My Side, 1963.
Times, They Are A-Changin', The,
1963.
Tip of My Fingers, The, 1960.
Tip of My Tongue, 1963.
Tired of Waiting for You, 1964.
To Be Alone with You, 1963.
To Kill a Mockingbird, 1963.
To Life, 1964.
To Look upon My Love, 1961.
To Ramona, 1964.
Tobacco Road, 1960.
Today, 1964.
Together, Supplement.
Together Again, 1963.
Togetherness, 1960.
Toki's Theme, 1964.
Tommy, Tommy, 1960.
Tomorrow, see Will You Love Me
Tomorrow, 1960.
Tonight, 1961.
Tonight at Eight, 1963.
Too Big for Her Bikini, 1961.
Too Busy Saying Goodbye, 1964.
Too Late To Try Again, 1963.
Too Many Fish in the Sea, 1964.
Too Many Rivers, 1964.
Too Many Times, 1961.
Too Much To Lose, 1960.
Topkapi, 1964.
Torture, 1962.
Tossin' and Turnin', 1961.
Touch Me, 1961.
Tous les Chemins, 1962.
Tower of Strength, 1961.
Town without Pity, 1961.
Toys in the Attic, 1963.
Tracy's Theme, 1960.
Tradition, 1964.
Tragedy, Supplement.
Transistor Sister, 1961.
Travelin' Man, 1960.
Treat Him Nicely, 1963.

306

Triangle, 1963.
Tribute, 1963.
Trouble in Paradise, 1960.
Trouble's Back in Town, 1961.
Truck Driving Man, 1962.
True Love Ways, Supplement.
True, True Love, A, 1962.
Trust in Me, Supplement.
Try It Baby, 1964.
Try To Remember, 1960.
Tuff, 1961.
Turn Around, Supplement.
Turn on the Sunshine, 1960.
Turn on Your Love Light, 1961.
Turn! Turn! Turn! (To Everything
   There Is a Season), 1962.
Twelfth Rose, The, 1960.
Twelve Days of Christmas, The,
   1962.
12 O'Clock High, 1964.
20 Miles, 1963.
25 Minutes To Go, 1962.
Twenty-four Hours from Tulsa,
   1963.
Twinkle Lullaby, 1963.
Twist, The, Supplement.
Twist and Shout, 1960.
Twist, Twist Senora, 1962.
Twistin' the Night Away, 1962.
Twistin' U.S.A., 1960.
Twisting Matilda, 1963.
Two Faces Have I, 1963.
Two Lovers, 1962.
Two of a Kind, 1960.
Two of Us, 1962.
Typically English, 1961.

U

Uh-Oh!, 1963.
Um Um Um Um Um Um, 1963.
Unchain My Heart, 1960.
Under the Boardwalk, 1964.
Under the Influence of Love, 1961.
Under the Yum-Yum Tree, 1963.
Understand Your Man, 1964.
Unforgiven, The (The Need for
   Love), 1960.
Unh Unh Unh, see Um Um Um
   Um Um Um, 1963.
Universal Soldier, The, 1963.
Unless You Care, 1964.
Unloved, Unwanted, 1962.
Unsquare Dance, 1961.
Up on the Roof, 1962.

Uptown, 1962.
Use Your Head, 1964.
Use Your Noggin', 1964.
Utopia, 1960.

V

V-A-C-A-T-I-O-N, 1962.
Venice Blue, 1964.
Venus in Blue Jeans, 1961.
Vespa Song, The, 1962.
Village of St. Bernadette, The, 1960.
Violet and a Rose, The, Supplement.
Viva Las Vegas, 1964.
Volare, 1960.
Volunteer, The, 1963.

W

Wah-Watusi, The, 1962.
Wait Till My Bobby Gets Home,
   1963.
Waitin' for the Evening Train,
   1963.
Wake Me When It's Over, 1960.
Walk, Don't Run, 1960.
Walk — Don't Run '64, see Walk,
   Don't Run, 1960.
Walk in the Black Forest, A, 1962.
Walk Like a Man, 1963.
Walk Me to the Door, 1962.
Walk On, Boy, 1960.
Walk on By, 1961, 1963.
Walk on the Wild Side, 1961.
Walk Out Backwards, 1960.
Walk Right Back, 1960.
Walk Right In, Supplement.
Walkin' Back to Happiness, 1961.
Walkin' Down to Washington, 1960.
Walkin', Talkin', Cryin', Barely
   Beatin' Broken Heart, 1963.
Walkin' with Peninnah, 1964.
Walking Away Whistling, 1960.
Walking Happy, 1962.
Walking in the Rain, 1964.
Walking Proud, 1963.
Walking the Dog, 1963.
Walking the Streets, Supplement.
Walking to New Orleans, 1960.
Wall to Wall Love, 1962.
Waltz de Funk, 1960.
Waltz for Debby, 1964.
Waltz from *The Cardinal*, 1963.
Wanderer, The, 1960.

Titles

Warmer Than a Whisper, 1962.
Was She Prettier Than I?, 1964.
Washington Square, 1963.
Washington Twist, The, 1962.
Watch What Happens, 1964.
Watching the World Go By, see
  The Luck of Ginger Coffey, 1964.
Watermelon Man, 1962.
Waves Roll Out, The, 1963.
Way Down East, 1960.
Way Down Yonder in New Orleans,
  Supplement.
Way of a Clown, The, 1960.
Way You Do the Things You Do,
  The, 1964.
We Got Us, 1960.
We Love You Beatles, 1964.
We Missed You, 1962.
We Must Have Been Out of Our
  Minds, 1963.
We Shall Overcome, 1960.
Wedding, The (La Novia), 1961.
Week in the Country, A, 1963.
Week-End, The, 1964.
Welcome to My World, 1961.
We'll Sing in the Sunshine, 1963.
We're the Talk of the Town, 1963.
What a Country!, 1962.
What a Night This Is Going To
  Be!, 1964.
What a Sweet Thing That Was,
  1961.
What a Way To Go, 1964.
What a Wonderful World, see
  Wonderful World, 1960.
What Are They Doing to Us Now?,
  1962.
What Did I Ever See in Him, 1960.
What Did You Learn in School
  Today?, 1962.
What Do the Simple Folks Do?,
  1960.
What Do You Want with Me, 1964.
What Happened to Me Tonight?,
  1961.
What Have They Done to the
  Rain?, 1962.
(How Can I Write on Paper) What
  I Feel in My Heart, 1961.
What I Need Most, 1964.
What in the World's Come Over
  You, 1960.
What Is This Feeling in the Air?,
  1961.
What Kind of Fool Am I?, 1961.
What Kind of Fool Do You Think

I Am?, 1963.
What Kind of Love Is This?, 1962.
What Makes a Man Wander?, 1964.
What Now My Love, 1962.
What Will My Mary Say?, 1961.
What You're Doing, 1964.
Whatever Happened to Baby
  Jane?, 1963.
What's Easy for Two Is So Hard
  for One, 1963.
What's in It for Me?, 1962.
What's New at the Zoo?, 1960.
What's That I Hear, 1963.
What's Wrong with Me?, 1961.
What's Your Name?, 1961.
Wheeler Dealers, The, 1963.
Wheels, 1960.
When Everything Was Green, 1964.
When I Fall in Love, 1962.
When I Get Home, 1964.
When I Get Thru with You, You'll
  Love Me Too, 1962.
When I Grow Up To Be a Man,
  1964.
When I'm Gone, 1964.
When in Rome (I Do As the
  Romans Do), 1964.
When My Little Girl Is Smiling,
  1961.
When the Boy in Your Arms Is the
  Boy in Your Heart, 1961.
When the Girl in Your Arms Is the
  Girl in Your Heart, see When
  the Boy in Your Arms Is the
  Boy in Your Heart, 1961.
When the Ship Comes In, 1963.
When Two Worlds Collide, 1961.
When We Get Married, 1961.
When Will I Be Loved, 1960.
When Will I Find Love, 1961.
When You Want Me, 1961.
When You're in Love (The Whole
  World Is Jewish), 1961.
When You're Young and in Love,
  1964.
Whenever a Teenager Cries, 1964.
Whenever He Holds You, 1964.
Where Did Our Love Go, 1964.
Where Do You Come From?, 1962.
Where Does a Little Tear Come
  From, 1964.
Where Have All the Flowers
  Gone?, 1961.
Where I Oughta Be, 1962.
Where Is Love?, 1960.
Where Love Has Gone, 1964.

Where or When, Supplement.
Where Shall I Find Him?, 1961.
Where the Boys Are, 1960.
Where the Hot Wind Blows, 1960.
While the City Sleeps, 1964.
Whipped Cream, 1964.
White on White, 1963.
White Rose of Athens, see Athina, 1961.
White Silver Sands, 1960.
Who Are You Now?, 1964.
Who Can I Turn To (When Nobody Needs Me), 1964.
Who Killed Norma Jean?, 1963.
Who Knows?, 1962.
Who Knows What Might Have Been?, 1961.
Who Put the Bomp (In the Bomp Ba Bomp Ba Bomp), 1961.
Who Will Buy?, 1960.
(It All Depends) Who Will Buy the Wine, see Who'll Buy the Wine, 1960.
Who'll Buy the Wine, 1960.
Who's Been Cheatin' Who, 1962.
Who's Been Sleeping in My Bed?, 1963..
Why, 1960, 1964.
Why Can't You Feel Sorry for Me, 1964.
Why Do Lovers Break Each Other's Hearts?, 1962.
Why Do the Wrong People Travel?, 1961.
Why I'm Walkin', 1960.
Wild in the Country, 1961.
Wild One, 1960, 1964.
Wild Weekend, 1960.
Wild Weekend Cha Cha, see Wild Weekend, 1960.
Wildwood Days, 1963.
Wilkes-Barre, Pa., 1963.
Will He Like Me?, 1963.
Will You Love Me Tomorrow?, 1960.
Will You Remember, 1962.
Will Your Lawyer Talk to God, 1961.
Willa, Willa, 1964.
Willie the Weeper, 1962.
Willing and Eager, 1962.
Willingly, 1961.
Willow, The, see Theme from The V.I.P.'s, 1963.
Willow, Willow, Willow, 1961.

Window Up Above, The, 1961.
Wine, Women, and Song, 1963.
Wings of a Dove, Supplement.
Wipe Out, 1963.
Wishful Thinking, Supplement.
Wishin' and Hopin', 1963.
Wishing Star, The, see Theme from Taras Bulba, 1962.
With God on Our Side, 1963.
With So Little To Be Sure Of, 1964.
Without You, 1961.
Wives and Lovers, 1963.
Wolverton Mountain, 1962.
Woman, a Lover, a Friend, A, Supplement.
Woman's Intuition, A, Supplement.
Wonder of You, Supplement.
Wonderful Day Like Today, A, 1964.
Wonderful Summer, 1963.
Wonderful To Be Young, 1962.
Wonderful, Wonderful!, 1963.
Wonderful World, 1960.
Wonderful World of Love, 1963.
Wonderful World of the Young, The, 1962.
Wonderland by Night, 1960.
Wooden Heart, 1960.
Wooly Bully, 1964.
Words, Supplement.
Work Song, 1960.
Working for the Man, 1962.
World I Can't Live In, A, 1960.
World I Used To Know, The, 1963.
World of Love, A, 1963.
World So Full of Love, A, 1960.
World without Love, 1964.
Worlds Apart, 1963.
Worried Guy, 1964.
Wound Time Can't Erase, A, Supplement.
Wreck on the Highway, Supplement.
Writing on the Wall, 1961.
Wrong for Each Other, 1964.

X

X-Ray Blues, 1962.

Y

Ya Ya, 1961.
Yakety Axe, see Yakety Sax, 1963.
Yakety Sax, 1963.

Titles

Yassu, 1961.
Yeh Yeh, 1963.
Yellow Bandana, The, 1960.
Yellow Bird, 1961.
Yes, My Heart, 1961.
Yesterday's Memories, 1962.
Yet . . . I Know, 1963.
Yogi, 1960.
You Are My Flower, Supplement.
You Are My Sunshine, Supplement.
You Are Woman, I Am Man, 1964.
You Beat Me to the Punch, 1962.
You Belong to Me, 1962.
You Can Depend on Me, Supplement.
You Can Have Her, 1960.
You Can't Do That, 1964.
You Can't Pick a Rose in December, Supplement.
You Can't Roller Skate in a Buffalo Herd, 1964.
You Can't Sit Down, 1960.
You Can't Take a Dream from a Dreamer, 1961.
You Comb Her Hair, 1963.
You Don't Know, 1961, 1963.
You Don't Know Me, 1962.
You Don't Know What You've Got, 1961.
You Don't Own Me, 1963.
(In the Summer Time) You Don't Want My Love, 1960.
You Got What It Takes, Supplement.
You Love Me, 1963.
You Mean Everything to Me, 1960.
You Must Have Been a Beautiful Baby, Supplement.
You Mustn't Feel Discouraged, 1964.
You Really Got Me, 1964.
You Talk Too Much, 1960.
You Took Her off My Hands (Now Please Take Her off My Mind), Supplement.
You Were Made for All My Love, see All My Love, 1960.
You Were Made for Me, 1963.

You Were on My Mind, 1964.
You'd Better Go, 1964.
You'd Better Love Me, 1964.
You'll Always Be the One I Love, Supplement.
You'll Answer to Me, 1961.
You'll Drive Me Back (Into Her Arms Again), 1963.
You'll Lose a Good Thing, 1962.
You'll Never Get a Better Chance Than This, 1962.
Young Emotions, 1962.
Young Lovers, 1963.
Young Ones, The, 1961.
Young Only Yesterday, 1963.
Young World, 1962.
Your Heart Turned Left (And I Was on the Right), 1964.
Your Old Love Letters, Supplement.
Your Old Standby, 1963.
Your Old Used To Be, 1960.
Your Other Love, 1963.
Your Used To Be, 1962.
You're a Wonderful One, 1964.
You're for Me, Supplement.
You're My World, 1964.
You're Sixteen, You're Beautiful and You're Mine, 1960.
You're the Devil in Disguise, 1963.
You're the Only Good Thing (That's Happened to Me), Supplement.
You're the Only World I Know, 1964.
You're the Reason, 1960.
You're the Reason I'm Living, 1962.
You've Come Home, 1960.
You've Got What It Takes, see You Got What It Takes, Supplement.
You've Lost That Lovin' Feelin', 1964.
You've Really Got a Hold on Me, 1963.

Z

Zip-a-Dee-Doo-Dah, Supplement.

List of Publishers

This is a list of the publishers of the songs included in Volume 3 of *Popular Music*. Publishers who are members of the American Society of Composers, Authors and Publishers or whose catalogs are available under ASCAP license are indicated by the designation, (ASCAP). Publishers who have granted performing rights to Broadcast Music, Inc. are designated by the notation, (BMI). Publishers whose catalogs are represented by SESAC, Inc. are indicated by the designation, (SESAC).

A

Aba, Inc. (BMI)
1421 South Michigan Avenue
Chicago, Illinois 60605

Abigail Music Co. (BMI)
2027 Parker Street
Berkeley, California 94704

Abilene Music, Inc. (ASCAP)
c/o Orland, Chase & Mucci
48 West 48th Street
New York, New York 10036

Acclaim Music, Inc. (BMI)
Post Office Box 128
Madison, Tennessee 37115

Ace Publishing Co., Inc. (BMI)
Suite 900
Vincent Building
203 West Capitol Street
Jackson, Mississippi 39201

Acorn Music Corp. (BMI)
Suite 2160
10 Columbus Circle
New York, New York 10019

Acuff-Rose Publications, Inc. (BMI)
2510 Franklin Road
Nashville, Tennessee 37204

Adaris Music, Inc. (BMI)
c/o T.M. Music, Inc.
Suite 906
1619 Broadway
New York, New York 10019

Advanced Music Corp. (ASCAP)
488 Madison Avenue
New York, New York 10022

Algrace Music Co. (BMI)
c/o Larry Shayne Music
Suite 1003
Sunset-Vine Tower Building
6290 Sunset Boulevard
Hollywood, California 90028

Alibri Music Co. (BMI)
93 East Alexandrine Street
Detroit, Michigan 48201

Almo Music Corp. (ASCAP)
8255 Sunset Boulevard
Hollywood, California 90046

American Metropolitan Enterprises
of New York, Inc. (BMI)
Room 1920
135 West 50th Street
New York, New York 10020

American Music, Inc. (BMI)
9109 Sunset Boulevard
Hollywood, California 90069

311

Publishers

Andor Music Co. (ASCAP)
6381 Hollywood Boulevard
Hollywood, California 90028

Annette Music, Inc. (BMI)
1440 North Highland Avenue
Hollywood, California 90028

Appleseed Music, Inc. (ASCAP)
Suite 1304
200 West 57th Street
New York, New York 10019

April Music, Inc. (ASCAP)
Suite 201
1650 Broadway
New York, New York 10019

Apt Music Corp. (ASCAP)
150 West 55th Street
New York, New York 10019

Arc Music Corp. (BMI)
1619 Broadway
New York, New York 10019

Arch Music Co., Inc. (ASCAP)
25 West 56th Street
New York, New York 10019

Armo Music Corp. (BMI)
c/o Lois Publishing Co.
1540 Brewster Avenue
Cincinnati, Ohio 45207

Artists Music, Inc. (ASCAP)
250 North Canon Drive
Beverly Hills, California 90210

Arvee Music (BMI)
Division of Hi Fi Records, Inc.
10920 Wilshire Boulevard
Los Angeles, California 90024

Ashland Music Corp. (BMI)
136 East 57th Street
New York, New York 10022

Ashna Music Corp. (BMI)
c/o Mr. R. Murray Nash
115½ Third Avenue North
Nashville, Tennessee 37201

At Last Publishing Co. (BMI)
Post Office Box 78191
Los Angeles, California 90016

Atlantic Music Corp. (BMI)
6124 Selma Avenue
Hollywood, California 90028

Atrium Music Corp. (ASCAP)
1631 Broadway
New York, New York 10019

Atzal Music, Inc. (BMI)
c/o Hill and Range Songs, Inc.
11th Floor
1619 Broadway
New York, New York 10019

Audre Mae Music (BMI)
34 Dogwood Drive
Smithtown, New York 11787

B

BNP Music Publishing Co.
(ASCAP)
c/o Mr. Alfred Perry
4030 Radford Avenue
North Hollywood, California
91604

Bais Music (BMI)
c/o East Publications
926 East McLemore Avenue
Memphis, Tennessee 38106

Bamboo Music, Inc. (BMI)
Suite 308
7033 Sunset Boulevard
Hollywood, California 90028

The Barclay Music Corp. (ASCAP)
c/o Shapiro, Bernstein & Co., Inc.
666 Fifth Avenue
New York, New York 10019

Barnaby Music Corp. (ASCAP)
1500 North Vine Street
Hollywood, California 90028

Bar-Thel Music Corp. (BMI)
69-45 108th Street
Forest Hills, New York 11375

Bayou State Publishing Co. (BMI)
Box 115
Madison, Tennessee 37115

Beckie Publishing Co., Inc. (BMI)
801 Dupont Building
22 South Second Street
Memphis, Tennessee 38103

Becks Music Co. (BMI)
c/o Mr. Patrick Ferraro
2834 Shillington Road
Sinking Spring, Pennsylvania
19608

Beechwood Music Corp. (BMI)
1750 Vine Street
Hollywood, California 90028

Belmar Music Publishing Co.
(BMI)
c/o Aronstein & Aronstein
1650 Broadway
New York, New York 10019

Benday Music Corp. (BMI)
c/o A. Halsey Cowan, Esq.
1740 Broadway
New York, New York 10019

Benders Music, Inc. (BMI)
c/o Marshall, Vigoda & Bomser
130 West 57th Street
New York, New York 10019

Bendig Music Corp. (BMI)
Suite 514
Sunset-Vine Tower Building
6290 Sunset Boulevard
Hollywood, California 90028

Ben-Ghazi Enterprises, Inc. (BMI)
c/o Jack Pearl, Esq.
515 Madison Avenue
New York, New York 10022

Bennie Benjamin Music, Inc.
(ASCAP)
1619 Broadway
New York, New York 10019

Bentley Music Co. (BMI)
Box 1170
Chapel Hill, North Carolina 27514

Berkshire Music, Inc. (BMI)
Room 1920
135 West 50th Street
New York, New York 10020

Irving Berlin Music Corp. (ASCAP)
41st Floor
1290 Avenue of the Americas
New York, New York 10019

Betalbin Music Publishing Corp.
(BMI)
c/o Mr. Alan Klein
Time and Life Building
Rockefeller Center
New York, New York 10020

Bexhill Music Corp. (ASCAP)
c/o Mr. Norman Gimbel
Apartment 13A
15 West 81st Street
New York, New York 10024

B-Flat Publishing Co. (BMI)
c/o Mr. Robert Lee Geddins
408 60th Street
Oakland, California 94609

Big Billy Music Co. (BMI)
c/o Mr. Bill Cook
205 Reynolds Street
Orange, New Jersey 07050

Big Bopper Music Co. (BMI)
Post Office Box 849
Beaumont, Texas 77704

Big "D" Music, Inc. (BMI)
Spartatorium Cadiz Industrial
Building
Dallas, Texas

Big Seven Music Corp. (BMI)
c/o Patricia Music Publishing
Corp.
1631 Broadway
New York, New York 10019

Bib Top Records, Inc. (BMI)
c/o Hill and Range Songs, Inc.
11th Floor
1619 Broadway
New York, New York 10019

Blackwood Music, Inc. (BMI)
Room 201
1650 Broadway
New York, New York 10019

Blen Music, Inc. (ASCAP)
Apartment 302
11670 Sunset Boulevard
Los Angeles, California 90049

Blue Book Music Co. (BMI)
Post Office Box 2387
Bakersfield, California 93303

Blue Grass Music Co. (BMI)
Room 100
157 West 57th Street
New York, New York 10019

Blue Indigo Music Co. (BMI)
3330 Barham Boulevard
Hollywood, California 90028

Publishers

Blue Seas Music, Inc. (ASCAP)
166 East 61st Street
New York, New York 10021

Bob-Dan Music Co. (BMI)
29 West 125th Street
New York, New York 10027

Boulder Music Corp. (ASCAP)
9 Rockefeller Plaza
New York, New York 10020

Bourne-Rank Music, Inc. (ASCAP)
136 West 52nd Street
New York, New York 10019

Brakenbury Music, Inc. (BMI)
c/o Hill and Range Songs, Inc.
11th Floor
1619 Broadway
New York, New York 10019

Bramble Music Publishing Co., Inc.
(BMI)
913 17th Avenue South
Nashville, Tennessee 37212

Branston Music, Inc. (BMI)
1631 Broadway
New York, New York 10019

Brazos Valley Music, Inc. (BMI)
Box 74A
Route 1
Park Hill, Oklahoma 74451

Brenner Music, Inc. (BMI)
11th Floor
1619 Broadway
New York, New York 10019

Briarcliff Music, Inc. (BMI)
c/o Miss Gladys Knochelman
1540 Brewster Avenue
Cincinnati, Ohio 45207

Brighton Music Co., Inc. (ASCAP)
Suite 804
1780 Broadway
New York, New York 10019

Bright-Tunes Music Corp. (BMI)
c/o Seymour Barash, Esq.
1 Hanson Place
Brooklyn, New York 11217

Broadway Music Corp. (ASCAP)
Suite 1920
135 West 50th Street
New York, New York 10020

Samuel Bronston Music Publishing,
Inc. (ASCAP)
10 Columbus Circle
New York, New York 10019

Brookville Music, Inc. (BMI)
817 16th Avenue South
Nashville, Tennessee 37203

Ray Brown Music (BMI)
Post Office Box 1254
Hollywood, California 90028

Bryden Music, Inc. (BMI)
157 West 57th Street
New York, New York 10019

Buckhorn Music Publishers (BMI)
812 17th Avenue South
Nashville, Tennessee 37203

Budd Music Corp. (ASCAP)
Room 501
1619 Broadway
New York, New York 10019

Buna Music Corp. (BMI)
Post Office Box 8
Santa Claus, Indiana 47579

Fred Burch Music (BMI)
2805 Shauna Court
Nashville, Tennessee 37214

Burlington Music Corp. (ASCAP)
539 West 25th Street
New York, New York 10001

Burthen Music Co., Inc. (ASCAP)
609 Fifth Avenue
New York, New York 10017

Buttercup Music (BMI)
Suite 200
801 17th Avenue South
Nashville, Tennessee 37203

Butterfield Music Corp. (BMI)
c/o Mr. Norman Gimbel
15 West 81st Street
New York, New York 10024

C

C. C. Publishing Co., Inc. (ASCAP)
309 South Broad Street
Philadelphia, Pennsylvania 19107

Cajun Publishing Co., Inc. (BMI)
Post Office Box 1130
Shreveport, Louisiana 71102

Cameo-Parkway Publishing Co.,
Inc. (BMI)
309 South Broad Street
Philadelphia, Pennsylvania 19107

Camp and Canyon Music Co. (BMI)
c/o Central Songs, Inc.
6357 Selma Avenue
Hollywood, California 90028

Campbell-Connelly, Inc. (ASCAP)
565 Fifth Avenue
New York, New York 10017

Capizzi Music (BMI)
1615 North Lima Street
Burbank, California 91505

Carolintone Music Co., Inc. (BMI)
1040 North Las Palmas Avenue
Hollywood, California 90038

Johnny Cash Music, Inc. (BMI)
11th Floor
1619 Broadway
New York, New York 10019

Cash Songs (BMI)
1065 East Vernon Avenue
Los Angeles, California 90011

Cavalcade Music Corp. (ASCAP)
136 East 57th Street
New York, New York 10022

Cedarwood Publishing Co., Inc.
(BMI)
815 16th Avenue South
Nashville, Tennessee 37203

Central Songs, Inc. (BMI)
6357 Selma Avenue
Hollywood, California 90028

Cetra Music Corp. (BMI)
c/o Mr. Morton A. Kaplan
The University of Chicago
1126 East 59th Street
Chicago, Illinois 60637

Chad & Jeremy Music, Inc. (BMI)
c/o Julius Lefkowitz & Co.
Suite 420
9171 Wilshire Boulevard
Beverly Hills, California 90210

Champion Music Corp. (BMI)
322 West 48th Street
New York, New York 10036

Channel Music Co. (ASCAP)
1926 North St. Andrews Place
Hollywood, California 90028

Chappell & Co., Inc. (ASCAP)
609 Fifth Avenue
New York, New York 10017

Chappell-Styne, Inc. (ASCAP)
609 Fifth Avenue
New York, New York 10017

Cherio Music Publishers, Inc.
(BMI)
c/o Mr. Lee V. Eastman
39 West 54th Street
New York, New York 10019

Cherry Lane Music, Inc. (ASCAP)
142 East 34th Street
New York, New York 10016

Cherrybell Music Co. (ASCAP)
Suite 201
1615 Westwood Boulevard
West Los Angeles, California
90025

Chesnick Music, Inc. (ASCAP)
c/o Mr. Norman Rosemont
The Plaza
Fifth Avenue and Central Park
South
New York, New York 10019

Chevis Publishing Corp. (BMI)
2120 South Michigan Avenue
Chicago, Illinois 60616

Cigma Music Co., Inc. (BMI)
Suite 300-02
806 17th Avenue South
Nashville, Tennessee 37203

Cinema Songs, Inc. (ASCAP)
c/o A. J. Silverman & Co.
12412 Ventura Boulevard
Studio City, California 91604

Cireco Music, Inc. (BMI)
c/o Mr. Max Weiss
855 Treat Avenue
San Francisco, California 94110

Clara Music Publishing Corp.
(ASCAP)
120 West 57th Street
New York, New York 10019

Publishers

Claridge Music, Inc. (ASCAP)
Suite 1528
250 West 57th Street
New York, New York 10019

Colby Music, Inc. (ASCAP)
c/o Mr. Samuel Jesse Buzzell
460 Park Avenue
New York, New York 10022

Colgems Music Corp. (ASCAP)
711 Fifth Avenue
New York, New York 10022

Columbia Pictures Music Corp.
(ASCAP)
666 Fifth Avenue
New York, New York 10019

Columbine Music Corp. (BMI)
22 West 48th Street
New York, New York 10036

Combine Music Corp. (BMI)
530 West Main Street
Hendersonville, Tennessee 37075

Comet Music Corp. (ASCAP)
Suite 1220
250 West 57th Street
New York, New York 10019

Commander Publications (ASCAP)
1610 North Argyle Avenue
Hollywood, California 90028

Compton Music Corp. (ASCAP)
Room 409
1733 Broadway
New York, New York 10019

Concertone Songs, Inc. (ASCAP)
161 West 54th Street
New York, New York 10019

Conrad Publishing Co., Inc. (BMI)
1449 South Michigan Avenue
Chicago, Illinois 60605

Cornerstone Publishing Co. (BMI)
c/o Metric Music Co.
1556 North La Brea Avenue
Los Angeles, California 90028

Correct-Tone Publishing Co. (BMI)
8912 West Grand River Street
Detroit, Michigan 48204

Cotillion Music, Inc. (BMI)
1841 Broadway
New York, New York 10023

Cousins, Inc. (BMI)
c/o Copyright Service Bureau,
Ltd.
221 West 57th Street
New York, New York 10019

Cramart Music, Inc. (BMI)
Suite 300-02
806 17th Avenue South
Nashville, Tennessee 37203

Crazy Cajun Music Co. (BMI)
The Music Building
227 East Sterling Avenue
Pasadena, Texas 77502

Cricket Music, Inc. (BMI)
c/o Mr. Jack Miller
8150 Beverly Boulevard
Hollywood, California 90048

Criterion Music Corp. (ASCAP)
150 West 55th Street
New York, New York 10019

Cromwell Music, Inc. (ASCAP)
Suite 2160
10 Columbus Circle
New York, New York 10019

Crystal Music Publishers, Inc.
(ASCAP)
Suite 312
Wilshire-Rexford Building
9301 Wilshire Boulevard
Beverly Hills, California 90210

Curtain Call Productions, Inc.
(ASCAP)
c/o Becker & London
300 Park Avenue
New York, New York 10022

Curtom Publishing Co., Inc. (BMI)
2203 Spruce Street
Philadelphia, Pennsylvania 19103

D

Damian Music Publishing Co.
(ASCAP)
Box 592
Blackhorse Pyke
Williamstown, New Jersey 08094

Darwood Music Corp. (ASCAP)
Apartment 8D
10 West 74th Street
New York, New York 10023

Davon Music Corp. (BMI)
Suite 823
Sunset-Vine Tower Building
6290 Sunset Boulevard
Hollywood, California 90028

Day Music Co. (ASCAP)
c/o Mr. Mort Garson
Apartment 1G
409 West 57th Street
New York, New York 10019

Dayben Music Corp. (ASCAP)
Room 405
39 West 55th Street
New York, New York 10019

Daywin Music, Inc. (BMI)
250 North Canon Drive
Beverly Hills, California 90210

Debmar Publishing Co., Inc.
(ASCAP)
1320 Vine Street
Philadelphia, Pennsylvania 19107

Deep Fork Music, Inc. (ASCAP)
15 East 48th Street
New York, New York 10017

Denslow Music, Inc. (ASCAP)
c/o Miss Peggy Lee
2345 Kimridge Drive
Beverly Hills, California 90210

Derry Music Co. (BMI)
240 Stockton Street
San Francisco, California 94108

Desmond Music Co. (BMI)
c/o Mr. Paul Desmond
Apartment 21G
77 West 55th Street
New York, New York 10019

Devon Music, Inc. (BMI)
Suite 2160
10 Columbus Circle
New York, New York 10019

Dijon Music (BMI)
Division of Donna Music
Publications
7165 Sunset Boulevard
Los Angeles, California 90046

Ding Dong Music Corp. (BMI)
Apartment 3B
116 Central Park South
New York, New York 10019

Disal Music Corp. (ASCAP)
Suite 1106
119 West 57th Street
New York, New York 10019

Dolfi Music, Inc. (ASCAP)
c/o Ross Jungnickel, Inc.
11th Floor
1619 Broadway
New York, New York 10019

Don Music Co. (BMI)
2809 Erastus Street
Houston, Texas 77026

Downey Music Publishing Co.
(BMI)
13117 Lakewood Boulevard
Downey, California 90242

Dragonwyck Music (BMI)
c/o Mr. David A. Gates
4373 Lemp Avenue
Studio City, California 91604

Duchess Music Corp. (BMI)
445 Park Avenue
New York, New York 10022

Dundee Music (BMI)
Box 926
1313 West Seventh Street
Clovis, New Mexico 88101

Dymor Productions, Inc. (ASCAP)
c/o Jerome B. Lurie, Esq.
717 Fifth Avenue
New York, New York 10022

E

Eager Music (BMI)
Post Office Box 287
Forest Park, Georgia 30050

East Publications (BMI)
c/o Satellite Records
926 East McLemore Avenue
Memphis, Tennessee 38106

East-West Music, Inc. (ASCAP)
1619 Broadway
New York, New York 10019

Eclectic Music Co. (BMI)
c/o Mr. Barry Kornfeld
190 Waverly Place
New York, New York 10014

Publishers

Eden Music, Inc. (BMI)
Suite 802
1697 Broadway
New York, New York 10019

Edville Publishing Co. (BMI)
10 Lynwood Court
Hurst, Texas 76053

Efsee Music, Inc. (BMI)
c/o Mr. George Scheck
161 West 54th Street
New York, New York 10019

Eldorado Music Co. (BMI)
1717 North Vine Street
Hollywood, California 90028

Eleventh Floor Music, Inc.
 (ASCAP)
1619 Broadway
New York, New York 10019

Elm Drive Music Corp. (ASCAP)
c/o Mr. Frank R. Cohen
608 Fifth Avenue
New York, New York 10020

Elmwin Music, Inc. (BMI)
c/o Robert Mellin, Inc.
9th Floor
1650 Broadway
New York, New York 10019

Elsher Music Co. (BMI)
Room 611
250 South Broad Street
Philadelphia, Pennsylvania 19102

Emanuel Music Corp. (ASCAP)
641 Lexington Avenue
New York, New York 10022

Embassy Music Corp. (BMI)
33 West 60th Street
New York, New York 10023

Empress Music, Inc. (ASCAP)
119 West 57th Street
New York, New York 10019

Englewood Publications, Inc. (BMI)
c/o Baude Music
c/o Mr. Morris Rubenstein
56 West 45th Street
New York, New York 10036

English Music, Inc. (BMI)
Post Office Box 6277
Nashville, Tennessee 37212

Epps Music Co. (BMI)
511 Brooklyn Avenue
San Antonio, Texas 78215

Escort Music Co. (BMI)
c/o Mr. Clifford L. Goldsmith
3009 West Pico Boulevard
Los Angeles, California 90006

Essex Music, Inc. (ASCAP)
Suite 2160
10 Columbus Circle
New York, New York 10019

Esteem Music Corp. (BMI)
c/o Ziv-World
729 Seventh Avenue
New York, New York 10019

Excellorec Music Co. (BMI)
177 Third Avenue North
Nashville, Tennessee 37201

F

Fairlane Music Corp. (ASCAP)
8625 Santa Monica Boulevard
Los Angeles, California 90069

Fajob Music Publishing Co.
 (ASCAP)
Suite 1111
1420 Walnut Street
Philadelphia, Pennsylvania 19102

Fall River Music, Inc. (BMI)
Room 602
200 West 57th Street
New York, New York 10019

Fame Publishing Co. (BMI)
c/o Mr. Rick Hall
Post Office Box 2238
Muscle Shoals, Alabama 35660

Famous Music Corp. (ASCAP)
1619 Broadway
New York, New York 10019

Leo Feist, Inc. (ASCAP)
1540 Broadway
New York, New York 10036

Fidelity Music Co. (BMI)
c/o Jobete Music Co., Inc.
2648 West Grand Boulevard
Detroit, Michigan 48208

318

Figure Music, Inc. (BMI)
c/o Mr. Jack Hooke
1631 Broadway
New York, New York 10019

Fred Fisher Music Co., Inc.
(ASCAP)
1619 Broadway
New York, New York 10019

Flanka Music Corp. (ASCAP)
119 West 57th Street
New York, New York 10019

Flatt and Scruggs Publishing Co.
(BMI)
201 Donna Drive
Madison, Tennessee 37115

Flomar Music Publishing, Inc.
(BMI)
254 West 54th Street
New York, New York 10019

Florence Music Co., Inc. (ASCAP)
609 Fifth Avenue
New York, New York 10017

Folkways Music Publishers, Inc.
(BMI)
Suite 2160
10 Columbus Circle
New York, New York 10019

Forrest Hills Music, Inc. (BMI)
1607 Hawkins Street
Nashville, Tennessee 37203

Forshay Music (BMI)
1631 Broadway
New York, New York 10019

Four Star Music Co., Inc. (BMI)
Suite 312
9220 Sunset Boulevard
Los Angeles, California 90069

Four Star Television Music Co.,
Inc. (BMI)
c/o Mr. Alfred Perry
4030 Radford Avenue
North Hollywood, California
91604

Sam Fox Publishing Co., Inc.
(ASCAP)
1841 Broadway
New York, New York 10023

Francon Music Corp. (ASCAP)
c/o Mr. George Scheck
161 West 54th Street
New York, New York 10019

Frank Music Corp. (ASCAP)
119 West 57th Street
New York, New York 10019

Frigate Music Corp. (BMI)
c/o Farber, Cohen & Diamond
608 Fifth Avenue
New York, New York 10020

Frost Music Corp. (BMI)
1631 Broadway
New York, New York 10019

G

Al Gallico Music Corp. (BMI)
101 West 55th Street
New York, New York 10019

Garpax Music Publishing Co.
(BMI)
Post Office Box 669
Hollywood, California 90028

Gavadima Music, Inc. (ASCAP)
c/o Mr. Felix Gaudio
Room 1202
161 West 54th Street
New York, New York 10019

Geld-Udell Music Corp. (ASCAP)
Room 301
200 West 57th Street
New York, New York 10019

General Music Publishing Co., Inc.
(ASCAP)
53 East 54th Street
New York, New York 10022

Genius Music Corp. (ASCAP)
1841 Broadway
New York, New York 10023

Gil Music Corp. (BMI)
c/o Mr. George Pincus
1650 Broadway
New York, New York 10019

Giovanni Music, Inc. (ASCAP)
157 West 57th Street
New York, New York 10019

Publishers

Glad Music Co. (BMI)
314 East 11th Street
Houston, Texas 77008

Gladstone Music, Inc. (ASCAP)
c/o Vee Jay Records, Inc.
1449 South Michigan Avenue
Chicago, Illinois 60605

Gladys Music, Inc. (ASCAP)
11th Floor
1619 Broadway
New York, New York 10019

Glamorous Music, Inc. (ASCAP)
c/o Mr. Klaus Ogermann
1619 Broadway
New York, New York 10019

Glaser Publications (BMI)
801 16th Avenue South
Nashville, Tennessee 37203

Glo-Mac Music (BMI)
c/o Metric Music Co.
1556 North La Brea Avenue
Los Angeles, California 90028

Glorste, Inc. (ASCAP)
175 South Mapleton Drive
Los Angeles, California 90024

Golden West Melodies, Inc. (BMI)
3rd Floor
1313 North Vine Street
Hollywood, California 90028

Gower Music, Inc. (BMI)
711 Fifth Avenue
New York, New York 10022

Groton Music, Inc. (BMI)
c/o Talent Associates-Paramount,
Ltd.
444 Madison Avenue
New York, New York 10022

Guild Music Co. (BMI)
2511 Mayberry Street
Los Angeles, California 90026

Gunston Music, Inc. (ASCAP)
c/o Mr. Arnold Roseman
Suite 302
9350 Wilshire Boulevard
Beverly Hills, California 90212

Gypsy Boy Music, Inc. (BMI)
Suite 1202
161 West 54th Street
New York, New York 10019

H

Hancock Music Co. (BMI)
c/o Mr. Hubert J. Hancock
Apartment 3C
202 Riverside Drive
New York, New York 10025

Charles H. Hansen Music Corp.
(ASCAP)
601 Fifth Avenue
New York, New York 10017

Harborn Music, Inc. (BMI)
136 West 52nd Street
New York, New York 10019

Harms, Inc. (ASCAP)
488 Madison Avenue
New York, New York 10022

Harold and Dimple Publishing Co.
(BMI)
c/o Mr. George Harold Jackson
Post Office Box 20710
Pico Heights Station
Los Angeles, California 90006

Harvard Music, Inc. (BMI)
33 West 60th Street
New York, New York 10023

Hawaii Music Co., Inc. (BMI)
c/o Revue Studios
Universal City, California 91608

Harwin Music Corp. (ASCAP)
31 West 54th Street
New York, New York 10019

Hastings Music Corp. (BMI)
1540 Broadway
New York, New York 10036

Helios Music Corp. (BMI)
Room 604
1619 Broadway
New York, New York 10019

Hendricks Music, Inc. (ASCAP)
90 State Street
Brooklyn, New York 11201

Hi Lo Music, Inc. (BMI)
639 Madison Avenue
Memphis, Tennessee 38103

Hidle Music (BMI)
c/o Mr. Hidle Brown Barnum
1600 North La Brea Avenue
Hollywood, Colifornia 90028

Hill and Range Songs, Inc. (BMI)
11th Floor
1619 Broadway
New York, New York 10019

Hilliard Music Co. (BMI)
c/o Mr. Maury Foladare
1717 North Highland Avenue
Hollywood, California 90028

Bob Hilliard Music Co. (ASCAP)
360 Allaire Avenue
Leonia, New Jersey 07605

Hollis Music, Inc. (BMI)
Suite 2160
10 Columbus Circle
New York, New York 10019

Hotpoint Music, Inc. (BMI)
Post Office Box 6277
Nashville, Tennessee 37212

Hullabaloo Music Co. (BMI)
8814 Trask Avenue
Playa del Rey, California 90291

Husky Music Co., Inc. (BMI)
816 16th Avenue South
Nashville, Tennessee 37203

I

In Music Co. (ASCAP)
2101 Ivar Avenue
Hollywood, California 90028

Integrity Music Corp. (ASCAP)
Apartment 14A
1050 Fifth Avenue
New York, New York 10028

International Korwin Corp.
(ASCAP)
45 West 56th Street
New York, New York 10019

International Pauline Corp.
(ASCAP)
45 West 56th Street
New York, New York 10019

Ipanema Music Co. (ASCAP)
1700 Rising Glen Road
Los Angeles, California 90069

J

Jac Music Co., Inc. (ASCAP)
c/o Mr. Hal David
Elm Drive
East Hills
Roslyn, New York 11576

Jack Music, Inc. (BMI)
Post Office Box 1333
Nashville, Tennessee 37202

Jaep Music, Inc. (BMI)
c/o Walter Hofer, Esq.
221 West 57th Street
New York, New York 10019

Jalynne Corp. (BMI)
2203 Spruce Street
Philadelphia, Pennsylvania 19103

Dick James Music, Inc. (BMI)
c/o Walter Hofer, Esq.
221 West 57th Street
New York, New York 10019

Jamie Music Publishing Co. (BMI)
919 North Broad Street
Philadelphia, Pennsylvania 19123

January Music Corp. (BMI)
25 West 56th Street
New York, New York 10019

Jarb Publishing Co. (BMI)
Division of Alon Music, Inc.
4318 MacArthur Boulevard
New Orleans, Louisiana 70114

Jat Music, Inc. (BMI)
c/o Four Star Music Co., Inc.
Suite 312
9220 Sunset Boulevard
Los Angeles, California 90069

Jay-Boy Music Corp. (BMI)
c/o Mr. Danny Kessler
Suite 1920
135 West 50th Street
New York, New York 10020

Jec Publishing Corp. (BMI)
c/o Mr. J. Cuoghi
308 Poplar Avenue
Memphis, Tennessee 38103

321

Jerryco Music Co. (ASCAP)
c/o Edwin H. Morris & Co., Inc.
31 West 54th Street
New York, New York 10019

Jimskip Music, Inc. (BMI)
c/o Mr. Larry Taylor
Apartment 20M
165 West End Avenue
New York, New York 10023

Jobete Music Co., Inc. (BMI)
c/o Mr. Berry Gordy, Jr.
2648 West Grand Boulevard
Detroit, Michigan 48238

Johnstone-Montei, Inc. (BMI)
Division of Beechwood Music
Corp.
1750 Vine Street
Hollywood, California 90028

Jonathan Music Co., Inc. (ASCAP)
c/o Bud Granoff Associates
45 West 56th Street
New York, New York 10019

Jonware Music Corp. (BMI)
c/o Jack Pearl, Esq.
515 Madison Avenue
New York, New York 10022

Joy Music, Inc. (ASCAP)
1790 Broadway
New York, New York 10019

Ross Jungnickel, Inc. (ASCAP)
11th Floor
1619 Broadway
New York, New York 10019

Just Music, Inc. (BMI)
35 West 45th Street
New York, New York 10036

K

Kags Music (BMI)
Room 301
6425 Hollywood Boulevard
Hollywood, California 90028

Kalmann Music, Inc. (ASCAP)
300 Farwood Road
Philadelphia, Pennsylvania 19151

Les Kangas Music Publishing Co.
(BMI)
7902 Dewey Street
San Gabriel, California 91776

Kavelin Music (BMI)
9341½ Olympic Boulevard
Beverly Hills, California 90212

Kemo Music Co. (BMI)
Room 205
6087 Sunset Boulevard
Hollywood, California 90028

Kentucky Music, Inc. (BMI)
11th Floor
1619 Broadway
New York, New York 10019

Keva Music Co. (BMI)
c/o Mr. Richard Becker
7 Queen Anne Drive
Deal, New Jersey 07723

Keymen Music (BMI)
c/o Copyright Service Bureau,
Ltd.
221 West 57th Street
New York, New York 10019

Kilynn Music Publishing, Inc.
(BMI)
c/o Mr. Curtis Ousley
392 Central Park West
New York, New York 10025

Kingsley Music, Inc. (ASCAP)
Room 501
1619 Broadway
New York, New York 10019

Knox Music, Inc. (BMI)
639 Madison Avenue
Memphis, Tennessee 38103

L

LDJN Music Corp. (ASCAP)
c/o Leeds Music Corp.
445 Park Avenue
New York, New York 10022

Lar-Bell Music Corp. (BMI)
Suite 140
9110 Sunset Boulevard
Los Angeles, California 90069

Larrabee Music, Inc. (BMI)
c/o Mr. Maurice M. Kahn
6381 Hollywood Boulevard
Hollywood, California 90028

Larrick Music Co. (BMI)
806 16th Avenue South
Nashville, Tennessee 37203

Laurel Music Corp. (ASCAP)
22 West 48th Street
New York, New York 10036

Le Bill Music, Inc. (BMI)
Suite A
4930 Camp Bowie Boulevard
Fort Worth, Texas 76107

Lear Music, Inc. (ASCAP)
1270 Avenue of the Americas
New York, New York 10020

Leeds Music Corp. (ASCAP)
445 Park Avenue
New York, New York 10022

Le Jean Music (BMI)
c/o Mr. Don Sessions
6110 Mayflower
Maywood, California 90270

Lena Music, Inc. (SESAC)
Suite 507
1619 Broadway
New York, New York 10019

Lescay Music, Inc. (BMI)
c/o Beltone Recording Corp.
Room 1006
1650 Broadway
New York, New York 10019

Levine-McHugh Music
International, Inc. (ASCAP)
Time and Life Building
Rockefeller Center
New York, New York 10020

Lewis Music Publishing Co., Inc.
(ASCAP)
39 West 60th Street
New York, New York 10023

Limax Music, Inc. (BMI)
618 South Ridgeley Drive
Los Angeles, California 90036

Linduane Corp. (BMI)
c/o Mr. Al Wilde
25 Central Park West
New York, New York 10023

Lion Publishing Co., Inc. (BMI)
c/o Mr. Don D. Robey
2809 Erastus Street
Houston, Texas 77026

Little Dipper Music Corp. (BMI)
1631 Broadway
New York, New York 10019

Livingston & Evans, Inc. (ASCAP)
Suite 1003
Sunset-Vine Tower Building
6290 Sunset Boulevard
Hollywood, California 90028

Llee Corp. (BMI)
c/o Mr. Lee V. Eastman
39 West 54th Street
New York, New York 10019

Lloyd and Logan, Inc. (BMI)
c/o Mr. Andrew J. Feinman
424 Madison Avenue
New York, New York 10017

Lois Publishing Co. (BMI)
1540 Brewster Avenue
Cincinnati, Ohio 45207

Lola Publishing Corp. (BMI)
457 West 45th Street
New York, New York 10036

Lonzo & Oscar Music Publishing
Co., Inc. (BMI)
Route 1
Tinnin Road
Goodlettsville, Tennessee 37072

Loring Music Co. (BMI)
Division of Loring Productions,
Inc.
1048 North Carol Drive
Los Angeles, California 90069

Lowe Music Corp. (ASCAP)
1405 Locust Street
Philadelphia, Pennsylvania 19102

Lowery Music Co., Inc. (BMI)
c/o Mr. Bill Lowery
Post Office Box 9687
Atlanta, Georgia 30319

Low-Twi Music (BMI)
c/o Mr. Bill Lowery
Post Office Box 9687
Atlanta, Georgia 30319

Ludix Publishing Co., Inc. (BMI)
c/o Mr. Albert R. Gaines
422 Madison Avenue
New York, New York 10017

Ludlow Music, Inc. (BMI)
Suite 2160
10 Columbus Circle
New York, New York 10019

Publishers

Lupercalia Music Publishing Co.
(ASCAP)
c/o Purcell
210 East 53rd Street
New York, New York 10022

Lupine Music (BMI)
c/o West
1008 South Holt Street
Montgomery, Alabama 36108

Luristan Music, Inc. (ASCAP)
723 Seventh Avenue
New York, New York 10019

Lyle Music, Inc. (ASCAP)
120 East 34th Street
New York, New York 10016

Lynlou Music, Inc. (BMI)
c/o Mr. Peter Paul
84-19 63rd Avenue
Queens, New York 11379

M

MCA, Inc. (ASCAP)
445 Park Avenue
New York, New York 10022

M.J.Q. Music, Inc. (BMI)
200 West 57th Street
New York, New York 10019

M.R.C. Music, Inc. (BMI)
35 East Wacker Drive
Chicago, Illinois 60601

Mabs Music Co. (ASCAP)
8721 Sunset Boulevard
Los Angeles, California 90069

John D. MacArthur Music Corp.
(BMI)
1631 Broadway
New York, New York 10019

Jimmy McHugh Music, Inc.
(ASCAP)
6381 Hollywood Boulevard
Hollywood, California 90028

McLaughlin Publishing Co. (BMI)
1300 Arborview Boulevard
Ann Arbor, Michigan 48103

Maclen Music, Inc. (BMI)
c/o Walter Hofer, Esq.
221 West 57th Street
New York, New York 10019

Macon Music Co. (BMI)
c/o Lois Publishing Co.
1540 Brewster Avenue
Cincinnati, Ohio 45207

Mainstay Music, Inc. (BMI)
c/o Mr. Al Gallico
101 West 55th Street
New York, New York 10019

Mallory Music Publications (BMI)
c/o Woodhaven Farms
Route 1
Little New York Road
Alexander City, Alabama 35010

Mansion Music Corp. (ASCAP)
136 West 52nd Street
New York, New York 10019

Maravilla Music, Inc. (BMI)
6277 Selma Avenue
Hollywood, California 90028

Maraville Music Corp. (ASCAP)
1619 Broadway
New York, New York 10019

Marbill Music (BMI)
Suite A
4930 Camp Bowie Boulevard
Fort Worth, Texas 76107

Maricana Music, Inc. (BMI)
713 18th Avenue South
Nashville, Tennessee 37203

Marimba Music Corp. (ASCAP)
c/o Orland, Chase & Mucci
48 West 48th Street
New York, New York 10036

Mariposa Music, Inc. (BMI)
713 18th Avenue South
Nashville, Tennessee 37203

Marizona Music (BMI)
713 18th Avenue South
Nashville, Tennessee 37203

Edward B. Marks Music Corp.
(BMI)
136 West 52nd Street
New York, New York 10019

Marson Music Co. (BMI)
c/o Mr. Archie L. Loden
Hackleburg, Alabama 35564

Marty's Music Corp. (BMI)
713 18th Avenue South
Nashville, Tennessee 37203

Mary Jane Music (ASCAP)
c/o Mrs. Florence Greenberg
Room 1410
1650 Broadway
New York, New York 10019

Maureen Music, Inc. (BMI)
c/o Old Town Record Corp.
1697 Broadway
New York, New York 10019

The Peter Maurice Music Co., Ltd.
(ASCAP) ,
101 West 55th Street
New York, New York 10019

Maverick Music, Inc. (BMI)
c/o Mr. Gary S. Paxton
Box 669
Hollywood, California 90028

Maxana Music Corp. (ASCAP)
729 Seventh Avenue
New York, New York 10019

Ray Maxwell Music Publishing Co.
(BMI)
6359 Selma Avenue
Hollywood, California 90028

Mayfair Music Corp. (ASCAP)
31 West 54th Street
New York, New York 10019

Maygar Publishing Co. (BMI)
c/o Mr. Garry Sherman
Apartment 12D
165 West End Avenue
New York, New York 10023

Meadowlark Music (ASCAP)
1481 Vine Street
Hollywood, California 90028

Medal Music, Inc. (BMI)
234 West 56th Street
New York, New York 10019

Robert Mellin, Inc. (BMI)
1650 Broadway
New York, New York 10019

Melody Trails, Inc. (BMI)
Suite 2160
10 Columbus Circle
New York, New York 10019

Melrose Music Corp. (ASCAP)
31 West 54th Street
New York, New York 10019

Mercedes Music Co. (BMI)
c/o Mr. Robert Davenport
Suite 323
Sunset-Vine Tower Building
6290 Sunset Boulevard
Hollywood, California 90028

Merjoda Music, Inc. (BMI)
35 East Wacker Drive
Chicago, Illinois 60601

Merrimac Music Corp. (BMI)
1619 Broadway
New York, New York 10019

Mesquite Music Corp. (ASCAP)
31 West 54th Street
New York, New York 10019

Metorion Music Corp. (BMI)
117 West 48th Street
New York, New York 10036

Metric Music Co. (BMI)
1556 North La Brea Avenue
Los Angeles, California 90028

Miller Music Corp. (ASCAP)
1540 Broadway
New York, New York 10036

Mills Music, Inc. (ASCAP)
1619 Broadway
New York, New York 10019

Mimosa Publishing Co. (BMI)
c/o Mr. Bob L. Moore
905 17th Avenue South
Nashville, Tennessee 37212

Minit Music Co. (BMI)
c/o Metric Music Co.
1556 North La Brea Avenue
Los Angeles, California 90028

Miraleste Music (BMI)
c/o Mr. Richard Delvy
2525 West Ninth Street
Los Angeles, California 90006

Mixer Music (BMI)
c/o Mr. George John Morris
729 Park Avenue
Covina, California 91723

Publishers

Modern Music Publishing Co.
(BMI)
5810 South Normandie Avenue
Los Angeles, California 90044

Ivan Mogull Music Corp. (ASCAP)
Room 804
1619 Broadway
New York, New York 10019

Monarch Music Corp. (ASCAP)
465 South Beverly Drive
Beverly Hills, California 90212

Mongo Music (BMI)
c/o Copyright Service Bureau,
Ltd.
221 West 57th Street
New York, New York 10019

Morley Music Co., Inc. (ASCAP)
31 West 54th Street
New York, New York 10019

Edwin H. Morris & Co., Inc.
(ASCAP)
31 West 54th Street
New York, New York 10019

Morro Music Corp. (BMI)
Suite 1531-32
250 West 57th Street
New York, New York 10019

Moss Rose Publications, Inc. (BMI)
806 16th Avenue South
Nashville, Tennessee 37203

Mother Bertha Music, Inc. (BMI)
9130 Sunset Boulevard
Los Angeles, California 90069

Mountain City Publishing Co.
(BMI)
Dome Building
738 Gerogia Avenue
Chattanooga, Tennessee 37402

Mured Publishing Co. (BMI)
8008 Rodgers Road
Elkins Park, Pennsylvania 19117

Music World Corp. (BMI)
Suite 409
6087 Sunset Boulevard
Hollywood, California 90028

Musical Comedy Productions, Inc.
(BMI)
Suite 2160
10 Columbus Circle
New York, New York 10019

Myto Music, Inc. (BMI)
c/o Miss Joanne Jackson
4039 West Buena Vista Street
Detroit, Michigan 48238

N

Nancy Music Co. (ASCAP)
24 Chandler Drive
Emerson, New Jersey 07630

Neillrae Music (BMI)
4714 Greenville Street
Dallas, Texas 75206

Nelson Music Publishing Co.
(ASCAP)
Suite 307
1717 North Highland Avenue
Hollywood, California 90028

Nep Music, Inc. (ASCAP)
Box 926
1321 West Seventh Street
Clovis, New Mexico 88101

New Christy Music Publishing Co.
(BMI)
10513 Santa Monica Boulevard
Los Angeles, California 90025

Newkeys Music, Inc. (BMI)
1531 Demonbreun Street
Nashville, Tennessee 37203

Nicolet Music (BMI)
328 East 58th Street
Chicago, Illinois 60637

Nom Music, Inc. (BMI)
1631 Broadway
New York, New York 10019

Noma Music, Inc. (BMI)
11th Floor
1619 Broadway
New York, New York 10019

Nor Va Jak Music, Inc. (BMI)
1313 West Seventh Street
Clovis, New Mexico 88101

North & Son Music, Inc. (ASCAP)
666 Fifth Avenue
New York, New York 10019

Northern Music Corp. (ASCAP)
445 Park Avenue
New York, New York 10022

Northridge Music, Inc. (ASCAP)
Suite 1003
Sunset-Vine Tower Building
6290 Sunset Boulevard
Hollywood, California 90028

Noslen Music Co. (BMI)
110-05 173rd Street
St. Albans, New York 11412

O

Octave Music Publishing Corp.
(ASCAP)
520 Fifth Avenue
New York, New York 10036

Odin Music Co. (ASCAP)
Suite C
1708 Pandora Avenue
Los Angeles, California 90024

Old Lyne Music (BMI)
Room 1100
1650 Broadway
New York, New York 10019

Olimac Music, Inc. (BMI)
130 Belmont Street
Englewood, New Jersey 07631

Olivia Publishing Co. (BMI)
c/o Mr. Waymon Glasco
604 Bergen Street
Newark, New Jersey 07108

Open Road Music, Inc. (BMI)
Post Office Box 123
Madison, Tennessee 37115

Owen Publications (BMI)
Post Office Box 842
Bakersfield, California 93302

Don Owens Music, Inc. (BMI)
c/o Mr. Robert Buckalew
219 Adams Avenue
Memphis, Tennessee 38103

P

Pacemaker Music Co., Inc. (BMI)
c/o Walter Hofer, Esq.
221 West 57th Street
New York, New York 10019

Painted Desert Music Corp. (BMI)
666 Fifth Avenue
New York, New York 10019

Pambill Music, Inc. (ASCAP)
c/o Carlton Record Corp.
345 West 58th Street
New York, New York 10019

Pamco Music, Inc. (BMI)
1501 Broadway
New York, New York 10036

Pamper Music, Inc. (BMI)
Post Office Box 96
119 Two Mile Pike
Goodlettsville, Tennessee 37072

Panther Music Corp. (ASCAP)
c/o Southern Music Publishing
Co., Inc.
1619 Broadway
New York, New York 10019

Paramount Music Corp. (ASCAP)
1619 Broadway
New York, New York 10019

Paris Music Co., Inc. (ASCAP)
Room 1115
1650 Broadway
New York, New York 10019

Pattern Music, Inc. (ASCAP)
Suite 201
6515 Sunset Boulevard
Hollywood, California 90028

George Paxton Corp. (ASCAP)
1619 Broadway
New York, New York 10019

Paxwin Music Corp. (BMI)
c/o Mr. George Paxton
1619 Broadway
New York, New York 10019

Peach Music (SESAC)
806 17th Avenue South
Nashville, Tennessee 37203

Publishers

Pearl Dee Publishing Co. (BMI)
Route 1
Franklin, Tennessee 37064

Pearl Music Co., Inc. (BMI)
Suite 1012
1619 Broadway
New York, New York 10019

Peer International Corp. (BMI)
1619 Broadway
New York, New York 10019

Penny Music Co. (BMI)
130 South Fourth Street
Las Vegas, Nevada 89101

Pepamar Music Corp. (ASCAP)
488 Madison Avenue
New York, New York 10022

Phalanx Music, Inc. (ASCAP)
c/o Pryor, Braun & Cashman
640 Fifth Avenue
New York, New York 10019

Piccadilly Music Corp. (BMI)
Room 1920
135 West 50th Street
New York, New York 10020

Pickwick Music Corp. (ASCAP)
445 Park Avenue
New York, New York 10022

Picturetone Music Publishing Corp.
(BMI)
1650 Broadway
New York, New York 10019

Piedmont Music Co., Inc. (ASCAP)
136 West 52nd Street
New York, New York 10019

George Pincus & Sons Music Corp.
(ASCAP)
Room 601
1650 Broadway
New York, New York 10019

Placid Music (BMI)
c/o A. Halsey Cowan, Esq.
1740 Broadway
New York, New York 10019

Plainview Music, Inc. (BMI)
Suite 1106
119 West 57th Street
New York, New York 10019

Plan Two Music, Inc. (ASCAP)
1619 Broadway
New York, New York 10019

Planetary Music Publishing Corp.
(ASCAP)
1631 Broadway
New York, New York 10019

Play Music, Inc. (BMI)
Suite 802
1697 Broadway
New York, New York 10019

The Players Music Corp. (ASCAP)
609 Fifth Avenue
New York, New York 10017

Ponderosa Music Co., Inc. (BMI)
666 Fifth Avenue
New York, New York 10019

Post Music, Inc. (ASCAP)
1556 North La Brea Avenue
Hollywood, California 90028

Premier Music Publishing Co.
(BMI)
Post Office Box 338
East Pasadena, California 91107

Elvis Presley Music, Inc. (BMI)
11th Floor
1619 Broadway
New York, New York 10019

Prestige Music Co., Inc. (BMI)
203 South Washington Avenue
Bergenfield, New Jersey 07621

Prigan Music Corp. (BMI)
c/o Mr. Andrew J. Feinman
424 Madison Avenue
New York, New York 10017

Print Music Co., Inc. (ASCAP)
c/o Jepalana Productions
723 Seventh Avenue
New York, New York 10019

Progressive Music Publishing Co.,
Inc. (BMI)
11th Floor
1619 Broadway
New York, New York 10019

Purchase Music, Inc. (ASCAP)
1650 Broadway
New York, New York 10019

Q

Quartet Music, Inc. (ASCAP)
1619 Broadway
New York, New York 10019

R

R-T Publishing Co. (BMI)
c/o Lois Publishing Co.
1540 Brewster Avenue
Cincinnati, Ohio 45207

RTD Music (BMI)
c/o Mr. Richard T. Drury
WBRB
Colonial Hotel
Mount Clemens, Michigan 48043

Raleigh Music, Inc. (BMI)
817 16th Avenue South
Nashville, Tennessee 37203

Ralph's Radio Music (BMI)
Demorest, Georgia 30535

Rambed Publishing Co., Inc. (BMI)
Penthouse A
116 Central Park South
New York, New York 10019

Randy-Smith Music Corp. (ASCAP)
3941 Woodlawn Drive
Nashville, Tennessee 37205

Walter Reade-Sterling Music Corp.
(ASCAP)
119 West 57th Street
New York, New York 10019

Recherche Music Corp. (ASCAP)
473 West End Avenue
New York, New York 10024

Recordo Music Publishers (BMI)
c/o Mr. Leon René
2124 West 24th Street
Los Angeles, California 90018

Red River Songs, Inc. (BMI)
1001 North Lincoln Street
Burbank, California 91506

Red Stick Publishing Co. (BMI)
Post Office Box 2306
100 Spain Street
Baton Rouge, Louisiana 70802

Regent Music Corp. (BMI)
1619 Broadway
New York, New York 10019

Herb Reis Music Corp. (BMI)
Room 516
1619 Broadway
New York, New York 10019

Remick Music Corp. (ASCAP)
488 Madison Avenue
New York, New York 10022

Rice Mill Publishing Co., Inc.
(BMI)
c/o Mr. Bernard Lowe
1411 Walnut Street
Philadelphia, Pennsylvania 19102

Ridge Music Corp. (BMI)
c/o Mr. Paul Tannen
Suite 7A
850 Seventh Avenue
New York, New York 10019

Rinimer Corp. (ASCAP)
c/o Julius Lefkowitz & Co.
9171 Wilshire Boulevard
Beverly Hills, California 90210

Ripley Music, Inc. (BMI)
c/o Jerome B. Lurie, Esq.
717 Fifth Avenue
New York, New York 10022

Rittenhouse Music (BMI)
Division of Seri Music
Publishing, Inc.
219 West 79th Street
New York, New York 10024

Ritvale Music Corp. (ASCAP)
608 Fifth Avenue
New York, New York 10020

Rob-Ann Music, Inc. (BMI)
254 West 54th Street
New York, New York 10019

Robbins Music Corp. (ASCAP)
1350 Avenue of the Americas
New York, New York 10019

Don Robertson Music Corp.
(ASCAP)
Room 426
1651 Cosmo Street
Hollywood, California 90028

Publishers

Robin Hood Music Co. (BMI)
c/o Mr. John Marascalco
5531 Tuxedo Terrace
Hollywood, California 90028

Rock Masters, Inc. (BMI)
177 Route 304
New City, New York 10956

Rock Music Co. (BMI)
444 North Camden Drive
Beverly Hills, California 90210

Romance Music, Inc. (BMI)
850 Seventh Avenue
New York, New York 10019

Roncom Music Co. (ASCAP)
Suite 1602
405 Park Avenue
New York, New York 10022

Rondell Music (BMI)
c/o Mr. James J. Lee
Suite 303
6515 Sunset Boulevard
Los Angeles, California 90028

Ronnat Music Co. (BMI)
c/o Mr. Nat Margo
45-55 41st Street
Long Island City, New York
11104

Roosevelt Music Co., Inc. (BMI)
Room 408
1050 Broadway
New York, New York 10019

Fred Rose Music, Inc. (BMI)
2510 Franklin Road
Nashville, Tennessee 37204

David Rose Publishing Co.
(ASCAP)
c/o Gilbert & Levine
Suite 229
9601 Wilshire Boulevard
Beverly Hills, California 90212

Rosemeadow Publishing Corp.
(ASCAP)
1619 Broadway
New York, New York 10019

Rosewood Music Corp. (ASCAP)
136 East 57th Street
New York, New York 10022

Rumbalero Music, Inc. (BMI)
c/o Hill and Range Songs, Inc.
11th Floor
1619 Broadway
New York, New York 10019

Ryerson Music Publishers, Inc.
(BMI)
154 West 14th Street
New York, New York 10011

Rytvoc, Inc. (ASCAP)
39 West 54th Street
New York, New York 10019

S

S & J Music Publishing Co.
(ASCAP)
c/o Schwartz Music Co., Inc.
35 West 45th Street
New York, New York 10036

S-P-R Music Corp. (BMI)
c/o Dunes Records, Inc.
1619 Broadway
New York, New York 10019

Sage and Sand Music Publishers
(SESAC)
5653½ Hollywood Boulevard
Hollywood, California 90028

Sahara Music, Inc. (ASCAP)
609 Fifth Avenue
New York, New York 10017

St. Nicholas Music, Inc. (ASCAP)
11th Floor
1619 Broadway
New York, New York 10019

Salaam Music Co. (BMI)
c/o Mr. John Lewis
8211 South Maryland Avenue
Chicago, Illinois 60619

Samos Island Music, Inc. (BMI)
c/o Record Industries
801 16th Avenue South
Nashville, Tennessee 37203

Sanga Music, Inc. (BMI)
Suite 1304
200 West 57th Street
New York, New York 10019

Saran Music Co. (BMI)
Box 17014
Dallas, Texas 75217

Saturday Music, Inc. (ASCAP)
1841 Broadway
New York, New York 10023

Saturn Music, Inc. (BMI)
265 West 54th Street
New York, New York 10019

Saunders Publications, Inc.
(ASCAP)
119 West 57th Street
New York, New York 10019

Saxon Music Corp. (BMI)
Suite 1920
135 West 50th Street
New York, New York 10020

Peter Schaeffers Music Corp.
(BMI)
Room 1920
135 West 50th Street
New York, New York 10020

Schroder Music Co. (ASCAP)
c/o Mr. William Reynolds
2027 Parker Street
Berkeley, California 94704

Schwartz Music Co., Inc. (ASCAP)
c/o Laurie Records
35 West 45th Street
New York, New York 10036

Screen Gems-Columbia Music, Inc.
(BMI)
711 Fifth Avenue
New York, New York 10022

Sea of Tunes Publishing Co. (BMI)
9042 La Alba Drive
Whittier, California 90603

Sea-Lark Enterprises, Inc. (BMI)
25 West 56th Street
New York, New York 10019

Seasons Four Music Corp. (BMI)
c/o Martin J. Machat, Esq.
1501 Broadway
New York, New York 10036

Selma Music Corp. (BMI)
c/o Mr. Morton Craft
Apartment 1P
225 East 57th Street
New York, New York 10022

Serendipity Publishing Corp.
(BMI)
c/o Pryor, Braun & Cashman
640 Fifth Avenue
New York, New York 10019

Sergeant Music Co. (ASCAP)
c/o Sinatra Enterprises
4000 Warner Boulevard
Burbank, California 91505

Seven Arts Music Corp. (BMI)
270 Park Avenue
New York, New York 10017

Shake-Well Music, Inc. (BMI)
c/o Mr. George Scheck
161 West 54th Street
New York, New York 10019

Shapiro, Bernstein & Co., Inc.
(ASCAP)
666 Fifth Avenue
New York, New York 10019

Eddie Shaw Music Co. (ASCAP)
9128 Sunset Boulevard
Los Angeles, California 90069

Sherlyn Publishing Co. (BMI)
c/o Mr. Henry Stone
495 South East 10th Court
Hialeah, Florida 33010

Sherman-De Vorzon Music Corp.
(BMI)
6290 Sunset Boulevard
Hollywood, California 90028

Sherwin Music, Inc. (ASCAP)
c/o Mr. Robert Mellin
Room 901
1650 Broadway
New York, New York 10019

Shoe-String Music, Inc. (BMI)
c/o Copyright Service Bureau,
Ltd.
221 West 57th Street
New York, New York 10019

Showboat Songs, Inc. (ASCAP)
c/o Paris Music Co., Inc.
Room 1115
1650 Broadway
New York, New York 10019

Sigma Music, Inc. (ASCAP)
11th Floor
1619 Broadway
New York, New York 10019

Publishers

'62 Revue Publishers, Inc. (ASCAP)
240 West 55th Street
New York, New York 10019

Skidmore Music Co., Inc. (ASCAP)
666 Fifth Avenue
New York, New York 10019

Songfest Music Corp. (ASCAP)
Room 1210
1650 Broadway
New York, New York 10019

Songs Music, Inc. (ASCAP)
Post Office Box 102
Scarborough, New York 10582

Sonlo Publishing Co. (BMI)
c/o Lois Publishing Co.
1540 Brewster Avenue
Cincinnati, Ohio 45207

Soon Music Co. (ASCAP)
4055 Wilshire Boulevard
Los Angeles, California 90005

South Coast Music (BMI)
314 East 11th Street
Houston, Texas 77008

South Mountain Music Corp. (BMI)
2nd Floor
1631 Broadway
New York, New York 10019

Southdale Music Corp. (ASCAP)
Suite 1003
Sunset-Vine Tower Building
6290 Sunset Boulevard
Hollywood, California 90028

Southern Music Publishing Co., Inc.
(ASCAP)
1619 Broadway
New York, New York 10019

Southside Music Corp. (BMI)
1650 Broadway
New York, New York 10019

Spanka Music Corp. (BMI)
Suite 1510
200 West 57th Street
New York, New York 10019

Spectorious Music Corp. (BMI)
Suite 1200
1780 Broadway
New York, New York 10019

Starday Music (BMI)
Division of Madison Music
Publisher, Inc.
c/o Mr. Don Pierce
Post Office Box 115
Madison, Tennessee 37115

Starflower Music Co. (BMI)
c/o Mr. Phil Medley
1225 Avenue of the Americas
New York, New York 10019

Starrite Publishing Co. (BMI)
314 East 11th Street
Houston, Texas 77008

Stratford Music Corp. (ASCAP)
609 Fifth Avenue
New York, New York 10017

Summit Music Corp. (ASCAP)
c/o Mr. Herb Reis
1619 Broadway
New York, New York 10019

Sunbeam Music Corp. (BMI)
22 West 48th Street
New York, New York 10036

Sun-Vine Music Co. (BMI)
1507 North Vine Street
Hollywood, California 90028

Sure-Fire Music Co., Inc. (BMI)
801 16th Avenue South
Nashville, Tennessee 37203

Sweco Music Corp. (BMI)
250 West 57th Street
New York, New York 10019

Sylvia Music Publishing Co., Inc.
(BMI)
Room 510
1650 Broadway
New York, New York 10019

Symphony House Music Publishers
Corp. (ASCAP)
c/o Paul Siegel Productions
Tauentzien Strasse 16
Berlin W. 30, Germany

T

T.M. Music, Inc. (BMI)
Suite 906
1619 Broadway
New York, New York 10019

Tangerine Music Corp. (BMI)
c/o Mr. Joe Adams
2107 West Washington Boulevard
Los Angeles, California 90018

Tannen Music Enterprises (BMI)
Suite 7A
850 Seventh Avenue
New York, New York 10019

Taracrest Music, Inc. (BMI)
Studio Three
70 Dorman Avenue
San Francisco, California 94124

Larry Taylor Music Corp.
(ASCAP)
136 West 52nd Street
New York, New York 10019

Tee Pee Music Co., Inc. (ASCAP)
Room 715
1650 Broadway
New York, New York 10019

Teena Music Corp. (ASCAP)
142 East 34th Street
New York, New York 10016

Tempo Music (ASCAP)
13310 Caine Avenue
Cleveland, Ohio 44105

Tender Tunes Music (BMI)
Division of Kama-Sutra
Productions, Inc.
Room 303
1650 Broadway
New York, New York 10019

Texoma Music Corp. (ASCAP)
Box 74A
Route 1
Park Hill, Oklahoma 74451

Thelonious Music (BMI)
Division of Bar-Thel Music Corp.
69-45 108th Street
Forest Hills, New York 11375

Tiger Music, Inc. (BMI)
c/o Hill and Range Songs, Inc.
11th Floor
1619 Broadway
New York, New York 10019

Tobi-Ann Music Publishing Corp.
(BMI)
1650 Broadway
New York, New York 10019

Tod Music, Inc. (ASCAP)
632 Winchester Avenue
Union, New Jersey 07083

Topper Music Publishing Corp.
(ASCAP)
Room 610
119 West 57th Street
New York, New York 10019

Towne Music Corp. (ASCAP)
Room 906
1619 Broadway
New York, New York 10019

Travis Music Co. (BMI)
c/o Metric Music Co.
1556 North La Brea Avenue
Los Angeles, California 90028

Tredlew Music, Inc. (BMI)
200 West 57th Street
New York, New York 10019

Tree Publishing Co., Inc. (BMI)
905 16th Avenue South
Nashville, Tennessee 37212

Trio Music Co., Inc. (BMI)
1619 Broadway
New York, New York 10019

Trousdale Music Publishers, Inc.
(BMI)
c/o Copyright Service Bureau,
Ltd.
221 West 57th Street
New York, New York 10019

Troy Martin Music, Inc. (BMI)
Post Office Box 58
Nashville, Tennessee 37202

Ernest Tubb Music, Inc. (BMI)
11th Floor
1619 Broadway
New York, New York 10019

Tuckahoe Music, Inc. (BMI)
Post Office Box 128
Madison, Tennessee 37115

Tune Publishers, Inc. (BMI)
123 East Alabama Street
Florence, Alabama 35630

Tune-Kel Publishing Co., Inc.
(BMI)
4318 MacArthur Boulevard
New Orleans, Louisiana 70114

Publishers

Tunetime Music, Inc. (BMI)
c/o Mr. George Pincus
1650 Broadway
New York, New York 10019

Tuneville Music, Inc. (BMI)
812 17th Avenue South
Nashville, Tennessee 37203

Tupper Publishing Co. (BMI)
959 Main Street
Buffalo, New York 14203

Twist Music (BMI)
Post Office Box 2921
Hollywood, California 90028

Tyler Publishing Co. (BMI)
Post Office Box 231
325 South Bois d'Arc Avenue
Tyler, Texas 75701

U

U.S. Songs, Inc. (ASCAP)
c/o Quartet Music, Inc.
1619 Broadway
New York, New York 10019

Unart Music Corp. (BMI)
c/o United Artists Corp.
729 Seventh Avenue
New York, New York 10019

United Artists Music Co., Inc.
(ASCAP)
c/o Sidney Semel, Esq.
729 Seventh Avenue
New York, New York 10019

United International Copyright
Representatives, Ltd. (ASCAP)
c/o B. Stollman, Esq.
120 East 56th Street
New York, New York 10022

Upam Music Co. (BMI)
119 West 57th Street
New York, New York 10019

V

Valiant Music Co., Inc. (ASCAP)
1619 Broadway
New York, New York 10019

Valjo Publishing Co. (BMI)
c/o Lois Publishing Co.
1540 Brewster Avenue
Cincinnati, Ohio 45207

Valley Publishers, Inc. (BMI)
c/o Hill and Range Songs, Inc.
11th Floor
1619 Broadway
New York, New York 10019

Valley Spring Music Corp. (BMI)
c/o A. Halsey Cowan, Esq.
1740 Broadway
New York, New York 10019

Van Heusen Music Corp. (ASCAP)
250 West 57th Street
New York, New York 10019

Vanadore Publications, Inc. (BMI)
1537 McGavock Pike
Nashville, Tennessee 37216

Vanguard Songs (BMI)
Division of Beechwood Music
Corp.
1750 Vine Street
Hollywood, California 90028

Vaughn Publishing Co., Inc. (BMI)
812 17th Avenue South
Nashville, Tennessee 37203

Venice Music, Inc. (BMI)
8300 Santa Monica Boulevard
Hollywood, California 90069

Vicki Music, Inc. (BMI)
c/o Mr. Irving Micahnik
850 Seventh Avenue
New York, New York 10019

Viva Music, Inc. (BMI)
c/o Harvard Music, Inc.
33 West 60th Street
New York, New York 10023

Vogue Music Co. (BMI)
2444 Wilshire Boulevard
Santa Monica, California 90403

Vonglo Music Co. (BMI)
1674 Broadway
New York, New York 10019

W

Walden Music Corp. (ASCAP)
1841 Broadway
New York, New York 10023

Walnut Music Corp. (BMI)
c/o Kenny's Record Shop
148 West 125th Street
New York, New York 10027

Kitty Wells Publications (BMI)
1302 Saunders Avenue
Madison, Tennessee 37115

Wemar Music Corp. (BMI)
1619 Broadway
New York, New York 10019

Western Hills Music, Inc. (BMI)
1758 Oak Hill Road
Fort Worth, Texas 76112

Westside Music, Inc. (BMI)
c/o G.L.G. Productions
600 Madison Avenue
New York, New York 10022

Wilderness Music Publishing Co.
(BMI)
Division of Harlan Howard, Inc.
913 17th Avenue South
Nashville, Tennessee 37212

Kae Williams Music, Inc. (BMI)
3214 West York Street
Philadelphia, Pennsylvania 19132

Williamson Music, Inc. (ASCAP)
609 Fifth Avenue
New York, New York 10017

Window Music Publishers (BMI)
720 17th Avenue South
Nashville, Tennessee 37203

Windsong Music (BMI)
2811 Wilton Road
West Columbia, South Carolina
29169

Winlyn Music, Inc. (BMI)
c/o Lawrence J. Greene, Esq.
Room 710
200 West 57th Street
New York, New York 10019

M. Witmark & Sons (ASCAP)
488 Madison Avenue
New York, New York 10022

Wolf-Mills Music, Inc. (ASCAP)
8814 Trask Avenue
Playa del Rey, California 90291

Wonderland Music Co., Inc. (BMI)
800 Sonora Avenue
Glendale, California 91201

B. F. Wood Music Co., Inc.
(ASCAP)
1619 Broadway
New York, New York 10019

Woodcrest Music, Inc. (BMI)
300 Farwood Road
Philadelphia, Pennsylvania 19151

Woodmere Music (BMI)
c/o Douglas Horn, Esq.
730 Bunker Road
North Woodmere, New York
11598

Wrist Music Co. (BMI)
6830 Pacific View Drive
Los Angeles, California 90028

Wyncote Music Publishing Co., Inc.
(ASCAP)
c/o Cameo-Parkway Records, Inc.
1405 Locust Street
Philadelphia, Pennsylvania 19102

Y

Yonah Music, Inc. (BMI)
806 16th Avenue South
Nashville, Tennessee 37203

Z

Zann Music, Inc. (BMI)
c/o Scepter Records, Inc.
254 West 54th Street
New York, New York 10019

Zodiac Music Corp. (BMI)
250 West 57th Street
New York, New York 10019

About the Editor

Nat Shapiro is co-editor of two standard jazz works, *Hear Me Talkin' to Ya* and *The Jazz Makers;* a frequent contributor to periodicals in the United States and abroad; and a prolific annotator of record albums. For two decades, he has been active in the creation, promotion, and production of popular music as press agent, artists' representative, editor, music publisher, and artists and repertoire director. He has produced and co-produced popular, classical, folk, jazz, and spoken word recordings in the United States, France, England, Holland, Germany, Italy, Spain, Argentina, Brazil, and Mexico with such artists as Lotte Lenya, Marlene Dietrich, Yves Montand, Mahalia Jackson, Michel Legrand, Miles Davis, Juliette Greco, and Barbra Streisand. Currently involved in the preparation of two musicals for the Broadway theater, he is also working on a long-range project, a "nostalgic history" of American popular songs, as well as on the subsequent volumes of *Popular Music*.